Behavioural Finance for Private Banking

For other titles in the Wiley Finance series
please see www.wiley.com/finance

Behavioural Finance for Private Banking

**Thorsten Hens
and
Kremena Bachmann**

WILEY
A John Wiley and Sons, Ltd, Publication

Copyright © 2008   John Wiley & Sons Ltd, The Atrium, Southern Gate, Chichester,
                      West Sussex PO19 8SQ, England
                      Telephone   (+44) 1243 779777

Email (for orders and customer service enquiries): cs-books@wiley.co.uk
Visit our Home Page on www.wiley.com

All Rights Reserved. No part of this publication may be reproduced, stored in a retrieval system or transmitted in any form or by any means, electronic, mechanical, photocopying, recording, scanning or otherwise, except under the terms of the Copyright, Designs and Patents Act 1988 or under the terms of a licence issued by the Copyright Licensing Agency Ltd, 90 Tottenham Court Road, London W1T 4LP, UK, without the permission in writing of the Publisher. Requests to the Publisher should be addressed to the Permissions Department, John Wiley & Sons Ltd, The Atrium, Southern Gate, Chichester, West Sussex PO19 8SQ, England, or emailed to permreq@wiley.co.uk, or faxed to (+44) 1243 770620.

Designations used by companies to distinguish their products are often claimed as trademarks. All brand names and product names used in this book are trade names, service marks, trademarks or registered trademarks of their respective owners. The Publisher is not associated with any product or vendor mentioned in this book.

This publication is designed to provide accurate and authoritative information in regard to the subject matter covered. It is sold on the understanding that the Publisher is not engaged in rendering professional services. If professional advice or other expert assistance is required, the services of a competent professional should be sought.

Other Wiley Editorial Offices

John Wiley & Sons Inc., 111 River Street, Hoboken, NJ 07030, USA

Jossey-Bass, 989 Market Street, San Francisco, CA 94103-1741, USA

Wiley-VCH Verlag GmbH, Boschstr. 12, D-69469 Weinheim, Germany

John Wiley & Sons Australia Ltd, 42 McDougall Street, Milton, Queensland 4064, Australia

John Wiley & Sons (Asia) Pte Ltd, 2 Clementi Loop #02-01, Jin Xing Distripark, Singapore 129809

John Wiley & Sons Canada Ltd, 6045 Freemont Blvd. Mississauga, Ontario, L5R 4J3, Canada

Wiley also publishes its books in a variety of electronic formats. Some content that appears in print may not be available in electronic books.

Library of Congress Cataloging-in-Publication Data

Hens, Thorsten.
  Behavioural finance for private banking / Thorsten Hens, Kremena Bachmann.
    p. cm. — (The Wiley finance series)
  Includes bibliographical references and index.
  ISBN 978-0-470-77999-6 (cloth)
  1. Private banks. 2. Investments—Psychological aspects. 3. Finance—Psychological aspects. 4. Banks and banking—Customer services. 5. Wealth—Management. I. Bachmann, Kremena. II. Title. III. Title: Behavioral finance for private banking.
  HG1978.H46 2008
  332.1′230688—dc22
                                                                                        2008038617

A catalogue record for this book is available from the British Library

ISBN 978-0-470-77999-6 (H/B)

Typeset in 10/12pt Times by Integra Software Services Pvt. Ltd, Pondicherry, India
Printed and bound in Great Britain by CPI Antony Rowe, Chippenham, Wiltshire

To Britta, Jerome and Annabelle,
as well as to Christoph and Vivien.

Contents

List of Figures	ix
List of Tables	xiii
Notation	xv
Preface	xxi

1 Introduction — 1
1.1 The private banking business — 1
1.2 Current challenges in private banking — 3
1.3 Improving service quality with behavioural finance — 6
1.4 Conclusion — 9

2 Decision Theory — 11
2.1 Introduction — 12
2.2 Mean-variance analysis — 14
2.3 Expected utility theory — 22
2.4 Prospect theory — 35
2.5 Prospect theory and the optimal asset allocation — 50
2.6 A critical view on mean-variance theory — 59
2.7 A critical view on expected utility axioms — 63
2.8 Comparison of expected utility, prospect theory, and mean-variance analysis — 64
2.9 Conclusion — 65

3 Behavioural Biases — 67
3.1 Information selection biases — 68
3.2 Information processing biases — 70
3.3 Decision biases — 82
3.4 Decision evaluation biases — 87
3.5 Biases in intertemporal decisions — 88
3.6 Behavioural biases and speculative bubbles — 91
3.7 Cultural differences in the behavioural biases — 95

4 Risk Profiling — 105
- 4.1 Dealing with behavioural biases — 105
- 4.2 The risk profiler and its benefits — 106
- 4.3 Designing a risk profiler: Some general considerations — 108
- 4.4 Implemented risk profilers: Case study of the former Bank Leu — 109
- 4.5 A risk profiler based on the mean-variance analysis — 114
- 4.6 Integrating behavioural finance in the risk profiler — 117
- 4.7 Case study: Comparing risk profiles — 127
- 4.8 Conclusion — 134

5 Product Design — 135
- 5.1 Case study: "Ladder Pop" — 136
- 5.2 Case study: "DAX Sparbuch" — 143
- 5.3 Optimal product design — 149
- 5.4 Conclusion — 155

6 Dynamic Asset Allocation — 157
- 6.1 The optimal tactical asset allocation — 158
- 6.2 The optimal strategic asset allocation — 171
- 6.3 Conclusion — 184

7 Life Cycle Planning — 187
- 7.1 Case study: Widow Kassel — 187
- 7.2 Main decisions over time — 189
- 7.3 Consumption smoothing — 189
- 7.4 The life cycle hypothesis — 190
- 7.5 The behavioural life cycle hypothesis — 192
- 7.6 The life cycle asset allocation problem — 194
- 7.7 The life cycle asset allocation of an expected utility maximizer — 195
- 7.8 The life cycle asset allocation of a behavioural investor — 198
- 7.9 Life cycle funds — 202
- 7.10 Conclusion — 206

8 Structured Wealth Management Process — 207
- 8.1 The benefits of a structured wealth management process — 209
- 8.2 Problems implementing a structured wealth management process — 210
- 8.3 Impact of the new process on conflicts of interests — 210
- 8.4 Learning by "cycling" through the process — 211
- 8.5 Case study: Credit Suisse — 211
- 8.6 Mental accounting in the wealth management process — 217
- 8.7 Conclusions — 226

9 Conclusion and Outlook — 229
- 9.1 Recapitulation of the main achievements — 229
- 9.2 Outlook of further developments — 229

References — 231

Index — 237

List of Figures

1.1	Efficiency and profitability of local and foreign banks in Switzerland	2
1.2	ROE weighted by the capitalization level of different countries	3
1.3	Differentiation drivers	5
1.4	Segmentation criteria	6
2.1	The lottery given by the returns of a fund of hedge funds	13
2.2	Mean-variance representation of the risk premium	16
2.3	The efficient frontier	16
2.4	Risk aversion and risk premium	17
2.5	Selecting the optimal portfolio	17
2.6	Two-fund-separation	19
2.7	Illustration of the certainty equivalent, risk premium, and risk aversion	29
2.8	Jensen's inequality	30
2.9	The value function	39
2.10	The probability weighting function	42
2.11	Return of hedge funds as they are and as seen by a prospect theory investor	45
2.12	Return probabilities	46
2.13	Risk taking conditions	49
2.14	Mean-variance preferences, based on the piecewise power value function of Kahneman and Tversky	51
2.15	Mean-standard deviation diagram with PT-indifference curves based on the piecewise exponential value function	51
2.16	Reward-risk perspective on the prospect theory	55
2.17	Cumulative gross returns (1993–2006)	56
2.18	Asset returns in a mean-variance diagram	56
2.19	Asset returns in an average-gain-loss diagram	57
2.20	Mean-variance tangential portfolio	57
2.21	Optimal asset allocation of a behavioural investor with $\beta = 2$	58
2.22	Optimal asset allocation of a behavioural investor with $\beta = 5$	58
2.23	Optimal asset allocation of a behavioural investor with $\beta = 10$	58
2.24	Two quite different structured products with the same mean and variance	59
2.25	The mean-variance paradox	60
2.26	The tangent portfolio without SPI+	61
2.27	The tangent portfolio with SPI+	61
2.28	Optimal asset allocation of a behavioural investor without SPI+	61

x   List of Figures

2.29	Optimal asset allocation of a behavioural investor with SPI+	62
2.30	The Ellsberg paradox	64
2.31	Similarities and differences of expected utility, prospect theory, and mean-variance	65
3.1	A typical decision-making process	68
3.2	Illustration of conditional probability	71
3.3	Experimental results on the gambler's fallacy	73
3.4	Performance of LGT-GST fund and its benchmark	74
3.5	Ideal growth stock purchase according to Fuller and Thaler Asset Management	77
3.6	The overconfidence effect in the case of forecasting	79
3.7	Hazardous trading	80
3.8	Average return per information level	80
3.9	Exploiting the favourite long-shot bias	82
3.10	Portfolio pyramid	83
3.11	Disposition effect	84
3.12	Equity portfolio weights of U.S., Japanese and British investors (Based on French and Poterba (1991))	85
3.13	Investor's payoff over time	91
3.14	Cultural differences according to Hofstede's "Uncertainty Avoidance Index"	95
3.15	Value functions of students in different countries based on the results of Bontempo *et al.* (1997)	96
3.16	Value functions of students in different countries based on the results of Weber and Hsee (1998)	97
3.17	Inflation rate versus degree of patience in several countries	99
3.18	Income per capita versus degree of patience in several countries	99
3.19	Individualism versus loss aversion index (theta)	100
3.20	Trend chasing and individualism around the world	101
3.21	Ambiguity aversion and the equity premium	104
4.1	Different advice from various banks according to *Stocks* magazine 41–42, 2003	107
4.2	An experimental laboratory at the University of Zurich	109
4.3	Risk ability in the mean-variance analysis	116
4.4	Mean-variance analysis with risk ability	116
4.5	Heterogeneity in the individuals' risk and loss aversion assessed in a study at ZKB	118
4.6	Heterogeneity in the individuals' risk aversion over gains α^+ and losses α^-	118
4.7	Heterogeneity in the individuals' perception of probabilities	119
4.8	Time diversification: The longer the investment horizon, the better the return-risk ratio	123
4.9	Probability for bonds beating stocks for portfolios with different time horizons	124
4.10	Optimal asset allocation over different time horizons	124
4.11	Investment advice of the former Bank Leu	130
4.12	Optimal asset allocation of Christine Kuhn according to BhFS	133
4.13	Client's classification based on predefined risk profiles	133

5.1	Optimal payoff from the perspective of behavioural investors	136
5.2	Payoff of the Ladder Pop at maturity	138
5.3	SMI and Ladder Pop prices (indexed) from 15.01.2002 to 12.12.2006	138
5.4	Two ways of achieving 8.1 % return after two years: Investing at 4 % each year or changing to 10 % after the first year	139
5.5	Scenarios setup	140
5.6	Payoff DAX Sparbuch per month	145
5.7	Payoff of a barrier-like structured product	149
5.8	Optimal structured-product of a CRRA investor with $\alpha = 0.8$	151
5.9	Optimal structured product for a mean-variance investor	152
5.10	Optimal structured product for a behavioural investor with $\beta = 2$	152
5.11	Optimal structured product for a behavioural investor with $\beta = 1$	153
5.12	Optimal structured product of an investor with biased perception of probabilities	153
5.13	Interactive multi-touch table	154
6.1	Example of Markov matrices	158
6.2	The CRRA investor on a random walk	162
6.3	TAA of the CRRA investor on mean reversion after "good" times	164
6.4	TAA of the CRRA investor on mean reversion after "bad" times	164
6.5	TAA of the behavioural investor on a random walk	167
6.6	TAA of the behavioural investor on mean reversion after "good" times	168
6.7	TAA of the behavioural investor on mean reversion after "bad" times	169
6.8	Sample paths of a random walk without drift	172
6.9	Variance of random walks over time	172
6.10	An example of mean-variance ratios of a random walk over different time horizons	173
6.11	Mean-variance ratio of S&P 500 annual logarithmic returns (1871–2007)	173
6.12	Variance ratios for S&P 500 annual logarithmic returns (1871–2007)	174
6.13	Asset allocation of the CRRA investor on a random walk	176
6.14	Asset allocation of the CRRA investor on mean reversion after "bad" times	177
6.15	Asset allocation of the CRRA investor on mean reversion after "good" times	178
6.16	Asset allocation of the CRRA investor on mean reversion after "good" times (fix-mix)	179
6.17	Asset allocation of the CRRA investor on mean reversion after "bad" times (fix-mix)	180
6.18	Asset allocation of the behavioural investor under a random walk	181
6.19	The behavioural investor on mean reversion after "good" times	182
6.20	The behavioural investor on mean reversion after "bad" times	183
7.1	Performance of German stocks (DAX) versus German government bonds (REX index)	188
7.2	Cumulative dividends from DAX versus interest earnings from REX	188
7.3	Consumption smoothing	190
7.4	Utility derived from consumption drawn from different mental accounts	192
7.5	Separating risk preference from risk ability	194
7.6	Perfect consumption smoothing	196
7.7	The impact of the discount factor on current consumption	196

7.8	The impact of asymmetric returns on consumption and asset allocation of a CRRA investor	198
7.9	Impact of human capital on consumption and asset allocation of a CRRA investor	199
7.10	Impact of required consumption on the optimal asset allocation of a CRRA investor	200
7.11	The behavioural investor and consumption smoothing	201
7.12	The habit formation effect on the optimal consumption over time	201
7.13	The effect of hyperbolic discounting on consumption	202
7.14	The effect of asymmetric returns	203
7.15	The effect of asymmetric returns with a less attractive risky asset	204
7.16	The cumulative effect of human capital, hyperbolic and intertemporal discounting, and habit formation	205
8.1	Exploiting the comparative advantage of the relationship manager (RM); vis-à-vis the investment committee (IC)	210
8.2	The wealth management process of Credit Suisse	211
8.3	Example of a personal balance sheet	213
8.4	Assets split	213
8.5	The asset split protects the client from a collapse of diversification	214
8.6	Finding an optimal investment strategy for the client	215
8.7	Integrated goal-based wealth management approach	226

List of Tables

1.1	Total wealth of high net worth individuals worldwide	4
1.2	Wealth management versus brokerage	4
2.1	Historical equity premiums of different countries	15
2.2	The asset allocation puzzle	19
2.3	An example of prospect theory violating Axiom 0	43
2.4	Risk taking behaviour in the face of gains and losses with small and moderate probabilities	50
2.5	Mean-variance violating the independence axiom	62
2.6	Advantages and disadvantages of the three theories of choice	64
3.1	Descriptive statistics of the 1-year annual real returns of the value weighted CRSP all-share market portfolio, the intermediate government bond index of Ibbotson, one month T-Bill as risk-free rate, and the size and value docile portfolios from 1927 to 2007 (81 yearly observations)	69
3.2	The splitting bias	78
3.3	Famous bubbles (Shleifer, 2000) continued by ourselves	92
3.4	Fitting prospect theory parameters of the results of Weber and Hsee (1998) and Bontempo *et al.* (1997)	97
3.5	Volatility and market returns in different countries	102
3.6	Value and glamour stocks performance from 1975 to 1995	103
4.1	Fighting against biases leading to irrational decisions	105
4.2	Summary investment advice of BhFS and the former Bank Leu	133
5.1	Final wealth with the underlying, the Ladder Pop, and a bond	141
5.2	Expected utility and certainty equivalents of a CRRA investor	142
5.3	Product returns	142
5.4	Prospect utility and certainty equivalents of a behavioural investor	142
5.5	DAX return per month and DAX bonus for that month (Nov. 2006–Dec. 2007)	144
5.6	DAX return and DAX bonus per month (Nov. 2006–Dec. 2007)	144
5.7	DAX return and DAX Sparbuch return on annual basis	145
5.8	Final wealth of a CRRA investor	147
5.9	Expected utilities and certainty equivalents of CRRA investors	147
5.10	Minimum appreciation of the underlying required by CRRA investors	147
5.11	Prospect utility of behavioural investors with an absolute reference point	148

5.12	Prospect utility of behavioural investors with a relative reference point	148
5.13	Minimum appreciation of the underlying required by behavioural investors with an absolute reference point	148
5.14	Structured products chosen by participants of a field study where structured products could be designed freely with a special editor	155
6.1	The tactical asset allocations of CRRA and behavioural investors under a random walk and a mean reversion	170
6.2	Strategic asset allocations of CRRA and behavioural investors under a random walk and mean reversion	184
6.3	Optimal asset allocations of myopic investors under a random walk and mean reversion	184
8.1	Asset payoffs	218
8.2	Prospect utilities and certainty equivalents with different mental accounting rules	219
8.3	Asset returns	224

Notation

The following symbols are used in this book.

$ARA(.)$ absolute risk aversion
α^+, λ^+ risk aversion over gains
α^-, λ^- risk aversion over losses
α^i risk aversion parameter of investor i

b^g budget for goal g
β loss aversion

$c = 1, \ldots, C$ consequences
$CARA(.)$ constant absolute risk aversion
CE, X certainty equivalent
$const$ a constant
$\text{cov}_{k,j}$ covariance of the returns of asset $k = 1, \ldots, K$ and $j = 1, \ldots, J$
$CRRA(.)$ constant relative risk aversion

d return
$DARA(.)$ decreasing absolute risk aversion
$DRRA(.)$ decreasing relative risk aversion
δ exponential discount factor
δ^g relative importance of goal g
δ^g weight of goal g
Δx change in the realisations of a random variable x

e return
E_U expected utility

$F(c)$ cumulative distribution function F at some point c

$g = 1, \ldots, G$ investment goals
γ^+ probability weighting factor over gains
γ^- probability weighting factor over losses

h habit formation factor

$i = 1, \ldots, I$ investors
$IARA(.)$ increasing absolute risk aversion

i.i.d. independent and identically distributed
IRRA(.) increasing relative risk aversion

$j = 1, \ldots, J$ mental accounts

$k = 0, 1, \ldots, K$ (risky) assets
K^j subset of assets in mental account j
λ asset allocation
λ_0 portfolio weight of the risk-free asset
λ_k portfolio weight of asset k
λ^{opt} optimal asset allocation
λ_k^T assets weights in the tangent portfolio T
λ_k^g asset weight for asset k serving the goal g
L lottery

m return

μ expected value of a random variable
μ_λ expected return of a portfolio λ

p_i probability for consequence c_i
p_s probability for state s
P^n probability for a sequence of outcomes of order n
$p(.|.)$ conditional probability
$p(. \cap .)$ joint probability of events
PT_v expected prospect value
pt^+ average gain utility
pt^- average loss utility

R, r return
R_f risk-free return
R_s^k return of asset $k = 1, \ldots, K$ in state $s = 1, \ldots, S$
R_s^M return of the market portfolio M in state $s = 1, \ldots, S$
RRA(.) relative risk aversion
RP reference point

$s = 1, \ldots, S$ or $s = u, d$ states of nature
σ^2 variance of asset returns
σ_λ^2 variance of portfolio return λ

$t = 0, \ldots, T$ time period

$u(.)$ utility function; $u^i(.)$ utility of investor i
U^g utility from achieving goal g
$u'(.)$ first derivative of a function
$u''(.)$ second derivative of a function
u return

V mean-variance utility function
$v(.)$ value function; $v^i(.)$ value function of investor i

$w(p)$ probability weighting function
$w^*(p)$ normalized probability weighting function
$w(K^j)$ weight of mental account K^j
$\underline{w}$ minimum wealth or a 'safety first' constraint
w_s^g wealth in state s associated with the goal g
$\widetilde{w}_s^g$ state-dependent exogenous wealth
w_t wealth in period t

«Wir können sie jetzt nicht stören. – Sie sind mitten in der neuen Anlagestrategie!»
We can't bother them now – they are working on a new investment strategy!
Source: Felix Schaad in *Tages-Anzeiger*, 28.05.2004

Preface

Behavioural finance is an interdisciplinary research area that combines psychology and finance. It originated from decision theory – most notably the psychological traps that occur in making decisions under uncertainty. Private banking consists of a collection of services that banks offer on a more personal basis to wealthy investors. In particular, these services include investment advice given by relationship managers helping clients to achieve their financial goals without falling into psychological traps when investing their wealth on financial markets. Hence, behavioural finance is an appropriate framework to give private banking a scientific foundation.

The high wealth of private banking clients makes it possible to give tailor-made advice that best suits the risk ability, risk preference, and risk awareness of the client. Within the bank, the relationship manager has a key role in providing this important service to clients. He needs to have a good knowledge of both the financial markets and the individual client. While traditional finance with its cornerstones of mean-variance analysis, efficient market hypothesis, and derivative pricing has provided good models to understand the market, it is not appropriate for understanding clients. On the one hand, traditional finance has ignored behavioural biases so that the relationship manager is unable to understand many of the reactions his clients show in the course of making investments. On the other hand, traditional finance has focused on a simplified notion of risk – the variance – that is neither appropriate for most private investors nor leads to rational decisions when applied to modern assets like hedge funds or structured products. Hence, in order to provide the best service quality to their clients, most relationship managers need some knowledge of behavioural finance. Without this knowledge, relationship managers who are trained only in traditional finance would be left unprepared for their task to optimally position their clients on the trade-offs financial markets provide.

The purpose of this book is to close this gap by providing advisors of private clients with both the appropriate framework for their task as well as a collection of practical tools to support their work.[1] To achieve this goal we structure the book as follows.

After a brief introduction into the current challenges of the private banking industry, we go extensively into the foundations of behavioural finance: decision theory. Decision theory has three broad paradigms: expected utility theory, prospect theory, and mean-variance analysis. Expected utility theory clarifies which decisions are rational, prospect theory describes which decisions are most often observed, and mean-variance analysis is the best known decision model in practice. As we will show, in special cases like normally distributed returns, the three decision models coincide, but in general they are mutually distinct. In particular, it is possible that prospect theory decisions are rational while mean-variance decisions are irrational; i.e., the naïve classification "behavioural is equal to irrational" and "mean-variance is equal to rational" can be totally wrong.

---

[1] Please visit our webpage www.bfpb.ch to download the Excel tools created for this book.

Chapter 3 goes through the many psychological traps (behavioural biases) that are commonly observed along a typical decision-making process. In particular, we show how these biases differ across different cultures, which is of vital importance to any bank offering private banking services worldwide. Chapter 4 then shows how to integrate the insights achieved thus far into an important tool of highly practical relevance: a risk profiler. A risk profiler is a well-designed questionnaire that assesses the client's risk ability, risk preferences, and his risk awareness. Besides choosing the most appropriate questions, behavioural finance helps to evaluate the answers in a consistent way. In many countries, risk profilers are required by law. We see this regulatory requirement as a chance for any bank to improve the quality of its advisory process.

In Chapter 5 we analyze the colourful world of structured products, a business of increasing importance to many banks. We show how to evaluate structured products both from an expected utility theory perspective and from a prospect theory point of view. Moreover, we explain how to design structured, tailor-made products for private clients. After this, in Chapter 6, we go into the dynamics of investing. We show which investor will rebalance his portfolio during the course of investments and which one will take his profits or increase risks. Moreover, we give a foundation for common investment advice like the age rule, according to which the share of risky assets ought to increase with the investment horizon. In the following chapter we look at the life cycle investment problem. Besides the time horizon effect, the flow of exogenous income and the consumption needs influence the asset allocation over the life cycle. In particular, we study behavioural effects such as habit formation and hyperbolic discounting and how they influence clients' investing decisions.

The final chapter, Chapter 8, wraps up the main contents of the book in the form of the practical problem of wealth management. We show how a typical advisory process should be structured to make the best use of the services the bank can offer. Such a process needs to integrate personal asset-liability management, life cycle aspects, a risk profiler, a strategy implementation, and a well-suited documentation. In particular, we highlight the relevance of framing effects in documentation and the importance of mental accounting in advising clients how to invest their wealth optimally.

The style of the book is mixed. Besides intuitive written explanations, examples, and case studies, we also deepen the understanding by using some mathematics. Case studies and mathematics are highlighted in boxes. One can also understand the book on a more general level without going into these boxes. We hope that, in this way, this book is appropriate for a broader audience. Certainly the book is suitable for master classes both at business schools and universities in the primary studies, but it is also suitable for executive master programmes.[2] Independent of organized courses, our book can be used as self-study material to obtain a Behavioural Finance Upgrade for anyone trained in traditional finance.

Even though by now there are quite a few good books on behavioural finance – such as the two brilliant books by Hersh Shefrin, and also the two excellent books by James Montier in this series – our book is unique since it focuses more on client advisory than on asset pricing. This focus makes use of our comparative advantage of being in one of the world's first-class centres for private banking. Indeed, our book benefitted a lot from projects we have done for the former Bank Leu, Credit Suisse (CS), Union Bank of Switzerland (UBS), and Zürcher Kantonalbank (ZKB), to name just a few.

---

[2] Indeed, the content has been taught for many years at the Norwegian Business School (NHH) in Bergen, at the University of Zurich (UZH), and also at executive programmes of the Swiss Training Centre for Investment Professionals (AZEK), the Swiss Banking School (SBS), and now the Swiss Finance Institute (SFI).

Naturally, our book has some overlaps with other books on behavioural finance but the core ideas are based on our own research done in NCCR-Finrisk and the Research Priority Program Finance (RPPF) at the University of Zurich. We are indebted to our collaborators in these projects: foremost, Enrico De Giorgi, Marc Oliver Rieger, János Mayer, and Mei Wang. Moreover, we would like to thank the above-mentioned research networks, in particular their directors, Rajna Gibson and Marc Chesney, for intellectual as well as financial support. The generous support from NCCR-Finrisk was not obvious, given the focus of that network, which is more on traditional finance. We are grateful to the International Scientific Council of NCCR-Finrisk and to the Director of NCCR-Finrisk, Rajna Gibson, for their tolerance. Last but not least, we would like to express our gratitude to many people who provided advice and comments during the development of this book. Without the help of the editors of Wiley Finance, most notably Peter Baker and Aimée Dibbens, we would not have finalized this book. Moreover, the book benefitted greatly from comments from Peter Wüthrich, Doris Schönemann, Mila Winter, Christoph Bachmann, Nilüfer Caliskan, Martine Baumgartner, Martin Vlcek, Andreas Kamm, Philippe Martin, Richard Meier, Alfons Cortes, Thierry Bonnas and Amelie Brune. Finally, without the feedback from many students at the Norwegian business school (NHH), University of Zurich (UZH), Swiss Training Centre for Investment Professionals (AZEK), and Swiss Finance Institute (SFI), the book would not have reached its current level of pedagogical excellence.

Last but not least, we are indebted to our families, as writing a book puts an extra burden on our close relatives – a burden that is heavily under-weighted. Hence having written this book reveals that we are ourselves of the behavioural type described in our book – not always totally rational and also motivated by things other than money.

1
Introduction

In this chapter we summarize the current challenges in private banking and explain why wealth managers need behavioural finance. The concepts and insights suggesting how to transfer the research results into practical solutions are discussed in great detail in the rest of the book.

1.1 THE PRIVATE BANKING BUSINESS

Private banking offers exclusive wealth-related services to high net worth individuals.[1] The term "private" refers to the more personalized and exclusive nature of the offer as compared to the mass-market services accessible for other individuals such as retail clients and also as compared to services offered to institutional clients.

Private banking services can be offered by any financial intermediary whose main activity is the supply of exclusive financial and advisory services to wealthy private clients. Such financial intermediaries call themselves either "private banks" or they have a separate "private banking" or "wealth management" department serving the needs of wealthy private clients.

Case Study 1.1: Swiss private banking

Many financial institutes all over the world provide private banking services, but Swiss financial intermediaries have an indisputable leading position. Private banking has been a Swiss competence for more than 300 years. Today, almost one third of the international assets under management are with Swiss private banks, which makes the country the principle platform for private banking.[2] With 9 % of global assets under management, Switzerland is also the third largest wealth management centre in the world behind the US and the UK.[3]

Several factors contribute to Switzerland's emergence as a leader in private banking. The country is famous not only for its neutrality and economic stability, but also for its liberal capital markets. In particular, private banking in Switzerland has a long tradition of confidentiality related to the Swiss banker's professional duty of client privacy.[4] Its outstanding reputation is also supported by the tradition of high-end services and committed staff. In Switzerland, a "private banker" is not simply an expert in a private

---

[1] Although high net worth is not defined, it generally refers to individuals with net worth greater than $1 million.
[2] See www.swissprivatebankers.com.
[3] See www.swissprivatebankers.com.
[4] The Swiss banker's professional duty of client confidentiality is rooted in Article 47 of the Federal Law on Banks and Savings Banks, which came into force on 8 November 1934.

Case Study 1.1: (Continued)

bank or in a wealth management department of a universal bank. The term refers to a specific definition in the Swiss Banking Law. In the words of Alfred E. Sarasin,

> "A private banker is an entrepreneur in the privately-owned banking sector who conducts his business using his own assets, assuming unlimited liability with his entire fortune and exercising his independent power of decision."

The Swiss banking sector plays also a very important role for the Swiss economy. At the end of 2005, banking balance sheet assets totalled 2.8 trillion Swiss francs, corresponding to six times the GDP of the country[5] and wealth management alone accounts for more than half of the banks' value–added.[6]

The long tradition in private banking has an important role for the success of Swiss private banks. In a recent study Cocca and Geiger (2007) compare different private banks in Switzerland and 10 other countries.[7] They find that Swiss banks surpass foreign competitors in Switzerland in profitability (compare return-on-equity ratios, ROE) as well as in operational efficiency (compare cost/income ratios in Figure 1.1).

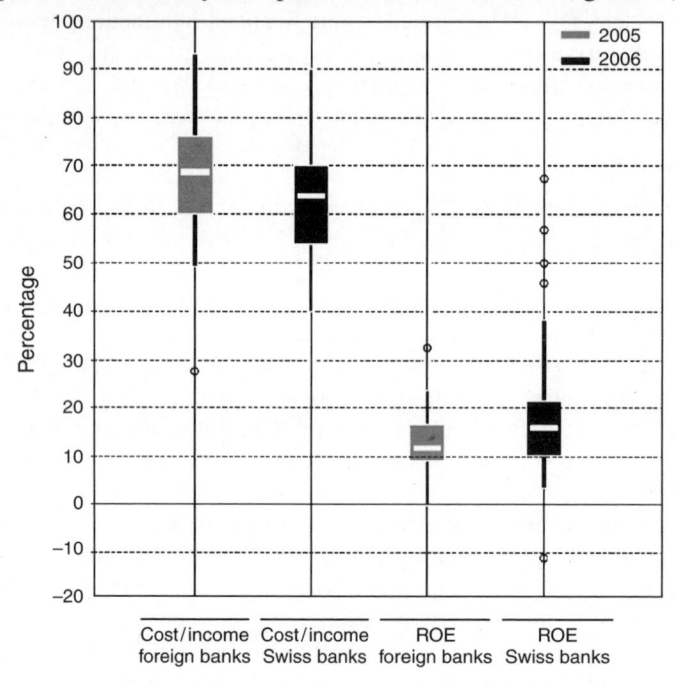

Figure 1.1 Efficiency and profitability of local and foreign banks in Switzerland

---

[5] See www.snb.ch.
[6] See www.swissprivatebankers.com.
[7] "The International Private Banking Study 2007" by Cocca, T.D. and H. Geiger is available at www.isb.uzh.ch.

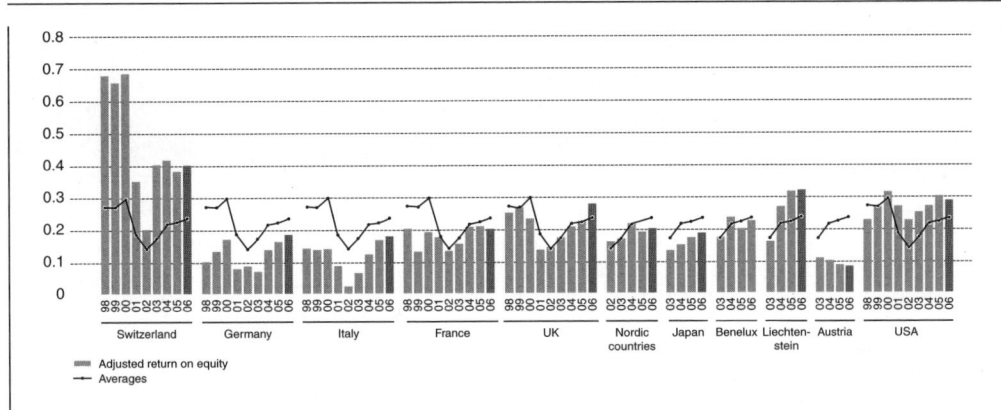

Figure 1.2 ROE weighted by the capitalization level of different countries

Compared to private banks in other countries, Swiss private banks are far more profitable. Their adjusted return-on-equity (return-on-equity weighted by the capitalization level of the country) remains far above the average for the last 10 years (see Figure 1.2).

On the one hand, the success of Swiss private banking in the future relies on external factors such as the Swiss banker's professional duty of client privacy, which recently has been under heated debate, particularly in the context of severe cases of tax evasion. On the other hand, the future of Swiss private banking depends on the banks' ability to keep improving the quality of professional services in a business where knowledge and intellectual advancement gain stronger recognition. To ensure the advancement of knowledge creation and of knowledge transfer for banks in Switzerland, the banking sector has created the Swiss Finance Institute, SFI, which supports the Swiss Universities in building up their finance departments to international excellence.[8]

As illustrated above, the Swiss business model belongs to the most important case studies in private banking. Other small countries like Luxembourg, Monaco, Austria, and Singapore, and even smaller entities like the British Virgin Islands, have already tried to emulate the Swiss model. Looking forward, however, there are some important challenges for all of them. While players compete aggressively, clients' expectations shift and regulatory pressures increase the need for financial centres to continue their transformation in order to sustain the growth potential of wealth management activities. The following section discusses these issues in more detail and argues that behavioural finance can help wealth managers to deal with them.

1.2 CURRENT CHALLENGES IN PRIVATE BANKING

In this section we refer to two recent surveys on private banking: The Global Private Banking/Wealth Management Survey 2007 by PricewaterhouseCoopers (PwC) and the World Wealth Report 2007 and 2008 by Capgemini and Merrill Lynch. The first one focuses on evaluating important industry trends from the perspective of senior management in private

---

[8] See www.sfi.ch.

banks, the second one surveys the behaviour of private banking clients. The main conclusion of these surveys is that private banking will probably continue to be a highly profitable business with strong growth. This is based on the observation that world wealth continues to grow despite fluctuations in markets and economic conditions. As clients demand comprehensive and tailor-made services, wealth managers are making strategic investments to differentiate themselves. In the resulting competition, the pressure on the firms to understand the essence of clients' needs and ultimately improve the quality of their advisory services is increasing. In this section we claim that wealth managers need behavioural finance to manage these tasks successfully. The rest of the book details the transfer of this knowledge into practical solutions.

1.2.1 Growth prospects

The business of private bankers depends ultimately on the size of the assets under management. Worldwide, there are 10.1 million high net worth individuals living predominantly in Europe (30%), North America (33%) and Asia-Pacific (28%) (see Table 1.1). In 2007, the global high net worth wealth totalled $40.7 trillion and is expected to reach $59.1 trillion by 2012, growing at an annual rate of 7.7% per annum.

Table 1.1 Total wealth of high net worth individuals worldwide (*Source*: Capgemini)

Year HNWIs	Total Million	Europe %	North America %	Asia Pacific %	Latin America %	Others %
1997	5.2	30.7	36.4	23.1	3.8	7.8
1998	5.9	31.0	36.2	22.4	3.4	7.0
1999	7.0	31.4	35.7	24.3	2.9	6.7
2000	7.0	35.7	31.4	22.9	4.3	5.7
2001	7.1	35.2	31.0	23.9	4.2	5.7
2002	7.2	34.7	30.6	26.4	4.2	4.2
2003	7.7	32.5	32.5	27.3	3.9	3.9
2004	8.3	31.3	32.5	27.7	3.6	4.8
2005	8.7	32.2	33.3	27.6	3.4	4.6
2006	9.5	30.5	33.7	27.4	4.2	4.2
2007	10.1	30.7	32.7	27.7	4.0	5.0

The growing pool of high net worth individuals means enormous profit potential for private banking firms. Most private bank players achieve net profit margins per asset of at least 25 basis points (bps) compared to net profit margins of 5 bps in the institutional asset management business. Table 1.2 gives an example from the annual report of Credit Suisse in 2007.

Given the profitability of the business and the increasing number of wealthy people, it is not surprising that private banking experts look ahead to strong industry growth. In the recent

Table 1.2 Wealth management versus brokerage (*Source*: Credit Suisse annual report (2007))

	Private Banking	Institutional Asset Management
Net revenues (million Swiss francs)	9583	2577
Cost/income ratio	59.6	82.2
Pre-tax income margin (%)	40.3	17.8
Gross margin (bps)	115	36
Net margin (bps)	47	5
Number of employees	14 300	3600

Wealth Management Survey by PwC, CEOs and wealth managers of 265 private banks expect the assets under management (AuM) in the industry to grow at 23 % per annum over the next three years. Surprisingly, both CEOs and financial directors expect their own businesses to grow at an even higher rate of 30 %. But how do the banks intend to fulfil these ambitious plans? Clearly, some of them either underestimate the growth potential of their competitors or overstate their own prospects.

1.2.2 Improving clients' experience and differentiation strategies

Overall, there are three strategies to increase the assets under management: through performance, through the acquisition of new clients, or through attracting new assets of existing clients. As the achievement of superior performance depends mainly on the advisors' view on the financial markets, which is not (and should not be) their primary domain of specialization, we focus our discussion on the last two strategies. The second strategy is probably more costly than the last one as the bank needs to hire and train more advisors who can take care of the increased number of clients. Hence, the most attractive growth strategy is the attraction of new assets from existing clients. Indeed, 96 % of the surveyed managers view increasing the shares of the existing clients' wallets as more important than gaining new assets through acquisitions, especially during the next three years. How can this goal be achieved? Clearly, banks need to convince their clients that there is no better placement for their assets. Hence, to gain a larger share of clients' wallets, banks need to improve the clients' experience and find a way to differentiate themselves from their competitors.

From the clients' perspective, the most important factor influencing them to stay with their wealth managers is the service quality. Furthermore, when choosing a wealth manager, high net worth individuals rely more on personal experience than on any marketing efforts. This suggests that wealth managers, who focus on the clients' needs when designing and implementing their advisory strategy, are expected to be more successful in improving clients' experience, thus increasing the share of clients' wallets.

Wealth managers see this point similarly. They perceive the difference among banks in the brand, the personal relationships, and the quality of the advisory services. In addition, the provision of a comprehensive, integrated planning approach is perceived as far more important than product development and investment performance (see Figure 1.3). In fact, as the wealth

Differentiation driver	Sum of weighted ranked responses
Brand value	186
Quality of professional advice	180
Personal relationships	180
Provision of comprehensive, integrated wealth management planning approach for clients	146
Knowledge of local markets	83
Best-in-class products	74
Product innovation and development	73
International know-how	68
Investment performance	64
Breadth of product range	52
Availability of non-proprietary products from an external provider	38
Research and analysis	20

Source: PricewaterhouseCoopers

Figure 1.3 Differentiation drivers

management market matures and products are becoming more commoditized, differentiation strategies based on specific products are turning out to be less successful.

1.3 IMPROVING SERVICE QUALITY WITH BEHAVIOURAL FINANCE

The recent surveys on wealth management and their clients point out a clear call for service quality along an integrated wealth management approach with a strong focus on clients' needs. Three factors play a significant role in its implementation: understanding, anticipation, and monitoring of clients' needs and behaviour. In the following section we also show that behavioural finance is of particular importance to them.

1.3.1 Understanding clients

In general, understanding the client means understanding the essence of his individual needs. Although needs are, by their nature, an individual circumstance and thus unique, most advisors try to reach a certain degree of standardization in order to keep the complexity of the advisory process low. One simple mechanism is to build different segments of clients. Clients within a segment build a homogenous group with similar needs and expectations toward the services of their advisor. Possible criteria are:

- geographic (e.g. place of domicile);
- demographic (e.g. income, education);
- psychographic (e.g. motives, ethical values, life style);
- client's profitability (e.g. assets, client's value);
- client's bankable assets (e.g. current and potential assets).

The most commonly used metric is, however, the current and potential assets as the PwC Wealth Management Survey documents (see Figure 1.4).

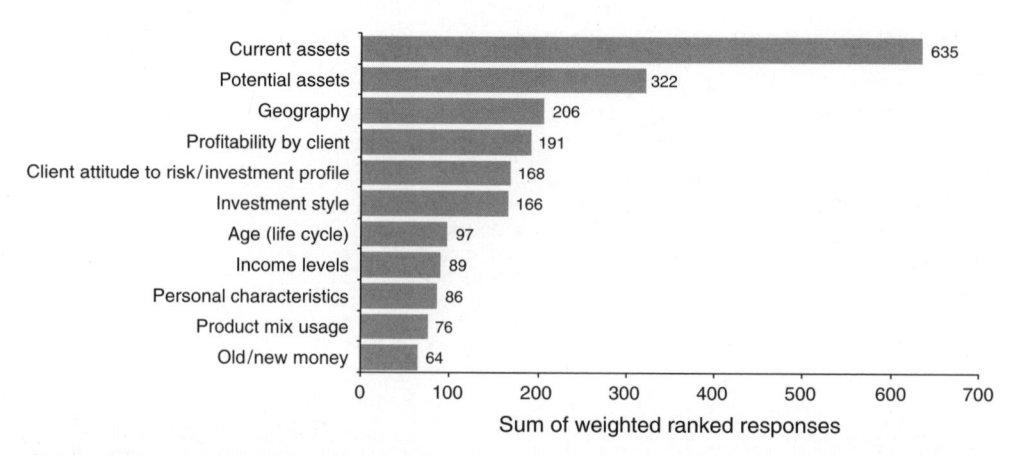

Source: PricewaterhouseCoopers

Figure 1.4 Segmentation criteria

While clients' wealth is important as a factor to help banks to differentiate clients and determine the intensity of the advisory relationship in each segment, wealth is less helpful to understand clients' needs and differentiate between clients' preferences. In fact, most economic models within traditional finance suggest the same solution for clients since preferences do not depend on their wealth. In other words, if the clients do not differ with respect to their aversion toward uncertainty, which is the main feature of their preferences, they should also receive the same advice independently on their wealth. Hence, to understand the clients' needs, advisors should take a closer look at the determinants of clients' preferences and the drivers of clients' financial decisions.

Clients' preferences are important in order to understand clients' needs because they determine how comfortable the clients feel with the outcome of a particular decision. Hence, knowing clients' preferences is important for advisors aiming to improve clients' experience. A crucial point thereby is the distinction between clients' decisions, which are driven by their preferences and those that are driven by psychological biases. This is also the reason why it is important for advisors to understand how their clients make financial decisions. At this stage, advisors can benefit enormously from the vast experimental and theoretical research in behavioural finance. Since the time when Vernon Smith introduced laboratory experiments into economics, experimental studies have amassed evidence that actual behaviour under uncertainty and risk contradicts the idealized behaviour postulated by traditional finance. Kahneman and Tversky have developed theoretical models of behavioural finance that can compete with traditional finance also on the analytical level.[9] Their prospect theory addresses the question of aggregation and segregation of assets, reference point dependent behaviour, loss aversion, asymmetric uncertainty aversion, and biased probability perception. A theoretical framework integrating these issues, such as prospect theory, provides a much richer foundation on which to assess clients' preferences than traditional finance models.

This perspective is important for establishing a link between the clients' needs and certain financial objectives because the typical perception is that traditional finance defines a rational benchmark, and all behaviourally motivated decisions of the clients are irrational. Hence, good advice is one that helps clients to reach this rational benchmark. However, this is not necessarily true. Some aspects of clients' behaviour are rational and other aspects are not. A good advisor helps clients make rational decisions, which are consistent with their needs and preferences but never forces them to accept the result of a theory that does not fit with the clients' understanding of a good investment. Once the advisors develop understanding on this important issue, they can continue with the next implementation step, i.e. the anticipation of clients' needs along a comprehensive wealth management planning approach.

1.3.2 Anticipation of clients' needs along the wealth management process

A comprehensive wealth management planning approach is seen by the managers as an important differentiation device (see Figure 1.3). As with every decision problem, its basic structure consists of the following three basic steps: assessment of the clients' profiles (needs, wishes, experience, financial strength), development and implementation of an optimal investment solution (in accordance with the clients' profiles), and monitoring of the match between the clients' profiles and the suggested solution. Thus, a planning approach can work as a differentiation

---

[9] In 2002, Daniel Kahneman and Vernon Smith received the Nobel Prize in economics for their extraordinary achievements.

device and serves to improve the clients' experience only if, in each step, the managers find the best way to define financial objectives based on clients' needs. This depends on two factors. The first one is the advisors' understanding of the clients as discussed in the previous step. The second one is the systematic acquisition and intelligent use of clients' information. This is of particular relevance for formulating investment advice that is not only theoretically correct but also optimal from the clients' perspective.

Behavioural finance provides clear advantages compared to traditional finance for managers aiming to reach this goal. The most important advantages are summarized as follows.[10]

First, traditional finance often works with overly simplified parametric models of risk attitudes such as the assumption that clients' risk aversion does not depend on their wealth. It is important to note here that this assumption does not follow from rationality considerations and thus cannot be used as an argument for using traditional finance as a rational benchmark. In contrast to this, behavioural finance develops a rich model of risk attitudes that is derived relative to reference points. Relaxing the assumption that the clients' risk aversion does not depend on their wealth, key aspects of behavioural finance – like loss aversion and asymmetric risk aversion – can be incorporated into a rational model.[11]

Second, traditional finance requires integrating all assets into one huge account so that a clever investor can always benefit from the diverging movements of the various components. An important aspect of behavioural finance is *mental accounting*. The basic idea of mental accounting is that the grand asset allocation problem can be split up into a couple of smaller problems across which the diversification may not be optimally adjusted. The question of whether mental accounting is irrational depends on whether the advantage of diversification is worth risking mistakes due to the increased complexity of the grand asset allocation problem. Additionally, the idea of mental accounting can be used to take into account the observation that clients may have particular financial goals. For these clients, an optimal advice does not maximize the overall performance of their portfolios as the traditional finance would suggest, but helps clients to make financial decisions that can be classified as optimal because they are designed to reach their predefined goals.

Finally, traditional finance has proposed variance as the unique risk measure. This is fine when markets are efficient and hence returns are normally distributed. However, the returns of stocks of individual firms or the returns of hedge funds, for example, deviate considerably from being normally distributed. Hence, other features of risk, in particular downside measures, come into play. Moreover, with downside risk measures like "Short Fall Probabilities" or "Conditional Value at Risk", holding more risk-free assets may actually increase the risk, if risk is measured as a fall below a target return that exceeds the risk-free rate.

These examples illustrate that the simple dichotomy that traditional finance equals rational finance and behavioural finance equals irrational finance, has to be taken with a pinch of salt. A good advisor will have to assess the various aspects of his clients' needs based on the background of the understanding that behaviourally motivated decisions are not always irrational. The advisor will then have to distinguish those aspects which are a matter of the clients' preference from those he has to correct because they are irrational and will be regretted by the client later on. This task has to be completed in each step of the advisory process in order to make sure that the clients' needs are anticipated extensively.

---

[10] The next chapter elaborates these points in more detail.
[11] Reference point based behaviour is not irrational when the reference points are given by aspiration levels and hence are determined by forward looking planning and not by backward looking considerations. This point is discussed in the following chapter.

1.3.3 Monitoring clients' behaviour

The final step of the implementation strategy is monitoring. Its aim is to supervise two features of clients' behaviour. The first one is the changes in clients' needs over time. Over the life cycle clients usually have different needs that have to be considered (e.g. marriage, children, house purchase, or unexpected job loss). Further, the needs of the clients might also change with the clients' experience with financial matters (e.g. after crises in the stock and mortgage markets). The second feature of clients' behaviour over time is related to its rationality. The rational benchmark is time consistency, i.e. clients' preferences should not change simply because the decisions are made at different points of time. In reality, individuals behave differently.

Behavioural finance provides useful insights into the drivers of time-inconsistent preferences and the determinants of individuals' financial decisions over time and over the life cycle. Using these insights, advisors will be able to help clients avoid irrational decisions and determine an asset allocation that is optimally adjusted to their changing needs over time. In particular, advisors will be able to judge whether it is wise to lock clients into investment products that adjust optimally over time and to determine how to design pension plans for clients with time-inconsistent preferences.

1.4 CONCLUSION

Private banking is a highly profitable business, which is expected to grow strongly with the increasing size of worldwide wealth. Looking forward, however, there is no lack of challenges. While players aggressively compete, clients' expectations shift toward higher service quality. The main success factor will therefore be the improvement of clients' experience by focusing more sharply on clients' needs. The goal can be reached only if advisors correctly understand what determines the clients' needs and drives their financial decisions. Clients' experience will barely be improved by guiding them toward decisions derived by nice analytical models but not necessarily motivated by rational considerations. Moreover, if advisors do not help clients to avoid irrational decisions, they are going to regret them and in their disappointment the clients may decide to withdraw their assets and change the advisor. Thus, an essential success factor in private banking is the development of an understanding of clients' behaviour. This understanding needs to be anticipated in all steps of the advisory process, from gathering the relevant information about the client to its intelligent evaluation. In fact, using clients' information in the wrong context is more dangerous than giving random advice as it generates potential for regret when clients face the result. Finally, clients' needs should be monitored over time as they are likely to change with the clients' life cycle and their experience. A failure to perform these tasks successfully will probably lead to a loss of clients to competitors in the mid- or long-term.

Behavioural finance provides valuable insights into the determinants of individuals' behaviour. These insights are particularly important for the advisor's understanding of his clients and the quality of his advice as perceived by the clients. The main reason is that not all psychologically determined decisions as documented by the behavioural finance research are irrational. Some of these decisions need to be taken seriously as part of clients' preferences; others need to be corrected because clients will regret them. This book helps the reader to understand the difference and to implement the knowledge gained in structuring the wealth management process in order to reach a solution that is in line with the clients' expectations.

2
Decision Theory

Decision theory is concerned with how investors make decisions and with how investors should make decisions. More than two hundred years of excellent research has resulted in the formulation of decision theory. The following box summarizes the basic insights.[1]

Two hundred years of decision theory

Most of decision theory is normative or prescriptive, i.e. it is concerned with identifying the best decision to take, assuming an ideal decision-maker who is fully informed, able to compute with perfect accuracy, and is fully rational. The practical application of this prescriptive approach (how people should make decisions) is called *decision analysis*, and is aimed at finding tools, methodologies, and software to help people make better decisions. The most systematic and comprehensive software tools developed in this way are called *decision support systems*.

Since it is obvious that people do not typically behave in optimal ways, there is also a related area of study, which is a positive or descriptive discipline that attempts to describe what people actually do. Since normative decision theory often creates hypotheses for testing against actual behaviour, the two fields are closely linked. Furthermore, it is possible to relax the assumptions of perfect information, rationality and so forth in various ways, and produce a series of different predictions about behaviour, allowing for further tests of the kind of decision-making that occurs in practice.

The heartland of decision theory is the choice under uncertainty. The procedure now referred to as *expected value* was known from the 17th century. Blaise Pascal invoked it in his famous wager, published in 1670. The idea of expected value is that, when faced with a number of actions, each of which could give rise to more than one possible outcome with different probabilities, the rational procedure is to identify all possible outcomes, determine their values (positive or negative) and the probabilities that will result from each course of action, and multiply the two to give an expected value. In 1738, Daniel Bernoulli published an influential paper entitled "Exposition of a New Theory on the Measurement of Risk", in which he shows that expected value theory must be normatively wrong. He gives an example in which a Dutch merchant is trying to decide whether to insure a cargo being sent from Amsterdam to St Petersburg in winter, when it is known that there is a 5 % chance that the ship and cargo will be lost. In his solution, he defines a utility function and computes expected utility rather than expected financial value. However, it took almost 200 years to end this debate: In 1948,

---
[1] The history of decision theory is adapted from Wikipedia.

> (Continued)
>
> von Neumann and Morgenstern gave an axiomatic foundation of expected utility theory that precisely lays down its normative content.
>
> In the 20th century, it was generally assumed in economics that people behave as rational agents and thus expected utility theory also provided a theory of actual human decision-making behaviour under risk. The work of Maurice Allais and Daniel Ellsberg showed that this was clearly not the case. The prospect theory of Daniel Kahneman and Amos Tversky placed behavioural economics on a more evidence-based footing. It emphasized that in actual human (as opposed to normatively correct) decision-making "losses loom larger than gains"; people are more focused on changes in their utility states than the states themselves and estimation of subjective probabilities is severely biased.

This chapter aims to lay the foundation for the entire book. It focuses on three renowned models of decision theory: mean-variance analysis, expected utility theory, and prospect theory. We show how these theories differ and how to apply them to private banking.

2.1 INTRODUCTION

Investing in financial markets amounts to selecting and combining lotteries. A lottery is described as "a set of consequences and the probability thereof". Simple lotteries arise, for example as the result of a coin tossing experiment. Say you gain $1 if "heads" comes up and you lose $1 if "tails" comes up. If the coin is fair, the lottery is described by the following information: ($1, 0.5; -$1, 0.5). With many outcomes, lotteries can be described by histograms, i.e. a figure that shows the likelihood of obtaining each outcome. Returns from the stock market, the bond market and any other investment are usually described by their histograms. Figure 2.1, for example, shows the return distribution of a fund of hedge funds based on monthly data from January 1993 to January 2006.

Decision theory is concerned with how to select and combine lotteries. Hence, it lays the foundation for any investment decision. Up to the 1950s, mathematicians like Feller and Hirsh claimed that selecting among lotteries must be done by "objective" statistical criteria like the expected value and the variance, and that vague criteria based on utility are not appropriate here. However, if one looks at applications such as investment decisions it is obvious that any payoff has to be evaluated in the light of what it buys. Hence, utility considerations cannot be avoided. Psychological laws will ultimately play a role in the selection of lotteries.

Daniel Bernoulli has used the law of *decreasing marginal utility from wealth* to explain the St Petersburg Paradox. In the St Petersburg Paradox, a fair coin is tossed until it shows tails for the first time. The payoff is 1 if the game ends after the first toss of the coin. It is 2 if tails shows up at the second coin tossing; it is 4 when tails comes at the third tossing of the coin and so on. Hence, the payoff is doubled as long as the coin does not show tails. In general, if tails comes up after k times, the payoff of this lottery is 2^{k-1}.

On the other hand, the probability is halved as long as tails does not show up. The probability of tails coming up after one coin toss is 1/2. The probability of getting tails after the second

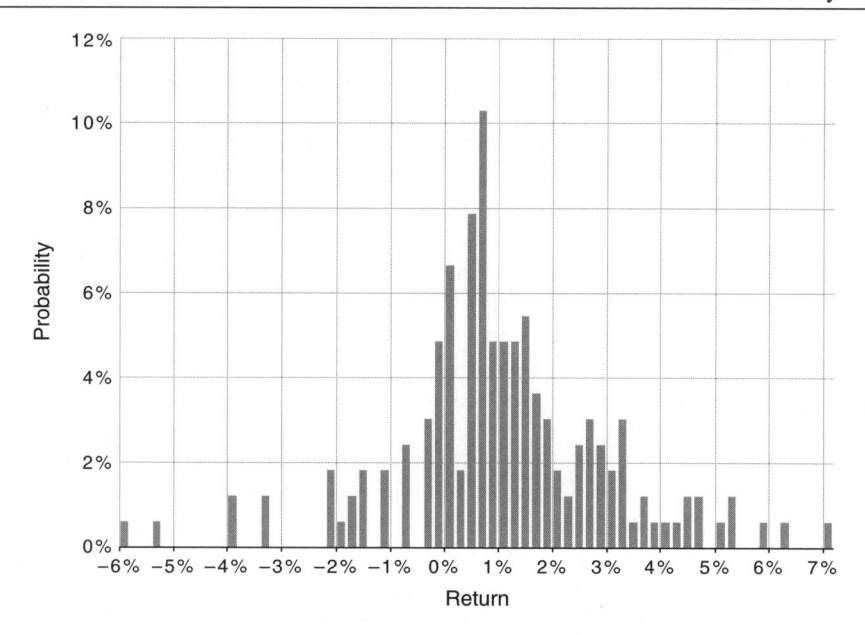

Figure 2.1 The lottery given by the returns of a fund of hedge funds

tossing is 1/2 multiplied by 1/2 for having tails in the first toss, which is equal to 1/4. In general, the probability for tossing tails after k tosses is $\frac{1}{2^k}$.

The funny thing about this lottery is that it has an infinite expected value. The expected value is $1\frac{1}{2} + 2\frac{1}{4} + \ldots + 2^{k-1}\frac{1}{2^k} = \sum_k 2^{k-1}\frac{1}{2^k} = \sum_k \frac{1}{2} = \infty$. But if people are asked how much they would be willing to pay in order to be allowed to participate in this game, the amount is typically rather small. Daniel Bernoulli explained this observation with the law of *decreasing marginal utility from wealth*. He said: "There is no doubt that a gain of one thousand ducats is more significant to a pauper than to a rich man though both gained the same amount." In particular he suggested evaluating the payoffs according to a logarithmic utility function. Hence, the subjective value of the St Petersburg Paradox, the *expected utility*, is $\sum_{t=1}^{n} \frac{1}{2^t} \ln(2^t) = \sum_{t=1}^{n} \frac{t}{2^t} \ln(2) = 2\ln(2) = 1.3863$.

By inverting the function we get that Bernoulli investors are ready to pay only \$4 to participate in a game with an infinite expected value, i.e. $\ln(4) = 1.3863$.

In 1944, von Neumann and Morgenstern freed expected utility theory from criticism of its subjective nature by founding it on a set of axioms with which almost any rational decision-maker would agree. Although expected utility theory has long since been used as a descriptive model for preferences under uncertainty, it has always been criticized as not fully describing actual behaviour. The paradox of Allais and that of Ellsberg showed this nicely.[2] Some 35 years later, two psychologists, Kahneman and Tversky, published a paper in *Econometrica* in which they proposed a descriptive theory of choice, *prospect theory*. Prospect theory resolves the

---
[2] See Sections 2.4.2 and 2.7.

Allais paradox and is well in line with a lot of evidence found in laboratory experiments. For a long time the debate between expected utility and prospect theory was simply ignored in finance literature.

Ever since Markowitz (1952), choices between financial investment alternatives have been based on seemingly objective criteria like the mean-variance principle. As a justification, finance researchers refer to Merton (1969) who showed that the related two-fund separation property can be derived from constant relative risk aversion and normally distributed log-returns. However, both of these assumptions seem quite restrictive. According to von Neumann and Morgenstern's theorem, *any* utility that is increasing in wealth is a rational utility function, and from looking at data one easily observes that returns on financial markets are not normally distributed (see Figure 2.1 above).

As a result, choices taken on the basis of the mean-variance principle can violate expected utility. These choices may even violate the idea that *more wealth is not worse than less wealth*, as the mean-variance paradox shows (see Section 2.8 and Figure 2.24). On the other hand, some aspects of prospect theory are well in line with expected utility theory. Hence, when advising a client, one cannot dismiss prospect theory as being irrational—it may be even more rational than the mean-variance principle.

In the next section, we describe the mean-variance principle of portfolio choice. Then, we explain some fundamental concepts that are needed in order to understand the theory of decision-making and outline the theorem of von Neumann and Morgenstern. Thereafter, we present prospect theory and show how to use it in order to build optimal portfolios. Finally, we consider choices in which the probabilities of the outcomes are unknown to the decision maker as in the case of private equity, antiques, gems, etc. We will see that the investment decision in such situations raises new challenges for decision theory and only experienced investors (like the endowment funds of Yale, Harvard, etc.) will be found to invest in these assets.

2.2 MEAN-VARIANCE ANALYSIS

A basic investment decision for many investors is the question of whether or not to hold their wealth in a bank account, which can be considered as riskless, or to buy risky assets in the financial market. One possible way to make such a decision is to compare the past returns of both alternatives. For long periods, the data shows that investments in risky assets get a higher return than investments in riskless assets.

Case Study 2.1: Equity premium

The difference between the expected return on the market portfolio of common stocks and the risk-free interest rate is the *equity premium*. A good proxy for the expected return on the market portfolio is the average return of a broad portfolio of stocks. Table 2.1 shows the historical equity premium for 16 countries over the 103-year period 1900–2002. The columns marked "SD" give the standard deviations of the equity premiums relative to bills and bonds.

Table 2.1 Historical equity premiums of different countries (*Source*: Dimson, Marsh and Staunton (2003))

| | Equity risk premiums (percent per year) ||||||
| | Relative to bills ||| Relative to bonds |||
	Geometric Mean	Arithmetic Mean	SD	Geometric Mean	Arithmetic Mean	SD
Australia	6.8	8.3	17.2	6.0	7.6	19.0
Belgium	2.2	4.4	23.1	2.1	3.9	20.2
Canada	4.2	5.5	16.8	4.0	5.5	18.2
Denmark	2.2	3.8	19.6	1.5	2.7	16.0
France	6.4	8.9	24.0	3.6	5.8	22.1
Germany	3.9	9.4	35.5	5.7	9.0	28.8
Ireland	3.6	5.5	20.4	3.2	4.8	18.5
Italy	6.3	10.3	32.5	4.1	7.6	30.2
Japan	6.1	9.3	28.0	5.4	9.5	33.3
The Netherlands	4.3	6.4	22.6	3.8	5.9	21.9
South Africa	5.9	7.9	22.2	5.2	6.8	19.4
Spain	2.8	4.9	21.5	1.9	3.8	20.3
Sweden	5.2	7.5	22.2	4.8	7.2	22.5
Switzerland	3.2	4.8	18.8	1.4	2.9	17.5
United Kingdom	4.2	5.9	20.1	3.8	5.1	17.0
United States	5.3	7.2	19.8	4.4	6.4	20.3
Average	4.5	6.9	22.8	3.8	5.9	21.6
World	4.4	5.7	16.5	3.8	4.9	15.0

The equity markets in the United States and in the United Kingdom have performed well in the past. However, the difference from other countries is not large. Over the entire 103-year period, the annualized equity premium relative to Treasury bills (i.e. government bonds) was 5.3 % for the United States and 4.2 % for the United Kingdom. The average risk premium across all 16 countries was 4.5 %. The equity premium measured relative to long-term bonds is similar.

In the past, equities paid more than less risky assets such as government bonds. Why should a long-term investor hold anything else but stocks?

The answer to this question can be found in portfolio theory. Its origin is the mean-variance analysis of Harry Markowitz (1952). In his work "Portfolio Selection" he recommends the use of an expected return versus variance of return rule,

> "... both as a hypothesis to explain well-established investment behavior and as a maxim to guide one's own action."

The portfolio theory of Markowitz was groundbreaking. Indeed, if one represents the risk premium of different countries in a mean-variance diagram (see Figure 2.2), one can see that a

Equity Risk Premium Relative to Bills   **Equity Risk Premium Relative to Bonds**

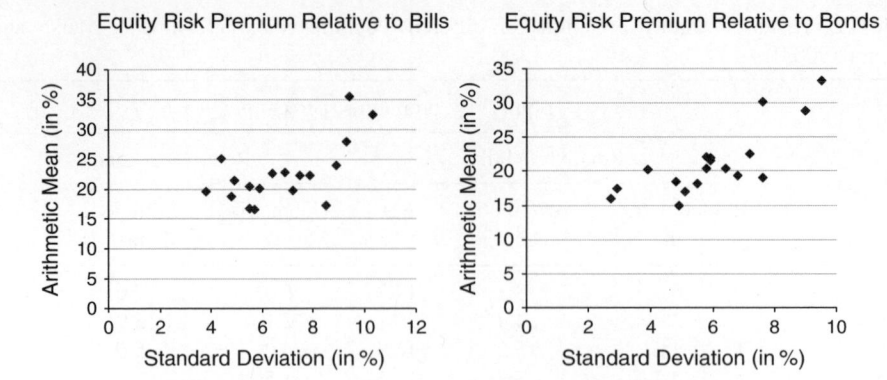

Figure 2.2 Mean-variance representation of the risk premium

higher equity premium is typically associated with a higher standard deviation. Thus, investors may not necessarily go for a higher equity premium.

The mean-variance analysis and its equilibrium implication, the Capital Asset Pricing Model (CAPM), are widely praised in finance literature. For example Jagannathan and Wang (1996) consider them " . . . the major contributions of academic research in the post-war era". Further, Campbell and Viceira (2002) write:

> "Most MBA courses, for example, still teach mean-variance analysis as if it were a universally accepted framework for portfolio choice."

In general, the best portfolio for an investor is determined by two factors – the risk-return opportunities on the market and the investor's preferences. The risk-return opportunities on the market determine the set of *efficient portfolios*, i.e. the portfolios of risky assets with the minimum risk for a given expected return level (or the maximum return for a given risk level). The set of efficient portfolios build the *efficient frontier* (Figure 2.3).

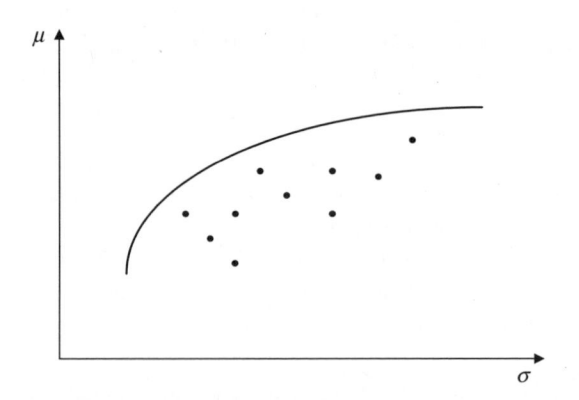

Figure 2.3 The efficient frontier

Within the mean-variance framework, the investor's preferences are given by the utility function $u^i(\mu, \sigma^2) = \mu - \frac{\alpha^i}{2}\sigma^2$ where $\alpha^i > 0$ is a parameter describing the risk aversion of investor i. The higher this parameter is, the higher the slope of the utility function.[3] The higher the risk aversion, the higher is the required expected return for a unit increase in risk, i.e. the required risk premium (see Figure 2.4).

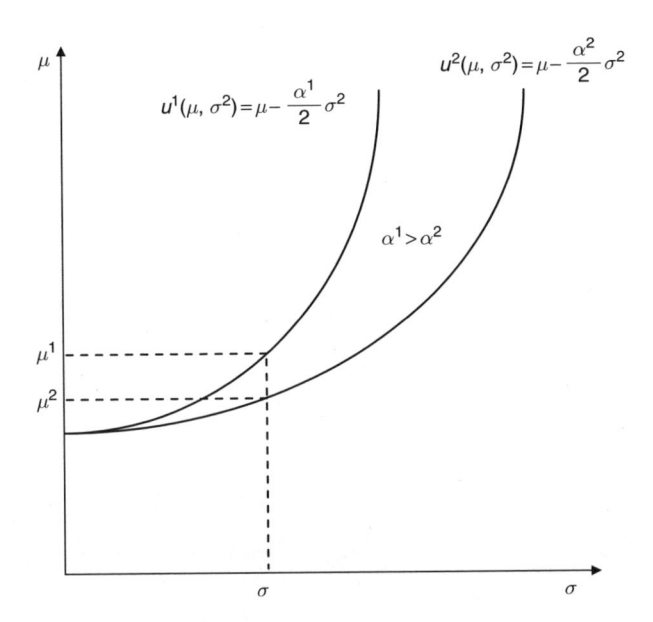

Figure 2.4 Risk aversion and risk premium

Different investors have different risk-return preferences. Investors with a higher level of risk aversion choose portfolios with a low level of expected return and variance, i.e. their portfolios move down the efficient frontier. Conversely, investors with a lower level of risk aversion choose portfolios with a high level of expected return and variance, i.e. their portfolios move up the efficient frontier (Figure 2.5).

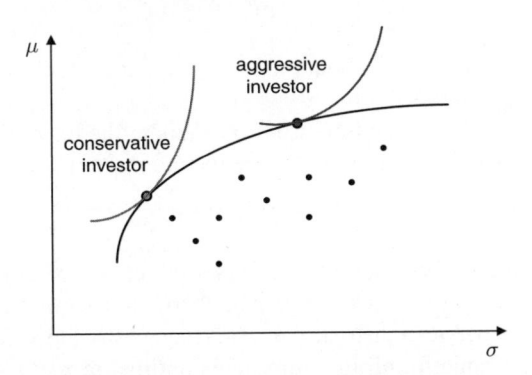

Figure 2.5 Selecting the optimal portfolio

---

[3] The risk aversion concept is often discussed in the expected utility context, where the (absolute) risk aversion is measured by the curvature of a utility function (see Section 2.3.6).

Case Study 2.2: Asking for the mean-variance trade-off

To estimate the investor's preferences within the mean-variance analysis, a large Swiss bank uses the following two questions:

Question 1: What is your main objective with respect to your wealth?

a) capital protection (limited risk but also limited return)
b) a mix of capital protection and wealth growth
c) wealth growth (higher wealth growth but also higher risk for losses)

Question 2: Which range of expected annual return and wealth changes do you prefer?

a) from -5% to 10%
b) from -10% to 20%
c) from -20% to 35%

Suppose the answers of Question 2 describe binary lotteries with equally likely outcomes. Then the alternatives a), b), and c) encode the following mean-variance combinations: a) $\mu = 2.5\%, \sigma = 7.5\%$, b) $\mu = 5\%, \sigma = 15\%$ and c) $\mu = 7.5\%, \sigma = 27.5\%$. The next figure illustrates them graphically.

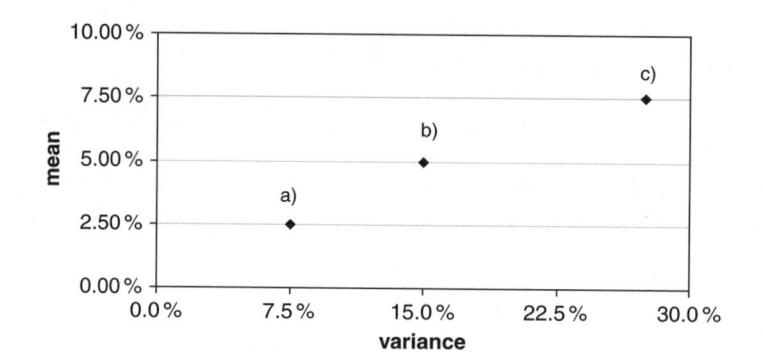

Question 1 can be seen as a validation question, since Question 2 may be too mathematical for many clients.

Note that these questions cannot be used to calculate the exact risk aversion of the investor but they are helpful to classify the clients into three risk classes.

Within the mean-variance analysis the optimal asset allocation of any investor follows the *two-fund-separation theorem* of James Tobin. The theorem says that differently risk-averse investors should diversify between the risk-free asset (e.g. cash) and a single optimal portfolio of risky assets that is the same for all investors. This optimal mix of risky assets is given by the *tangent portfolio,* point (T) in Figure 2.6, i.e. the portfolio on the efficient frontier at the point of tangency between the efficient frontier and a line starting at the risk-free rate of return. This line is called the *Capital Market Line* (CML). The slope of the CML is $\frac{\mu - R_f}{\sigma}$, which is called the *Sharpe ratio*.

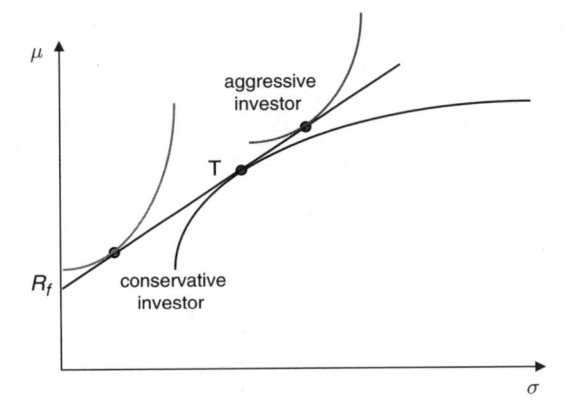

Figure 2.6 Two-fund-separation

Thus, according to the two-fund-separation theorem, different attitudes toward risk result in different combinations of the risk-free asset and the tangent portfolio. All investors can improve on the mean-variance trade-off given by the efficient frontier. More conservative investors, for example, should put a higher fraction of their wealth in the risk-free asset; respectively, more aggressive investors should borrow capital on the money market (go short in risk-free assets) and invest it in the tangent portfolio.

Note that the two-fund-separation theorem reduces the heterogeneity of clients to a single dimension: the mix of the risk-free asset and the tangent portfolio. It is, however, well known that advisors do not follow two-fund-separation theorem, as Table 2.2 shows.

Table 2.2 The asset allocation puzzle (*Source*: Canner, Mankiw and Weil (1997))

Advisor in investor type	% of portfolio			Ratio of bonds to stocks
	Cash	Bonds	Stocks	
(a) *Fidelity*				
Conservative	50	30	20	1.50
Moderate	20	40	40	1.00
Aggressive	5	30	65	0.46
(b) *Merrill Lynch*				
Conservative	20	35	45	0.78
Moderate	5	40	55	0.73
Aggressive	5	20	75	0.27
(c) *New York Times*				
Conservative	20	40	40	1.00
Moderate	10	30	60	0.50
Aggressive	0	20	80	0.25

This is the so-called *asset allocation puzzle*. It describes the finding that professional advisors adjust the recommended mix of risky assets according to the risk preferences of their clients. For example, in the advice given by the *New York Times* the ratio of the portfolio weight of S&P 500 to bonds changes from 0.25 to 1.0 in aggressive, moderate, and conservative portfolios. This is in contradiction to the two-fund-separation theorem that says that the asset allocations of investors with different risk attitudes should differ only by the percentage of wealth invested in the mix of risky assets. However, the mix of risky assets should be the same for everyone. The question that arises then is "Who is right?—Tobin or the practitioners?" As we see below, while traditional finance sides with Tobin, behavioural finance gives support to the practitioners.

Math Box 2.1: The mathematics of the mean-variance analysis

Before we do the general case, let's look at a simple example. Suppose there are just two assets: one is risk-free, paying R_f whatever happens and the other is risky because its return can either be R_u or R_d. Let λ be the percentage of wealth that one invests in the risky asset. Then the return of a portfolio with λ invested in the risky asset and $1-\lambda$ invested risk-free is: $R_f + (R_u - R_f)\lambda$ in the "up" state and $R_f + (R_d - R_f)\lambda$ in the "down" state. Supposing that the up state realizes the probability p, the resulting mean return is $\mu_\lambda = R_f + (\mu - R_f)\lambda$, where $\mu = pR_u + (1-p)R_d$. The variance is accordingly $\sigma_\lambda^2 = \left[p(R_u - \mu)^2 + (1-p)(R_d - \mu)^2\right]\lambda^2$.

Suppose the investor maximizes the mean-variance utility $\mu - \frac{\alpha}{2}\sigma^2$. Then the first order condition reads as: $(\mu - R_f) = \alpha \left[p(R_u - \mu)^2 + (1-p)(R_d - \mu)^2\right]\lambda$.

Thus the optimal portfolio is $\lambda = \dfrac{\mu - R_f}{\alpha\left[p(R_u - \mu)^2 + (1-p)(R_d - \mu)^2\right]} = \dfrac{\mu - R_f}{\alpha\sigma^2}$. We see that the investor takes more risk the higher the expected return μ. The investor avoids risk the higher his risk aversion α and the higher the variance of the risky asset σ^2.

To generalize this result to $k = 1, 2, \ldots, K$ assets and $s = 1, \ldots S$ states of the world, let the gross return of asset k in state s be R_s^k. As before $\mu_k = E\left(R^k\right)$ is the expected return[4] and $\sigma_k^2 = \text{var}\left(R^k\right)$ is the variance of the gross return of asset k. As above, all assets can be represented in a two-dimensional diagram with an expected return as a reward measure and standard deviation $\sigma_k = \sqrt{\text{var}\left(R_s^k\right)}$ as the risk measure on the axes.

Consider the case of two assets k and j. The expected return of a portfolio of them is equal to $\mu_\lambda = \lambda \mu_k + (1-\lambda)\mu_k$, where $0 \leq \lambda \leq 1$ is the portfolio weight of asset k. The variance of the portfolio is equal to $\sigma_\lambda^2 = \lambda^2 \sigma_k^2 + (1-\lambda)\sigma_k^2 + 2\lambda(1-\lambda)\text{cov}_{kj}$.

The expected return of a portfolio of K assets is equal to $\mu_\lambda = \sum_k \lambda_k \mu_k$. Its variance is

$$\sigma_\lambda^2 = \sum_k \sum_j \lambda_k \text{cov}_{k,j} \lambda_j.$$

Calculating the efficient frontier

The efficient frontier can be determined by minimizing the portfolio variance for a given level of portfolio return under the restriction that all wealth is spent, i.e.

$$\min_\lambda \sum_k \sum_j \lambda_k \text{cov}_{k,j} \lambda_j$$

---

[4] Expected returns are usually calculated using historical return values or asset pricing models.

$$\text{s.t.} \sum_K \lambda_k \mu_k = const$$

$$\text{and} \sum_K \lambda_k = 1.$$

Calculating the tangent portfolio

The structure of the tangent portfolio can be found either by maximizing the Sharpe Ratio subject to a budget constraint[5] or by solving the simplest[6] $\mu - \sigma$ maximization problem.

$$\max_{\lambda \in R^{K+1}} u(\mu_\lambda, \sigma_\lambda^2) = \mu_\lambda - \frac{\alpha}{2}\sigma_\lambda^2$$

$$\text{s.t.} \sum_{k=0}^K \lambda_k = 1.$$

In this equation, λ_0 denotes the fraction of wealth invested in the riskless asset. λ_0 can be eliminated from the optimization problem by substituting the budget constraint $\lambda_0 = 1 - \sum_{k=1}^K \lambda_k$ into the utility function. Using the definition of μ_λ and σ_λ^2 we get:

$$\max_\lambda R_f + (\mu - R_f)\lambda - \frac{\alpha}{2}\lambda' \text{cov} \lambda,$$

where λ is the vector of risky assets in the tangent portfolio, μ is the vector of risky assets returns, and cov is their variance-covariance matrix. The first order condition of the maximization problem is:

$$\text{cov}\,\lambda = \frac{1}{\alpha}(\mu - R_f).$$

If there are no constraints on λ, then the solution is: $\lambda = \frac{1}{\alpha}\text{cov}^{-1}(\mu - R_f)$

From this result, the two-fund-separation property can be easily seen. The asset allocations of different investors $i = 1 \ldots, I$ are vectors with K components that only differ by one scalar α^i. With short-sales constraints, $\lambda \geq 0$, for example, one can apply standard algorithms for linear equation systems to solve the problem. Note that the higher the risk aversion parameter α^i, the smaller the fraction of risky assets the investor holds.

Say the solution to the first order condition is λ^{opt}, then the tangent portfolio can be found by a renormalization: $\lambda_k^T = \frac{\lambda_k^{opt}}{\sum_j \lambda_j^{opt}}$. Note that the risk aversion parameter α^i cancels out after the renormalization, which yields again the two-fund-separation property.

Having reviewed the basic principles of portfolio choice, we turn our focus to the question of how to make rational decisions when there is a risk.

---

[5] This approach is cumbersome since the portfolio weight λ appears both in the numerator and in the denominator.
[6] By the two-fund-separation theorem, any other $\mu - \sigma$ utility would lead to the same tangent portfolio.

2.3 EXPECTED UTILITY THEORY

The analysis of decision-making under risk is to a large extent dominated by the expected utility theory. Even Kahneman and Tversky (1979) acknowledge:

> "It [the expected utility theory] has been generally accepted as a normative model of rational choice, and widely applied as a descriptive model of economic behavior. Thus, it is assumed that all reasonable people would wish to obey the axioms of the theory, and that most people actually do, most of the time."

To illustrate the normative appeal of the expected utility approach, we derive it from a set of axioms that everyone agrees to. We will argue that these axioms should be followed if one wants to take rational decisions. However, it will also be important that these axioms exhaust the requirements of rational decision-making. That is to say, imposing any specific assumptions on the agent's risk aversion may be nice for practical purposes but cannot be justified by referring to rationality.

2.3.1 Lottery approach to expected utility

Consider a set of possible choices X with $i = 1, \ldots, I$ elements. For example, X can be a set of lotteries L defined over the set of consequences C. The probability of occurrence of a particular consequence c_i from C is denoted by p_i. For example, a lottery is described by the consequences $C = \{-100\$, 0\$, 100\$\}$ with probabilities $p = \{0.25, 0.25, 0.5\}$, meaning that there are three possible outcomes $c_1 = -100\$$, $c_2 = 0\$$ and $c_3 = 100\$$ and each of them occurs with the probability $p_1 = 0.25$, $p_2 = 0.25$, and $p_3 = 0.5$, respectively. To reduce the notation we will represent lotteries as sequence of pairs of consequences and probabilities. For example the lottery above is then written as: $L = \{-100\$, 0.25; 0\$, 0.25; 100\$, 0.5\}$.

Lotteries can be also described using the *state-preference approach*, which defines the consequences $c_1, \ldots, c_S$ over a set of scenarios in the future $S = \{1, \ldots, S\}$ occurring with the probabilities $\{p_1, \ldots, p_S\}$. Mapping the state preference approach on to the lottery approach, the probability for a certain consequence is defined by the sum of probabilities of scenarios delivering the particular consequence, i.e. $p_i = \sum_{\substack{s=1 \\ c_i = c_s}}^{S} p_s$. To get a better understanding of the lottery and state-preference approach, consider the following example.

Example 2.1: The lottery and the state-preference approach

Assume that there is a fair dice, offering the following payoff scheme:

Dice outcome	1	2	3	4	5	6
Payoff scheme	$500	$700	$500	$300	$500	$300

The probability for each state is $p_s = 1/6$ since the dice is fair. To calculate the probability of a particular outcome, we first determine the set of possible consequences. In the example above, there are three possible consequences, i.e. $c_1 = 300$, $c_2 = 500$ and $c_3 = 700$. The probabilities of all scenarios delivering these consequences are $p_1 = 1/3$, $p_2 = 1/2$, and $p_3 = 1/6$, respectively. Thus, in the state-preference approach the lottery can be written as
$$L = \left\{300, \frac{1}{3}; 500, \frac{1}{2}; 700, \frac{1}{6}\right\}.$$

This correspondence between the lottery and the state-preference approach is innocuous if the probabilities of the states $\{p_1, \ldots, p_S\}$ are known by the decision-maker. In this case, we say that the decision is made under *risk*. If, however, the probabilities are formed as beliefs by the decision-maker, then a second degree of uncertainty occurs, the uncertainty of having formed correct beliefs. In this case one speaks of *ambiguous* situations. The main focus of this section will be on decisions under risk.

2.3.2 The axioms of rationality

Decisions under risk can be very successful, in particular if the state with the best outcome is realized. However, this fact does not mean that the decision was good. Without additional information we can only say that the decision-maker was lucky. To distinguish between good and lucky decisions, we need the concept of *rationality*.

We start by introducing the concept of a preference. This is a binary relation $\succcurlyeq$ on the choice set X. A preference $x \succcurlyeq y$ means that the alternative x is at least as good as the alternative y. Accordingly, $x \succ y$ means that the alternative x is, strictly speaking, better than the alternative y, and $x \sim y$ means that both alternatives x and y are equally good.

The first hypothesis of rationality is embodied in two basic assumptions about the preference relation: completeness and transitivity. The assumption that a preference relation is **complete** means that between any two possible alternatives the individual has a well-defined preference, i.e. for all alternatives $x, y \in X$ we have that either $x \succcurlyeq y$ or $y \succcurlyeq x$ (or both). In the latter case, we call the two alternatives "indifferent". The assumption of completeness is violated if the investor has no opinion about which alternative he prefers and cannot even say that the two alternatives are equivalent to him. The strength of this assumption should not be underestimated. In many circumstances, it is difficult to evaluate alternatives that are far from common experience. For example, it is questionable which alternative is better if the set of lotteries is based on consequences as $C = \{$die in car crash, die in plane crash$\}$ and one might also hesitate to state indifference. Fortunately, in finance, the outcomes considered are easier to compare because they are all measured in terms of money. Hence we require completeness of preferences as an axiom of rationality in finance.

The *transitivity* assumption says for all $x, y, z \in X$ if $x \succcurlyeq y$ and $y \succcurlyeq z$, then $x \succcurlyeq z$, i.e. the decision-maker does not face choices in which his preferences appear to cycle: for example, feeling that coffee is at least as good as cappuccino and cappuccino is at least as good as tea, then one should not prefer tea over coffee.

An old fairy tale by Jacob and Wilhelm Grimm illustrates the meaning of the transitivity axiom.

> **"Lucky Hans"**
>
> Lucky Hans changed his whole wages earned from seven years hard work for a piece of gold, the gold for a horse, the horse for a cow, the cow for a pig, the pig for a goose, the goose for grindstones. Each time he was convinced that he made a good deal, but, in the end, the grindstones fell into the water as he tried to drink from a well. Then Hans, having watched them disappear, jumped for joy, and thanked his lucky stars that he had been fortunate to get rid of the stones that had weighed upon him so long without any effort of his own. "I really think," he cried, "I am the luckiest man under the sun" and he went, free from care, until he reached his mother's house. His mother, however, made clear to him that a piece of gold would have been very desirable.

Alternatives can also be compared by assigning numerical values to them. The utility function establishes a link between the decision-maker's preferences and the numerical values. To ensure that a utility function exists, we need the preference relation on X to be **continuous,** i.e. the preferences cannot exhibit erratic behaviour like sudden "jumps" in the portfolio caused by minor changes in the data. For example, a preference relation on a set of lotteries is continuous, if for all lotteries x, y and z, $x \succ y \succcurlyeq z$, there exists $\alpha \in (0,1)$ such that $\alpha x + (1-\alpha)z \succ y$. In other words, there is no lottery that is infinitely better or worse than other lotteries, i.e. lottery z is not so bad that it "poisons" any compound lottery in which it is included.

Summarizing these axioms on rational choice, we can state that preferences $\succcurlyeq$ defined over pairs of alternative outcomes $x, y \in X$, can be represented by a utility function, i.e. $u(x) \geq u(y)$, if and only if the preference relation is continuous, complete, and transitive.

We need to make one additional assumption on the decision-maker's preferences in order to represent his preferences by a continuous utility function with the expected utility form. This is the ***independence axiom***. The preference relation $\succcurlyeq$ satisfies it, if for all lotteries x, y and z and for all numbers $0 \leq \alpha \leq 1$, we have $x \succcurlyeq y$ if and only if $\alpha x + (1-\alpha)z \succcurlyeq \alpha y + (1-\alpha)z$. In other words, if we mix each of two lotteries with the same third one, then the preference ordering of the two resulting mixtures is ***independent*** of the particular third lottery used.

2.3.3 The expected utility representation

As we have just argued, to assign numerical values to the outcomes of lotteries in order to compare them, the preference relation must be complete, transitive, and continuous. If in addition, the preference order $\succcurlyeq$ satisfies the independence axiom, it can be represented by an *expected utility function*. More precisely, the expected utility representation states that a decision-maker who prefers the lottery x over the lottery y has a greater expected utility with the lottery x than with the lottery y and vice versa, i.e.

$$x \succ y \Leftrightarrow E_u(x) > E_u(y),$$

where the expected utility of a lottery is the sum of utilities derived from each of the n consequences c_i that the lottery offers, weighted with their probabilities p_i, i.e.

$$E_u(x) = p_1 u(c_1) + p_2 u(c_2) + \ldots + p_n u(c_n) = \sum_{i=1}^{n} p_i u(c_i).$$

The representation theorem goes back to von Neumann and Morgenstern (1944).

> **Theorem of von Neumann and Morgenstern (1944):**
>
> Let $\succeq$ be a preference order that is complete, transitive, and continuous, then $\succeq$ can be represented by an expected utility function, i.e. $x \succ y \Leftrightarrow E_u(x) > E_u(y)$ if and only if $\succeq$ satisfies the independence axiom.

The reader may be easily convinced that an expected utility function does indeed satisfy the independence axiom.[7] The hard part of the proof is to show that the independence axiom is only satisfied in the expected utility case.

This representation theorem is based on the lottery approach. Similar axioms can be given for the *state-preference approach*.[8] In that case the utility representation becomes

$$E_u(x) = p_1 u(c_1) + p_1 u(c_2) + \ldots + p_S u(c_S) = \sum_{s=1}^{S} p_s u(c_s).$$

To illustrate the expected utility representation, consider once again the example of a fair dice.

Dice outcome	1	2	3	4	5	6
Scheme C	$500	$700	$500	$300	$500	$300

Assume that $u(.) = \ln(.)$. Then,

$$E_u = \sum_{s=1}^{S} p_s u(c_s) = \frac{1}{6}\big[\ln(500) + \ln(700) + \ln(500) + \ln(300) + \ln(500) + \ln(300)\big]$$

$$= \frac{1}{3}\ln(300) + \frac{1}{2}\ln(500) + \frac{1}{6}\ln(700) = \sum_{i=1}^{n} p_i u(c_i)$$

One of the advantages of the expected utility representation is that it provides a valuable guide for action. People often find it hard to think systematically about risky alternatives. But if the individual believes that his choices should satisfy the axioms on which the theorem is based (in particular, the independence axiom), then the theorem can be used as a guide in the decision process. It facilitates decisions because it separates beliefs from risk attitudes. In an advisor–client relationship, the client will then determine the risk preferences while the advisor should choose the most realistic expectations. Note that the von Neumann and Morgenstern theorem does not restrict the form of the risk utility, u. It does not even restrict it to steadily increasing. We will thus have to include this desirable property as a separate axiom.

---

[7] This is because the expected utility is linear in the probabilities. Hence any mixture of lotteries results in the sum of expected utility terms so that a common component can be cancelled.
[8] For a derivation see Savage (1954) and Hens (1992).

2.3.4 Axiom 0: More is better

The four axioms of rationality can be used to distinguish whether someone's preferences are rational or not. However, they do not include a more basic axiom, which Woody Allen states as

"More money is better, if only for financial reasons".

We call this *Axiom 0*. The proper name of Axiom 0 is "state dominance" since it says that a lottery A that in each state pays off at least as much as a lottery B is preferable to B if it pays off more than B in at least one state. Moreover, it says that the investor should be indifferent to identical lotteries. If someone's decision violates this axiom, we may also conclude that it is not rational. The next two examples demonstrate how individuals may behave irrationally by violating Axiom 0.

Example 2.2: Violation of Axiom 0

There is a fair dice with outcomes from 1 to 6. Consider the two schemes A and B available with the payoffs:

Dice outcome	1	2	3	4	5	6
Scheme A	$600	$700	$800	$900	$1000	$500
Scheme B	$500	$600	$700	$800	$900	$1000

Which scheme do you prefer?

Evaluation: The typical answer to this question is the following: "I prefer scheme A to scheme B because in 5 out of 6 cases I get a higher payoff in A than in B." However, the schemes A and B represent exactly the same lotteries and should be ranked identically. If scheme A is the payoff of a product offered at a higher price than another product with a payoff scheme B, then the difference in the prices of the products is a loss that one will make by preferring scheme A to scheme B.

The next example illustrates a situation where individuals violate Axiom 0 when their choice is a combination of two lotteries.

Example 2.3: Violation of Axiom 0

First choice:

(A) a guaranteed gain of $2400 or
(B) a 25 % chance of a $10 000 gain and a 75 % chance of winning nothing at all

Then choose:

(C) a guaranteed loss of $7500 or
(D) a 75 % chance of a $10 000 loss and a 25 % chance of losing nothing at all. Your payoff is the combination of the two lotteries you have chosen!

The typical choice is A and D. Lottery A is usually chosen because the expected payoff of B is $2500 and the extra $100 is not enough to tempt people into taking a chance. Lottery D is typically preferred to C because it offers a chance to avoid a loss.

Evaluation: The combined expected payoff from choosing A and D is a 75 % chance of −$7600 and a 25 % chance of $2400 and that from B and C is a 75 % chance of −$7500 and a 25 % chance of winning $2500. Thus, in either case it is better to choose B and C instead of A and D if one prefers more money to less.

Irrational decisions result also when individuals violate the axioms of rationality as discussed in Chapter 2.3.2. The next example shows how individuals' decisions may violate the transitivity axiom.

Example 2.4: Violation of the transitivity axiom
Consider five lotteries with the following payoffs:[9]

Lottery	Probability	Gain	Expected gain
A	7/24	5.00	1.46
B	8/24	4.75	1.58
C	9/24	4.50	1.69
D	10/24	4.25	1.77
E	11/24	4.00	1.83

Question 1: If you have the choice between lottery A and B, which one would you prefer?
Question 2: Compare then the lotteries B and C, C and D, and D and E. Which lotteries of the listed pairs do you prefer?
Question 3: If you have the choice between lottery A and E, which one would you prefer?

Evaluation: The typical answer of the first two questions is the lottery with the higher gain as the small difference in the probabilities is not sufficient to differentiate among the lotteries. However, the typical answer of the third question is lottery E, i.e. the lottery with the higher probability of a gain, as in the beginning individuals focus on the gain, but later on they shift their focus to the differences in probabilities, so they prefer A to B, B to C, C to D, D to E, but also E to A, which is inconsistent with the transitivity axiom.

If investors make decisions that violate the transitivity axiom, they will systematically lose money. To see how this may happen, suppose that your preferences are not transitive, i.e. $x \succ y$, $y \succ z$ but $z \succ x$ and the lotteries x, y, and z represent investment products offered by a bank. Suppose that you get product z. The bank offers you product z for $1 in exchange for product y. Since $y \succ z$ you accept the deal. Now you own y. The bank offers to sell y for $1 and get x instead. Since $x \succ y$ you accept the deal. Now you own x and you are ready to pay $1 again to get z since $z \succ x$. As a result, you own product z as in the beginning but you paid $3 to the bank.

---

[9] The example is based on an experiment conducted by Tversky (1969).

In other words, if one's preferences are not transitive, one will systematically lose money by paying for something without improving the initial position.

Finally, we show an example where a violation of the independence axiom means also a violation of Axiom 0.

Example 2.5: Violation of the independence axiom
Assume that a bank offers the assets A and B with the following payoffs:

Probabilities	Asset A	Asset B
0.7	100 %	20 %
0.2	−50 %	−10 %
0.1	−100 %	−100 %

Suppose that the investor prefers asset A to asset B. Then an advisor might recommend that the client buys asset A and sells short asset B. The net payoff in each state is then as follows.

Probabilities	Buy asset A	Sell asset B	Net payoff
0.7	100 %	−20 %	80 %
0.2	−50 %	10 %	−40 %
0.1	−100 %	100 %	0 %

Assume that there is another bank offering products A' and B'. These products have the same payoffs as assets A and B but in the case of default (−100 %) the bank offers a 100 % capital protection for both products. The products' payoffs are summarized as follows.

Probabilities	Product A'	Product B'
0.7	100 %	20 %
0.2	−50 %	−10 %
0.1	0 %	0 %

If the investor now prefers product B' to product A' his decision would violate the independence axiom. This is because in the first two states products A' and B' have identical payoffs as assets A and B and in the default state, both products return 0 %. Thus, the preference order should not change because of the capital protection offered by the bank.

If the investor prefers product B' to product A', while preferring asset A to asset B, he will lose money. To see why, consider the net payoff of the investor who buys product B' and sells short product A'.

Probabilities	Sell asset A'	Buy asset B'	Net payoff
0.7	−100 %	20 %	−80 %
0.2	50 %	−10 %	40 %
0.1	0 %	0 %	0 %

Comparing the net payoffs from the deals with both banks, one can easily see that the investor pays transaction fees but does not improve his initial position. In each state the cumulated net payoff is equal to 0 %.

2.3.5 Certainty equivalent, risk premium, and risk aversion

As we have just argued, the standard way of applying expected utility is to narrow it down to a specific functional form and then to estimate the parameters that best describe the clients' choices between simple lotteries. Note that these functional forms are very useful in applications because they are simple to estimate and also to maximize. However, they cannot themselves be derived from a rationality postulate. In order to understand the use of such functional forms one needs to define the notions of *certainty equivalent, risk premium,* and *risk aversion*.

A general definition that does not presume an expected utility formulation is based on the idea of comparing preferences on a lottery and a certain payoff. The certain payoff that is regarded as good as the lottery itself is known as the *certainty equivalent*. Consider for example a lottery with equally likely payoffs $0 or $1 (see Figure 2.7). On average, this lottery pays $\mu = \$0.5$. The amount that a decision-maker is ready to pay for this lottery is his certainty equivalent. It is denoted by X. It can be greater, smaller, or equal to the expected value of the lottery depending on the decision-maker's preferences. In the case that only the average payoff of the lottery is known, the certainty equivalent of the decision-makers is the subjective belief that the lottery pays something.

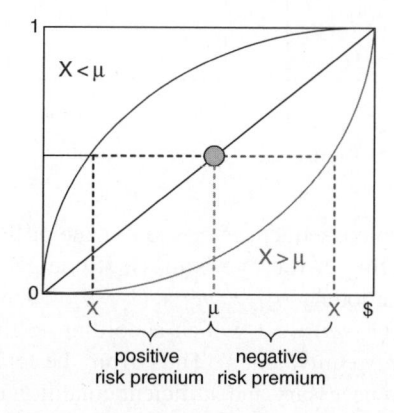

Figure 2.7 Illustration of the certainty equivalent, risk premium, and risk aversion

The difference between the expected value of the lottery μ and the certainty equivalent X is the *risk premium* that the decision-maker requires for playing the lottery. *Risk-averse* decision-makers require a positive risk premium for playing a lottery, i.e. their certainty equivalent is lower than the expected value of the lottery. Risk-averse decision-makers who do not know how likely it is that they will get $1, believe that the lottery pays something in less than 50 % of the cases. In contrast, *risk-loving* decision-makers are ready to pay a positive risk premium for playing the lottery, i.e. their certainty equivalent is higher than the expected value of the lottery.

In the context of expected utility theory, risk aversion (or risk-loving) is equivalent to the concavity (convexity) of the utility function. Strict concavity (convexity) means that the *marginal utility of money* is *decreasing (increasing)*. Hence, at any level of wealth, the utility gain from an extra unit of money is less (higher) than the utility loss of having a small unit of money. A decision-maker is *risk-neutral* if the utility function of money is linear (see Figure 2.7).

If the utility function $u(.)$ is concave, then the utility of the expected value of the lottery is greater than the expected utility from playing the lottery, i.e.

$$\underbrace{u\left(pc_1 + (1-p)c_2\right)}_{u(\mu)} \geq \underbrace{pu(c_1) + (1-p)u(c_2)}_{Eu}$$

The opposite is true if the utility function is convex. This property is known as *Jensen's inequality*. Figure 2.8 illustrates it graphically.

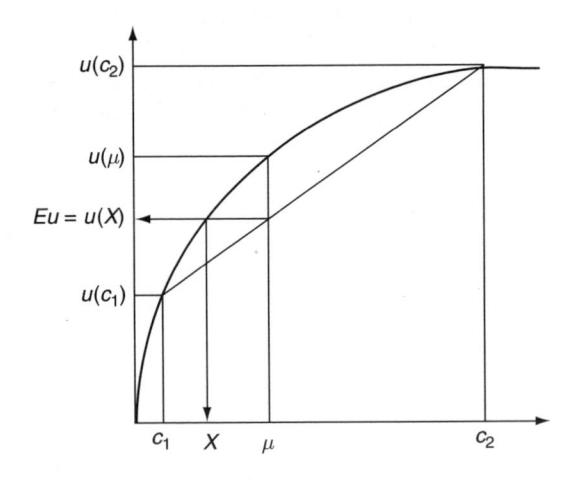

Figure 2.8 Jensen's inequality

Consider a lottery with two consequences c_1 and c_2. The utility of receiving c_1 for sure is $u(c_1)$ and the utility of receiving c_2 for sure is $u(c_2)$. If one gets c_1 with a probability of p, then the expected value of the lottery is $\mu = pc_1 + (1-p)c_2$. The expected utility of playing the lottery is $E_u = pu(c_1) + (1-p)u(c_2)$, which according to the definition is equal to the utility received by the certainty equivalent X. Thus, from the Jensen's inequality, we get that a concave utility function is a necessary and sufficient condition to describe risk aversion.

To illustrate the idea consider Example 2.6.

Example 2.6: Certainty equivalent, risk premium

An investor with a logarithmic utility function faces two different scenarios (boom and recession). Assume that the probability for a boom is 25 %. There are also two different risky assets: stocks and bonds. Their payoffs are summarized in the following table.

	Boom	Recession
Stocks	10	5
Bonds	5	7

If the investor holds stocks or bonds, his expected utility is:

$$E_u(stocks) = 0.25\ln(10) + 0.75\ln(5) = 1.7827$$
$$E_u(bonds) = 0.25\ln(5) + 0.75\ln(7) = 1.8618$$

To calculate the certainty equivalent, we search for the two values of X that solve:

$$\ln(X_{stocks}) = 1.7827$$
$$\ln(X_{bonds}) = 1.8618$$

The certainty equivalent for stocks is equal to 5.946 and the certainty equivalent for bonds is equal to 6.435. In our example, the expected payoff is:

$$\mu(stocks) = 0.25 \cdot 10 + 0.75 \cdot 5 = 6.25$$
$$\mu(bonds) = 0.25 \cdot 5 + 0.75 \cdot 7 = 6.5$$

Thus, the risk premium for stocks and bonds is equal to $6.25 - 5.95 = 0.30$ respectively $6.50 - 6.44 = 0.06$.

2.3.6 Measuring risk aversion

We can measure the degree of risk aversion by the curvature of the utility function $u(.)$. One possible measure of the curvature is its second derivative $u''(.)$. However, it is not invariant under positive affine transformations of the utility function, i.e. if we multiply $u(.)$ by a positive number, we change its second derivative $u''(.)$, although we do not change the preferences. To find a way to measure the risk aversion, the simplest way is to use the ratio $u''(.)/u'(.)$. If we change the sign to have a positive number for an increasing and concave utility function, we get the *Arrow-Pratt measure of absolute risk aversion*: $ARA(w) = -\dfrac{u''(w)}{u'(w)}$. It determines the asset allocation in terms of monetary units when income changes. The *relative risk aversion* is obtained by simply multiplying the absolute risk aversion with the wealth w, i.e. $RRA(w) = ARAw = -\dfrac{u''(w)}{u'(w)}w$. It determines the asset allocation in terms of shares when wealth changes.

Consider some examples. The quadratic utility function $u = w - \beta w^2$ is concave for positive β. The absolute and the relative risk aversion increase with the wealth w, i.e.

$$ARA = -\frac{u''(w)}{u'(w)} = -\frac{-2\beta}{1-2\beta w} \text{ (IARA)}$$

$$RRA = ARAw_0 = \frac{2\beta}{1-2\beta w}w \text{ (IRRA)}$$

The logarithmic utility function $u(w) = \ln(w)$ exhibits a decreasing ARA and a constant RRA.

$$ARA = -\frac{u''(w)}{u'(w)} = -\frac{-1/w^2}{1/w} = \frac{1}{w} \text{ (DARA)}$$

$$RRA = ARAw = 1 \text{ (CRRA)}$$

The same properties can be found for the power utility function $u = \beta w^\beta$, i.e.

$$ARA = -\frac{u''(.)}{u'(.)} = -\frac{\beta(\beta-1)w^{\beta-2}}{\beta w^{\beta-1}} = \frac{1-\beta}{w} \text{ (DARA)}$$

$$RRA = ARAw = 1 - \beta \text{ (CRRA)}$$

These specific functional forms are convenient to calculate asset allocations but they are not more rational than any other utility function $u(.)$. We conclude this section by mentioning the connection of risk measures and the resulting asset allocation. One can show the following properties:[10]

- If the investor's preferences are such that he has a decreasing (increasing) ARA, he has to increase (decrease) the monetary units invested in risky assets as he becomes richer. If the investor has a constant ARA utility, he must hold the same amount of risky assets when increasing income.
- If the investor is interested in knowing how to adjust the exposure in risky assets as a percentage of his wealth, he has to pay attention to his RRA. The fraction of wealth invested in risky assets increases with income if and only if RRA decreases with income. If an investor has constant relative risk aversion (CRRA), he would hold the same shares of risky assets as his income increases.
- Overall, if an agent has constant absolute risk aversion (CARA), then he will invest the same absolute amount in risky assets when his wealth changes. If an agent has constant relative risk aversion (CRRA), then he will invest the same relative amount in risky assets, i.e. he holds the share of wealth invested in risky asset constant.

2.3.7 Intertemporal decisions and updating

Most economic choices yield costs and benefits that are incurred at different points in the future. To make choices, people must weigh the utilities of these future costs and benefits in some way. Rational evaluation of future consequences assumes *exponential discounting*—future utilities $u(x_t)$ are discounted by a weight δ^t which is an exponentially declining function of t. Exponential discounting makes the strong prediction that the relative evaluation of two payments depends *only* on the amount of delay between the two payments.

Exponential discounting is important because it implies *time consistency*. This means that if one prefers the sequence $x_t, x_{t+1}, \ldots$ to $y_t, y_{t+1}, \ldots$ from the point of view of period 0, then one

---

[10] For a proof see Eichberger and Harper (1997), Section 1.4.3.

has the same preferences also from the point of view of any period later on. In other words, if an individual has time consistent preferences, he would not reverse his decisions later. This is, if $\sum_{s=0}^{T} \delta^{t+s} u(x_{t+s}) > \sum_{s=0}^{T} \delta^{t+s} u(y_{t+s})$ then $\sum_{s=0}^{T} \delta^{s} u(x_{t+s}) > \sum_{s=0}^{T} \delta^{s} u(y_{t+s})$. For example, if people prefer getting $100 now over getting $110 in a week, they should also prefer $100 in 10 weeks to $110 in 11 weeks, since both choices involve waiting an extra week to get $10 more. If they behave differently, their preferences are said to be not time-consistent and their behaviour is considered as not rational. As in the concept of hyperbolic discounting, explained in the next chapter, people indeed often violate time-consistency.

If future payments are uncertain, individuals' decisions are determined on the one hand by the payoff size and on the other hand by the probability that the state delivering this payoff will occur. These probabilities reflect the individuals' expectations. Classical statistical inference tells us how to adjust expectations to a new sample of evidence. Roughly speaking, one needs to revise prior probabilities upward for outcomes that are relatively likely to have produced the new data, and revise prior probabilities downward for outcomes that are relatively unlikely to have produced the new data. The following case study illustrates how to update expectations in the face of new information, which is not always easy.

Case Study 2.3: A car or a goat?

In a game show you are given a choice of three doors. Behind one is the main prize, a car; behind the others are goats. Suppose you pick door 1, and the host, who knows what's behind them, opens (according to the rules of the game) one of the other doors, which has a goat, say door 3. He then asks if you want to pick door 2. Should you stay with your choice of door 1 or should you switch to door 2?

The right action is "to switch". To see why, consider three possible scenarios, i.e. the car might be behind door 1, 2 or 3. If the car is behind door 1 and you choose to stay, you win; if you change, you get the goat. If the car is behind door 2 and you stay, you get the goat; if you change, you win. If the car is behind door 3, the host would open door 2. Then, if you choose to stay, you get the goat again. If you switch, you win. Thus, the strategy to stay before door 1 is a winning strategy only if the car is indeed behind door 1, which is possible in 1 of 3 cases. However, if you switch to the other closed door, you get the car if it is indeed behind door 2 but also if it is behind door 3, since the game master knows where the car is and has to open a door with a goat. Thus, if you switch you will get the car in two of three cases, which is better than the choice not to switch. These arguments are summarized in the following table.

Scenarios	Strategies	
	"Stay with door 1"	"Switch to the other closed door"
"The car is behind door 1"	car	goat
"The car is behind door 2"	goat	car
"The car is behind door 3"	goat	car
Probability to get the car	1/3	2/3

Case Study 2.3: (Continued)

Nevertheless, most of the people (even some mathematicians!) would decide not to switch since they think that the odds of winning a car have increased from 1/3 to 1/2 just because the show host has opened a losing door. This reasoning ignores that by his choice the show host reveals some of his information.[11]

The best decision in the case study can also be found by computing the probability that the car is behind one of the two unopened doors. The tool for this is called *Bayes rule*.

Math Box 2.2: Bayesian updating

To apply the Bayes rule in order to solve the case study problem, we need to introduce the concept of *conditional probability*. This is the probability that given all possible states where B is true, A is also true, i.e. $P(A|B)$. To calculate this conditional probability, we need the fraction of states where both A and B are true, i.e. $P(A \cap B)$ and the fraction of states where B is true, i.e. $P(B)$. Then, the Bayes rule says that

$$P(A|B) = \frac{P(A \cap B)}{P(B)}$$

or $P(A \cap B) = P(A|B)P(B) = P(B|A)P(A)$ so that

$$P(A|B) = \frac{P(B|A)P(A)}{P(B)}.$$

Now, let D_t stand for the case that "the car is behind door t" and O_t is the case that "the host opens door t" with $t \in \{1,2,3\}$.

To decide whether to switch to door 2, we need to calculate the probability that the car is behind door 2, given that door 3 has been opened, i.e. $P(D_2|O_3)$. Applying the Bayes rule, we get:

$$P(D_2|O_3) = \frac{P(D_2 \cap O_3)}{P(O_3)} = \frac{P(O_3|D_2)P(D_2)}{P(O_3)}.$$

In this equation, $P(O_3|D_2)$ is the probability that the host opens door 3 given that the car is behind door 2. Since the host will not open the door with the car behind it, we get $P(O_3|D_2) = 1$. Further, $P(D_2)$ is the prior probability that the car is behind door 2, which is equal to 1/3. Finally, we need to calculate the prior probability that the host will open door 3 or $P(O_3)$. To calculate this probability, recall that there are three possible states: the car is behind door 1 (D_1), the car is behind door 2 (D_2) and the car is behind door 3 (D_3). Then, the probability that the host opens door 3 is $P(O_3) = P(O_3 \cap D_1) + P(O_3 \cap D_2) + P(O_3 \cap D_3)$. If we apply the Bayes rule once again, then we get: $P(O_3) = P(O_3|D_1)P(D_1) + P(O_3|D_2)P(D_2) + P(O_3|D_3)P(D_3)$.

---

[11] This problem is discussed in the literature as the "Monty Hall Problem".

Since the host knows where the car is, he will not open the door with the car behind it, i.e. $P(O_3|D_3) = 0$. Therefore, $P(O_3|D_2) = 1$ and $P(O_3|D_1) = 1/2$. The prior probabilities are $P(D_1) = P(D_2) = P(D_3) = 1/3$. Thus, we get $P(O_3) = \frac{1}{2} \cdot \frac{1}{3} + 0 \cdot \frac{1}{3} + 1 \cdot \frac{1}{3} = \frac{1}{2}$.

Therefore, $P(D_2|O_3) = \dfrac{P(D_2 \cap O_3)}{P(O_3)} = \dfrac{P(O_3|D_2)P(D_2)}{P(O_3)} = \dfrac{1 \cdot \frac{1}{3}}{\frac{1}{2}} = \dfrac{2}{3}.$

In other words, given the information revealed by the host that the car is not behind door 3, the probability that the car is behind door 2 increases from 1/3 to 2/3. Therefore, one should switch and bet on door 2.

2.4 PROSPECT THEORY

A central issue of optimal decision-making is the notion of risk. There are quite different opinions about the meaning of risk. For some economists, risk has a neutral meaning. In other words, risk is associated with the uncertain (positive or negative) outcomes of decisions. For financial economists, risk is related to something negative such as the possibility of losses. It is not surprising that the question of how to measure risk is at least as unclear as the definition of risk. Nevertheless, using a risk measure which does not match an investor's essential understanding about risk would lead to investment decisions which are sub-optimal from the investor's point of view.

Traditional finance uses the variance as a risk measure and suggests that individuals weight negative returns equally with positive returns. In particular, the mean-variance analysis assumes further that the volatility is the unique risk factor driving decisions under uncertainty. Behavioural finance research has a slightly different perspective. It claims that individuals perceive risk differently so that individual risk preferences are not determined solely by deviations from the mean, but depend significantly on gains and losses with respect to a certain reference point. If, in addition, clients form beliefs that do not correspond to the statistical probabilities, their perception of the risks associated with particular decisions would be biased. It is the advisor's duty to respond to clients' preferences and correct biases if necessary. Prospect theory provides some useful insights on how to perform this task successfully.

Prospect theory is the most well-known descriptive decision theory. In 2002, its authors were awarded the Nobel Prize in economics. Prospect theory has two phases. In Phase I, a given decision problem is framed and processed so that it can be evaluated in Phase II. The way decisions are framed can make a huge difference. We will, however, postpone framing effects to the chapter on behavioural biases and on wealth management processes. Here we will therefore only consider the evaluation phase of prospect theory.

2.4.1 The value function

When studying how individuals evaluate different alternatives in order to make a decision, several experimental studies document that (1) gains are treated differently to losses and (2) outcomes received with small probability are over-weighted relative to more certain outcomes.

Based on these observations, Kahneman and Tversky (1979) and Tversky and Kahneman (1992) offered a theory that can predict individual choices even in cases where expected utility is violated. In prospect theory, the objective probabilities are replaced by subjective decision weights and the utility function is substituted by a *value function* that is defined over changes in wealth rather than over the final wealth.

The value function has three important properties:

- It is defined over gains and losses with respect to some natural reference point.
- It is concave in gains and convex for losses.
- The function is steeper for losses than for gains.

Property 1: Gains versus losses and the reference point

The first valuation principle concerns the finding that individuals think in terms of gains and losses rather than in total wealth. Whether a certain outcome is a gain or a loss depends on the individual's *reference point*. Typical reference points are the price at which an asset was bought,[12] the initial wealth multiplied by the risk-free rate, or the wealth multiplied by the return of a benchmark. Moreover, people can have multiple reference points. Below each reference point an investment is considered as a loss; however, each of the losses is perceived differently. One reference point is called *aspiration level*. Returns above the aspiration level are considered as totally satisfactory, returns slightly below it are disappointing but not as much as in the case of falling below the initial reference point, e.g. the buying price. Returns below the aspiration level but above the initial reference point can be still perceived as a gain, depending on which reference point is more important for the investor. However, returns far below the initial reference point are usually considered as totally disappointing - so much so that further losses no longer change the evaluation.

The best established finding on how to define aspiration levels is that they are closely correlated with past achievements (e.g. current income or the average assets' performance in the past). This aspiration level represents an absolute reference point. An alternative way to define an aspiration level is to refer to the performance of a suitable benchmark (e.g. a broadly diversified index). The benchmark represents a relative reference point. The following example illustrates the importance of absolute and relative reference points.

Example 2.7: Absolute and relative reference points

Suppose that there is a hedge fund achieving a positive return in each market phase and an index fund following the movements of the market. The returns are given as:

	Market	
Returns	8 %	−5 %
Probabilities	0.5	0.5
Hedge fund	2 %	1 %
Index fund	8 %	−5 %

---

[12] Note that the choice of this reference point is typically enforced by banks: on their account statements it is pointed out at which price an asset has been bought.

Which asset is more attractive, depending on the investor's reference point?

Evaluation: If the client has an absolute reference point, then, given that each market phase is equally likely, he would better invest in the hedge fund. With this investment he will never make a loss and the 8 % gain of the index fund does not outweigh the 5 % loss because, according to prospect theory, losses usually count more than twice. However, if the client has a relative reference point, i.e. he evaluates investments relative to the performance of the market, investing into the hedge fund would not be attractive. In good times, the performance of the hedge fund is four times lower than the performance of the market. For an investor with a relative reference point, this is equivalent to failing to reach an aspiration level, i.e. to making a loss. In the example above, the loss of achieving 2 % instead of 8 %, i.e. 6 %, cannot be compensated for by a gain of 1 % instead of -5%, i.e. 6 % given that the investor is loss averse, i.e. he puts more weight on losses.

As we said in the introduction, basing one's decision on reference points is not necessarily irrational. When reference points are realistic and stable, goals that will be achieved in the future do not contradict rational decision-making. If, however, the reference point is used to justify previous decisions or if the reference point changes very often in the course of the investment, then irrational decisions may result.

Decisions based on gains and losses can differ substantially from decisions based on the total payoff. The next example illustrates this point.

Example 2.8: Decisions based on gains and losses versus decisions based on total wealth

In addition to whatever you own, you have been given $1000. You are now asked to choose between

A = a guaranteed gain of $500 and
B = a 50 % chance to gain $1000 and a 50 % chance to gain nothing.

In addition to whatever you own, you have been given $2000. You are now asked to choose between

A' = a guaranteed loss of $500 and
B' = a 50% chance to lose $1000 and a 50% chance to lose nothing.
How would you decide?
The typical answer in the first case is A and in the second one B'.

Evaluation: This result occurs because people do not integrate the lump sum with the lotteries. That is to say that they do not base their decisions on total wealth but on gains and losses.

The result in Example 2.8 cannot be explained by the expected utility model, because from a total wealth perspective both situations are the same and decisions shouldn't change. If we believe in the standard normative model, then we should: "...judge a portfolio by its total value, rather than by the values of the individual assets it contains, and should ultimately be based on the standard of living that the portfolio supports" (Campbell and Viceira, 2002). It is a framing effect that can be revealed by integrating the upfront payment with the lotteries.

Property 2: Different attitude toward risk
The second valuation principle suggested by the prospect theory is that individuals' attitudes toward risk differ in the context of gains and losses. This yields different predictions when applying expected utility theory or prospect theory. The classical theory predicts risk aversion independent of reference points whereas prospect theory predicts risk aversion in the domain of gains and risk seeking in the domain of losses (except for small probabilities). The phenomenon is illustrated in the following example.

Example 2.9: Risk-taking behaviour over gains and losses

Consider the following two choices:

$A = (\$0, 50\%; \$1000, 50\%)$

Do you prefer Lottery A to the guaranteed payoff of $500?

$B = (-\$1000, 50\%; \$0, 50\%)$

Do you prefer Lottery B to the guaranteed loss of $500?

The typical answer in the first case is "no" in the second case "yes".

As the example above shows, one is willing to gamble only to avoid losses.

Risk-taking to avoid sure losses

Nick Leeson, at the time an investment officer at Barings, had been continuously making (and disguising) losses (£21m in 1993; £185m in 1994) but on 23 February 1995, the pressure had reached boiling point (in the first two months of 1995 his losses amounted to £619m). In order to recover his initial losses, Leeson had been betting on the Japanese stock market to rise and the Japanese government bonds to fall. However, he did not do anything to limit his liability, i.e. the potential losses if the market went in the opposite direction. As his position deteriorated, Leeson doubled up his bets in an effort to recover his losses. In his words, "I gambled on the stock market to reverse my mistakes and to rescue the bank." The markets continued to move the wrong way. The result was a total loss of £830m, which finally broke the bank.

Even though the outcome of Nick Leeson's investments was not lucky, he had taken rational decisions. At some point his losses were so severe that further losses did not matter as much as getting a chance to break even. However, one may argue that he violated the risk ability of the bank, which was a management mistake of the bank since it should have controlled its traders in this respect.

The case of Nick Leeson seems not to be as unusual as was thought until recently: in January 2008 Jerome Kerviel caused losses of 4.9 billion Euro to his bank, Société Générale, when speculating illegally on higher and higher stakes in order to recover his initial losses.

Decision Theory

Property 3: Loss aversion

The third property of the value function is that it is steeper for losses than for gains. This means that individuals making a loss of $100 need to gain more than $100 as compensation. The higher an individual's aversion to losses, the higher is the required compensation. Alternatively, if an average loss-averse investor is offered a 50% chance to double his income (100% gain) or lose part of it, he would decide to secure at least 77% (lose no more than 23%) in case the chance turns against him. In contrast, a Bernoulli investor, an investor with a logarithmic utility function, would choose to secure 50%.

One consequence of loss aversion is the following.

"Good news is no news; no news is bad news; bad news is good news"

(Jim Morgan, Chairman, Applied Materials)

Each news channel needs to fight for attention. As people dislike negative events much more than they feel pleased by positive ones, it is no surprise that news agencies have developed a bias toward negative stories. For example, in the 1990s, the national murder rate in the United States of America fell by 20 percent. But the number of murder stories on network newscasts rose by roughly 600 percent (according to David Altheide, a professor at the School of Justice at Arizona State University).

These properties of the value function are illustrated graphically in Figure 2.9, where Δx represents a gain or a loss and $v(\Delta x)$ is the prospect utility derived from this gain or loss.

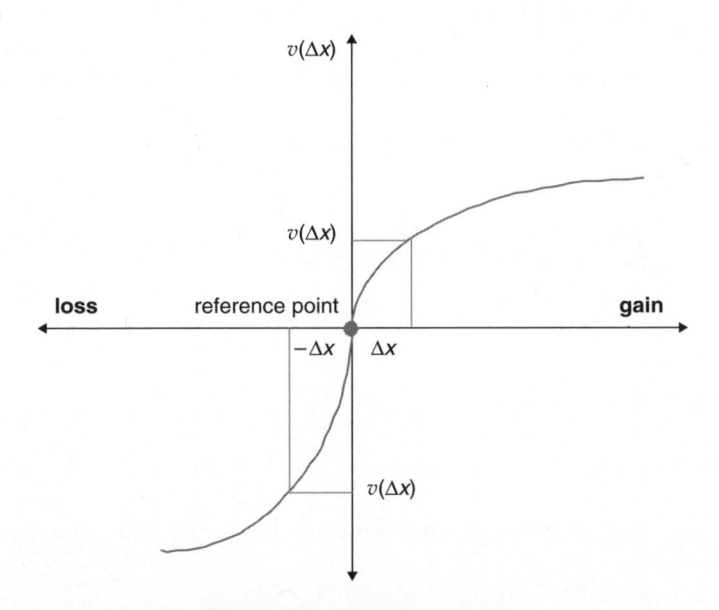

Figure 2.9 The value function

One function of these properties is for example the piecewise power function of Tversky and Kahneman (1992).

$$v(\Delta x) = \begin{cases} \Delta x^\alpha & \text{for } \Delta x \geq 0 \\ -\beta(-\Delta x)^\alpha & \text{for } \Delta x < 0 \end{cases}$$

Based on experimental evidence they suggest that the median risk and loss aversion of individuals are $\alpha = 0.88$ and $\beta = 2.25$.

To check your understanding of the properties of the value function, consider the following case study.

Case Study 2.4: Credit cards

Daniel Bernoulli, one of the founders of expected utility theory, and Daniel Kahneman, one of the founders of prospect theory, go on vacation. Both have two credit cards and two purses in which to keep them. Suppose the chance of losing a purse is 25 % and it is independent of the chance of losing the other purse. Further, suppose that the loss of one card is as bad as the loss of the other card. Who will put both credit cards into the same purse and who will put one credit card into each purse?

Clearly, Daniel Bernoulli will diversify his risk by putting one credit card into each purse. However, Daniel Kahneman will put both credit cards into one purse in order to minimize the chance of losing some of the cards. Note that both Daniels are perfectly rational because risk aversion is a matter of a person's preferences.

To see this, consider the formal solution of the problem. Overall, there are four possible states: lose the left purse (L), lose the right purse (R), lose both purses (L&R), lose neither of the purses (0). Depending on the decision of the agents, i.e. to put both credit cards in one purse (*concentration*) or to put each card in separate purses (*diversification*), the payoffs are as follows (assume that the loss of one credit card is equivalent to -1 and the loss of two credit cards is equivalent to -2):

Strategies/State	L	R	L&R	0
Diversification D	-1	-1	-2	0
Concentration L	-2	0	-2	0
Concentration R	0	-2	-2	0

The probabilities for the four states are:

$$p(L) = p(R) = 1/4 \cdot 3/4, \ p(L\&R) = 1/4 \cdot 1/4 \text{ and } p(0) = 3/4 \cdot 3/4.$$

To decide between the strategies (diversification or concentration), the agents compare the expected utilities associated with each of the strategies and choose the strategy providing the highest expected utility.

Let w be the initial wealth of Daniel Bernoulli. Then his expected utility from the diversification strategy is

$$E_U(D) = \frac{1}{16}\big[3u(w-1) + 3u(w-1) + u(w-2) + 9u(w)\big]$$

$$= \frac{1}{16}\big[6u(w-1) + u(w-2) + 9u(w)\big]$$

and his expected utility from the concentration strategy (in the left purse) is[13]

$$E_U(L) = \frac{1}{16}\big[3u(w-2) + 3u(w) + u(w-2) + 9u(w)\big]$$

$$= \frac{1}{16}\big[4u(w-2) + 12u(w)\big].$$

To decide which strategy delivers a higher expected utility recall Jensen's inequality saying that for each risk-averse decision-maker, the utility of the expected value of a lottery is higher than the expected utility from sure outcomes. Thus, the risk-averse Daniel Bernoulli would choose the diversification strategy since he prefers to lose one card instead of betting on the chance of losing neither of them. This is true since $E_U(D) > E_U(L)$ or $u(w-1) > \frac{1}{2}u(w-2) + \frac{1}{2}u(w)$, which is true for risk-averse decision-makers (with a concave utility function).

Daniel Kahneman would prefer the concentration strategy because his utility is determined by gains and losses and not by final wealth and he is risk-seeking when he makes losses (his utility or value function $v(.)$ is convex for losses). To see this, compare again Daniel's expected prospect utility associated with the diversification strategy

$$PT_v(D) = \frac{1}{16}\big[3v(-1) + 3v(-1) + v(-2) + 9v(0)\big]$$

$$= \frac{1}{16}\big[6v(-1) + v(-2) + 9v(0)\big]$$

and the concentration strategy

$$PT_v(L) = \frac{1}{16}\big[3v(-2) + 3v(0) + v(-2) + 9v(0)\big] = \frac{1}{16}\big[4v(-2) + 12v(0)\big].$$

Since Daniel Kahneman is risk-seeking over losses, $PT_v(D) < PT_v(L)$

$$\text{or } v(-1) < \frac{1}{2}v(-2) + \frac{1}{2}v(0).$$

Thus, Daniel Kahneman would choose to bet on the chance to lose neither of the credit cards by putting both cards into one purse (concentration) instead of losing one card with high probability by putting one card into each of the purses (diversification).

2.4.2 Probability weighting

A further modification of the standard expected utility theory is the concept of perceived probabilities. According to Tversky and Kahneman (1992), investors react to probabilities in

---

[13] The expected utility from following a concentration strategy in the right purse is the same.

such a way that very rare events are over-weighted and events with a higher probability are under-weighted. Psychologically, the mathematical step from zero to one percent probability is a huge step since it is the step from an event being impossible to being possible. This is surely a larger step psychologically than a change from 49 % probability to 50 % probability, which might be described as the psychological step from "quite likely" to "a little more likely". Tversky and Kahneman (1992) suggested that the psychological probability weight should be analytically calculated using a ***probability weighting function***[14] $w(p)$ with

$$w(p) = \frac{p^\gamma}{(p^\gamma + (1-p)^\gamma)^{1/\gamma}}$$

The bias in the perception of probabilities is captured by the parameter of $0.27 \leq \gamma \leq 1$ with an average value of 0.65 found in experiments. The lower the parameter, the stronger is the distortion in the perceived probabilities. This is illustrated in Figure 2.10.

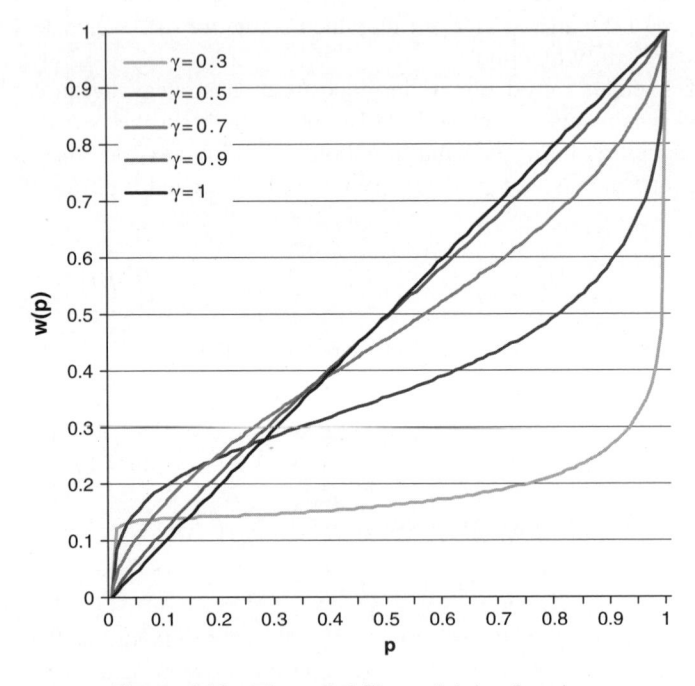

Figure 2.10 The probability weighting function

It is important to note that the weighting function is not a subjective probability, but rather a distortion of the given probability. An individual may agree that the probability of a fair coin landing twice on "heads" is 0.25, but in decision-making the individual acts as if the probability is $w(0.25)$.

---

[14] Other probability weighting functions have later been suggested by Prelec (1998) and Rieger and Wang (2006).

Prospect theory as a by-product of nuclear power

A funny story of decision theory is that prospect theory came as a by-product of nuclear power. When in the 1970s a scientist in physics convinced the US government that using nuclear power for the energy supply of the nation was a wise idea, the government was wondering why the general public protested so much at this decision. The government gave a grant to two young researchers at Carnegie Mellon, Daniel Kahneman and Amos Tversky to figure out what was wrong. The two found that the general public did not buy the argument that nuclear power is acceptable because the great catastrophe of a nuclear explosion would not count much because it was expected that there was only a very small probability of this occurring. Rather, envisioning the case of a nuclear catastrophe, the general public did not care much about the fact that the probability of this was very small. Over-weighting small probabilities became one of the cornerstones of prospect theory.

Taking expectations of a utility function with respect to weighted probabilities may, however, lead to counterintuitive effects.[15] Table 2.3 gives an example. The lottery with 10 different payoffs from 99 to 99.9 with a 10 % probability each has a higher prospect utility than the certain payoff 100. In the example we assumed the PT-parameter values $\alpha = 0.5$ and $\gamma = 0.65$.

Table 2.3 An example of prospect theory violating Axiom 0

Payoff	Probability	PT-weight	PT-utility
99	0.1	0.1787	1.7782
99.1	0.1	0.1787	1.7791
99.2	0.1	0.1787	1.7800
99.3	0.1	0.1787	1.7809
99.4	0.1	0.1787	1.7818
99.5	0.1	0.1787	1.7827
99.6	0.1	0.1787	1.7836
99.7	0.1	0.1787	1.7845
99.8	0.1	0.1787	1.7854
99.9	0.1	0.1787	1.7863
			17.8227
100	1		**10.0000**

What is disturbing in this example is that the certainty equivalent of the lottery is not in between the smallest and largest possible payoff of the lottery, but in fact is much larger than the largest possible payoff. To cure this counterintuitive effect of prospect theory (which is called a "violation of in-betweenness"), Tversky and Kahneman (1992) suggested cumulative prospect theory (CPT) that applies the probability weighting to the cumulative distribution function[16]

---

[15] For example violating state dominance and therefore also first-order stochastic dominance.
[16] The cumulative distribution function F at some point c gives the probability that the lottery has a payoff that is at most c:
$$F(c) = \sum_{\substack{i=1 \\ c_i \leq c}}^{I} p_i.$$

instead of the probabilities. An easier approach is, however, to normalize the decision weight $w(p)$ so that they add up to 1 and can again be interpreted as a probability distribution. This approach – sometimes called *normalized prospect theory* (NPT) – cures the violations of state-dominance for $S = 2$ and avoids violations of in-betweenness completely. In this book we will follow this approach that goes back to Karmakar (1978).[17] Given the biased perception of probabilities and the value function, the value of a lottery with s different outcomes x_s each occurring with a probability p_s is then equal to

$$PT_v = \frac{\sum_{s=1}^{S} w(p_s) v(x_s)}{\sum_{s=1}^{S} w(p_s)}$$

where the term in the denominator $\sum_{s=1}^{S} w(p_s)$ is a simple normalization in order to make sure that the sum of all weighted probabilities is equal to 1.

Math Box 2.3: Prospect theory, normalized prospect theory, and cumulative prospect theory in a nutshell

To explain the difference between prospect theory (PT), normalized prospect theory (NPT), and cumulative prospect theory (CPT), consider a simple binary lottery with payoffs $c_1 < c_2$ in the two states $s = 1$ and $s = 2$, respectively. Let p denote the probability of the first state and let w be the probability weighting function. Then prospect theory (PT) is given by

$$w(p)v(c_1) + w(1-p)v(c_2).$$

Normalizing the probabilities we obtain normalized prospect theory (NPT):

$$\frac{w(p)}{w(p) + w(1-p)} v(c_1) + \frac{w(1-p)}{w(p) + w(1-p)} v(c_2).$$

Finally, note that p is the probability to obtain at least c_1. Hence the cumulative distribution takes the values $0, p$ and 1 and is a step function increasing at c_1 and c_2. Cumulative prospect theory is given by

$$w(p)v(c_1) + (1 - w(p))v(c_2).$$

Figure 2.11 displays the histogram of the returns of a certain fund-of-fund investing in hedge funds both with and without probability weighting, where $w^*(p_s) = \dfrac{w(p_s)}{\sum_{s=1}^{S} w(p_s)}$.

---

[17] See Rieger and Wang (2006).

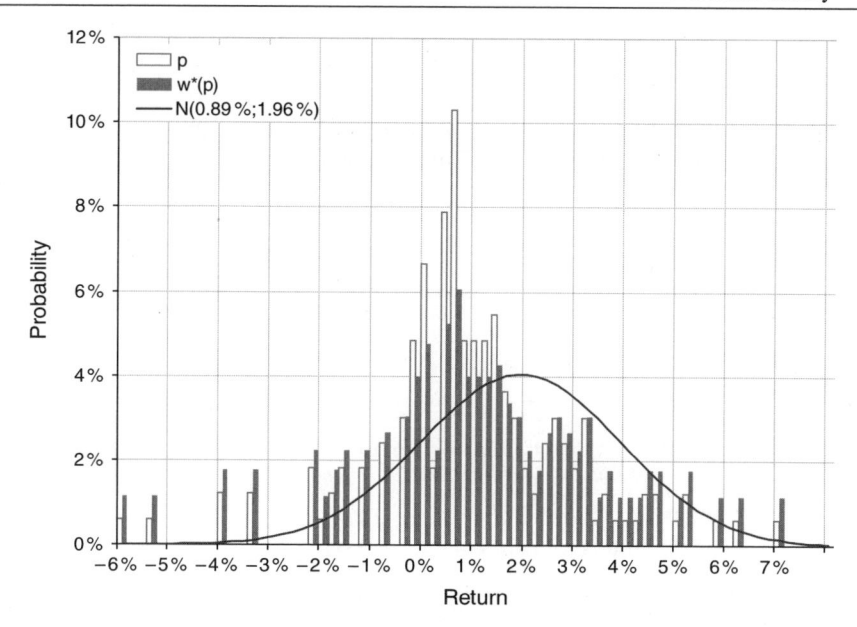

Figure 2.11 Return of hedge funds as they are and as seen by a prospect theory investor

We see that the extreme events get over-weighted at the expense of the medium events. This psychological effect should be taken into account in risk management, which tries to tame extremely negative events.

The next case study shows that the biased perception of probabilities may lead to irrational advice since it motivates decisions which are in contradiction with the expected utility theory and in particular with the independence axiom.

Case Study 2.5: Probability weighting

Financial advisor Professor Clever has two clients, Mrs Moderatio and Mr Moderate. Both have recently inherited some assets. Mrs Moderatio has inherited certificates of deposit (CD) earning a 2 % interest rate and Mr Moderate has inherited some stocks. They are not allowed to change their inheritance drastically. Mrs Moderatio considers including some bonds. Mr Moderate considers including some hedge funds. Professor Clever believes that three scenarios are most likely to happen in the next year:

Scenario 1: Interest rates increase.

Scenario 2: Interest rates decrease and the economy is stagnating.

Scenario 3: Interest rates remain unchanged and the economy stays in recession.

He guesses the probabilities of occurrence are 1 %, 10 %, and 89 %, respectively. He understands that both clients have the same risk preference and knows that their total wealth is also comparable. He recommends to Mrs Moderatio not to include bonds,

Case Study 2.5: (Continued)

but to Mr Moderate he suggests also investing in hedge funds. The payoffs in the three scenarios are as follows. Mrs Moderatio's payoff matrix is:

	Interest up 1%	Interest down 10%	Recession 89%
CD	+2%	+2%	+2%
+bonds	−5%	+6%	+2%

Mr Moderate's payoff matrix is:

	Interest up 1%	Interest down 10%	Recession 89%
Stocks	+2%	+2%	−5%
+hedge funds	−5%	+6%	−5%

Is advisor Clever rational? Clearly not! To see this, note that when there is a recession, for both clients both alternatives deliver the same payoff. Hence by the independence axiom, the choice between the two alternatives of each client should be independent from the recession scenario. However, if one cancels the recession scenario from the payoff matrices, then both clients are faced with exactly the same choices. Hence, there is no reason to advise them differently.

To understand why Professor Clever may have given this advice, let us reframe the problem using the lottery approach. Instead of defining the probabilities of different scenarios occurring and then defining the payoffs in each of the states, we first define the possible payoffs and then determine the probabilities of their occurrence. In the example above, there are three possible payoffs: −5%, 2%, and 6%. Mrs Moderatio investing in CDs would receive 2% in any case. If she adds bonds, she would achieve a return of −5% with 1% probability, a return of 2% with 89% probability, and a return of 6% with 10% probability. Using the same logic also for Mr Moderate, we can reframe the problem above as in Figure 2.12.

	−5%	+2%	+6%	
Mrs Moderatio	0%	100%	0%	CD
	1%	89%	10%	CD+Bonds
Mr Moderate	89%	11%	0	Stocks
	90%	0%	10%	Stocks+HF

Figure 2.12 Return probabilities

Decision Theory

Based on this framing, advisor Clever reasons that including bonds in Mrs Moderatio's CDs mainly opens the possibilities of losses while adding hedge funds to Mr Moderate's stocks mainly opens new chances. For this to be true, the expected utility of achieving 2 % for sure by investing in CDs only must be higher than the expected utility of investing in the mix of CDs and bonds. To see this, evaluate the lotteries with a generalized expected utility function in which probabilities p are replaced by decision weights $w(p)$. Clever's advice amounts to saying that

$$w(100\,\%)v(2\,\%) > \frac{w(1\,\%)v(-5\,\%) + w(89\,\%)v(2\,\%) + w(10\,\%)v(6\,\%)}{w(1\,\%) + w(89\,\%) + w(10\,\%)}.$$

Respectively, the expected utility of mixing stocks with hedge funds must be higher than the expected utility of investing in stocks only:

$$\frac{w(90\,\%)v(-5\,\%) + w(10\,\%)v(6\,\%)}{w(90\,\%) + w(10\,\%)} > \frac{w(89\,\%)v(-5\,\%) + w(11\,\%)v(2\,\%)}{w(89\,\%) + w(11\,\%)}.$$

If Professor Clever applies the same criteria in both cases, then his recommendation is consistent only if he does not consider the "real" probabilities, but a nonlinear weighting function $w(p)$ of them. To see why this is necessary, assume that $w(p) = p$. In this case we get,

$$v(2\,\%) > 1\,\%v(-5\,\%) + 89\,\%v(2\,\%) + 10\,\%v(6\,\%) \text{ and}$$

$90\,\%v(-5\,\%) + 10\,\%v(6\,\%) > 89\,\%v(-5\,\%) + 11\,\%v(2\,\%)$, showing a contradiction.

For these conditions to hold, Professor Clever must weight the probabilities using a nonlinear function $w(.)$. In particular, he responds more strongly to a probability increase from 0 % to 1 %, as in the case of Mrs Moderatio as compared to the numerically equivalent increase from 89 % to 90 % in the case of Mr Moderate. We use the probability weighting function with $\gamma = 0.35$ to check whether it helps to explain Professor Clever's advice.

γ: 0.35	α 0.88	β 2.25	
p	$w(p)$	R	NPT value
Investing in CDs and bonds			
1 %	0.1196	−5 %	−0.0302
10 %	0.1672	6 %	0.0220
89 %	0.3512	2 %	0.0176
sum	0.6380		**0.0094**
Holding only CDs, no bonds			
100%	1	2 %	**0.0320**
Investing in stocks only			
11 %	0.1689	2 %	0.0104
89 %	0.3512	−5 %	−0.1088
sum	0.5201		**−0.0984**

Case Study 2.5: (Continued)

Investing in stocks and hedge funds			
10 %	0.1672	6 %	0.0266
90%	0.3608	−5 %	−0.1101
sum	0.5280		**−0.0835**

Notation:
p: probabilility
$w(p)$: weighted probability
R: returns
NPT: Normalized Prospect Theory

The calculations show that the value of a portfolio with CDs only (NPT = 0.0320) is higher than the value of a portfolio including CDs and bonds (NPT = 0.0094). At the same time, adding hedge funds to a portfolio with stocks is associated with a higher value (NPT = − 0.0835) compared to a portfolio only with stocks (NPT = -0.0984).
Formally,

$$w(100\%)v(2\%) > \frac{w(1\%)v(-5\%) + w(89\%)v(2\%) + w(10\%)v(6\%)}{w(1\%) + w(89\%) + w(10\%)} \text{ or}$$

$$1*2\%^{0.88} > \frac{-0.1196*2.25*5\%^{0.88} + 0.3512*2\%^{0.88} + 0.1672*6\%^{0.88}}{0.638},$$

which is $0.032 > 0.0094$

and

$$\frac{w(90\%)v(-5\%) + w(10\%)v(6\%)}{w(90\%) + w(10\%)} > \frac{w(89\%)v(-5\%) + w(11\%)v(2\%)}{w(89\%) + w(11\%)} \text{ or}$$

$$\frac{-0.3608*5\%^{0.88} + 0.1672*6\%^{0.88}}{0.5280} > \frac{-0.3512*2.25*5\%^{0.88} + 0.1689*2\%^{0.88}}{0.5201},$$

which is $-0.0835 > -0.0984$.

The example and the case study above show that probability weighting is irrational. It may be avoided by separating beliefs from risk attitudes and then choosing the optimal portfolio using some algorithm instead of basing it on one's intuition.

While probability weighting should not be done when one selects a client's asset allocation, it is quite common in financial markets, and can explain a couple of asset pricing puzzles. Overweighting small probabilities means that investors over-weight the tails of the probability distribution, i.e. they are willing to pay very high prices for securities with skewed payoffs. Consider for example, Initial Public Offerings (IPOs). Their return distribution is positively skewed. Thus, investors with prospect theory preferences would require an average return that is lower than the market. This may be one explanation of the IPOs under-pricing puzzle (Barberis and Ming, 2004). Probability weighting can also explain the long-shot bias, i.e. on race-track betting markets higher average returns could be earned by betting on favourites (generally identified by lower odds) than by betting on losers with a lower probability to win (generally identified by higher odds). In other words, if gamblers are over-sensitive to the chances of winning on long-shots and over-sensitive to the chances of losing on favourites, the favourites would win more often than the market's estimate of their winning chances imply (Thaler and Ziemba, 1988).

2.4.3 Risk-taking: Buying lottery tickets and insurance

According to expected utility theory, an investor either takes risk or he insures against risk. This is the case since at the current wealth the agent has either a concave or a convex risk utility function. Actual investors, however, typically do both: they take risk, e.g. on the stock market and they insure against risk, e.g. they buy health insurance or insurance for their car. This can be explained by prospect theory.

Whether a prospect theory investor actually takes risks, as seen by an outside observer, depends on the curvature of his risk utility *and* the degree of probability weighting he applies. To see this, consider an elementary lottery with just two outcomes, e.g. c_1 and c_2. Recall also that, according to Jensen's inequality (see Section 2.3.4), a risk-loving decision-maker prefers the lottery to the guaranteed payoff equal to the expected value of the lottery, i.e.

$$v(pc_1 + (1-p)c_2) < w^*(p)v(c_1) + (1 - w^*(p))v(c_2), \text{ where } w^*(p) = \frac{w(p)}{w(p) + w(1-p)}.$$

Supposing furthermore that $c_2 = 0$ and $v(c_2) = 0$ then we get risk-taking as a combination of c_1 being negative or positive and the size of the probabilities. Rewriting the definition given above for this case leads to $v(pc_1) < w^*(p)v(c_1)$. If we replace the utility function with the piecewise power function of Kahneman and Tversky (1992), then we get $v(p)v(c_1) < w^*(p)v(c_1)$ which is equivalent to $p^\alpha v(c_1) < w^*(p)v(c_1)$ or

$$p^\alpha < w^*(p) \text{ for gains, i.e. } v(c_1) > 0 \text{ and}$$

$$p^\alpha > w^*(p) \text{ for losses, i.e. } v(c_1) < 0.$$

These conditions can be illustrated graphically for example for $\alpha = 0.88$ and $\gamma = 0.65$ as in Figure 2.13.

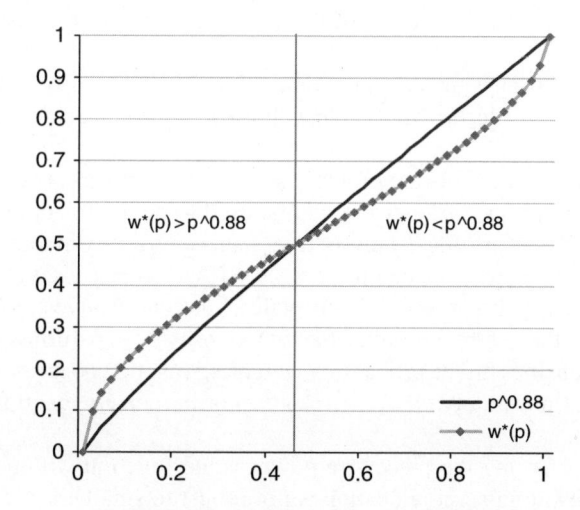

Figure 2.13 Risk taking conditions

Investor's risk taking behaviour in the face of gains and losses with small and moderate probabilities is then summarized in Table 2.4.

Table 2.4 Risk taking behaviour in the face of gains and losses with small and moderate probabilities

	Losses	Gains
Small probability	no risk-taking	risk-taking
Moderate probability	risk-taking	no risk-taking

Hence, if the investor has to decide whether to take a lottery paying 0 or more instead of a guaranteed payment he would decide to gamble if the probability for the gain is small. This is because the investor over-estimates the probability of reaching the utility level associated with the gain. The investor would buy a lottery ticket. For the same reason of probability over-estimation, investors facing losses would buy insurance, i.e. pay for avoiding the lottery.

2.5 PROSPECT THEORY AND THE OPTIMAL ASSET ALLOCATION

Essential for finding an asset allocation that reflects the investor's preferences is the choice of a utility function. To make an appropriate selection, one needs to define a catalogue of criteria that the utility function has to satisfy. Recalling the extensive experimental literature on individual decision-making under uncertainty, a common criterion for the utility function that one uses to define an optimal asset allocation is that it is *psychologically sound*. This means that individuals' behaviour resulting from maximizing this utility function has to be in consensus with the true behaviour of individuals observed in experimental laboratories or in reality. Furthermore, the asset allocation resulting from solving an optimization problem based on the utility function has to be *robust* to small changes in the functional parameters. Finally, asset allocations based on the utility function can be checked for the two-fund-separation theorem requiring that the weight and not the mix of risky assets adjust to changes in the investor's preferences.

In the following we discuss the advantages and disadvantages of several utility functions, which satisfy at least the criterion of being psychologically founded as the value function of Kahneman and Tversky.

Let us first assume that markets are efficient so that asset returns are normally distributed. In this case, the mean-variance framework can be used to define the optimal asset allocation of investors with different profiles. This is true since any utility integrated over normally distributed returns is a mean-variance utility since $PT_v(\mu, \sigma) = \int v^i(\Delta x) \, dT^i(N(\Delta x; \mu, \sigma))$. In this expression, $v^i(.)$ is the prospect theory value function of investor i, Δx is the change of wealth relative to the reference point, the function $T^i(.)$ transforms (for investor i) the cumulative normal densities (as the probability weighting function does) as required by Tversky and Kahneman (1992), and finally, $N(\Delta x; \mu, \sigma)$ is the normal density function of wealth changes with mean μ and risk σ.

The disadvantage of using the piecewise power value function within the mean-variance analysis is that the resulting asset allocation is not robust to small changes in the parameters

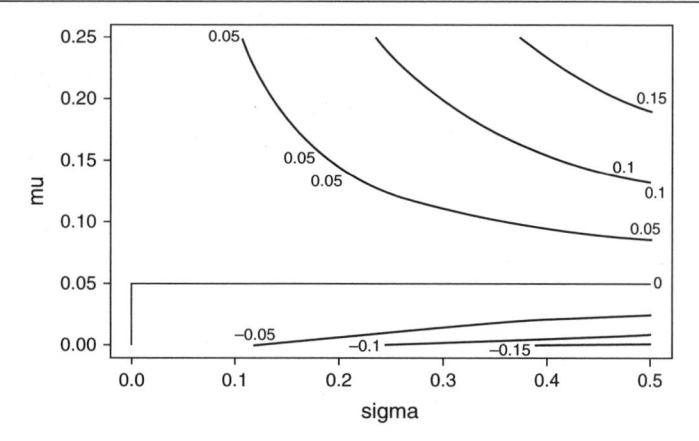

Figure 2.14 Mean-variance preferences, based on the piecewise power value function of Kahneman and Tversky

so that the mix of risk-free and risky assets may change abruptly when the parameters change, as the indifference curves in Figure 2.14 display.

To solve this problem, Levy, De Georgi, and Hens (2004) suggest the use of the piecewise exponential value function

$$v(\Delta x) = \begin{cases} -\lambda^+ \exp(-\alpha \Delta x) + \lambda^+ & \text{for } \Delta x \geq 0 \\ \lambda^- \exp(\alpha \Delta x) - \lambda^- & \text{for } \Delta x < 0 \end{cases}$$

where x is the gain (loss) and the ratio of the parameters λ^+ and λ^- determine the loss aversion of the decision-maker, i.e. $\beta = \dfrac{\lambda^+}{\lambda^-}$. Adopting the piecewise exponential value function for the prospect theory utility function v^i, the indifference curves of the decision-maker can be represented in the mean-standard deviation diagram as follows (see Figure 2.15; De Georgi, Hens and Levy, 2004).

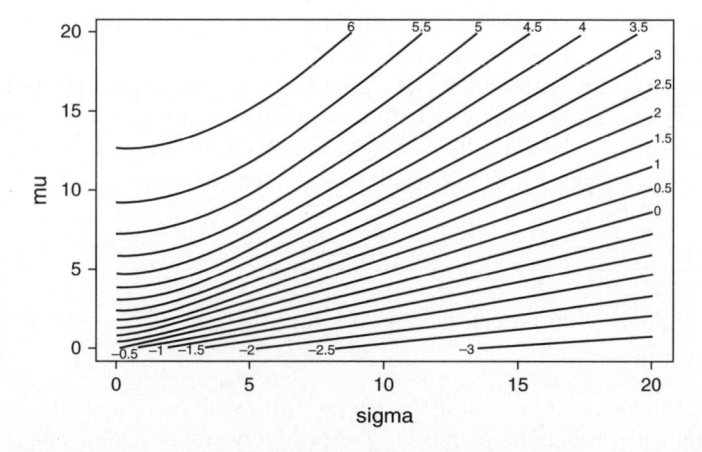

Figure 2.15 Mean-standard deviation diagram with PT-indifference curves based on the piecewise exponential value function

We see in Figure 2.15 that the indifference curves are now shaped in a way that gives robust solutions to the optimization problem applied on the efficient frontier or on the capital market line.

The higher the loss aversion, the steeper is the PT-indifference curve, the less risky the assets the loss-averse investor would hold. The effect is similar if the reference point increases. Both effects are illustrated with examples later on.

To make the choice of the behavioural investor compatible with the mean-variance framework for *any* return distribution, one can use a piecewise quadratic value function with the following form:

$$v(\Delta x) = \begin{cases} \Delta x - \dfrac{\alpha^+}{2}(\Delta x)^2 & \text{if } \dfrac{1}{\alpha^+} > \Delta x \geq 0 \\ \beta \left(\Delta x - \dfrac{\alpha^-}{2}(\Delta x)^2 \right) & \text{if } \dfrac{1}{\alpha^-} < \Delta x < 0 \end{cases}$$

where Δx is defined as the portfolio return R relative to the investor's reference point RP. Note that for $\alpha^+ > 0$ and $\alpha^- < 0$ the function is s-shaped, i.e. concave for $\Delta x \geq 0$ and convex for $\Delta x < 0$ as the piecewise power function of Kahneman and Tversky. The parameter $\beta > 1$ indicates again the degree of loss aversion.

The restrictions $\frac{1}{\alpha^+} > \Delta x \geq 0$ and $\frac{1}{\alpha^-} < \Delta x < 0$ are technical requirements that prevent the utility from falling (increasing) after the gain (loss) reaches the level $\frac{1}{\alpha^+}$, and $\frac{1}{\alpha^-}$ respectively. Beyond this gain (loss), we assume a constant utility of $v(\Delta x) = \frac{1}{2\alpha^+}$, respectively $v(\Delta x) = \frac{1}{2\alpha^-}$. Taking into account these considerations, the piecewise quadratic value function takes the form:

$$v(\Delta x) = \begin{cases} \dfrac{1}{2\alpha^+} & \text{if } \Delta x \geq \dfrac{1}{\alpha^+} \\ \Delta x - \dfrac{\alpha^+}{2}(\Delta x)^2 & \text{if } \dfrac{1}{\alpha^+} > \Delta x \geq 0 \\ \beta \left(\Delta x - \dfrac{\alpha^-}{2}(\Delta x)^2 \right) & \text{if } \dfrac{1}{\alpha^-} < \Delta x < 0 \\ \dfrac{1}{2\alpha^-} & \text{if } \Delta x \leq \dfrac{1}{\alpha^-} \end{cases}$$

Note that for the piecewise quadratic value function for $\beta = 1$, $\alpha^+ = \alpha^-$, and a reference point $RP = \mu$ where μ is the expected return of the investor's portfolio,[18] we get $v(\Delta x) + RP = \mu - \frac{\alpha}{2}\sigma^2$. Thus, the optimal asset allocations of an investor with a quadratic utility function as in the standard mean-variance analysis will be equivalent to the asset allocation of a specific behavioural investor maximizing the piecewise quadratic function suggested above. In the following math box we generalize this result to any reference point.

Math Box 2.4: Mean-variance as a special case of piecewise quadratic value function

To illustrate the idea assume that there is a portfolio with two possible returns R^+ and R^- occurring with probability p and $1 - p$ respectively. Suppose now that $\alpha^+ = \alpha^-$ and $\beta = 1$. Then, the expected utility of an investor holding this portfolio becomes:

---

[18] $E(v(R) \mid RP) = E(v(R)) - \frac{\alpha}{2} E(R - RP)^2 = \mu(R) - \frac{\alpha}{2}\sigma^2(R)$ where $RP = \mu$.

> $$PT_v(R) + RP = p(R^+ - RP) + (1-p)(R^- - RP) - \frac{\alpha}{2}\left(p(R^+ - RP)^2\right.$$
> $$\left. + (1-p)(R^- - RP)^2\right) + RP$$
> $$= \mu(R) - \frac{\alpha}{2}\mu(R - RP)^2.$$
>
> More generally, by definition of variance, i.e. $\mu(R-RP)^2 = \sigma^2(R-RP) + \mu^2(R-RP)$, we get
> $$PT_v(R) + RP = \mu(R) - \frac{\alpha}{2}\left[\sigma^2(R-RP) + \mu^2(R-RP)\right]$$
>
> Hence, $PT_v(R) + RP = \mu(R) - \frac{\alpha}{2}\left[\sigma^2(R) + \mu^2(R) - RP^2\right]$, i.e. the prospect theory objective function depends on the reference point, the degree of risk aversion, and on the first two points of the return distribution.
>
> In particular, if $RP = \mu$, then $PT_v(R) + RP = \mu(R) - \frac{\alpha}{2}\left[\sigma^2(R)\right]$; i.e. we would then get a very simple mean-variance objective function.

2.5.1 An explicit solution with the piecewise quadratic value function

Suppose that there are two assets, one risk-free with a return R_f and one risky with two possible returns, R_u and R_d. The probability that the return R_u is realized is p. Let λ be the percentage of wealth invested in the risky asset. Thus, the portfolio return can be either $R_f + (R_u - R_f)\lambda$ or $R_f + (R_d - R_f)\lambda$. Suppose also that there is an investor with a piecewise quadratic value function as suggested above, i.e.

$$v(R_s) = \begin{cases} R_s - RP - \frac{\alpha^+}{2}(R_s - RP)^2 & \text{if } R_s \geq RP \\ \beta\left(R_s - RP - \frac{\alpha^-}{2}(R_s - RP)^2\right) & \text{if } R_s > RP \end{cases}$$

where R_s is the return of the portfolio with risky assets (excess return).

Thus, assuming that $\frac{1}{\alpha^-} \leq R_s \leq \frac{1}{\alpha^+}$ and that PT_v is quasi-concave[19], the optimal percentage of wealth that should be invested in the risky asset when $RP = R_f$ is:

$$\lambda = \frac{p(R_u - R_f) + \beta(1-p)(R_d - R_f)}{\alpha^+ p(R_u - R_f) + \beta\alpha^-(1-p)(R_d - R_f)^2},$$

which is robust if the numerator stays positive.

Note that the percentage of wealth invested in the risky asset increases with the expected return of the risky asset, i.e. $\mu = pR_u + (1-p)R_d$, and decreases with the investor's loss aversion β but also with the investor's risk aversion α^+ and α^- if the latter is not too negative. Also note the similarity with the explicit solution for the mean-variance utility that we displayed earlier.

Generalizing this solution to the multiple assets case, we see that prospect theory does not satisfy the two-fund-separation theorem. This is illustrated in the Math Box 2.5. The two-fund-separation theorem does not hold, since neither the loss aversion nor the risk aversion parameters can be separated out of the asset allocation in a simple multiplicative way.

---

[19] Note that PT_v can be quasi-concave even if $v(.)$ is not concave everywhere. A function $f(x)$ is quasi-concave if its level sets $\{x|f(x) \succcurlyeq c\}$ are convex.

> **Math Box 2.5:** The piecewise quadratic value function and the two-fund separation theorem
>
> For the $s = 1,\ldots,S$ scenarios let
>
> $$\tilde{p}_s^+ = \begin{cases} p_s & \text{if } R_s^j > RP \\ 0 & \text{if } R_s^j < RP \end{cases} \quad \text{and} \quad \tilde{p}_s^- = \begin{cases} p_s & \text{if } R_s^j < RP \\ 0 & \text{if } R_s^j > RP \end{cases}$$
>
> Let $\tilde{R}_s^j = R_s^j - R_f$ and $\tilde{R}$ be the $S \times J$ matrix of excess returns and Λ a diagonal matrix with p on the main diagonal. Then under the same assumptions as above $\lambda^{opt} = \left[\alpha^+ \tilde{R}^T \Lambda (\tilde{p}^+) \tilde{R} + \beta \alpha^- \tilde{R}^T \Lambda (\tilde{p}^-) \tilde{R}\right]^{-1} \left[\tilde{p}^+ \tilde{R} + \beta \tilde{p}^- \tilde{R}\right]$.
>
> Hence the ratio of any two assets' budget share λ_k/λ_j depends on the loss – and the risk aversion parameters.

2.5.2 The preferences of the median behavioural investor

Tversky and Kahneman (1992) find that the median risk aversion over gains and losses is equal to 0.88 and the median loss aversion is equal to 2.25. These parameters are specific for the piecewise power function used by Kahneman and Tversky to represent the preferences of behavioural investors. If one wants to describe the median investor in the experiments of Kahneman and Tversky with the piecewise quadratic function, one needs to find the parameters $\alpha^+, \alpha^-, \beta, \gamma^+, \gamma^-$ that govern individuals' behaviour as observed in those experiments. In other words, we look for the set of parameters that motivate individuals to give the same answers (as certainty equivalents) as the answers to the lottery questions used by Kahneman and Tversky.

For payoffs between 0 and 400 the median investor of Kahneman and Tversky with piecewise quadratic value function has preferences described by $\alpha^+ = 0.00215$ and $\alpha^- = -0.00185$. The loss aversion parameter is still $\beta = 2.25$.

If the payoffs are in the form of returns between 10 % and 380 % (respectively between -10 % and -380 %), the parameters are: $\alpha^+ = 0.21512$, $\alpha^- = -0.18469$.

For low payoffs, i.e. between 1 % and 38 % (respectively between -1 % and -38 %), the parameters of the piecewise quadratic function are $\alpha^+ = 2.15114$, $\alpha^- = -1.84688$, and so forth.

2.5.3 Reward-risk perspective on prospect theory

A fundamental principle in financial economics is that there is no reward without risk. In the mean-variance framework, the reward-risk trade-off is implemented using the idea that investors who wish to increase the expected return of their investments must accept returns that deviate more strongly from the mean. Actually, the real ground-breaking idea of Markowitz (1952) was the suggestion of a simple reward-risk diagram. That he had chosen the mean return for the reward and the standard-deviation for the risk axis was more for convenience because, at the time it was not possible to efficiently deal with higher moments of the return distribution.

De Giorgi, Hens and Meier (2006) suggest a different perspective on implementing the reward-risk-principle. From the investor's point of view, the reward of an investment is not its expected return as in the mean-variance analysis but the expected return over his reference point or its *average gain*. It is defined as the sum of all portfolio returns over the investor's reference point, weighted with the corresponding probabilities as perceived by the investors. More precisely, the average gain is defined as

$$pt^+ = \sum_{\substack{s=1 \\ \Delta s > 0}}^{S} w(p_s) v(R_s - RP)$$

where R_s is the return of the portfolio in state s.

Respectively, the risk of the investment is not the deviation from the expected return as in the mean-variance analysis but the expected portfolio return below the investor's reference point. This is the portfolio's *average loss*, i.e.

$$pt^- = -\frac{1}{\beta} \sum_{\substack{s=1 \\ \Delta s < 0}}^{S} w(p_s) v(RP_s - R_s)$$

where β is the investor's loss aversion. Therefore, the utility over the average gains and losses is $PT = pt^+ - \beta pt^-$. Graphically, the return-risk perspective can be represented as in Figure 2.16.

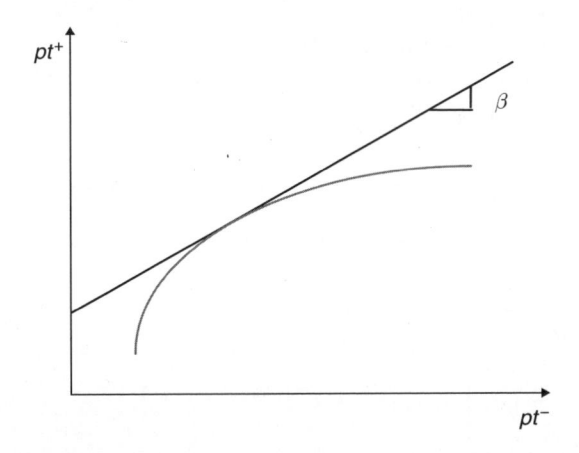

Figure 2.16 Reward-risk perspective on the prospect theory

2.5.4 Some examples

In the following example, we illustrate the optimal asset allocations of clients with different preferences using real data. In particular, we assume that there are five assets: four risky and one risk-free asset (cash). The risky assets include Swiss Government Bonds (SGB), Swiss Performance Index (SPI), commodities (Cdty), and a hedge fund offered by LGT (LGT Hedge). The cumulative gross returns of the assets in the period from 1993 to 2006 are summarized in Figure 2.17.

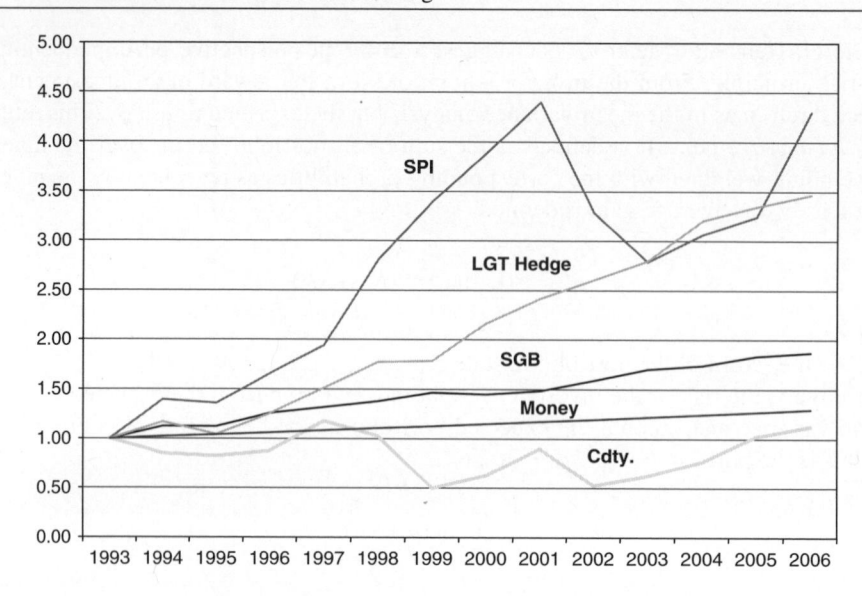

Figure 2.17 Cumulative gross returns (1993–2006)

The reward-risk trade-off of the assets can be analyzed in two different ways as previously discussed. First, one can use the variance as a risk measure and illustrate the asset returns in a mean-variance diagram (see Figure 2.18). In this case, the most unattractive assets are commodities - on average, an investor gets the same return as with Swiss Government Bonds (SGB) but with a greater uncertainty.

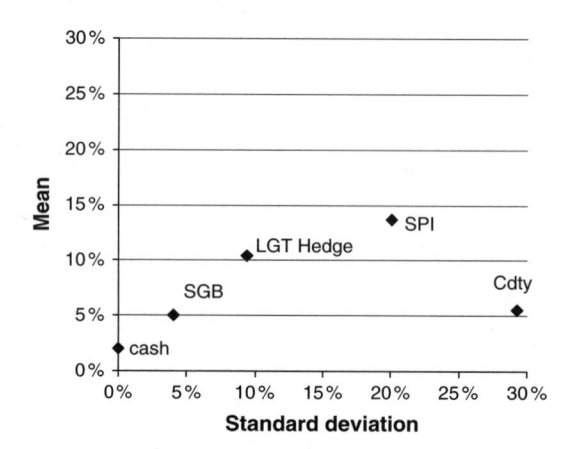

Figure 2.18 Asset returns in a mean-variance diagram

Second, if one uses the average loss as a risk measure and the average gain as a reward measure as defined above, one gets a different view on the assets (see Figure 2.19). In particular, commodities are not so unattractive anymore, i.e. an investment in commodities alone offers the largest average loss but also the largest average gain.

Decision Theory 57

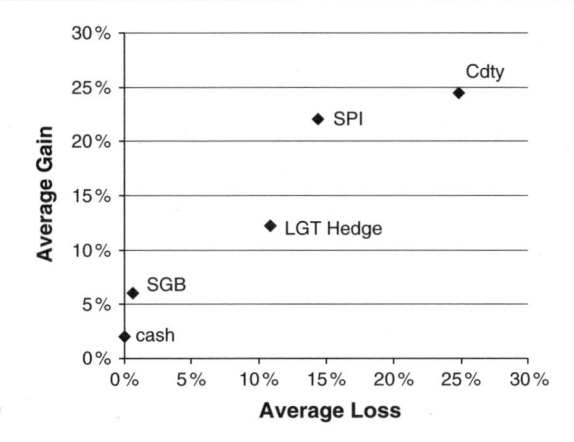

Figure 2.19 Asset returns in an average-gain-loss diagram

In the following example, we use the asset returns to determine the optimal asset allocation of different investors. In particular, we use the piecewise quadratic value function introduced above, where $\Delta x = R - RP$ with R defined as the portfolio return and RP defined as the investors' reference point to distinguish between two investors. The first one is the standard investor with a quadratic utility function. The second one is a behavioural investor. The difference in their preferences is the level of loss aversion defined by the parameter β and the choice of the reference point. Again, the typical investor with a quadratic utility function known from the standard mean-variance analysis has $\beta = 1$ and $RP = \mu$ where μ is the expected portfolio return. We assume also that $\alpha^+ = 11$, $\alpha^- = -11$. The optimal asset allocation of this investor is illustrated in Figure 2.20.

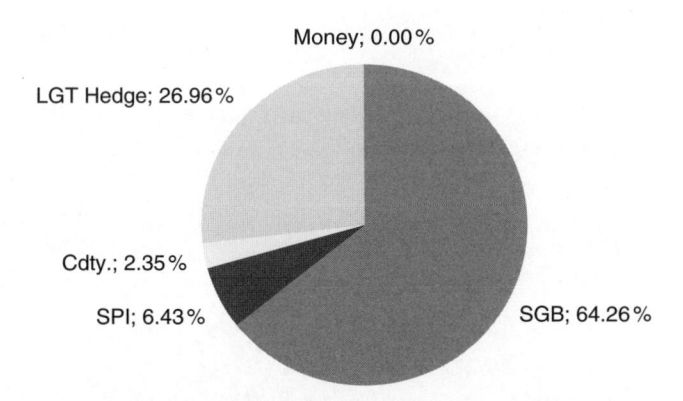

Figure 2.20 Mean-variance tangential portfolio

The optimal asset allocation of a behavioural investor with $\alpha^+ = 11$ and $\alpha^- = -11$ and a loss aversion $\beta = 2$ is illustrated in Figure 2.21.

A behavioural investor with a greater loss aversion, e.g. $\beta = 5$, prefers to decrease his exposure to risky assets such as SPI and hold more Swiss Government Bonds (SGB) instead (see Figure 2.22).

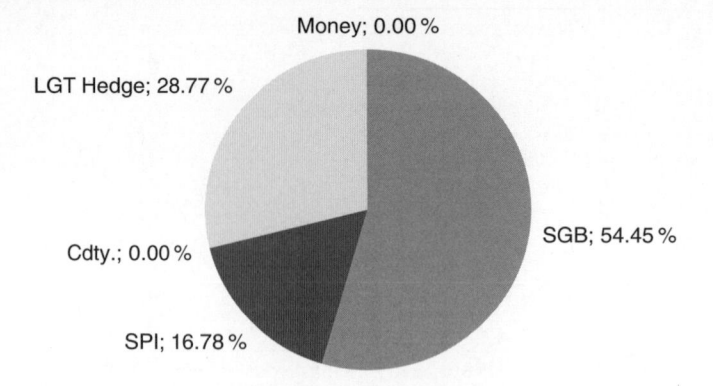

Figure 2.21 Optimal asset allocation of a behavioural investor with $\beta = 2$

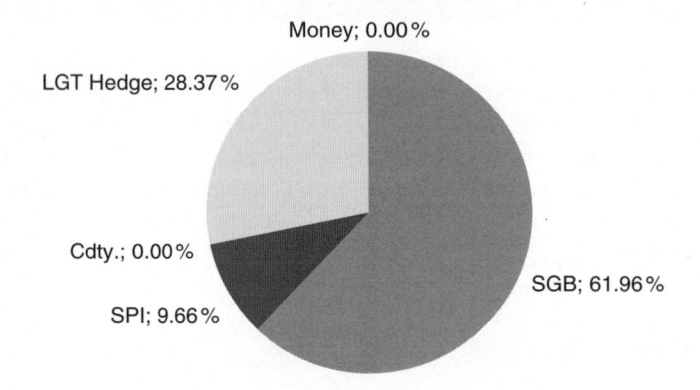

Pie chart values: Money 0.00%; LGT Hedge 28.77%; Cdty. 0.00%; SPI 16.78%; SGB 54.45%

Figure 2.22 Optimal asset allocation of a behavioural investor with $\beta = 5$

Pie chart values: Money 0.00%; LGT Hedge 28.37%; Cdty. 0.00%; SPI 9.66%; SGB 61.96%

The exposure in less risky assets such as Swiss Government Bonds (SGB) increases further with the investor's loss aversion (see Figure 2.23).

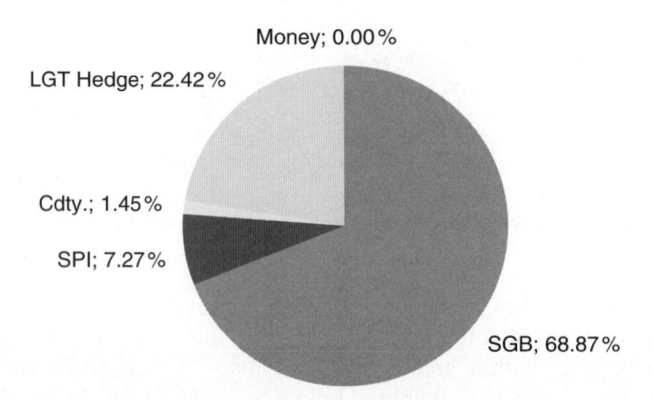

Figure 2.23 Optimal asset allocation of a behavioural investor with $\beta = 10$

Pie chart values: Money 0.00%; LGT Hedge 22.42%; Cdty. 1.45%; SPI 7.27%; SGB 68.87%

2.6 A CRITICAL VIEW ON MEAN-VARIANCE THEORY

In this section, we focus on the main disadvantages of the mean-variance analysis as a commonly used portfolio theory in private banking. The first problem when applying the mean-variance analysis is that it is not sensitive to higher moments of the probability distribution of the asset returns. This problem arises because the mean-variance analysis uses only the first two moments of the return distribution, i.e. its mean and variance. However, there are many different distributions, which have the same mean and same variance as illustrated in the next example.

Example 2.10: Mean-variance and higher moments of the probability distribution

Consider two lotteries: $A = \{27\%, 0.57; -20\%, 0.43\}$ and $B = \{85\%, 0.08; 0\%, 0.92\}$. Both lotteries have approximately the same mean, $\mu = 7\%$ and the same variance, $\sigma^2 = 23\%$. Suppose these lotteries represent products. Then an investor applying mean-variance analysis would be indifferent between them. However, if the investor cares about gains and losses, he would not consider both products as equally attractive.

The same point can be made in a more realistic setting by comparing the two structured products on the SMI displayed in Figure 2.24. Supposing the SMI has normally distributed returns with a mean of 7.5 % and a standard-deviation of 12 %, both products have a mean return of 2.7 % and a variance of 34.4 %. Thus they are indistinguishable for a mean-variance investor while typically investors would prefer the product with unlimited gains since it has capital protection and unlimited upside potential while the other has limited upside potential and unlimited loss potential.

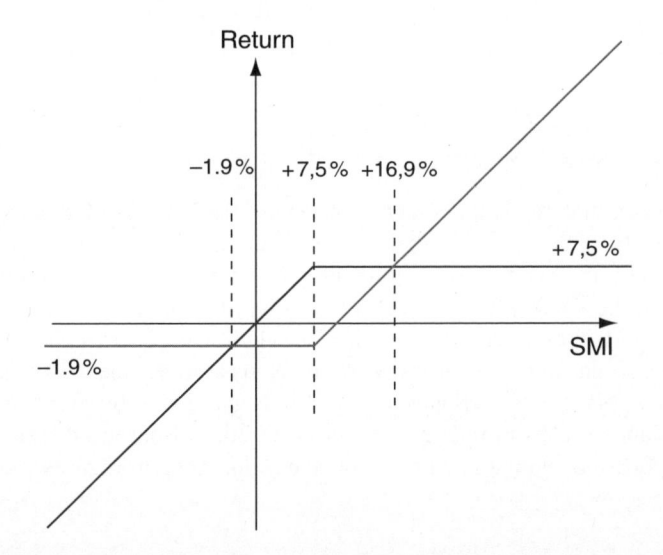

Figure 2.24 Two quite different structured products with the same mean and variance

The second problem of the mean-variance analysis is known as the mean-variance paradox that violates Axiom 0. The following example illustrates the effect.[20]

Example 2.11: The mean-variance paradox

Consider a binary lottery in which, with probability $p > 0$, you can get a prize $y > 0$. In the other state, the payoff is zero. Since one cannot lose in this lottery, any agent satisfying Axiom 0 would prefer it to a payoff of 0 in both states. This is, however, not clear for a mean-variance optimizer. To see this, let the probability p converge to zero while the payoff y increases so as to keep the expected value of the lottery $\mu = py$ constant. As an effect, the variance of the lottery $\sigma^2 = p(y-\mu)^2 + (1-p)(-\mu)^2 = \mu y - \mu^2$ tends to infinity (see Figure 2.25) so that any variance-averse investor will eventually prefer to get nothing rather than to play the lottery!

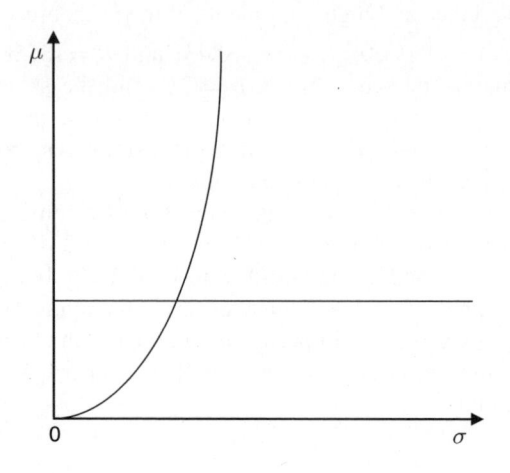

Figure 2.25 The mean-variance paradox

Case Study 2.6: Asset allocations with structured products

Consider an asset that pays the returns of the Swiss Performance Index (SPI), but only if they are positive. We use the label SPI+ for this asset. Without the risk of realizing negative returns, this asset is a quite attractive investment opportunity. However, investors using the mean-variance analysis have a different view. To be more precise, we build two portfolios of risky assets, i.e. one with and one without SPI+. Then we calculate the optimal portfolio of risky assets (Swiss Government Bonds, Swiss Performance Index, MSCI United States, Hedge Funds, and SPI+) by searching for the best (1) mean-variance trade-off and (2) gains-losses trade-off based on historical returns. The tangent portfolios with and without SPI+ are illustrated in Figures 2.26 and 2.27.

---

[20] A different example goes as follows: Consider the mean-variance utility $\mu(10-\sigma)$ and convince yourself that the 50:50 lottery of getting 10 or 20 is not preferred to the sure payoff of 10.

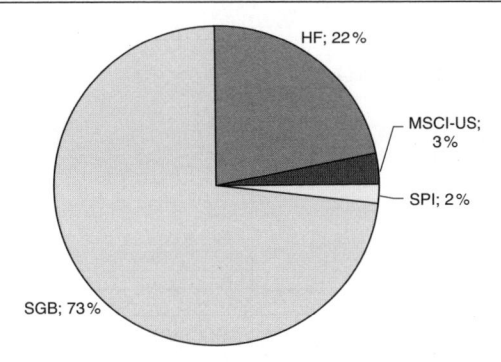

Figure 2.26 The tangent portfolio without SPI+

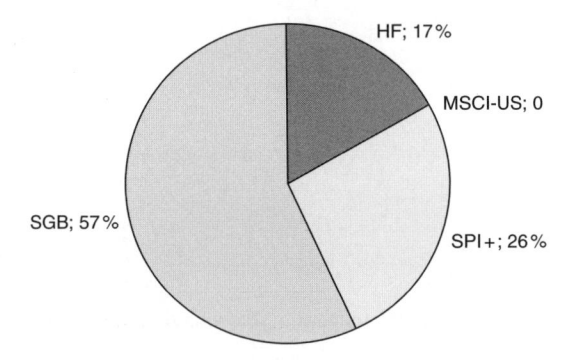

Figure 2.27 The tangent portfolio with SPI+

If there is an asset paying only the positive returns of SPI, then a mean-variance investor would increase his exposure to the Swiss market from 2 % to 26 %. In contrast, a behavioural investor with a piecewise quadratic value function would detect this arbitrage opportunity and invest all his wealth in SPI+ (see Figures 2.28 and 2.29).

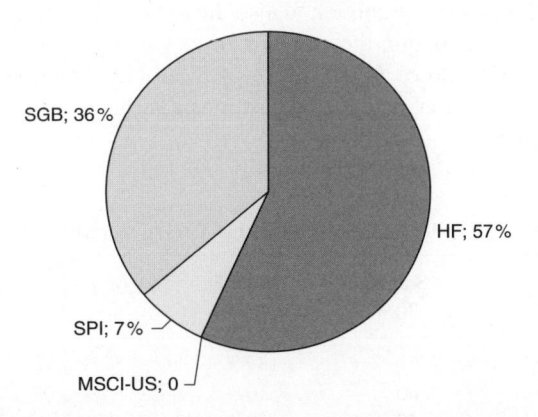

Figure 2.28 Optimal asset allocation of a behavioural investor without SPI+

Case Study 2.6: (Continued)

Figure 2.29 Optimal asset allocation of a behavioural investor with SPI+

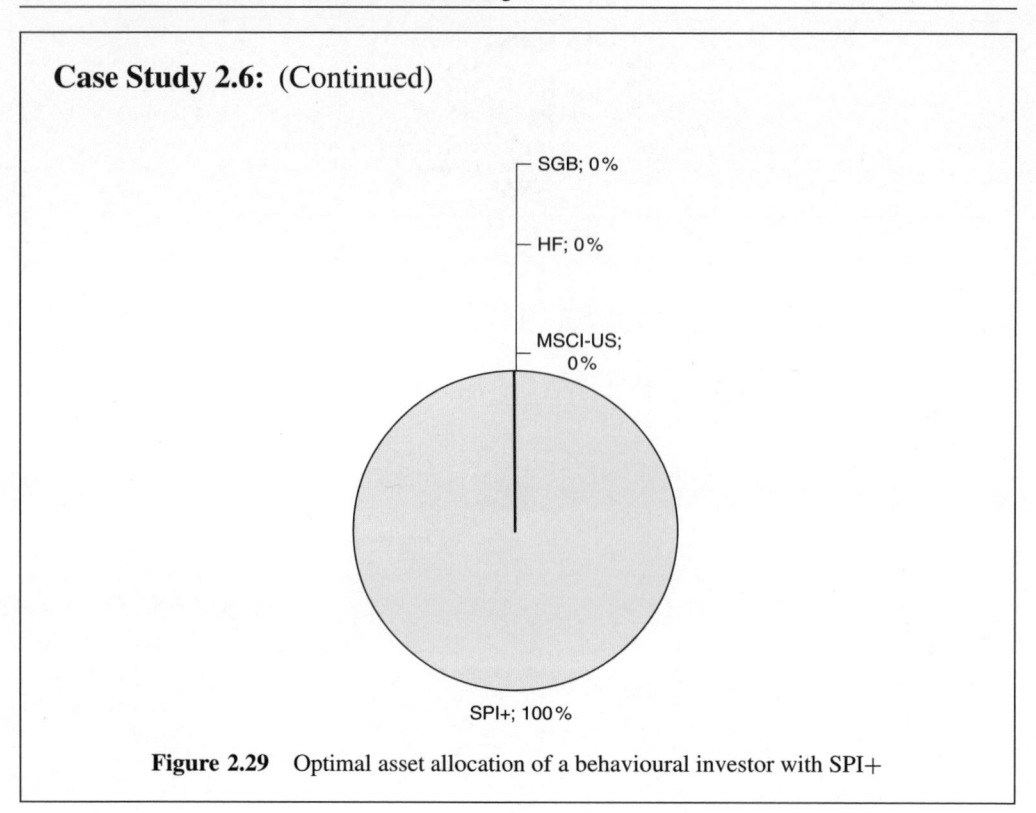

(Pie chart: SPI+; 100%, MSCI-US; 0%, HF; 0%, SGB; 0%)

In a final example we show that mean-variance may also violate the independence axiom.

Example 2.12: Mean-variance violating the independence axiom

Consider four lotteries A, B, A' and B' with payoffs in three states constructed in such a way that in the third state, the lotteries A and B and also the lotteries A' and B' have the same payoff. Hence, by the independence axiom, the comparison between the two should be independent of the third state. Hence, a choice $B \succ A$ and $A' \succ B'$ violates the independence axiom. But for some degree of risk aversion, α, the standard mean-variance utility $\mu - \frac{\alpha}{2}\sigma^2$ leads to this choice, as Table 2.5 shows.

Table 2.5 Mean-variance violating the independence axiom

Probability	State 1 10%	State 2 80%	State 3 10%	Mean	Variance	M/V
Lottery A	75%	50%	30%	51%	1.02%	49.39
Lottery B	40%	60%	30%	55%	1.05%	52.38
Lottery A'	75%	50%	0%	48%	3.06%	15.51
Lottery B'	40%	60%	0%	52%	3.36%	15.48

Note that the variance, i.e. $\sigma^2 = \sum_{s=1}^{S} p_s \left(x_s - \sum_{s=1}^{S} p_s x_s \right)^2 = \sum_{s=1}^{S} p_s x_s^2 - \left(\sum_{s=1}^{S} p_s x_s \right)^2$ is not linear in probabilities. Thus, in general mean-variance preferences are not consistent with the expected utility theory as the latter requires preferences to be linear in probabilities.

To summarize, the mean-variance analysis has a simplified notion of risk, which is the variance of returns. However, the variance treats gains and losses symmetrically. Moreover, variance-based preferences are not consistent with the expected utility theory; they may also lead an investor to reject investments even if they offer only non-negative and potentially high payoffs. These concerns suggest that the mean-variance analysis is not motivated by rationality considerations and should be used with some care. In particular, one should be aware that the mean-variance analysis works only for normally distributed returns, which is fine for the assets classes in the 1950s where hedge funds, structured products etc. had not yet been invented, but not for today. Overall, the mean-variance analysis is a good starting point, but one should keep in mind that it also represents the technology of the 1950s.

2.7 A CRITICAL VIEW ON EXPECTED UTILITY AXIOMS

The expected utility axioms and in particular the independence axiom, have been a subject of criticism by the behavioural finance research community. The main point of this criticism is that the axioms do not describe the real behaviour of decision-makers and this is why several paradoxes such as the *Allais paradox* emerge. While violations of the independence axiom remain, a paradox within the expected utility framework – the observation that people use weighted probabilities as implemented in the prospect theory – explains why people violate the independence axiom as documented in the Allais paradox (see Case Study 2.5).

Another violation of the expected utility axioms, which is not addressed by prospect theory, was observed in an experiment conducted by Daniel Ellsberg in 1961. Subjects are presented with an urn containing 90 balls. 30 are red and the rest are either yellow or black. The proportion of yellow to black balls is unknown. Subjects must bet on the colour that will be drawn. The payoff matrix is shown in Figure 2.30.

It is very common for individuals to prefer lottery A to B since A gives a 1:3 chance of winning $50, whereas the decision-maker does not know how likely the payoff is in the latter; the proportion of black balls can be very small. The second choice the decision-maker faces is between A' and B'. Most of the subjects in the experiment choose B', because it gives a 2:3 chance of winning $50 whereas A' can only be certain of a 1:3 chance of winning $50 and the proportion of yellow balls can be very small. The explanation for the preference reversal is that people always prefer definite information to indefinite: the urn may have more yellow balls than black, so in this case lottery A' is more attractive than lottery B', but people tend to prefer "the devil they know", i.e. lottery B' where they get $50 with 50 % probability.

The *Ellsberg paradox* casts doubt on the basic premise of subjective expected utility theory that subjective probabilities are equivalent to objective probabilities. Knight (1921) was the first who made a distinction between *risk* (lotteries with objective probabilities) and *uncertainty* (lotteries with subjective probabilities). In particular, when having to form subjective

	red	yellow	black
A	50$	0	0
B	0	0	50$
A'	50$	50$	0
B'	0	50$	50$

Figure 2.30 The Ellsberg paradox

probabilities, people will not make point estimates but consider a whole set of probabilities to be possible. Moreover, they do not assign likelihoods to the members of this set and then compute compounded probabilities to get point estimates. They would rather look at the worst-case scenario and maximize their insurance against that, so that their utility function can be expressed as: $\max_x \min_{p \in \Delta} E_p u(x)$. From this perspective, rationality is not necessarily violated and the Ellsberg paradox can be solved. One may further argue that with experience one learns the true probabilities so that ambiguity is reduced.

2.8 COMPARISON OF EXPECTED UTILITY, PROSPECT THEORY, AND MEAN-VARIANCE ANALYSIS

Expected utility has been derived as a prescriptive theory of choice but it does not always match with individuals' behaviour. In contrast, prospect theory has its main strength in its descriptive validity, but it is relatively complicated in deriving applications. The mean-variance analysis is a simple pragmatic decision theory that is often used in making practical decisions. However, it can give very wrong descriptions. These considerations are summarized in Table 2.6.

Table 2.6 Advantages and disadvantages of the three theories of choice

Approach	Advantages	Disadvantages
Expected utility theory	rational model prescriptive	not always good as a descriptive model
Mean-variance analysis	simple model can easily be applied	can lead to very wrong decisions
Prospect theory	descriptive, explains investors' behaviour well	not entirely prescriptive, relatively complicated

As all three theories have their advantages and disadvantages, one needs to take a deeper look into each of them in the context of the others in order to decide which one to apply. The similarities and the differences of the three models can be summarized as in Figure 2.31.

In the case of normally distributed returns, all three decision criteria only depend on the mean and the variance of asset returns since a normal distribution is totally described by the

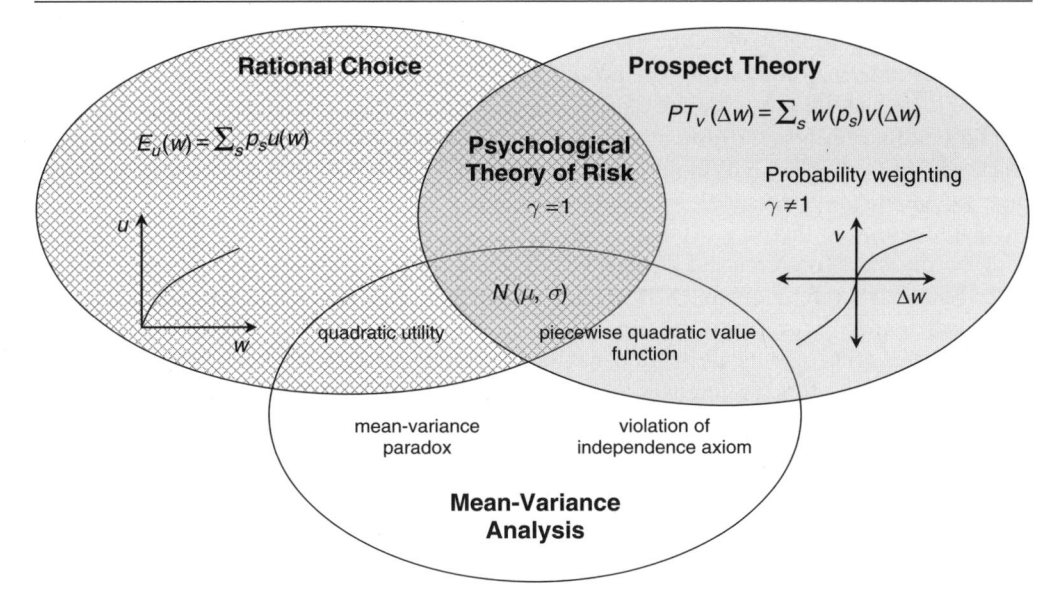

Figure 2.31 Similarities and differences of expected utility, prospect theory, and mean-variance

first two moments. In this case, a decision based on the mean-variance analysis is rational. Additionally, it can be in line with the investor's understanding of risk (see Section 2.5). However, if asset returns are not normally distributed, the decision criteria need to be studied more carefully. In this case, the mean-variance analysis can be applied without violating the axioms of rationality under the condition that the investor's utility is quadratic and returns are not too high so that the utility is still increasing. If this is true, for any return distribution the expected utility is actually a mean-variance utility function. In general, the mean-variance analysis is not appropriate as a rational benchmark for three reasons: first, not all investors have a quadratic utility and therefore, they do not perceive the variance as an appropriate risk measure (see Example 2.10); second, investors following the mean-variance may eventually prefer to get nothing than to play a lottery where they cannot lose anything (see Example 2.11); third, mean-variance-based decisions might violate the independence axiom and therefore the expected utility, as the variance is by definition not linear in probabilities (see Example 2.12).

An alternative model describing individuals' decision-making is prospect theory. It is consistent with expected utility theory in the absence of frame-dependence and probability weighting. In particular, reference point dependent behaviour, loss aversion, and asymmetric risk aversion need not violate the axioms of expected utility.[21] Moreover, these properties of individuals' preferences can be used within the mean-variance analysis whether or not asset returns are normally distributed (see first part of Section 2.5 and Subsection 2.5.1).

2.9 CONCLUSION

In this chapter, we reviewed the normative and descriptive theories of decision-making. Our main objective was to incorporate investors' preferences as documented by descriptive theories

---

[21] This is true as long as the reference point is not changed over time.

into the analytical framework of the normative reward-risk theory in order to derive an optimal asset allocation that is consistent with the investors' understanding of risk. To achieve this goal, we first reviewed the mean-variance theory, defining how investors with certain preferences should build portfolios of different assets. We agreed that (1) an optimal portfolio of risky assets should be efficient and (2) if investors hold cash, its weight in the asset allocation should increase with the investors' risk aversion.

Having reviewed the basic principles of portfolio choice, we focused on theories dealing with the investors' preferences. Within the expected utility theory, we have learned how to describe agents' preferences and how to judge whether a decision based on these preferences is rational or not. We used these criteria in the following analysis of prospect theory to evaluate which aspects of the agents' decision behaviour are rational. We agreed that (1) loss aversion is a part of the investors' preferences and (2) probability weighting is irrational.

Then we combined both the normative mean-variance and the descriptive prospect theory to determine an optimal asset allocation that is consistent with the risk-reward principle of portfolio choice and the investors' meaning of risk. To achieve this goal, we studied different value functions that reflect the notion of risk and loss aversion as suggested by prospect theory and agreed that the piecewise quadratic value function satisfies our criteria best.

Finally, we reviewed the critique on the expected utility theory motivated by individuals' ambiguity aversion. Our conclusion is that the expected utility theory does not fit with individuals' behaviour but it is a good normative framework for decision-making. Mean-variance analysis is a pragmatic approach, but it can deliver very wrong descriptions. Prospect theory describes individuals' behaviour well, and can be made consistent with both the mean-variance analysis and also with rational choice. We therefore recommend using prospect theory as a foundation for private banking.

Since our book uses decision theory as its foundation but is itself not a book on decision theory, we had to limit the part on decision theory. If this part has caught your interest and made you want to dig deeper into decision theory itself we refer you to Jungermann, Pfister and Fischer (1998) and Eisenführ and Weber (2003) for further reading.

3
Behavioural Biases

There are many forms of irrational behaviour, but there is only one way for people to engage in rational behaviour as that term is understood in the classical economic theory - they must hold and act on a set of consistent preferences, i.e. preferences that satisfy the axioms of rational choice (see previous chapter).[1] Additionally, people must form estimates of probabilities of uncertain events in a rational way, like Bayesian updating.

In the previous chapter, we saw that individuals' preferences may be described by risk and loss aversion. If these preferences motivate decision-making, the latter are no less rational than the decisions of a Bernoulli investor, for example. However, if the individual perceives probabilities in a biased way, his decision would be irrational as we have already seen in the previous section.

In this chapter, we analyze additional sources for biased decision-making related to the handling of information. Since no individual can perform calculations with the rapidity and accuracy of computers, people are constantly required to utilize information by using rough proxies, sometimes called "heuristics" or "rules of thumb".

Using heuristics does not necessarily lead to irrational decisions. In some instances, using common heuristics may lead to choices that are not biased in one direction or another. Chess players, for example, using certain rules of thumb when deciding their next move, are no less rational than a computer. In some cases, however, the biases are more severe. From an ex-ante perspective, individuals may adopt information-processing strategies that lead them to falsely estimate the properties of a distribution. From an ex-post perspective, individuals could miscalculate the underlying distribution from which the observations have been drawn. The central finding of the psychology of cognitive biases is that individuals use strategies that systematically violate the basic principles of rational behaviour and the accepted rules of probability, and do so even when the stakes are high and their motivations to succeed are unambiguous.

To show how this might happen, we consider a typical decision-making process and discuss how different heuristics might lead to biased decisions at each stage of the process. The structure of a typical decision-making process can be summarized as in Figure 3.1. First, decision-makers select the information that appears to be relevant to their decisions. Then, they process the selected information in order to form beliefs and compare alternatives. In the next step, individuals make decisions and receive feedback. This feedback influences the data the decision-maker uses when he is about to make his next decision.

The aim of this section is to provide a descriptive overview of the most important cognitive effects that influence an individual's behaviour at each level of the decision-making process. Further, this section aims to emphasize the relevance of these biases for individuals' investment behaviour in particular.

---

[1] Applying the axioms of intertemporal choice leads to exponential discounting (see Subsection 2.3.7).

```
                    ┌──────────────┐
              ┌────▶ │ Information  │
              │     │  Selection   │──────┐
              │     └──────────────┘      │
              │                           ▼
        ┌─────────┐              ┌──────────────┐
        │  Data   │              │ Information  │
        └─────────┘              │  Processing  │
              ▲                  └──────────────┘
              │                           │
        ┌──────────┐             ┌──────────────┐
        │ Feedback │ ◀───────────│   Decision   │
        └──────────┘             └──────────────┘
```

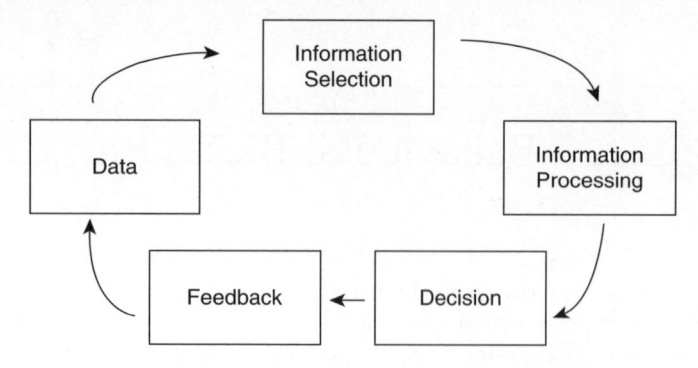

Figure 3.1 A typical decision-making process

3.1 INFORMATION SELECTION BIASES

Limited attention, memory, and processing capacities usually force individuals to base their decisions on a subset of information. Certain characteristics of the information flow can influence their judgment so that subsequent decisions become biased.

One of the most important information selection biases is the *availability bias*. It describes the tendency of individuals to judge the relevance of information depending on how easy it is to recall it. The availability bias leads to systematic errors when people need to estimate probabilities and judge the attractiveness of different alternatives.

To gain an understanding of how this may happen, consider the following example.

Example 3.1: Availability bias

Answer the following questions:

1. What was the more likely cause of death in a medieval siege: being killed by bullets, swords, knives etc., or being killed by a disease?
2. What has caused a higher increase in the life expectancy in the US: the discovery of antibiotics or the invention of the refrigerator?
3. What is more likely in the next 12 months: a crash in the stock market or a crash in the bond market?

Most people answer that you are more likely to be killed by bullets, swords, knives etc., that the discovery of antibiotics caused a higher increase in the life expectancy in the United States, and that a crash in the stock market is more likely in the next 12 months than a crash in the bond market. The reason for these answers is that these events have been in the news more often, i.e. the events are easily available.

The same effect can be observed when people select from among many different stocks. A recent study by Barber and Odean (2005) shows that individuals manage the problem of selecting among thousands of stocks by focusing on those that catch their attention. Examples are stocks in the news, stocks experiencing a high abnormal trading volume, or stocks with extreme one-day returns. Although experienced investors are less likely to purchase stocks simply because they have caught their attention, many individual investors tend to be net buyers on high attention days. However, they cannot benefit from doing so, i.e. attention-grabbing stocks do not outperform the market.

> **Case Study 3.1:** Value investing
>
> Since most investors have a tendency to buy stocks that catch their attention, one would expect that "boring stocks" are more valuable. The study of Barber and Odean (2006) confirms that individual and institutional investors tend to buy stocks that are in the news and have good stories. Over time, the market learns the real value of those stocks and hence market prices tend to return back to economic value. This tendency of markets to converge to their fundamental values is the source of the profits generated by "value" investors. Indeed, as Fama and French (1992, 1998) have shown, "value" is one of the key factors that, besides the market portfolio, is needed to explain the cross-section of stock returns. According to Fama and French, value is defined by book-to-market ratios. Other criteria like earnings yield (7 % p.a.) or price deterioration (6.6 % p.a.) generate even higher excess returns than book-to-market (3.6 % p.a.). One can find many value investors delivering their excess returns in a reliable way. The most prominent, of course, is Warren Buffet who, before Bill Gates entered the stage, was for a long time the richest man in the world. The connection between value investing and behavioural finance has materialized for example in the LSV-fund, founded by three prominent scholars of behavioural finance: Lakonishok, Shleifer, and Vishny, who published their results on value investing in the *Journal of Finance* (1994).
>
> Table 3.1 reports the annual real returns of the 10 book-to-market benchmark portfolios that can be found on Kenneth French's homepage. We see that indeed, over the period 1927–2007, portfolios with higher book-to-market ratios have outperformed those with lower such ratios and also outperformed the market. Note that the systematic profits from value investing seem to violate Fama's "Efficient Market Hypothesis" so that it is reasonable to look for a behavioural finance explanation. Given the stability of the excess returns of value investing, and also of its simple explanation, one might wonder why not everyone engages in value investing so that sooner or later the excess returns vanish. Recently, Caliskan et al. (2008) have given a prospect theory explanation for this puzzle. Realizing that value returns have a relatively high skewness, kurtosis, and a wide max–min spread, they show that for investors with loss aversion and asymmetric risk aversion value returns are not attractive. Since approximately 80 % of all investors are prospect theory investors, the high attractiveness of the Sharpe ratio that value returns possess is not sufficient to let all investors follow a value strategy.
>
> **Table 3.1** Descriptive statistics of the 1-year annual real returns of the value weighted CRSP all-share market portfolio, the intermediate government bond index of Ibbotson, one month T-Bill as risk-free rate, and the size and value docile portfolios from 1927 to 2007 (81 yearly observations)
>
> | | Mean | Std Dev | Skew | Kurt | Exc. Kurt | Min | Max |
> | --- | --- | --- | --- | --- | --- | --- | --- |
> | Equity | 8.82 | 20.55 | −0.21 | 2.68 | −0.32 | −40.28 | 56.74 |
> | Bond | 2.15 | 6.72 | 0.21 | 3.65 | 0.65 | −17.16 | 22.19 |

Case Study 3.1: (Continued)

Table 3.1 (Continued)

	Mean	Std Dev	Skew	Kurt	Exc. Kurt	Min	Max
Risk Free	0.60	4.11	−1.04	7.73	4.73	−17.77	11.22
Growth	7.97	22.96	0.02	2.46	−0.54	−45.29	60.75
2	8.87	20.06	−0.22	2.74	−0.26	−39.51	57.03
3	8.83	20.09	−0.14	2.57	−0.43	−38.70	50.67
4	8.97	22.00	0.37	4.90	1.90	−44.12	94.05
5	10.27	22.26	0.31	4.79	1.79	−52.68	92.51
6	10.58	22.92	0.35	3.98	0.98	−53.66	78.12
7	10.88	24.32	0.18	4.19	1.19	−53.07	97.87
8	12.90	26.29	0.64	4.88	1.88	−45.82	112.63
9	13.49	28.22	0.51	4.50	1.50	−47.16	119.17
Value	14.32	33.15	0.60	5.16	2.16	−60.70	149.10

One consequence of the availability bias is the investors' *overreaction* toward new information. This stronger-than-appropriate reaction to news occurs in situations when the price of a firm's share increases or decreases as a response to good or bad news, but then corrects in the opposite direction without any additional information. If investors overreact to recent news due to the availability bias for example, past winners or losers may become overpriced (winners) or underpriced (losers). This is a signal that investors react too strongly toward recent good or bad news reflected in the recent stocks' returns. Afterwards, investors realize that their optimism or pessimism was too strong, and the winners and loser begin to rebound.

This effect finds empirical support in several studies. De Bondt and Thaler (1985) for example, examined the returns of stocks listed on the New York Stock Exchange for a period of three years. At the beginning of the period, they separated the best 35 stocks into a "winners" portfolio and the worst 35 stocks into a "losers" portfolio. Tracking the performance of both portfolios against a representative market index for three years, the authors found that the "losers" portfolio consistently beat the market index, while the "winners" portfolio consistently underperformed. Overall, the difference between the "winners" and the "losers" portfolios accumulated to almost 25 % over the three year period.

3.2 INFORMATION PROCESSING BIASES

After selecting information that is considered relevant for the particular decision to be made, individuals focus on processing it in order to form or update their beliefs and/ or compare alternatives. Even if people avoid focusing on the information just because it is easy to recall, their estimates and subsequent decisions may be distorted by cognitive biases related to the processing of selected information. The most important examples are summarized hereafter.

3.2.1 Representativeness and gambler's fallacy

To make a judgment in reasonable time, people have developed a natural propensity for classifying information signals. While this classification reflex may be helpful to make a quick decision, in some circumstances it may lead to an incorrect understanding of the new information. The reason is a heuristic called *representativeness bias*.

The representativeness bias describes the tendency of individuals (1) to estimate probabilities depending on their pre-existing beliefs even if the conclusions are statistically invalid and (2) to believe that small samples (e.g. a sequence of returns) represent entire populations (e.g. all returns from which the realization is drawn). In the first case, the representativeness bias describes the individual's tendency to rely on stereotypes when judging whether a sample belongs to one population or another. In the second case, the representativeness bias describes the individual's tendency to treat the properties reflected in the small samples as properties that accurately describe the whole data pool. Investors can make significant errors due to the representativeness bias as the next two examples show.

Example 3.2: Representativeness bias: relying on stereotypes

Consider a small 20-year-old manufacturing company with the following characteristics: current assets are twice current liabilities, equity is equal to debt, and share price equals the book value of tangible assets. During the previous year, the company was reporting serious management inefficiencies. What is more likely: that the company belongs to group A (value stocks) or to group B (value stocks that go bankrupt)?

To answer this question, most investors try to judge whether the company is representative of group A or group B. After reading the headlines preoccupied with business difficulties, most investors would probably conclude that it is better to sell the company because it is more likely that it is a value company that will go bankrupt. In this case, they neglect the probability that there are many more viable value companies than value companies that go bankrupt. In fact, inefficient management usually causes companies to become takeover candidates. More precisely, if C is the group of all companies (value or not) that go bankrupt, then the probability that the company is a value stock that goes bankrupt is equal to $p(A \cap C)$. However, $p(A \cap C) < p(C)$ and $p(A \cap C) < p(A)$. Graphically, the relationship is illustrated in Figure 3.2.

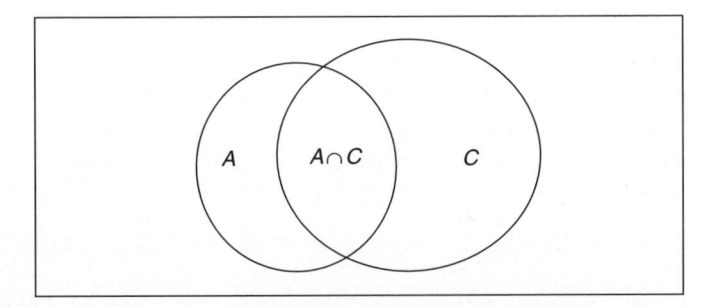

Figure 3.2 Illustration of conditional probability

Example 3.3: Representativeness bias: the problem of small samples

A fund manager is known to beat the market in two out of three years. Which of the following protocols is most likely (B: beat; L: lose)?

a) BLBBB   b) LBLBBB   c) LBBBBB

Given the sample sequences, BLBBB, LBLBBB and LBBBBB, people typically choose the sequence LBLBBB. The reason is that it is most similar or *representative* of the population probability, which is equal to 2/3, although, from a statistical perspective, the sequence BLBBB is more likely than the sequence LBLBBB, because the latter is the former *and* the condition that L comes before. The correct answer is BLBBB.[2]

Based on the representativeness bias, one can argue that after a relatively short sequence of good returns, investors believe that the process of returns has changed for the better. Why? Because when seeing the sample returns and applying the representativeness heuristic, one believes that the true population returns have to be similar to the sample returns. Hence the representativeness bias works both ways: from the population to the sample as in the example above, and from the sample to the population as in the case of real world returns. In particular, after a few good years on the stock market, investors may speak of "new era economics" meaning that fundamental laws of economics like "no returns without risk" no longer hold.

The representativeness bias has at least two implications for investors' behaviour on the financial market. First, the representativeness bias motivates investors to use the past performance of firms to place them into different categories. Extrapolating the past performance of the firms into the future, investors mistakenly believe that good performing firms are also good investments. This biased perception triggers prices too high or too low, which generates return reversals in the future. There is an *overreaction* on the market.

One can profit from investors' tendency to make categorical predictions and the resulting price overreaction by switching between momentum and contrarian investment strategies. Stock return continuation on horizons between 6 and 12 months is evident for the United States, Europe, and emerging markets (Jegadeesh and Titman, 1993, 2001; Rouwenhorst, 1998; Griffin et al., 2003) with historically earned profits of about 1 % per month over the following 12 months. After some time, investors realize that there is an overreaction on the market and stock returns reverse. Consequently, investment strategies buying the losers and selling the winners of the last three years for a horizon of three to five years become profitable (DeBondt and Thaler, 1985 and Lakonishok, Shleifer, and Vishny, 1994).

Second, the representativeness bias induces the wrong belief that a manager of a mutual fund has a "hot hand". Empirical evidence for example by Sirry and Tufano (1998) indicates increased flows into mutual funds with exceptional (but statistically short-lived) past performance.

---

[2] Since outcomes are assumed to be independent the probability for each sequence is $P(x_1 \ldots x_n) = \prod_{i=1}^{n} p(x_i)$ where x_i is a realization in a sequence and $p(x_i)$ is its probability. The probability of the first sequence is $P^1(x_1, \ldots, x_5) = (1/3)^1 (2/3)^4$, the second sequence has probability $P^2(x_1, \ldots, x_6) = (1/3)^2 (2/3)^4$ and the third $P^3(x_1, \ldots, x_6) = (1/3)^1 (2/3)^5$.

Misunderstanding of how randomness works can also cause the phenomenon of *gambler's fallacy*. It is the phenomenon where people inappropriately predict reversals in a random sequence because a mean reversion "looks" more similar to randomness than a trending regime. For example, when playing roulette, after a run of order at most seven spins, people think it is time for the other colour to come again although the outcomes are i.i.d (independent and identically distributed over the time), i.e. the roulette has no memory. Asking students to write down a sequence of heads and tails that they believe is generated by tossing a fair coin 100 times, we observe that people underestimate the frequency of long runs of the random walk process (see Figure 3.3). In the true random walk, the probability of the run of the next higher order is exactly half of the one before, so that the probabilities for runs of order 1, 2, 3, 4, 5 are 50 %, 25 %, 12.5 %, 6.25 %) and 3.125 % respectively. However, people rarely write down runs of order 4; they hesitate to write down runs of order 5 and they almost never write down runs of higher order.

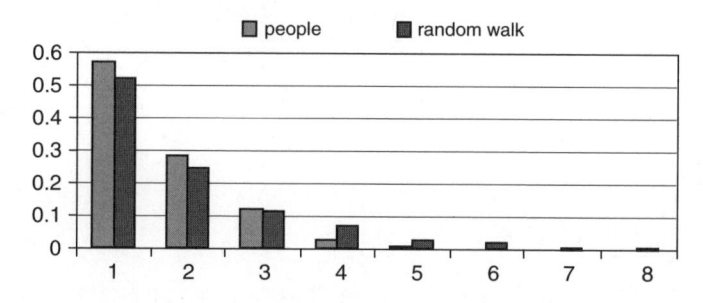

Figure 3.3 Experimental results on the gambler's fallacy

Hence, one may argue that after too many good returns, people become pessimistic for no good reason. For example, some scientists (see Pasteur, 2004) argue that even the extreme run up on the NASDAQ was fundamentally justified but people just became too pessimistic at the latest all-time highs.

Case Study 3.2: LGT Global Sector Trend Fund

As we have seen in the form of the representative bias, behavioural finance suggests searching for momentum in asset prices. Indeed, ever since Carhart (1997), it is well documented that momentum is one important factor that, besides the market, the size and the value factor helps to explain cross-sections of asset returns. However, trading on momentum is more difficult than holding a market portfolio or structuring a portfolio with a small cap or a value bias since trading on momentum amounts to good market timing.

The Global Sector Trend equity fund from LGT Capital Management is one of the most successful mutual funds based on momentum. Figure 3.4 shows its success as

Case Study 3.2: (Continued)

compared to its benchmark, the MSCI-world. The main idea of the GST-Fund is to identify momentum from relative price movements combined with a clever analysis of the news process.

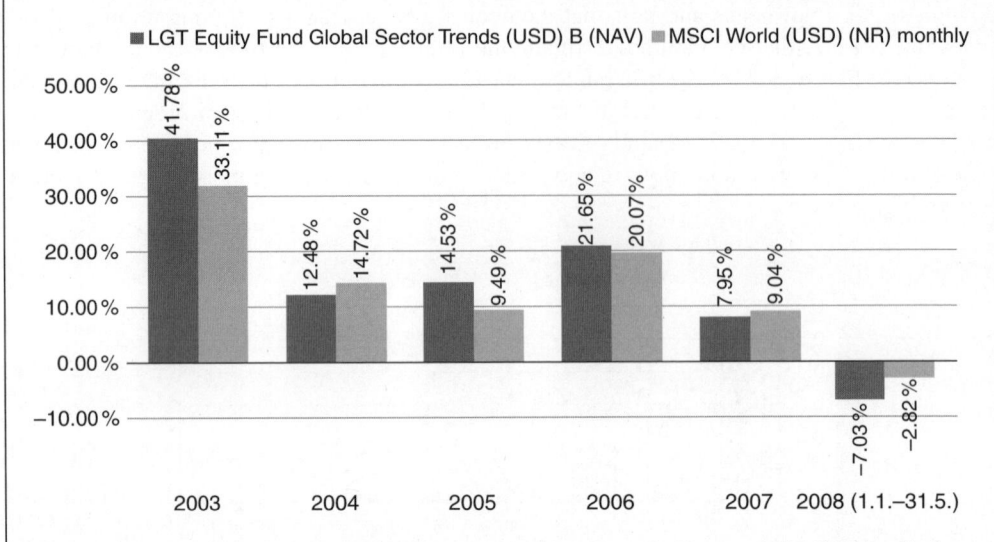

Figure 3.4 Performance of LGT-GST fund and its benchmark (*Source*: LGT-GST fund's fact sheet)

3.2.2 Anchoring and conservatism biases

As investors tend to overreact to particular information, due to the representativeness bias for example, there are circumstances where investors' reactions are too weak. This underreaction is usually caused by two heuristics: *anchoring* and *conservatism*. Anchoring is the phenomenon where people tend to be overly influenced in their assessment of some quantity by arbitrary quantities mentioned in the statement of the problem, even when the quantities are clearly not informative. To illustrate how decision-making may deviate from the rationality, consider Example 3.4.

Example 3.4: Anchoring

In an experiment, different groups of people are asked to provide a quick answer to the following questions:

A) What is the product of the following numbers: 1, 2, 3, 4, 5, 6, 7, 8, 9, and 10?
B) What is the product of the following numbers: 10, 9, 8, 7, 6, 5, 4, 3, 2, and 1?

The average answer to the first question is 150. In contrast, the average answer to the second question is 900.

The reason for observing this difference is that, in the first case people use 1 as an anchor and extrapolate, in the second case they use 10 as an anchor and extrapolate. The anchor influences the estimations.

Another experimental study with professional traders confirms that the anchoring effect is not an isolated finding (see also Stephan and Kiell, 1997).

Example 3.5: Anchoring by professional traders

One group of professional traders is asked:

A) Would the Dow Jones Industrial Index be above or below 6600 at the end of the year?

Another group of professional traders is asked:

B) Would the Dow Jones Industrial Index be above or below 8000 at the end of the year?

The average estimated value of the answers to question A) is 7214. In contrast, the average estimated value of the answers to question B) is 7650. The difference is statistically significant.

Additionally, the study shows that the shorter the estimation horizon, the stronger the anchoring effect, although the uncertainty for short-term estimates is lower compared to long-term estimates.

Typical anchors are the opinion of experts, consensus forecasts, and the status-quo.

The anchoring heuristic may lead to underreaction if people use the initial or current value and underweight new information. Conservatism can be seen as a consequence of anchoring upon an initial probability estimate. The next example illustrates the effect.

Example 3.6: Conservatism as a consequence of anchoring

The benchmark for assessing under- and overreaction in probability estimates is the *Bayes theorem*. It provides a rule for estimating combined probabilities.

Consider an investment in a foreign country. It is known that 45 of the 100 largest firms manipulate profits in 30 % of their units. The remaining 55 firms manipulate profits in 70 % of their units. What is the probability that a randomly selected firm manipulates profits in less than half of its units? The answer is clearly 45 %.

After some time, investors become concerned with the reporting situation in the country and decide to order an auditor. The latter picks a firm at random and checks 12 of its business units. He finds that four of them manipulate profits and the other eight units report truthfully. What is now the probability that a randomly selected large firm manipulates profits in less than half of its units? The typical answers to this question range between 45%, i.e. the posterior probability, to 67 %, as according to the auditor's report eight out of 12 units reported truthfully. However, the correct answer after applying the Bayes rule is 96.04 % as Math Box 3.1 shows.

Example 3.6: (Continued)

Math Box 3.1: Conservatism and the Bayes rule

To apply the Bayes rule, let $p(good\,|\,*)$ be the probability that a randomly selected firm manipulates profits in less than half of its units (a "good" firm), given the inspector's report. According to the Bayes rule, $p(good\,|\,*) = \dfrac{p(good)p(*\,|\,good)}{p(good)p(*\,|\,good)+p(bad)p(*\,|\,bad)}$, which is equivalent to $p(good\,|\,*) = \dfrac{1}{1+\dfrac{p(bad)p(*\,|\,bad)}{p(good)p(*\,|\,good)}}$. To calculate $\dfrac{p(bad)p(*\,|\,bad)}{p(good)p(*\,|\,good)}$, recall that $p(good) = 45\,\%$ respectively $p(bad) = 55\,\%$. Further, $p(*\,|\,good) = \binom{12}{8} 0.7^8 0.3^4$ and $p(*\,|\,bad) = \binom{12}{8} 0.3^8 0.7^4$.

Thus, $\dfrac{p(bad)p(*\,|\,bad)}{p(good)p(*\,|\,good)} = \dfrac{55}{45} \dfrac{\binom{12}{8} 0.3^8 0.7^4}{\binom{12}{8} 0.7^8 0.3^4} = \dfrac{11}{9}\left(\dfrac{0.3}{0.7}\right)^4 = 0.027$ so that $p(good\,|\,*) = \dfrac{1}{1.027} = 96.04\,\%$.

One explanation for conservatism is that processing new information and updating beliefs is costly. There is evidence that information that is presented in a cognitively costly form such as abstract and statistical information is weighed less.[3]

If investors' expectations are influenced by anchors, stock prices will need some time to fully incorporate new information such as, for example, earnings releases. Consequently, stocks with positive (or negative) earnings surprises earn abnormally high (or low) returns in the months after the announcement. This phenomenon is known as the *post-earnings-announcement-drift* (PEAD). Several studies provide empirical evidence on the existence of this phenomenon. For example, Bernard and Thomas (1990) investigate about 85 000 quarterly earnings announcements over the period from 1974 to 1986. Each calendar quarter, they rank stocks based on the unexpected earnings report and build 10 portfolios. Over the following 60 trading days, a long position in the top portfolio (with firms reporting positive earnings surprises) and a short position in the bottom one (with firms reporting negative earnings surprises) yields an abnormal return of 4.2 % or about 18 % on an annualized basis. After extending the holding period to 180 days, the difference between the return of the top and the bottom portfolios becomes 7.75 %.

The PEAD is successfully exploited by professional investors such as, for example, Fuller and Thaler Asset Management. Their strategy, Small/ Mid-Cap Growth Equity, invests in

---

[3] In contrast, if the information is easily processed, i.e. scenarios and concrete examples, people may overreact when processing the selected information.

American stocks that report large earnings surprises that are permanent (e.g. due to the introduction of a new product, new management or improved efficiency). The investors are likely to underreact to the reported earnings if the analysts covering the firm are biased by anchoring. This is estimated by analyzing the analysts' initial revisions and the questions they ask, i.e. if the analysts are more concerned with the past than with the future of the firm, they are more likely to raise their forecasts insufficiently. The perfect purchase opportunity is therefore the one illustrated in Figure 3.5.

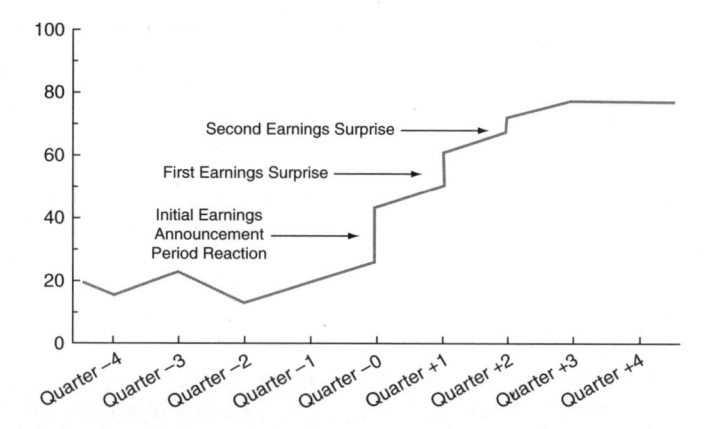

Figure 3.5 Ideal growth stock purchase according to Fuller and Thaler Asset Management (*Source*: Fuller and Thaler Asset Management, Inc.)

At the beginning of the announcement period, the price of the firm's shares increases as a response to investors' expectations of increasing earnings. However, if the investors' expectations are anchored to some past value, the stock price will exhibit a positive drift until the earnings are announced and analysts (and investors) are surprised positively. If the earnings growth is permanent and the expectations of the firm's outsiders are still biased toward the previous earnings as an anchor, there will be a second positive earnings surprise with the firm's prices continuing to drift in the same direction.

Typically, the drift lasts one year. Afterwards, there are no earnings surprises; the earnings fall below the analysts' expectations, which is a signal that the underreaction effect is over and it is time to sell the stock.

3.2.3 Framing

The anchoring bias as illustrated in Example 3.4 is related to the *framing bias*, i.e. when evaluating information, people fail to see through the way in which information is provided. Tversky and Kahneman (1981), for example, have shown that alternative descriptions of a decision problem may give rise to different preferences contrary to the principle of invariance underlying a rational choice. The intuition behind the normative concept is that variations of the form that do not affect the actual outcomes should not be relevant to the choice.

Although this rule appears to be simple, there are many cases where it is violated. Benartzi and Thaler (2001), for example, observe that employees planning their pension savings tend to split their funds equally (1/N) over the alternatives offered by their pension fund (see Table 3.2). Consider two pension funds aiming to hold on average 60 % in stocks and 40 % in bonds by investing in mutual funds. Depending on the array of equity and bond funds offered, pension funds managers seem to decide differently on the weights of their equity and bond exposure. In particular, asset classes offering more choices receive significantly more capital.

Table 3.2 illustrates the effect. If an attribute receives more weight in the decision problem simply because it is presented in more detail, then the final decision would be biased. The phenomenon is known as the *splitting bias*.

Table 3.2 The splitting bias

Employees of TWA		Employees of University of California	
choose from:	average % invested	choose from:	average % invested
Equity Fund 1	75 %	Equity Fund	34 %
Equity Fund 2		Bond Fund 1	66 %
Equity Fund 3		Bond Fund 2	
Equity Fund 4		Bond Fund 3	
Equity Fund 5		Bond Fund 4	
Bond Fund	25 %	Bond Fund 5	

3.2.4 Probability matching

Additional violations of rational choice theory emerging during the information process stage are reported in studies based on binary choice problems. In such tasks, people often tend to "match" probabilities, i.e. they allocate their responses to the two options in proportion to their relative payoff probabilities.

Suppose that a monetary payoff of fixed size is given with tossing a coin with a probability of 0.49 for "heads" and with a probability of 0.51 for "tails". *Probability matching* refers to behaviour in which "heads" is chosen in about 49 % of trials and "tails" in 51 %. On any coin toss, the expected pay-off for choosing "tails" is higher than the expected payoff for choosing "heads". Thus, the optimal choice is to always select "tails". The rational behaviour would not match the randomness of the choice problem. From a rational investor's perspective, the optimal decision whether to invest in an asset whose price increases with "heads" and decreases with "tails" is not to invest if the coin is fair and there are some transaction costs, but to follow a "buy and hold" strategy if the coin is worn as described above.

When people match the price process while targeting a market-timing strategy, they probably trade too much. The problem of excessive trading is that it leads to poor returns over time.

3.2.5 Overconfidence and the illusion of control

Excessive trading results not only if individuals wrongly estimate the process driving the prices but also if they overestimate the accuracy of their predictions. If individuals express confidence in their judgments that exceeds the accuracy of those judgments, they are *overconfident*. To get an understanding of the origins of this bias, consider the following examples.

Example 3.7: Better-than-average effect of the overconfidence bias

It is well known that more than 50% of car drivers think that they are a better driver than the average driver. Assuming that the population of drivers is normally distributed, only half of them can be above the average. Hence, the *group* of car drivers is overconfident.

A more subtle aspect of the overconfidence bias is the *miscalibration effect*. To see this, answer the questions in Example 3.8.

Example 3.8: Miscalibration effect of the overconfidence bias

Where will the SMI be at the end of the year? Please choose one of the following intervals: [5000, 5500], [5250, 5750], [5500, 6000], and [5750, 6250].

Also give the level of confidence for your forecast. The level of confidence is the percentage of cases in which your estimate is correct.

Typically, the percentage of correct answers sorted by the subgroups of similar confidence is much lower than the average correctness within each group. When participants say they are about 70 % sure they have the correct answer, they are right about 60 % of the time; when they say they are 90 % sure, they are right about 55 % of the time.

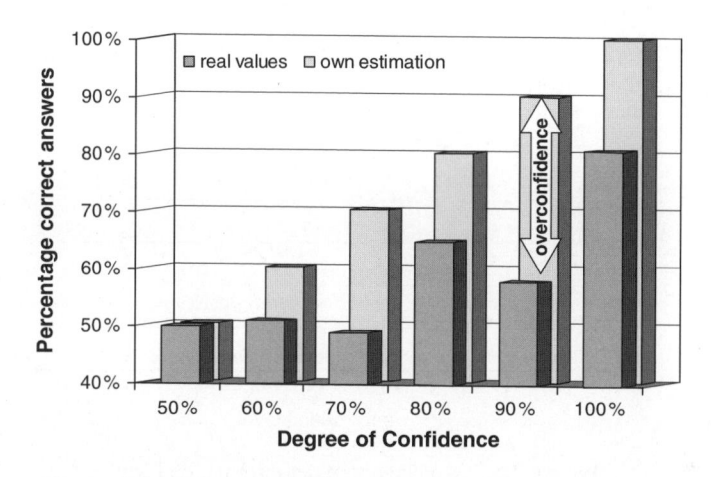

Figure 3.6 The overconfidence effect in the case of forecasting

---

Overconfidence with range questions may be even more extreme. Russo and Schoemaker (1992), for example, found that business managers asked to provide 90 % confidence ranges, supplied the correct answer within the stated range between 42 % and 62 % of the time, depending on the domain and the participant group.

Further, overconfident investors overestimate their stock-picking abilities, i.e. they overestimate the probability that their personal assessment on the value of a particular firm is more accurate than the assessment of other investors. As a consequence, individuals may even invest when the true expected returns are negative, which generates counter-productive excessive trading on the market. In fact, individuals turn over their common stock investment by about 70 % per year (see Barber and Odean, 2001). However, those individuals who trade most make the lowest profits (see Barber and Odean, 2000) as Figure 3.7 shows.

The disadvantages of being overconfident are further studied by Joachim Huber from Innsbruck University. In an experiment, Huber (2006) lets students trade a dividend-paying asset on a double auction for 10 periods. The students have different information levels. Some are told in advance the dividends of the next 9 periods, some get to know the dividends of the next 8, 7, ... etc. periods, and some only know the next period's dividends.

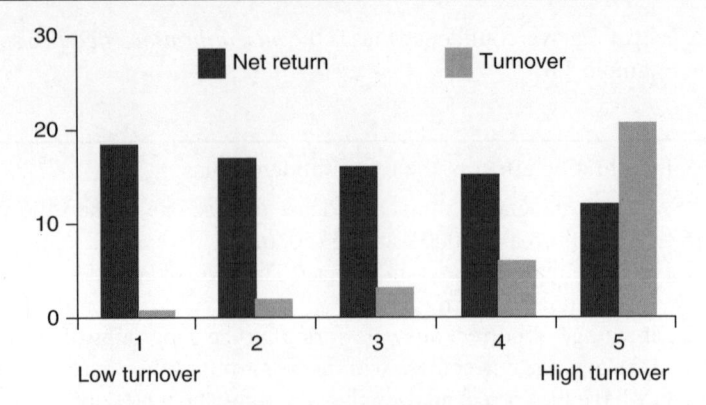

Figure 3.7 Hazardous trading

The interesting finding of Huber (2006) is a J-curve effect when displaying the returns the students make as of their information level (see Figure 3.8).

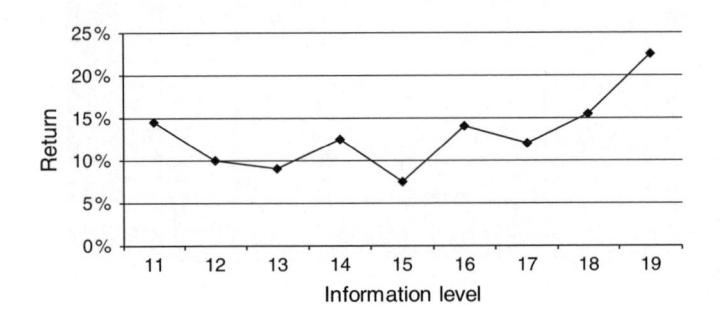

Figure 3.8 Average return per information level

The best informed students clearly make the highest returns but the medium well informed students do worst. When asked why they did the worst, the students with medium information level said that they tried to exploit the least informed students. But asking the least informed students, they say that they knew they are worst off from the outset and thus they did not engage in active trading. As an effect, the best informed students could exploit the medium informed ones.

The moral of this experiment is that it is fine to be incompetent if one is aware of this and invests accordingly, e.g. buy ETFs (Exchange Traded Funds) of a well diversified index. The worst is to be overconfident, i.e. to believe that "The best plan is ... to profit by the folly of others"[4] but then the fool is the one who acts according to this belief.

Overall, overconfident decision-makers overestimate the precision of information signals. This makes them feel more secure than they are. As a consequence, individuals are ready to take more risks than they actually can afford. This is particularly relevant for individuals who are incompletely informed, i.e. they engage in active strategies in the mistaken belief that they

---

[4] Pliny the Elder, from John Barlett, comp. *Familiar Quotations*, 9th ed. 1901.

can profit from non-informed market participants. As the latter know that they do not know anything and invest passively, the incompletely informed individuals lose against the informed traders.

Overconfident investors are expected to have a significant impact on the market prices. In particular, if investors are overconfident, they may overestimate the precision of their private information, causing the prices to overreact. As more public information arrives, prices eventually correct themselves (see Daniel *et al.*, 1998).

The effect is similar if individuals suffer from the *illusion of control*. Although the distinction between skill situations and luck is clear in principle, most people would agree there is much overlap between them and they behave as if chance events are the subject of control. In particular, when a chance situation mimics a situation requiring skills, people behave as if they have control over an uncontrollable event even if they know that success or failure depends on chance. The greatest satisfaction, or a feeling of competence, is achieved from being able to control the seemingly uncontrollable.

For example, when people are actively involved as participants in the market (e.g. via online trading) they may develop an illusion of full control of their assets. In 1997, for example, the amount of assets managed online went from near zero to $100 billion. In 1998, Internet stocks captured investors' attention, especially those of online traders. On the strength of investors' imaginations, Internet stock prices were propelled into orbit.

Case Study 3.3: Probability weighting and the favourite long-shot bias

When processing information in order to build beliefs, individuals tend to put too much weight on rare events and underestimate the probability of common alternatives. This probability weighting can be clearly observed on betting markets: long-shots are valued more highly than expected, given how rarely they win, and favourites are valued too little, given how often they actually win. This observation is known as the *favourite long-shot bias*. It may also be observed in the markets for derivatives. For example, Hodges, Tompkins and Ziemba (2008) study the prices of calls and puts on different stock index futures. They find that on the S&P 500, deep in-the-money call options (favourites) and out-of-the money call options yield a positive return, on average. However, on the FTSE 100 futures, with a higher proportion of retail investors, the favourites return less than the initial investments. In both markets, investors pay too much for deep out-of-the-money call options (long-shots) since from their perspective, these calls represent lottery tickets. Overall, an investment in calls makes slight profits but increasingly greater losses as calls go out-of-the-money. The average returns on the puts are all negative since hedging by insurance companies and other financial institutions creates a large demand for these puts, so they invariably tend to be overvalued.

To exploit the favourite long-shot bias on the market for derivates, one should sell the overpriced puts, hedge them with short futures, and use the proceeds of the put sale to buy calls, as William T. Ziemba does. Under strict risk control and employing precautionary crash risk measures, he achieves steady returns as the net value of his personal account at Vision and Man (and in an off-shore hedge fund) from December 2001 to December 2007 demonstrates (see Figure 3.9).

> **Case Study 3.3:** (Continued)
>
> **Index of Net Value Private Futures Account of William T. Ziemba at Vision and Man Financial, December 31, 2001 to December 31, 2007**
>
> **Figure 3.9** Exploiting the favourite long-shot bias

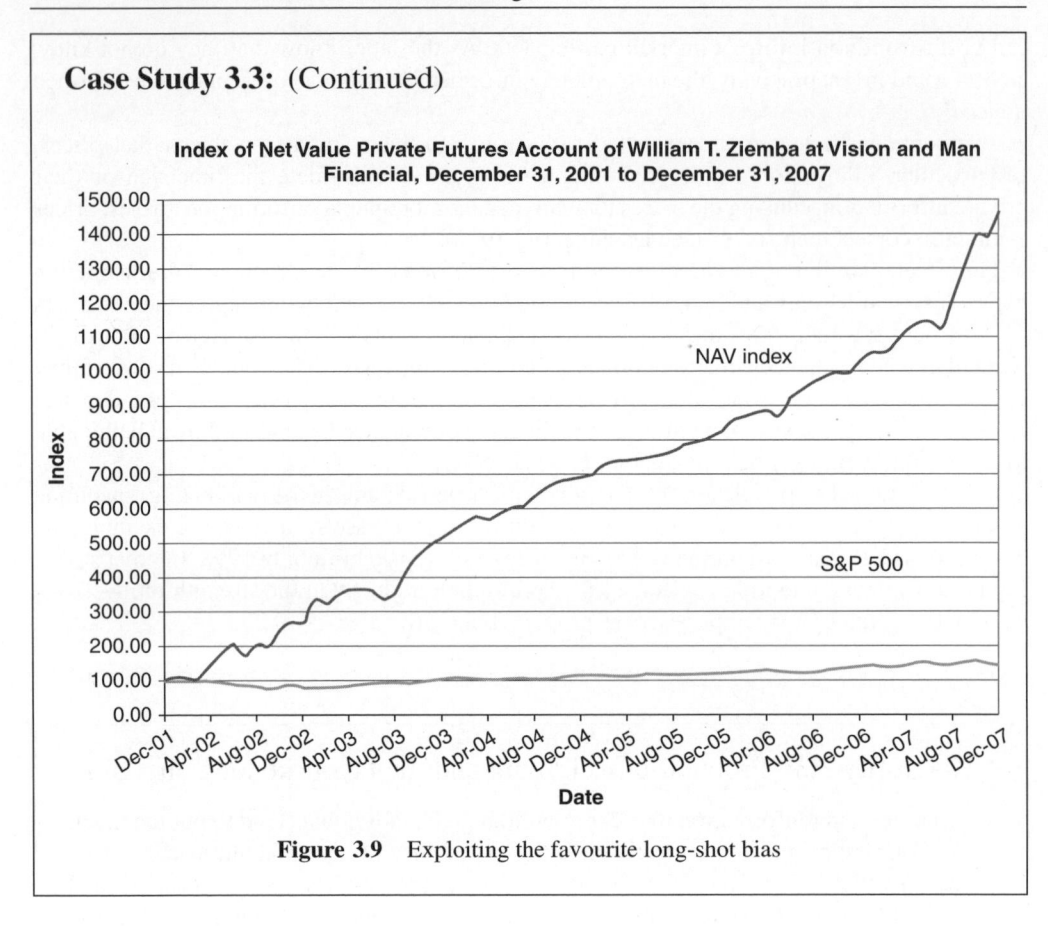

3.3 DECISION BIASES

Sub-optimal decisions may result not only from biased information processing but also as a consequence of other heuristics, which are not particularly related to the assessment of probabilities. The most prominent examples are summarized hereafter.

3.3.1 Mental accounting

If problems are analyzed in an isolated fashion, individuals' decisions may be biased by *narrow framing*. An example for this effect is using *mental accounting* as a heuristic used to organize, evaluate and keep track" of decisions (Thaler, 1999). For example, many people divide their household budget into expenses for food and expenses for entertainment. At home, where the food budget is applied, they eat fish instead of lobster because it is less costly. In a restaurant, however, they order a lobster, even though the costs are higher. If they ate lobster at home and fish in the restaurant, they would save money. Nevertheless, people choose to limit the food expenses at home, because they are thinking separately about food in a restaurant and at home.

As in the food example, individuals think differently about the way income is generated (work, gambling, bonus, etc.). They do not integrate all sources of income into one account. Similarly, they do not integrate all assets in one portfolio. Instead, individuals use layers in a pyramid format, each of them addressing different investment goals. The idea is illustrated in Figure 3.10

The problem with this investment approach is that investors make decisions within the layers. Neglecting the correlations between the returns of assets belonging to different layers may create sub-optimal inefficiencies.

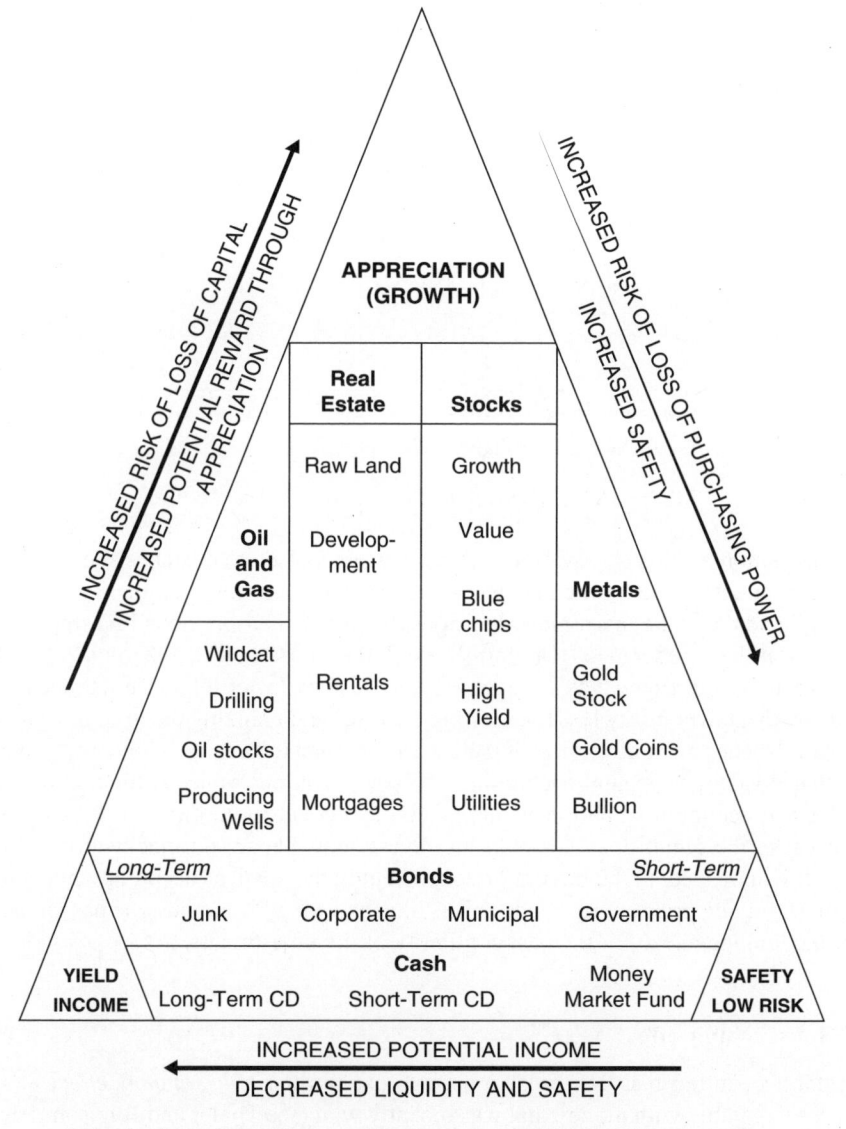

Figure 3.10 Portfolio pyramid (Courtesy of Ginita Wall CPA CEPR)

3.3.2 Disposition effect

Mental accounting may also explain the "disposition effect". It describes the investors' tendency to hold losing assets too long and sell winning stocks too early, given that these assets belong to different accounts. Empirical evidence for this effect is provided, for example, by Odean (1998). He finds that individual investors are more likely to sell stocks that have gone up in value, rather than stocks that have lost. This can be seen in Figure 3.11, where PGR is the number of realized gains divided by the number of total gains (realized and "paper" gains) and PLR is the number of realized losses divided by the number of total losses (realized and "paper" losses).

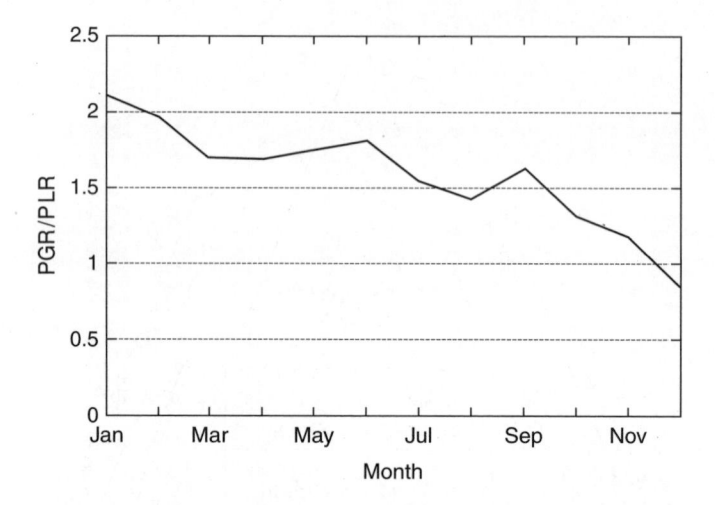

Figure 3.11 Disposition effect (*Source*: Odean (1998))

One explanation for this observation is that investors make two mistakes at once: they build two mental accounts – one for the realized gains (or losses) and another one for "paper" gains (or losses) – and they take investment decisions that make their previous investment decision (to buy an asset) look better (see Hens and Vlcek, 2005 and Barberis and Xiong, 2008). If a loss occurs, investors would keep it as a "paper" loss (investors do not sell the asset) because this is associated with a lower utility loss than selling the asset and realizing the loss. If a gain occurs, the investor is better off if he realizes it (sell the asset) than to keep the gain as a "paper" gain.

Note that this sort of mental accounting is clearly irrational since it hinders the client in facing the real economic situation of his assets. Moreover, note that the disposition effect occurs because the client does not plan his investments ahead, but backwards. Assets that made a loss with respect to the buying price are kept in the "paper" account, while gains with respect to the buying price are realized. This is like justifying the actions one has already taken and not like looking ahead for the best continuity of the investments.

3.3.3 House money effect

The mental accounting bias can be also used to explain the *house money effect* – a greater willingness to gamble with money that was recently won (see Thaler and Johnson, 1990). The reason is that the utility loss associated with a loss is diluted if the loss is aggregated with an earlier gain and the investor is ready to take more risks.

3.3.4 Home bias

One of the more prominent asset allocation puzzles is the degree to which investments are focused in home country equity as opposed to foreign investments. This phenomenon is called *home bias*. French and Poterba (1991) for example find that investors in the United States, Japan and United Kingdom allocate 94 % respectively 98 % and 82 % of their wealth in domestic equities (see figure 3.12). The home bias can be associated with the notion that people prefer familiar situations. They feel that they are in a better position than others to evaluate particular decision problems. However, one should be aware that the feeling of being better informed may be deceptive and lead to the illusory feeling of being on secure ground.

U.S. Investors
- Japan; 1.31%
- U.K.; 5.90%
- U.S.; 93.80%

Japanese Investors
- U.K.; 4.80%
- U.S.; 3.10%
- Japan; 98.11%

British Investors
- U.S.; 1.10%
- Japan; 0.19%
- U.K.; 82.00%

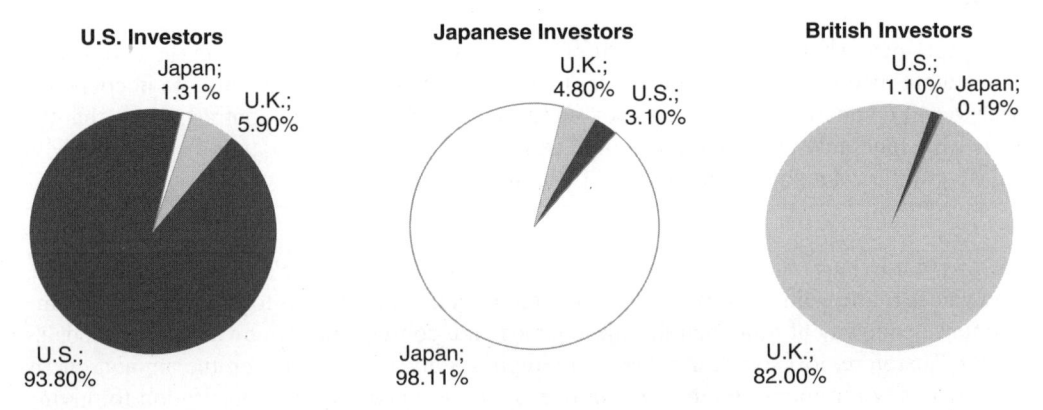

Figure 3.12 Equity portfolio weights of U.S., Japanese and British investors (Based on French and Poterba (1991))

The home bias can be also linked to *ambiguity aversion*; when faced with a choice between two lotteries with, say, a 50:50 chance of getting $100 or not getting anything, versus a lottery with the same outcome but with unknown probabilities, those people who never have invested in foreign stocks choose the lottery with known probabilities. In an experimental study, Ackert *et al.* (2004) show that providing participants with information about a firm's name and home base motivate them to increase their investments. The firm's name alone is not sufficient to change investment behaviour.

Note that ambiguity aversion may well be compatible with rational choice since markets will typically be incomplete for those states that give rise to ambiguity. However, given the current degree of globalization of financial markets, a strong home bias seems hard to justify.

3.3.5 Endowment bias

Although decision-makers are aware that their choice to take an action or not should depend only on the expected pay-offs, in many situations they cannot avoid taking into account previous decisions. Such behaviour may result from the endowment effect or the sunk costs effect. The *endowment bias* describes the reluctance of people to part from assets that belong to their endowments. If it is more painful to give up an asset than it is pleasurable to obtain it, then buying prices will be significantly lower than selling prices. In other words, the highest price an individual pays to acquire an asset will be smaller than the minimal compensation that would motivate the same person to give up that asset once acquired. To illustrate the point, consider once again the following example (see Kahneman, Knetsch and Thaler, 1990).

Example 3.9: Endowment bias

Suppose that you can choose between a mug and a chocolate bar, both with the same market value. Which one would you choose?

A) a mug   B) a chocolate bar

You own the good now.

Suppose that you can exchange what you have for the other good. Are you going to trade?

A) yes   B) no

The experiment shows that roughly half of the people prefer each good. After the goods were handed out, people are allowed to trade: those who had wanted mugs but got chocolate (or vice versa) could swap. Barely 10 % of students decided to trade. In contrast, given that the gifts were randomly allocated, one would expect 50 % to swap. Even after a short time with things of little value, ownership had overwhelmed the individuals' prior tastes.

In other words, if one must pay for goods and these goods are not in one's reference endowment, one values it as a gain.[5] But if one has the right to get compensation for giving them up, the reference endowment now includes these goods and, consequently, one values the goods as a loss. Therefore, loss aversion necessarily implies a divergence between the amount one is willing to pay for goods and the amount one is willing to accept as compensation for giving up the same goods.

The endowment bias may cause several investment mistakes. In particular, investors biased by their endowments may hold on to securities that they have inherited or have purchased regardless of whether it is wise to do so. As a result, investors caught by the endowment bias may feel compelled to continue holding a stock even if its economic prospects are not encouraging.

3.3.6 Sunk costs

The next bias that affects implementing decisions is the bias originating from past investments that are now irrevocable, i.e. the *sunk costs*. We know rationally that these costs are irrelevant to decision-making. Only incremental costs and benefits should influence future choices. Yet research shows that the more we invest in something (financially, emotionally, or otherwise), the harder it is to give up that investment. For example, in a telephone call, being on hold and hearing the recording "Please stay on the line" often means that it will probably take longer to get connected. Nevertheless, it's hard to hang up and call again later. Similarly, one may find it harder to terminate a project that is not profitable if the project has already required large investments. One reason why it is so difficult to free oneself from sunk cost reasoning is that people are unwilling to admit to a mistake. For example, by selling a poorly performing asset that was previously regarded as a great investment, one may feel that this is making a public admission of earlier poor judgment. This was also the reason for the disposition effect.

---

[5] The current endowment is the reference point.

3.4 DECISION EVALUATION BIASES

Each decision receives feedback depending on the results. This feedback reveals new information and determines whether the decision was successful or not. Thereby it gives rise to additional biases affecting the individual's decision-making behaviour, which are summarized below.

3.4.1 The hindsight bias

When evaluating past decisions, people often believe that one should have been able to anticipate events much better than was actually the case. In hindsight, people consistently exaggerate what could have been anticipated in foresight. They even wrongly remember their own predictions so as to exaggerate in hindsight what they knew in foresight. It appears that when we receive knowledge about the outcome, we immediately make sense out of it by integrating it into what we already know. The next example provides an explanation of how this might happen.

Example 3.10: Hindsight bias

Robert Citron, treasurer of Orange County,[6] said in September 1993, "We will have level, if not lower interest rates through this decade. Certainly, there is nothing that would indicate that we will have rising interest rates for a minimum of three years." In March 1994, he said, "The recent increase in rates was not a surprise to us; we expected it and were well prepared for it."

The problem with this bias is that even if one is aware of it, one may still be unaware of exactly what it is. Warnings about the danger have little effect. A more effective manipulation is forcing oneself to argue against the inevitability of the reported outcomes, i.e. trying to convince oneself that it might have turned out otherwise. One might further track down some of the uncertainty surrounding past events in their original form (see Fischhoff, 1980).

3.4.2 The psychological call option

Another impediment in achieving a rational assessment of previous decisions is the *psychological call option* the investor carries when hiring a financial advisor. If an investment decision turns out well, then the investor can take the credit, attributing the favourable outcome to his skills. On the other hand, if the decision turns out badly, then the investor can protect his ego and lower the regret by blaming the advisor.

The effect of *regret aversion* can be best illustrated with an example.[7]

Example 3.11: Regret aversion

Consider the following conversation between George, John, and Paul that took place in summer 2003. George holds many stocks and on the basis of his own analysis decided to sell stocks and buy bonds instead. John was in the same situation as George, and like him, switched to bonds.

---

[6] Orange County, California (USA), went bankrupt by speculation on interest rates.
[7] The example is adjusted from Shefrin (2000).

However, John based his decision on his financial adviser's recommendation rather than on his own analysis. Paul has traditionally held bonds. Paul thought that the market would rebound, and he considered changing his usual practice by purchasing stocks but at the end did not do so. From summer 2003 to the beginning of 2004 the market appreciated by 30 %.

Question: Whose self-image suffered the most:
(a) George, who traded out of stocks and into bonds based on his own analysis?
(b) John, who traded out of stocks and into bonds based on his advisor's recommendation?
(c) Paul, who continued to hold bonds?
(d) Nobody. Self-image doesn't matter in these situations.

Typical answer: 70 % choose George, 12 % choose John, 0 % choose Paul, and 18 % choose "nobody".

The intuition behind these results is that George has nobody to blame. He must accept 100 % responsibility. John can still blame his advisor, and Paul has continued with his conventional strategy.

In the short run, one regrets more what one has done (*error of commission*) than what one didn't do (*error of omission*): George and John took the wrong action (deviation from their conventional behaviour), while Paul didn't deviate (error of omission).[8] Hence George and John regret more than Paul. Moreover, John can blame his advisor. He holds a psychological call option.

In contrast to regret, where the investor realizes that other opportunities could have been better, disappointment arises when the results fall short of expectations. In the context of prospect theory, this is equivalent to not achieving a certain aspiration level defined at the beginning. Falling short of the aspiration level is then perceived as a loss.

3.5 BIASES IN INTERTEMPORAL DECISIONS

If individuals have to take subsequent decisions over time, their preferences are rational if they are time-consistent, i.e. if there are no preference reversals over time. Whether individuals behave rationally over time has been studied in several experiments. The cumulative evidence shows that individuals' decision patterns are dynamically inconsistent.

In dynamic models, it is usual to use the assumption that agents have a common discount rate applying for any t-period decision, starting now or starting in the future. This view, however, is inconsistent with the experimental evidence showing that people seem to discount the future differently, depending on the decision point of time. People may not go for a future gain at the cost of an immediate loss while they may find the same deal acceptable if both the gain and the loss period are in the future.

In order to explain this phenomenon, it was hypothesized that individuals' decisions are governed by a utility function of this type:

$$u_t(c_t, c_{t+1}, \ldots, c_T) = c_t + \beta \sum_{z=t+1}^{T} c_I \delta^{z-t}$$

---

[8] In the long run this is typically reversed. One regrets more the foregone opportunities.

where c_t is the consumption (or the payoff) in period t, $0 \leq \delta \leq 1$ is the discount factor reflecting an individual's preferences between any two periods and $0 \leq \beta \leq 1$ is the so-called "hyperbolic discount" factor reflecting the extra discounting between today and any later period. Note that since the notion of "today" changes from period to period, the hyperbolic discount factor $0 \leq \beta \leq 1$ leads to time-inconsistency in individuals' decisions. Overall, the idea of hyperbolic discounting can be summarized as follows (see Laibson, 1997): "From today's point of view one may find an action to be taken tomorrow profitable but when it comes to tomorrow this is no longer so."

Example 3.12: Hyperbolic discounting

Assume that you are required to save (consume less) today in order to consume more in the future. A bank offers you a contract requiring paying 5 in t and receiving 6 in the following period. The contract if started today is desirable if $-5 + \beta 6 \delta > 0$. Starting one period later from today's point of view, one would have decided to sign the contract if $\beta(-5\delta + 6\delta^2) > 0$. However, for $\beta = \delta = 0.9$, the second inequality is true but not the first. There is a preference reversal. The agent may have paid for a contract requiring 5 and delivering 6 in the subsequent period. However, one period later, the investor regrets his choice and is ready to pay for being able to sell the contract. Clearly, such preference reversal is costly and sub-optimal.

A person with time-inconsistent preferences may or may not be aware that his preferences would change over time. At the one extreme, people might be completely "naïve" and believe that their preferences in the future would be the same. At the other extreme, people might be completely "sophisticated", correctly predicting that their preferences change over time and anticipating this in their current choice. One way to identify the degree of sophistication is to look for evidence of *commitment*. Someone who is unsure about his preferences in the future might take steps to eliminate an option that does not look that attractive today but might tempt later.

Example 3.13: Lack of self-control and commitment

You have the choice *now* between:

A) $ 110 in 31 days   B) $ 100 in 30 days

In *a month* you have the choice again between:

A') $ 110 tomorrow   B') $ 100 immediately

If someone currently prefers option A but suspects that in *a month* he will prefer option B', he may decide to bind himself *now* to receive the $ 100 reward in 31 days. In this case, the person anticipates a lack of self-control and prevents a preference reversal by a commitment.

If people are sufficiently sophisticated about their own self-control problems, adopting a commitment device may be beneficial for them. However, if people are naïve, it might be better if they get either more education about the loss of control or are provided with incentives are to use commitment devices, even if people do not recognize the need for them.

When making decisions over time, the real investor differs from the expected utility maximizer in another way. Experimental studies suggest that the real investor evaluates consumption streams by *habit formation*, i.e. the utility of current consumption ("tastes") can be affected by the level of past consumption. The following example illustrates how habit formation affects individuals' decisions.

Example 3.14: Habit formation

Suppose that you could earn $ 1 million over the next 10 years. Which income profile would you prefer?

A) $1 million in year 10
B) $1 million in year 1
C) $100 000 each year
D) an increasing profile like $30 000, $70 000, $90 000, $110 000, $140 000, $160 000, $180 000, $220 000

Most people prefer option D.

Formally, the preferences including hyperbolic discounting and habit formation over consumption can be expressed as follows.

$$u(c) = u(c_0) + \beta \sum_{t=1}^{T} \delta^t \left[(1-h)u(c_t) + h\left(v(c_t - c_{t-1})\right) \right]$$

where β is the hyperbolic discount rate, δ is the exponential discount rate, h is a coefficient determining the degree of habit formation, and $v(.)$ is the value function. From the habit formation perspective, the reference point is the current period's consumption. Depending on the coefficient h, the client's utility depends on the one hand on the current consumption, and on the other hand on the consumption growth. For $h=0$, only current consumption matters, for $h=1$, only consumption growth is important.

Finally, inter-temporal decisions can be influenced by the way decision-makers frame the problem. A *framing bias* occurs when investors frame the problem *myopically*, i.e. when they frame an inter-temporal investment decision as a sequence of independent one-period problems. As a result, they may be very hesitant to invest in risky assets. This is illustrated in the next example (see Benartzi and Thaler, 1995).

Example 3.15: Myopic loss aversion

Compare two investors: Nick who calculates the gains and losses in his portfolio every day, and Dick who only looks at his portfolio once per decade. Since, on a daily basis, stocks go down in value almost as often as they go up, Nick's loss aversion will make stocks appear very unattractive to him. In contrast, loss aversion will not have much effect on Dick's perception of stocks since at 10-year horizons stocks offer only a small risk of losing money.

For example, consider an investment with a 50 % chance for a return of 20 % and 50 % chance for a loss of 10 %. If the initial value of the investment is 1000, then we get the following payoffs over three periods.

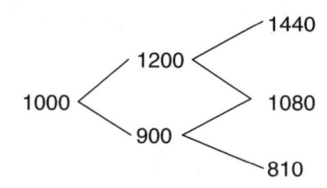

```
                    1440
              1200
        1000        1080
               900
                     810
```

Figure 3.13 Investor's payoff over time

Investors with a one-period horizon face a loss with a 50 % probability. In contrast, investors with a two-period horizon face a loss with a probability of 25 %. Using traders recruited from the CBOT, Haigh and List (2005) find that traders exhibit behaviour consistent with the myopic loss aversion even stronger than non-professionals. Recall that this behaviour is not shown by expected utility maximizers with CRRA.

3.6 BEHAVIOURAL BIASES AND SPECULATIVE BUBBLES

Experienced investors would probably say that investing is tough. Assets make moderate gains and sometimes their value decreases so that investors need to be very patient if they want to achieve their goals. However, in some periods investing appears very easy: market prices are rising and everyone makes a profit. In such periods, fundamental laws like "there is no free lunch" and "what comes up must come down" belong to what looks like the dark ages of investing while now a new era has begun promising a bright future for everyone. Unfortunately, these periods, called *stock market bubbles* (see Table 3.3 for a summary of famous bubbles), typically end in a collective disaster – stock market crashes.

According to Kindleberger (1978) a stock market bubble can be broken into five phases: displacement, take off, exuberance, critical stage, and crash. A speculative bubble starts from an atypical increase in the fundamental values, mostly triggered by innovations. The market reacts with a price increase. This well justified price movement is observed by trend chasers who, ignoring fundamental values, simply bet on further price increases. Attracted by high returns, more and more people join the crowd and push up prices further. At some point the return expectations of those who joined the crowd can no longer be satisfied by "even greater fools" jumping on the train later on. The bubble has reached its critical stage and a seemingly unimportant event can trigger its bursting.

Speculative bubbles show that individual behavioural biases like greed and overconfidence need not always be corrected by the market but the market itself can temporarily reinforce them. It is the social interaction via the stock market that makes a bubble so fascinating. From an individual point of view, it may well make sense to "ride a bubble". For example, Brunnermeier and Nagel (2004) have shown that even sophisticated investors favour hedge funds engaged in speculative buying behaviour during the TMT-bubble. Finding the right time to exit the bubble before it bursts is still a challenging task, even for experienced investors.

Table 3.3 Famous bubbles (Shleifer, 2000) continued by ourselves

Bubble	Initial displacement	Smart-money response	Sustaining the bubble	Authoritative blessing	Crash	Political reaction
Dutch Tulip mania (1630s)	Mosaic viruses produce interesting looking tulips; prosperity of Holland	Selective breeding of tulips; purchase by "insiders" of broken tulips that can only reproduce slowly and asexually	Development of tulip speculation contracts, which can be signed before notaries; appearance of trading	??	1637	??
South Sea bubble (1710–20)	Profits from conversion of government debt; supposed monopoly on trade with Spanish ruled parts of America	Insiders buy up debt in advance of the conversion scheme, then profit by presenting debt for full conversion	Development of coffee house network for speculation; new subscriptions	Government approval; royal involvement	1720	Ex post facto punishing directors; restrictions on the use of the corporate form
Mississippi bubble (1717–20)	Rapidly growing trade with the New World; Law's success as a financial organizer	Law's plan to make money and acquire power by securitizing the French debt	Government support; large expansion of credit by Law's bank to support further purchases	Official government support. Duke of Orleans imprisons critics of Law – the President of the Parlement de Paris and others	1720	Fall of Law; end of efforts to reform French finances until 1787
British First Railway boom (1845–6)	End of depression; excitement over the new means of transportation	Many new railroad projects	Ponzi schemes by George Hudson (i.e. use this railroad's capital to pay the last railroad's dividends)	Parliamentary Bills passed for every railroad suggesting government approval; close links between George Hudson and London Society	No crash, gradual decline	Reform of accounting standards; requirement that dividends be paid only out of earnings, not out of capital

US 1873 railway boom and crash	End of the Civil War; settlement of the American west	Construction of government subsidized railroads	Additional railroad charters; expectation that subsidies would continue	Henry Varnum Poor and Charles Frances Adams	1873 – Bankruptcy of Jay Cooke & Co., beginning of mid-1870s depression	??
Argentine loans (1880s)	Strong demand on world markets for the staple products of Argentinian agriculture; large profits made by early investors	Investment flows from Britain to Argentina; expansion of railway network; construction of social overhead capital	New issues on the London exchange; creation of joint-stock companies to speculate in Argentinian land	Foreign investors "grossly misled … by Argentinian President". Barings express optimism that the situation might improve (hoping to avoid bankruptcy)	Baring Bros. bankruptcy November 1890	Coup d'etat in Argentina; laws discriminating against foreign investment
1920s Florida land boom	Great winter climate; closeness to centres of American population; prosperity of the 1920s	Building of railroads; development of Miami; land development projects	Subdivisions; creation of a network of real estate offices selling Florida land	William Jennings Bryan boosts Florida land; close connections between mayors and developers	1926	Fraud prosecutions
1920s US Stock Market boom	Decade of fast growth in the 1920s; end of fears of post WWI deflation; rapid expansion of mass production	Expansion of supply of shares; creation of new closed end funds	Regional exchanges; growth of margin accounts and brokers' loans	Blessings from Coolidge, Hoover, Mellon and Irving Fisher	October 1929 and following	Glass-Steagall Act; creation of SEC; public utility holding company act; election of FDR
1920s US utility stocks boom	Expansion of demand for power; economies of scale	High leverage; expansion of scale to capture economies	Creation of public utility holding companies with cascades of control	??	October 1929 and following	Breakup of large utilities; TVA a byproduct; substantial government regulation of utility industries

Table 3.3 (Continued)

Bubble	Initial displacement	Smart-money response	Sustaining the bubble	Authoritative blessing	Crash	Political reaction
1960s conglomerate mergers in the US	Two decades of rising stock market prices during which investing in growth stocks had been profitable	Emergence of professional conglomerates; Harold Geneen's ITT, Textron, Teledyne, etc.	Stock swaps to create apparent earnings growth	Harvard endowment takes large positions in National Student Marketing; McGeorge Bundy urges institutions to invest aggressively	1970–1971	Reform of accounting practices; Williams Act
1990s TMT-bubble	Technological innovations like the Internet penetrate everyday life. Macroeconomic factors (high economic growth and low inflation) favour stocks	Creation of .com firms financed with easy money on new stock exchanges like Nasdaq (USA) and Neuer Markt (Germany)	Accounting fraud (Enron, World Com, EM-TV, etc.)	Acceptance of new valuation standards like comparative methods	2001–2003	Sarbanes Oxley Act prohibits synergies between auditing and consulting
2000s US housing bubble	Speculative money returning from the TMT-bubble goes into housing	Packaging of mortgage risks in new securities (MBS) that are sold outsourced in special investment vehicles (SIV) and sold worldwide	Rating agencies give highest ratings to MBS based on wrong assumptions on correlations	Accepting SIVs as legally sound	2007–2008	Banning SIVs since they effectively circumvent capital requirement regulations

3.7 CULTURAL DIFFERENCES IN THE BEHAVIOURAL BIASES[9]

There is only one way of being rational: maximizing an inter-temporal expected utility function with exponential discounting. But there are many ways of being irrational. In the following, we show that the deviations from the rational paradigm are not only systematic but also that they can be linked to cultural differences. Knowing these differences is essential for success in a global private banking market.

3.7.1 Cultural regions

Cultural regions are defined with respect to differences in the orientation towards performance and the future, as well as towards uncertainty aversion, individualism, and sexual equality of the people living there. Applying these criteria Gupta *et al.* (2002), for example, distinguish between the following cultural regions: Anglo-Saxon countries, Romanic Europe, Nordic Europe, German Europe, Eastern Europe, Latin America, Africa (south to Sahara), Arabic Cultures, South Asia, and Confucian Asia. Hofstede (2001) finds a similar fragmentation of cultural regions. Particularly interesting is the individualism index of Hofstede. The degree of individualism/ collectivism of a culture has a profound impact on risk attitudes, cognitive style, and the behavioural tendencies of its inhabitants, which we will discuss in more detail later on. Another important dimension discovered by Hofstede is the "Uncertainty Avoidance Index". It captures the attitudes towards ambiguous situations, which is also related to general risk attitudes. Figure 3.14 illustrates the Uncertainty Avoidance Index in a world map. The darker colour indicates a higher degree of uncertainty avoidance. For countries in white, we do not have data. Although Hofstede's cultural indexes have been widely accepted and used in various disciplines in social science, including economics and business, the applications to finance research are still new.

Some researchers approach cultural difference from the perspective of social-economic structure or cognitive thinking style. Douglas and Wildavsky (1982), for example, classify

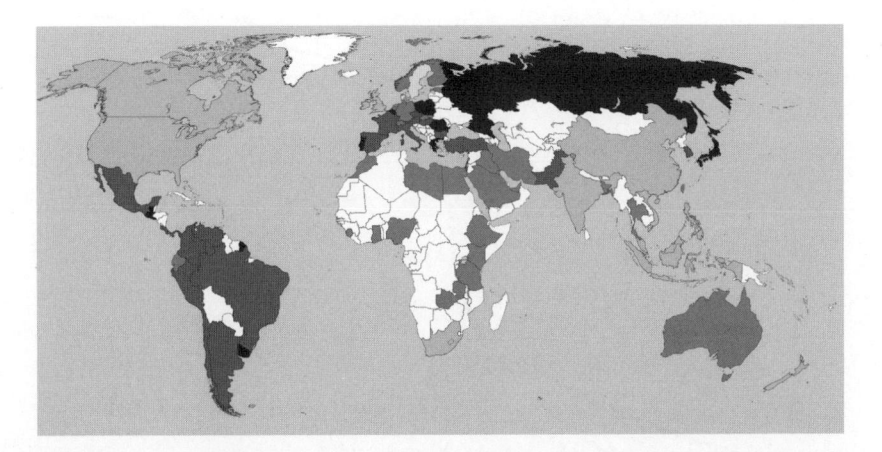

Figure 3.14 Cultural differences according to Hofstede's "Uncertainty Avoidance Index"

---

[9] This Section is based on Hens and Wang (2007).

cultural regions based on their market respectively on their hierarchic orientation. Nisbett *et al.* (2001) distinguish between regions based on their holistic and analytical thinking.

3.7.2 Cultural differences in the individual risk-taking behaviour

Studies on risk aversion show significant differences between the cultural regions described above. In general, these studies show that, compared to their counterparts from the US and European countries, Asian participants are more risk-tolerant and less loss-averse when facing financial risk (e.g. Fan and Xiao, 2005), which seems to contradict our stereotype. Bontempo *et al.* (1997) asked students in Hong Kong, Taiwan, Holland, and in the US to choose among different lotteries. They find that the risk aversion of the students in Hong Kong and Taiwan depends more on the level of the losses and less on the probability of the gains compensating the losses as compared to the students in Holland and in the US. Transferring this result into prospect theory, one gets the following students' value functions in the different countries (see Figure 3.15 and Table 3.4).

Weber and Hsee (1998) asked students in China, Germany, Poland, and the US to choose among different lotteries and found significant differences in their perception of risk. Using their result in applying prospect theory, one gets significant differences in the value function of students in different countries (see Figure 3.16 and Table 3.4).

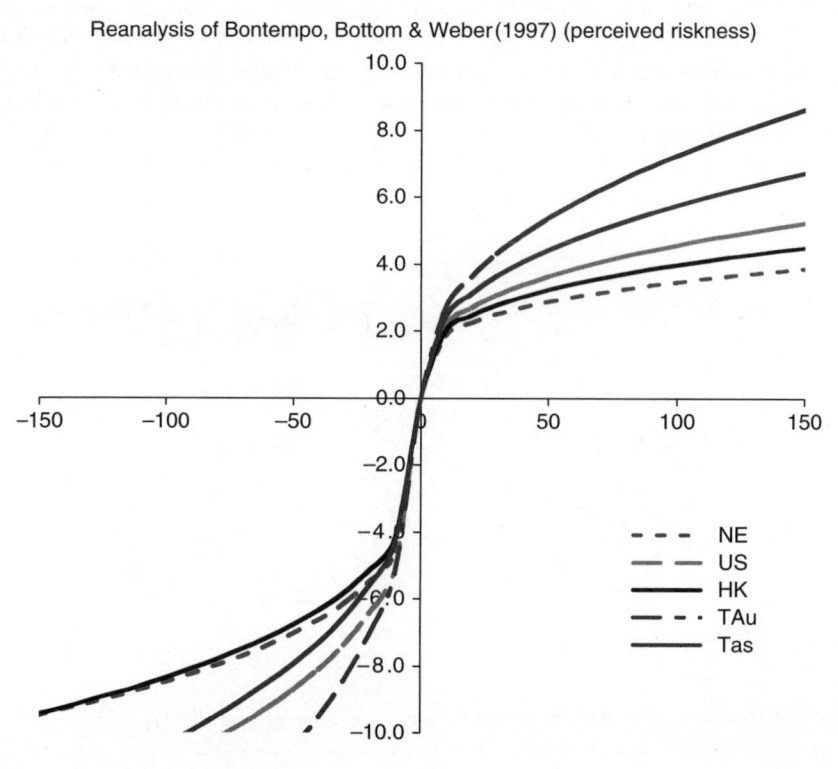

Figure 3.15 Value functions of students in different countries based on the results of Bontempo *et al.* (1997)

Table 3.4 Fitting prospect theory parameters of the results of Weber and Hsee (1998) and Bontempo et al. (1997)

Studies	Tasks	Parameters	Countries				
Weber & Hsee (1998)	Pricing		USA	Germany	Poland	China	
		Risk coefficient (α)	0.68	0.7	0.7	0.81	
		Loss aversion (β)	1.00	1.00	1.00	1.00	
		Probability weighting (γ)	0.77	0.73	0.73	0.82	
	Perceived risk		USA	Germany	Poland	China	
		Risk coefficient (α)	0.4	0.41	0.42	0.42	
		Loss aversion (β)	3.90	3.60	3.60	3.30	
		Probability weighting (γ)	0.88	0.80	0.83	0.77	
Bontempo et al. (1997)	Perceived risk		USA	Netherlands	Hong Kong	Taiwan University students	Security analysts
		Risk coefficient (α)	0.33	0.27	0.30	0.43	0.38
		Loss aversion (β)	2.10	2.45	2.10	1.95	1.80
		Probability weighting (γ)	0.60	0.63	0.60	0.66	0.62

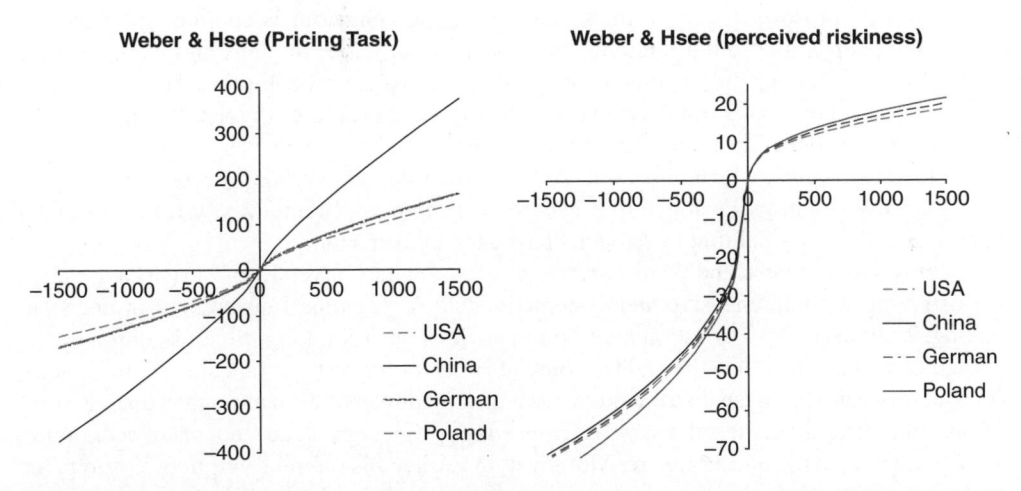

Figure 3.16 Value functions of students in different countries based on the results of Weber and Hsee (1998)

In general, these studies show that compared to their counterparts from the US and Europe, Asian participants are more risk-tolerant and less loss averse when facing financial risk (e.g. Fan and Xiao, 2005), which seems to contradict our stereotype. To account for the phenomenon that Asian participants are more risk-tolerant and less risk averse than their counterparts from the US and Europe, Weber and Hsee (1998) propose the "cushion hypothesis". They argue that in a collectivist society like China, the citizens can get more support from their families and friends when they are in financial troubles. As a result, they perceive less monetary risk. In other decision contexts (e.g. health risk), however, Asians tend to be more risk-averse, which is consistent with their high degree of Uncertainty Avoidance Index.

The culture in which the person lives exerts influences on his probabilistic thinking style. Wright and Phillips (1980) find that in probability judgment tasks, Hong Kong participants tend to assign more extreme probability estimations (e.g. "100 %" or "no chance"), whereas British participants can express their judgment with more differentiated numerical probabilities. These findings have been supported by more recent experiments conducted in the US, Japan, China, and other Asian countries. Yates, Lee and Shinotsuka (1996) suggest that this overconfidence bias in probability judgment may be caused by the collectivist culture, which emphasizes conformity and does not encourage counter-arguments in their education.

Since prospect theory defines the value function over gains and losses instead of final wealth, the reference point is important in determining one's risk attitude. A high reference point or aspiration level is more likely to induce risk-seeking attitudes, because the perceived outcomes are shifted to the more negative domain. For the same reason, a lower reference point or aspiration level may lead to a more risk-averse attitude. How people from different cultures choose their reference point or aspiration level is still an open research question. It was found, however, that Chinese people are more prone to the framing effect, and are more affected by the social context when evaluating insurance products or other objects (Wang and Fischbeck, 2004; Levinson and Peng, 2006). Potential reasons can be either that the Chinese still lack the experience with financial products and financial markets, or that their thinking style tends to be more holistic and less analytical so that they focus more on contextual cues. More research needs to be done to disentangle these alternative hypotheses.

In summary, prospect theory implies that risk-taking behaviour is conjointly determined by (1) how people choose the reference point, (2) risk attitudes in gains and losses, (3) the degree of loss aversion, and (4) how people judge and weight probabilities. This is far more complicated than the standard expected utility theory which captures the risk-taking tendency only through the concavity of the utility function. Prospect theory, however, offers much richer psychological insights, which allows us to deconstruct the underlying process of risk-taking behaviour. Investigating the above four aspects in a more systematic way will help us better comprehend the cross-cultural difference on risk-taking behaviour.

Recently, Hens, Rieger, and Wang (work in progress) at the University of Zurich have started one of the most comprehensive and systematic studies on cultural differences in decision-making. They designed a questionnaire with questions on risk taking, time discounting, and ambiguity aversion to which they added some of Hofstede's questions on cultural dimensions. This questionnaire has been distributed to more than 50 universities in more than 30 countries. In most of these universities, the same reference group, undergraduate students of economics, was asked to fill in the questionnaire. Moreover, in Zurich this reference group was compared to students from other majors as well as to practitioners from banks. The first results show interesting differences with respect to time preferences.

Figure 3.17 and Figure 3.18 show that the time preference is highly correlated with the inflation rate and income per capita. In a country with lower inflation rate and higher income per capita, people are more willing to wait and consume later. When controlling for the income and the inflation rate, it seems that participants from Anglo-Saxon countries (e.g. US, UK, Ireland, and Australia) are less patient, whereas participants from countries like Germany, Switzerland, and Austria are very patient.

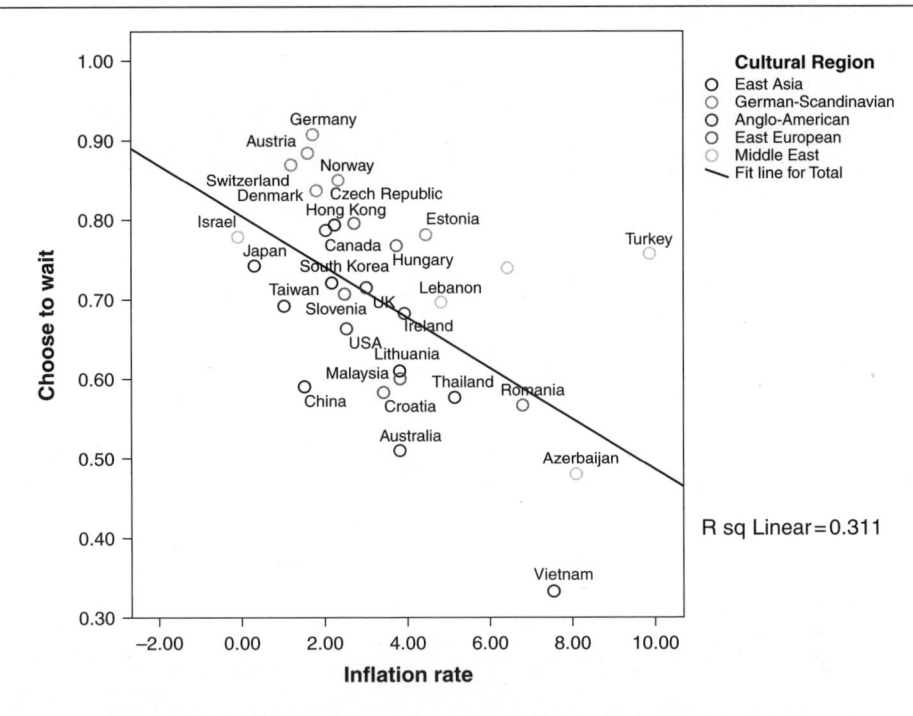

Figure 3.17 Inflation rate versus degree of patience in several countries

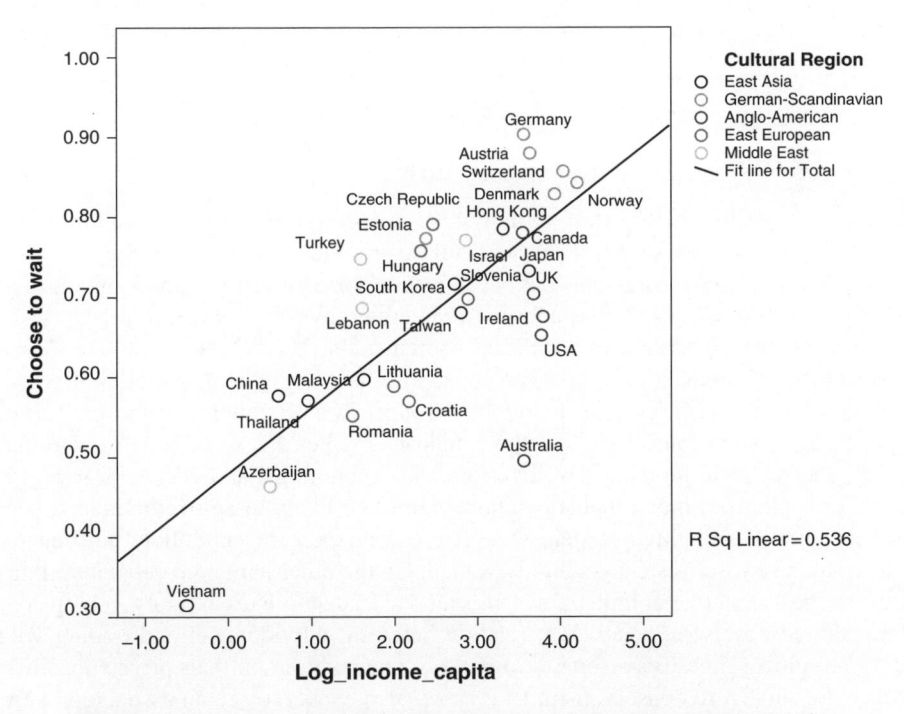

Figure 3.18 Income per capita versus degree of patience in several countries

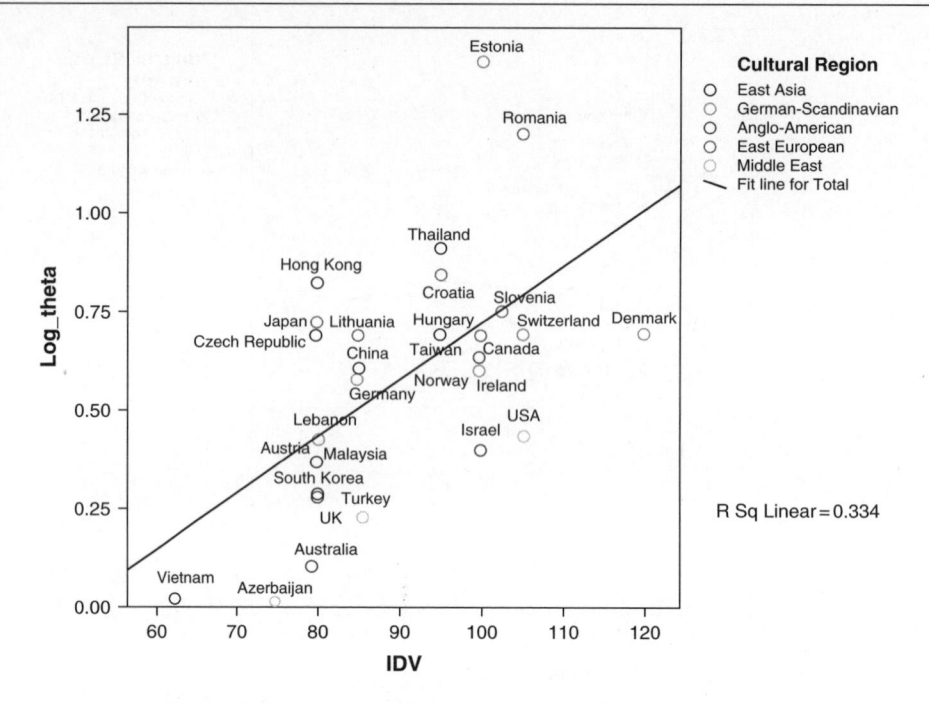

Figure 3.19 Individualism versus loss aversion index (theta)

Further differences among people in different countries can be observed by comparing their risk preferences and in particular, their loss aversion. Figure 3.19 shows that people from the more individualistic countries tend to be more loss averse, which is consistent with the cushion hypothesis proposed by Weber and Hsee (1998).

3.7.3 Cultural differences in the market returns

We have discussed how cultures affect individual decisions under risk. Can cultural dimensions predict aggregate market trend? For example, a profit to momentum strategy only weakly co-moves among 40 countries, and has virtually no correlation to macroeconomic factors (Griffin *et al.* 2003). Could culture add any predictive power to momentum profits? Using stock return data from 41 countries and the individualism index by Hofstede (2001), Chui *et al.* (2005) find that individualistic cultures tend to have higher trading volumes. They also find that momentum and long-term reversals tend to be stronger in individualistic cultures. These patterns persist even when controlling for other country variables that serve as a proxy for market efficiency, such as legal protection of investors and accounting standards. Chui *et al.* (2005) reason that people from individualistic cultures are more likely to be overconfident, because they are encouraged to distinguish themselves from others since their childhood and that in individualistic countries, self-esteem is highly valued. On the other hand, the behavioural finance literature suggests that overconfident investors tend to trade more excessively. If both are true, then one should observe a positive correlation between individualism and trading volume. Since overconfident investors also tend to put too much weight on their private information, and hence are subject to conservatism, Chui *et al.* also expect to see an association between mid-term momentum, long-term reversal, and individualism. Their results confirm these conjectures at the country level.[10] It would be interesting to see whether these patterns also emerge at the individual level, i.e. the investors who score higher in the individualism index are more likely to follow the momentum strategy and trade more often. This study is novel in the sense that, to our knowledge, it is the first study that links the cultural dimensions directly to the stock market data.

Culture may also influence how investors choose their stocks. In a study of Finnish firms, Grinblatt and Keloharju (2001) document how investors are more likely to hold and trade the stocks of companies that have chief executives of the same cultural background, that are located at a short distance, and that communicate in the investor's native language.[11] The influence of culture, language, and distance seem to be stronger for households and less investment savvy institutions. Chan, Covrig, and Ng (2005) examine mutual funds from 26 developed and developing countries, and confirm that "home bias" is a pervasive phenomenon. Although home bias may be related to availability bias, these studies only investigate the existence of home bias, instead of the psychological mechanism behind it.

International comparisons of financial markets have frequently been conducted (e.g. Dimson, Marsh, and Staunton, 2006; Papa, 2004). Few of them, however, have examined the impact of cultural factors. Cultural dimensions can be helpful to explain the differences in cross-national market behaviour, especially when institutional or macro-economic variables lack the ability to predict such heterogeneity (Griffin, Ji, and Martin, 2003; Chui, Titman, and Wei, 2005). The relationship between momentum returns and individualism based on the results of Chui *et al.* (2005) is illustrated in Figure 3.20. Each point shows the return achieved by a standardized momentum strategy depending on the score of the individualism index for

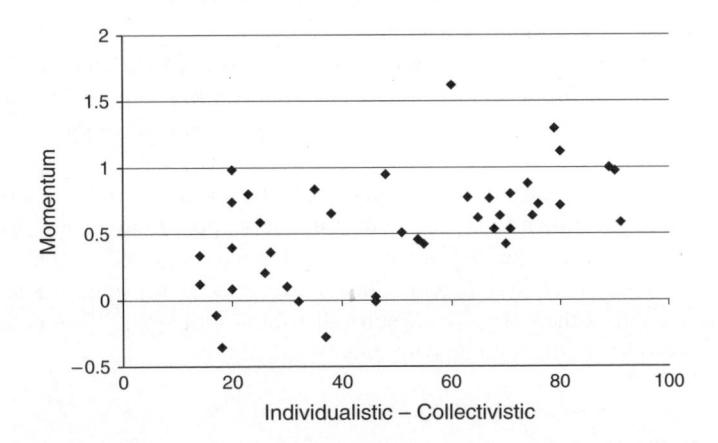

Figure 3.20 Trend chasing and individualism around the world

---

[10] Note that the concept of overconfidence here is different from the overconfidence in probability judgment that we discussed previously. The former refers to the self-evaluation of one's ability compared to other people, whereas the latter is defined as a too narrow confidence interval or miscalibration in probability judgment.

[11] Finnish firms are particularly interesting for cross-cultural studies because Finland has two official languages (Finnish and Swedish), and Finnish firms are also different in their communication languages (either exclusively Finnish, exclusively Swedish, or multiple languages). Actually, another interesting example is Switzerland, a country which has four diversified cultural-regions and correspondingly four official languages (German, French, Italian, and Rhaeto-romanic). But we are not aware of any cross-cultural studies of investment behaviour in Switzerland.

Table 3.5 Volatility and market returns in different countries (*Source*: Papa (2004))

		MSCI STOCKS INDEX						
	Sample period	Mean up	Mean down	Volatility up	Volatility down	Corr	Corr up	Corr down
World	1970.1–2003.10	21.00 %	−15.00 %	14.35	17.86	0.89	0.86	0.9
USA	1970.1–2003.10	24.00 %	−17.00 %	15.65	17.61	1	1	−1
GER	1970.1–2003.10	28.00 %	−23.00 %	19.63	22.62	0.51	0.35	0.6
UK	1970.1–2003.10	29.00 %	−21.00 %	22.3	23.3	0.61	0.47	0.66
CH	1970.1–2003.10	25.52 %	−19.90 %	17.9	21.15	0.64	0.5	0.7
CAN	1970.1–2003.10	25.73 %	−19.11 %	17.41	19.66	0.71	0.65	0.72
IT	1970.1–2003.10	35.89 %	−29.41 %	25.45	23.84	0.35	0.2	0.41
FR	1970.1–2003.10	32.94 %	−26.00 %	21.71	23.45	0.54	0.4	0.6
AUS	1970.1–2003.10	28.96 %	−23.53 %	20.42	23.74	0.53	0.33	0.62
JAP	1970.1–2003.10	27.45 %	−22.05 %	19.42	20.4	0.36	0.24	0.37

the different countries. On average, the momentum effect is stronger for countries with more individualists.

Some market anomalies are still unexplained perhaps because they are determined by cultural differences. The Italian stock market, for example, exhibits two anomalies compared to other western European countries. First, only in Italy is the volatility of stock returns higher for positive compared to negative returns (see Table 3.5).

Second, in the long run, Italian glamour (or growth) stocks achieve higher returns than value stocks, which is in contradiction to other countries, where value stocks, in the long run, achieve higher returns than glamour stocks (see Table 3.6).

In another ongoing project, Wang and Rieger at the University of Zurich look at the predictors of the various levels of equity risk premium at the county level. Figure 3.21 shows that the equity premium is higher in those countries with a higher tendency of ambiguity aversion. Here the ambiguity aversion is measured from a question in the previously mentioned international risk attitude study by Hens, Rieger, and Wang, which asked the students to choose between a lottery with known probabilities and a lottery with unknown probabilities (ambiguous option). From a theoretical point of view, ambiguity aversion has been suggested as a behavioural factor to explain the high equity premium: potential investors prefer to buy bonds rather than stocks, because they are afraid of the unspecified return distribution of stocks. The pattern shown in Figure 3.21 seems to be in line with this argument.

3.7.4 Further aspects

Culture is deeply rooted in every society, and every human being has to learn from the culture he lives in. Hence culture has relatively stable and long-term effects on how individuals perceive the world, think, and make decisions. Cultural differences, although acknowledged in many other contexts, have not yet gained enough attention from the finance research community. One main reason could be that, for a long time, finance was considered to be a discipline that only focuses on how rational agents make optimal decisions under perfect or imperfect conditions. With the emergence of behavioural finance, it is a natural step to include cultural factors in the analysis.

Table 3.6 Value and glamour stocks performance from 1975 to 1995 (*Source*: Fama and French (1998))

Market	Book-to-market Value	Book-to-market Glamour	Earnings-price Value	Earnings-price Glamour	Cash flow-price Value	Cash flow-price Glamour	Dividend-price Value	Dividend-price Glamour
U.S.	9.57 (14.64)	14.55 (16.92)	7.74 (15.79)	14.09 (18.10)	7.38 (15.23)	13.74 (16.73)	7.08 (15.99)	11.75 (13.89)	8.01 (17.04)
Japan	11.88 (28.67)	16.91 (27.74)	7.06 (30.49)	14.14 (26.10)	6.67 (27.62)	14.95 (31.59)	5.66 (29.22)	16.81 (35.01)	7.27 (27.51)
U.K.	15.33 (28.62)	17.87 (30.03)	13.25 (27.94)	17.46 (32.32)	14.81 (27.00)	18.41 (35.11)	14.51 (26.55)	15.89 (32.18)	12.99 (26.32)
France	11.26 (32.35)	17.10 (36.60)	9.46 (30.88)	15.68 (37.05)	8.70 (32.35)	16.17 (36.92)	9.30 (31.26)	15.12 (30.06)	6.25 (33.16)
Germany	9.88 (31.36)	12.77 (30.35)	10.01 (32.75)	11.13 (24.62)	10.58 (34.82)	13.28 (29.05)	5.14 (26.94)	9.99 (24.88)	10.42 (34.42)
Italy	8.11 (43.77)	5.45 (35.53)	11.44 (50.65)	7.62 (42.36)	12.99 (54.68)	11.05 (43.52)	0.37 (38.42)	10.07 (38.28)	12.68 (56.66)
Netherlands	13.30 (18.81)	15.77 (33.07)	13.47 (21.01)	14.37 (21.07)	9.26 (20.48)	11.66 (33.02)	11.84 (23.26)	13.47 (21.38)	13.05 (30.81)
Belgium	12.62 (25.88)	14.90 (28.62)	10.51 (27.63)	15.12 (30.47)	12.90 (27.88)	16.46 (28.84)	12.03 (25.57)	15.16 (26.47)	12.26 (29.26)
Switzerland	11.07 (27.21)	13.84 (30.00)	10.34 (28.57)	12.59 (31.44)	11.04 (28.81)	12.32 (36.58)	9.78 (27.82)	12.62 (31.00)	10.44 (27.83)
Sweden	12.44 (24.91)	20.61 (38.31)	12.59 (26.26)	20.61 (42.43)	12.42 (24.76)	17.08 (30.56)	12.50 (23.58)	16.15 (29.55)	11.32 (25.13)
Australia	8.92 (26.31)	17.62 (21.03)	5.30 (27.32)	15.64 (28.19)	5.97 (28.89)	18.32 (29.08)	4.03 (27.46)	14.62 (28.43)	6.83 (28.57)
Hong Kong	22.52 (41.96)	26.51 (48.68)	19.35 (40.21)	27.04 (44.83)	22.05 (40.81)	29.33 (46.24)	20.24 (42.72)	23.66 (38.76)	23.30 (42.05)
Singapore	13.31 (27.29)	21.63 (36.89)	11.96 (27.71)	15.21 (29.55)	13.12 (34.68)	13.42 (26.24)	8.03 (28.92)	10.64 (22.01)	13.10 (33.92)

As we have illustrated before, culture can influence risk attitudes, probabilistic thinking, and overconfidence tendency, which may in turn manifest itself as different patterns in investment behaviour as well as market trends across countries and regions. It opens the door to various research directions. We mention a few of them as a suggestion for future research.

(1) Are people from different cultures systematically subject to different cognitive biases? Each culture has its advantages and disadvantages. For example, people from an individualistic culture are more likely to be overconfident and subject to self-attribution bias, but are better in probability calibration. On the other hand, people from a collectivist culture are more likely to be affected by framing effects and hindsight bias, but are better in detecting correlation/covariance between variables because of their holistic thinking styles (Nisbett *et al.*, 2001; Choi and Nisbett, 2000). How do these propensities lead to different investment strategies and performances?
(2) Emotion plays a big role in making economic and financial decisions. Different emotions are related to different risk-taking tendencies. For example, anger may trigger risk-seeking

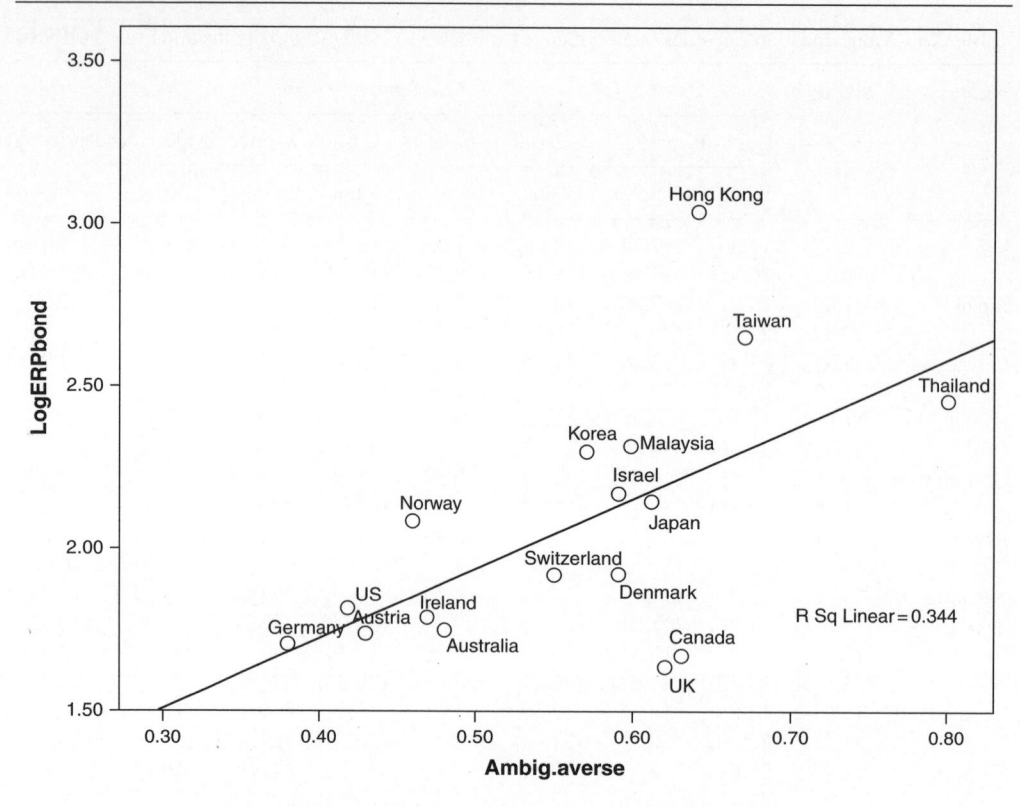

Figure 3.21 Ambiguity aversion and the equity premium

whereas sadness may lead to risk-avoidance. The fundamental emotions are universal across all societies, but different cultures may encourage some emotions but suppress others (Aaker and Williams, 1998; Berry, Dasen, and Sarawathi, 1997). To what extent are emotions contributing to cross-cultural differences in risk-taking behaviour and financial decision-making?

(3) How can financial products be constructed that are appealing to different cultures? For example, are high-risk products more attractive to Asian countries? Does experience with financial products change risk preferences over time?

With the rapid process of globalization, different cultures inevitably confront and interact with each other. This makes cross-cultural studies in finance and financial market more necessary and at the same time more feasible. We believe a deeper understanding of the impacts of cultural backgrounds will help us gain more insights into the development of financial markets, and facilitate higher efficiency.

4
Risk Profiling

4.1 DEALING WITH BEHAVIOURAL BIASES

Individuals are exposed to a number of biases that affect their decision-making behaviour. In financial matters, biased decisions lead to a systematic loss of money. It is one of the advisor's main duties to help clients avoid falling into psychological traps in the wealth management process.

To perform this task successfully, client advisors need to determine which part of the client's choice is driven by behavioural biases and which part mirrors behavioural aspects of the client's preferences. Based on Chapter 2, one must conclude that a choice driven by the risk and loss aversion of the client is not irrational. However, if the client develops a biased perception of probabilities, as described in the normalized prospect theory, or if he acts according to some of the behavioural biases summarized in Chapter 3, his decision becomes irrational. Hence Chapter 2 and Chapter 3 have the important role of helping the advisor distinguish between rational and irrational behaviour.

Once the advisor develops an understanding of how to distinguish rational from irrational aspects of his client's behaviour, the next problem he needs to solve is to help the client make rational choices. There are certainly many ways to deal with this problem. Some examples are given in Table 4.1. The best way, however, is to follow a structured process as outlined in Chapter 8, that advisors have to go through with the client again, when the client does not feel comfortable with the received recommendation. A risk profiler is at the centre of such a process.

Table 4.1 Fighting against biases leading to irrational decisions

Biases leading to an irrational choice	How to fight against the bias
Availability bias/ Attention bias	Show the client long-term results before letting him jump on the recent news in the media. Give examples of glamour stories that failed.
Representativeness/ Gambler's fallacy	Make sure that the client does not neglect statistically relevant results when he tries to see patterns in the data.
Anchoring / Conservatism	Make sure that the client's expectations respond adequately to new changes in fundamentals and do not stick to the last estimates.
Framing	Show an alternative representation of the problem and ask the client whether he will decide differently. Use a decision support tool for risk management.

Table 4.1 (Continued)

Biases leading to an irrational choice	How to fight against the bias
Overconfidence	Point out that the other investors also try to out-smart the client and that those investors who find the right balance between their skills and their investment style, perform best.[1]
Mental accounting	Point out the benefits of diversification.
Home bias	Show facts like the benefit from international diversification or the specific risk of your home country.
Self attribution bias	Point out that success/failure is most likely good/bad luck.
Emotions	Help the client to avoid spontaneous trades.
Hindsight bias	Take notes on the risks and chances when a decision is taken and recall them after the returns have realized.

4.2 THE RISK PROFILER AND ITS BENEFITS

In general, one can say that an asset allocation is optimal if it suits the client's preferences and his risk ability so that the client holds onto his strategy over time. This strategy should be free from behavioural biases but it should take into account behavioural aspects of the client's preferences such as loss aversion.

A risk profiler is a questionnaire that assesses the client's risk ability, his risk awareness, and his preference in a systematic way. Using a risk profiler has some important advantages, one of which is that it allows financial advisors to improve the conformability of their services with the requirements of the European Markets in Financial Instruments Directive (MiFID). The directive was designed to produce greater European harmonisation of laws and to encourage integration of the capital markets within the EU. In addition, MiFID ensures a higher level of protection for investors, particularly through best execution obligations, new rules for handling clients' orders, requirements for managing conflicts of interest, and obligations on transparency and the information to be provided to investors. For financial advisors (at least in the EU), the new directive aims at improving the service quality, in particular in terms of matching the bank's recommendation and the client's needs. According to the new directive, advisors are required to pay greater attention to the assessment of the client's profile in order to make sure that the recommended asset allocation best fits his individual needs and investment objectives. Even if the client's mandate does not include advisory services (the bank is only the executor of the client's transaction orders), the advisor responsible for the execution is required to make sure that the client is aware of the risks of the particular investment.

A further advantage of using a risk profiler is that it reduces the impression that the advice one gets from a bank is arbitrary. As the following case of Christine Kuhn shows, it is typically very difficult for an external observer to judge which bank gives the best advice.[2]

---

[1] In a great experiment Huber (2006) shows that those who know that they do not know anything typically perform better than those who are overconfident in their knowledge (see the previous chapter).

[2] In the scientific literature the Christine Kuhn problem has been shown to prevail also under clean experimental conditions. See Siebenmorgen and Weber (2003) for a recent study.

Case Study 4.1: Christine Kuhn

In the year 2003 the Swiss investment magazine *Stocks* sent a fictitious client, named Christine Kuhn, to a number of banks in Switzerland in order to ask for investment advice (see Strohm, 2003). Christine Kuhn was supposed to be a 40-year-old IT specialist, married and without children. Her yearly income was supposed to be CHF 203 000. Furthermore, it was said that she had recently inherited CHF 150 000, that her pension is well secured, and that she wants to invest the money over a horizon of at least seven years. Even though this data looks conclusive, Christine Kuhn got quite different advice from the various banks (see Figure 4.1). The percentage of money invested in stocks, for example, ranged from 50 % to 100 % and the share invested in her home currency ranged from 28 % to 90 %.

The problem of this case is the following: because the matching of the client to the bank is a random process[3] and because the advice of the various banks is so heterogeneous, the outcome of the advisory process is random. The bottom line of the article in *Stocks* was to ask why a customer should be willing to pay for random advice. The same heterogeneity of advice can be observed in a large organisation if the bank does not use a risk profiler and does not follow a structured process. This is because, without a risk profiler, the advice is left totally to the discretion of the relationship manager. Since different relationship managers have different views on the various asset classes and since they put different emphasis on the various aspects of the client, the resulting asset allocation is arbitrary.

Name	Cash	Equities	Bonds	Alternative	CHF	EUR	USD	Others
Bank Coop	4	74	22	–	28	24	34	14[1]
Bank Jura Laufen	10	50–60	30–40	–	50–60	30–40	10	–
Bank Linth	30	65	5	–	45	25	25	5[2]
Bank Sarasin	0–10	90–100	–	–	27	10	39	24[4]
Credit Suisse	10–15	50–55	15–20	15–20[3]	55–60	20–25	20–25	–
Graubündner Kantonalbank	13	54	27	6[4]	43	24	13	20[5]
Hypothekarbank Lenzburg	5–15	55–75	20–30	–	40–60	15–35	15–35	0–20
LGT Bank in Liechtenstein	0–5	45–55	45–55	–	75–90	15–25	3–10	0–5[2]
Liechtensteinische Landesbank	7	81	12	–	50	21	22	7[2]
Luzerner Kantonalbank	8	61	31	–	36	25	16	23[4]
Migrosbank	8	62	25	5[4]	50	24	18	8
Neue Aargauer Bank	0–10	90–100	–	–	50–55	20–25	15–20	5–10[2]
Raiffeisen/Cosba Private Banking	0–5	65–75	25–35	–	25–55		45–75[7]	
UBS	5	75	20	–	50	8	29	13[6]
Valiant	7	60	33	–	63	16	14	7[8]

1) NOK-bonds (funds in Pacific/Japan); 2) JPY; 3) structured products; 4) real estate; 5) NOK/GBP/JPY/CZK/HKD/TWD/CAD; 6) GBP/JPY/others; 7) currency bounds for EUR, USD, GBP, HKD, SGD, AUD, CAD, DKK, SEK; 8) Asia/AUD/NZD

Figure 4.1 Different advice from various banks according to *Stocks* magazine 41–42, 2003

---

[3] Similarly, the matching of the client with some client advisors within a big bank is random.

4.3 DESIGNING A RISK PROFILER: SOME GENERAL CONSIDERATIONS

Before applying a risk profiler the advisor should show the chances and risks of various asset classes over a long horizon. This is important since otherwise the risk appetite of the client will depend too much on the recent experience with his investments. However, when introducing a risk profiler, the bank has to take positions on several trade-offs.

Precise answers to quantitative questions allow the bank to give the best advice. However, some clients may give answers to quantitative questions that do not make sense, just because they are not used to thinking quantitatively. A solution to this problem could involve using a question that sorts the clients into a qualitative or quantitative part of the risk profiler.

Further, one needs to decide whether the questionnaire should be static, or whether later questions should be based on the answers of earlier ones. To facilitate this, an IT solution may be used. Next, one may ask for certain aspects in different ways. Introducing validation questions improves the quality of the questionnaire but will increase its length.

Finally, the decision has to be made whether back-tracks to earlier questions are allowed if one is not comfortable with the result. Going this way, the client can learn best the trade-offs that markets offer. However, there is a risk of re-engineering, i.e. deciding on the asset allocation and then filling in the questionnaire so that it is consistent with the asset allocation.

Once the risk profiler has been designed, the bank needs to decide how to make use of the information. In this evaluation phase, the bank may employ a scoring system, i.e. each answer gets a score and these points are aggregated into one number based on the experience of the bank. Further, the bank needs to decide whether the risk profiler should be used as a stand-alone solution or whether it should be integrated into some database with information that the bank already has about its clients. Also, the bank needs to decide whether information about the client's assets with other banks can and/or should be also considered when advising clients.

Designing risk profilers in the laboratory

Typically, risk profilers are created in banks by a team consisting of client advisors, business developers, and maybe also experts with a quantitative background. Some distinctions, like risk ability and risk tolerance, are made and then each participant suggests aspects that he finds most important. This process relies on the imagination and the intuition of the participants. Then the risk profiler is tested with other employees of the bank and finally it is first used on a small segment of the clients. Only after some years will one be able to see whether the new risk profiler has improved the investment decisions – if this is possible at all. The problem is that, in contrast to the necessary *ceteris paribus* clause (other things held fixed), when introducing the risk profiler many other things will have changed on the financial market. Thus, following this procedure of creating a risk profiler is a costly, time-consuming and unreliable process with a result that can hardly be validated.

An alternative to this process is used by BhFS[4], who designs risk profilers in an experimental laboratory (see Figure 4.2). In this setting, one has full control of the

---

[4] BhFS stands for Behavioural Finance Solutions (www.bhfs.ch), a spinoff firm of the University of Zurich.

ceteris paribus clause and can link the performance of the investors to the questionnaire. Moreover, by changing aspects of the questionnaire, one sees clearly whether these are improvements. In a typical laboratory experiment, the participants have to invest over several periods into some risky assets. Different groups (called "treatment group" and "control group") do this with different risk profilers. Moreover, the participants are recruited using a huge database so that their socio-economic characteristics are known before the experiment.

Figure 4.2 An experimental laboratory at the University of Zurich

4.4 IMPLEMENTED RISK PROFILERS: CASE STUDY OF THE FORMER BANK LEU[5]

To structure the discussion between the advisor and the client, a bank usually uses checklists or questionnaires. In some countries like Germany, this is even required by law.[6] Which questionnaire is best depends on the specific advisory process of the bank. Credit Suisse, for example, which follows a very structured advisors process,[7] uses only a few questions

---
[5] Clariden Leu Ltd came into being on 26 January 2007 as a result of the merger of Credit Suisse's four private banks – Clariden, Bank Leu, Bank Hofmann, and BGP Banca di Gestione Patrimoniale – as well as the securities dealer Credit Suisse Fides.
[6] Wertpapierhandelsgesetz, Wphg.
[7] We describe the Credit Suisse advisory process in Chapter 8.

to evaluate the risk profile of their clients. Another example is the Finter Bank, since it has a special focus on absolute return products; their risk profiler is extended in that direction. A further example is Arab Bank, whose risk profiler includes aspects of Sharia compliant investments.

Although banks differ with respect to the questions they ask, all of them need to assess at least the risk ability, the risk preference, and the risk perception of their clients. Moreover, introducing a risk profiler together with master portfolios to which clients are matched assures the homogeneity of the advice a large bank gives. The risk profiler helps to assess the client more objectively and the master portfolios are determined in a separate business unit such as, for example, the investment committee, so that the typical heterogeneity in the relationship manager's view on the financial markets is no longer reflected in the client's portfolios. We start with the risk profiler of the former Bank Leu as our first example because it was one of the first banks in Switzerland to introduce risk profilers into their advisory process.

Case Study 4.2: Questionnaire of the former Bank Leu

The following questionnaire was implemented by the former Bank Leu in 2001. Since that time Bank Leu, now Clariden Leu, has gained experience and adapted the questionnaire resulting in a more sophisticated concept. The original version of the questionnaire is shown below.[8] The questionnaire addresses the needs analysis, the investment horizon, the risk ability, the aspiration level and the loss aversion.

The needs of the client are assessed with the following question:

Question 6
In order to integrate the invested assets in an overall financial plan, we need the following personal information.

a) Your age in years		Points	b) Are you		Points	c) Number of children (young children or children in full-time education)		Points
Under 30	☐	0	Self-employed	☐	0	0	☐	0
30–60	☐	10	A retiree	☐	10	1–3	☐	–10
Over 60	☐	0	A blue-collar worker	☐	0	More than 3	☐	–20
			A salaried employee	☐	0			
			A manager	☐	10			

d) Do you own property?		Points	e) What is the proportion of your financial investments to your total assets (property, money investments)?		Points	f) What is the proportion of your investment assets to your annual income?		Points
Yes	☐	20	Less than 10%	☐	20	Less than 50%	☐	
No	☐	0	Less than 20%	☐	10	50–80%	☐	–10
			20% or more	☐	0	More than 80%	☐	–15

☐ Sum of answers to question 6
Transfer value to the box on the evaluation sheet

☐ Sum of answers to questions 6a) und 6d)
Transfer value to the box on the evaluation sheet

---

[8] To increase the comparability with the other questionnaires presented in this book we have changed the order of the bank's questions.

Risk Profiling 111

The following question has been used to determine the investment horizon:

Question 3
Possibly you may wish to be able to dispose of your invested assets* at a specific date in order to buy something, or there is a possibility you may need this sum again.
*By invested assets we mean the sum of securities and cash that you currently have invested with financial institutions.

°several answers per question possible

a) When do you plan to use or estimate that you will use your assets?

Definitely in...	Points°	Probably in...	Points°
Less than 3 years	☐ 40	Less than 3 years	☐ 40
3 years	☐ 30	3 years	☐ 30
4 years	☐ 20	4 years	☐ 20
5 years	☐ 10	5 years	☐ 10
6 years	☐ 5	6 years	☐ 5
8 years and over	☐ 0	8 years and over	☐ 0

☐ Highest number of points of all answers given

b) Amount of the sum invested I will need is

	Factor
a quarter	☐ ¼
a half	☐ ½
three quarters	☐ ¾
the entire sum	☐ 1

☐ Please multiply the points from question 3a) by the factor from question 3b)

Transfer value to the box on the evaluation sheet

The client's risk ability is checked by asking for events in which he would need to get the invested money back:

Question 4
In the course of a life unforeseen events occur. In such cases, money may be needed.

°several answers per question possible

a) In which of the following events would you need access to your financial engagements?

	Points°		Points°
Purchasing a house for an attractive price	☐ 10	Founding my own company	☐ 10
		If I was unable to work	☐ 10
Increase in mortgage interest rates	☐ 10	Serious illness	☐ 10
Marriage or divorce	☐ 10	Temporary loss of employment for about ½ year	☐ 10
In the event of my death, the heirs would need access to the sum	☐ 10	None of the above cases will occur	☐ 10
Children's education	☐ 10	I do not need the sum invested for any of the above reasons	☐ 10
Early retirement	☐ 10		

☐ Sum of answers to question 4a)

b) Amount of the sum invested I will need is

	Factor
a quarter	☐ ¼
a half	☐ ½
three quarters	☐ ¾
the entire sum	☐ 1

☐ Please multiply the points from question 4a) by the factor from question 4b)

Transfer value to the box on the evaluation sheet

Case Study 4.2: (Continued)

Question 5
Problems can occur in everyday life where you need to have access to your invested assets.

°several answers per question possible

a) In which of the following events would you need access to your financial engagements?

	Points°
Car accident where the insurance does not pay and I have to buy a new car	☐ 50
I make an expensive purchase for the home – furniture for example	☐ 50
Temporary loss of employment for about 1 month	☐ 50
None of the above cases will occur	☐ 0
I do not need the sum invested for any of the above reasons	☐ 0

b) Amount of the sum invested I will need is

	Factor
a quarter	☐ ¼
a half	☐ ½
three quarters	☐ ¾
the entire sum	☐ 1

☐ Please multiply the points from question 5a) by the factor from question 5b)
Transfer value to the box on the evaluation sheet

☐ Sum of answers to question 4a)

Risk awareness and the client's aspiration level are determined by the following question:

Question 1
Think about the largest investment in your portfolio that you have made in recent years:

*only one answer per question is possible

a) What return were you aiming to achieve with this investment?

	Points*
Less than 4%	☐ 10
4–6%	☐ 20
6–8%	☐ 30
8–10%	☐ 40
More than 10%	☐ 50

b) At the time, what did you estimate the maximum return to be?

	Points*
Less than 4%	☐ 10
4–6%	☐ 20
6–8%	☐ 30
8–10%	☐ 40
More than 10%	☐ 50

c) In your opinion at that time, what was the greatest loss that the investment could incur?

	Points*
0–6%	☐ 10
6–15%	☐ 20
15–25%	☐ 30
25–40%	☐ 40
More than 40%	☐ 50

☐ Smallest number of points of all answers given
Transfer value to the box on the evaluation sheet

Finally, one question tries to elicit the client's loss aversion:

Question 2
You would like to invest CHF 1,000,000. With this investment you have a 50% chance of either gaining CHF 1,000,000 within a year or ending up with less than CHF 1,000,000. How much of the CHF 1,000,000 would you need to be left with, in a worst case scenario, for you to continue to invest?

*only one answer per question is possible

	Points*		Points*
1,000,000	☐ 0	at least 750,000	☐ 30
at least 940,000	☐ 10	at least 600,000	☐ 40
at least 850,000	☐ 20	less than 600,000	☐ 50

☐ Points total for answer to question 2
Transfer value to the box on the evaluation sheet

Risk Profiling

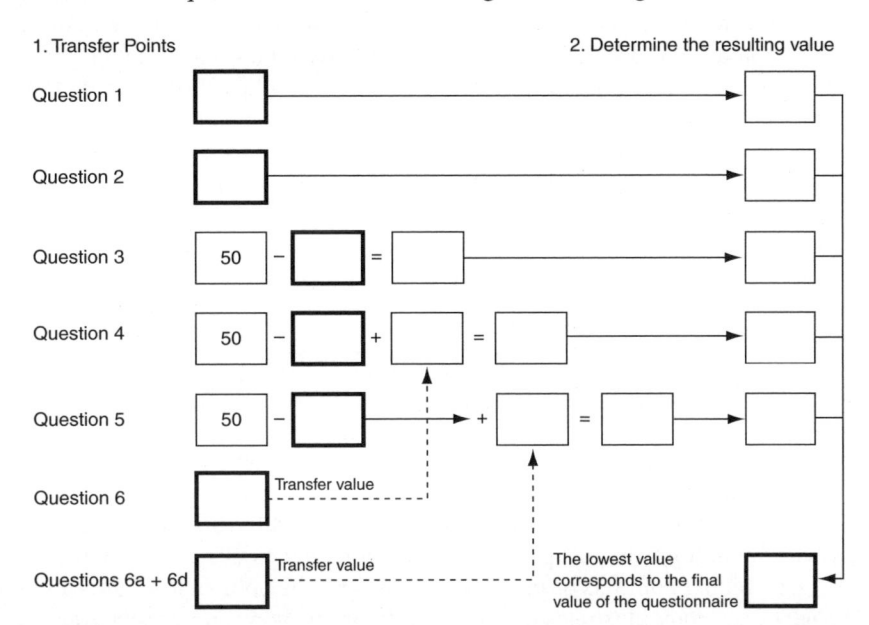

The answers to the questions are evaluated using the following scheme:

1. Transfer Points   **2. Determine the resulting value**

- Question 1 → □ → □
- Question 2 → □ → □
- Question 3: 50 − □ = □ → □
- Question 4: 50 − □ + □ = □ → □
- Question 5: 50 − □ → + □ = □ → □
- Question 6: □ (Transfer value)
- Questions 6a + 6d: □ (Transfer value)

The lowest value corresponds to the final value of the questionnaire.

The decisive factor for evaluation is the one with the lowest value. Consider, for example, an investor with high risk ability, i.e. an investor with high income and assets (question 6). As the investor correctly assessed his financial situation, his risk perception is also high (question 4). However, if the high equity allocation worries the investor because he is afraid to lose money, his risk preference is low (question 2 shows the lowest value).

This is a very prudent approach, which may imply that some questions become "bottlenecks" and therefore determine the asset allocation independently of the answers to the other questions.

On the basis of the evaluated answers, one can choose a suitable strategy among a few master portfolios. The percentage of equity increases with the risk tolerance of the investor. The following table is an example that reflects the bank's view on the financial markets as of summer 2003:

Points	Maximum 8 "100% Fixed Income"	8 to 18 "25% Equity"	18 to 28 "50% Equity"	28 to 40 "75% Equity"	more than 40 "100% Equity"
Breakdown by asset class in %					
Cash CHF	5	5	5	5	5
Bonds CHF	60	48	29	12	
Bonds EUR	35	22	16	8	
Equities Switzerland		10	19	27	33
Equities Europe		7	15	23	28
Equities USA		6	11	17	22
Equities Japan		2	4	6	8
Equities Emerging Markets			1	2	4

The former Bank Leu questionnaire is quite effective since it asks for difficult concepts like loss aversion and risk ability in an appropriate way. However, the evaluation of the answers, which gives the matching of the client with the master portfolios of the bank, looks quite ad hoc. In the meantime, Clariden Leu elaborated an improved questionnaire with 24 questions and included validation questions for important factors. Added questions refer to topics such as depletion of capital, past experiences regarding investments, and the preference regarding relative or absolute returns. All questionnaires are now analyzed by a specialist in order to use individual judgment of the client's investment profile. An automatic scheme to evaluate the profile is no longer in place.

In the following, we show how one can use mean-variance theory and prospect theory to compute a tailor-made asset allocation for each client.

4.5 A RISK PROFILER BASED ON THE MEAN-VARIANCE ANALYSIS

The optimal asset allocation is determined on the one hand by the risk and opportunities offered on the market, and on the other hand by the preferences and restrictions of the client. Questionnaires are helpful to elicit the latter. Previous return realizations of the assets included in the asset allocation, for example, provide information on the risks and the opportunities on the market.[9] Combining both sets of information, one gets the optimal asset allocation for the client. The next case study illustrates how to do this within the mean-variance framework.

Case Study 4.3: Risk profiling within the mean-variance analysis

Question 1: What is your main objective with respect to your wealth?

a) capital protection (limited risk but also limited return)
b) a mix of capital protection and wealth growth
c) wealth growth (higher wealth growth but also higher risk for losses)

Question 2: Which range of expected annual return and wealth changes do you prefer?

a) from -5% to 10%
b) from -10% to 20%
c) from -20% to 35%

Question 1 can be seen as a validation question, since question 2 may be too mathematical for many clients.

To see how these questions help to find the optimal asset allocation of the client, suppose the answers of question 2 describe binary lotteries with equally likely outcomes. Then the alternatives a), b), and c) encode the following mean-variance combinations:
a) $\mu = 2.5\%$, $\sigma = 7.5\%$, b) $\mu = 5\%$, $\sigma = 15\%$ and c) $\mu = 7.5\%$, $\sigma = 27.5\%$. The next figure illustrates them graphically.

---

[9] One can also use more sophisticated methods to forecast the moments of the return distribution of the assets than simply looking in the past.

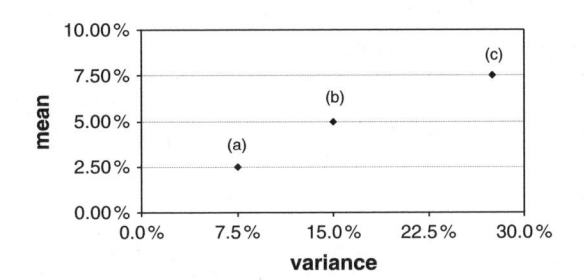

The optimal asset allocation is determined by the efficient portfolios. In general, they can be divided into groups. Within each group, a master portfolio defines the optimal asset allocation for a client with a risk tolerance that is closest to the risk-return characteristics of that master portfolio.

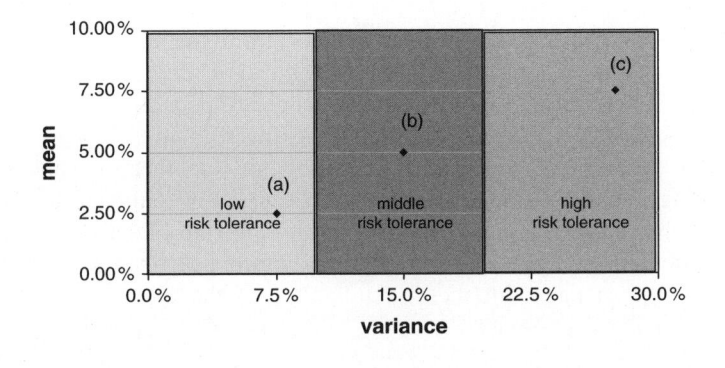

Within the mean-variance analysis, the risk ability of the client can be considered as a Value at Risk (VaR) constraint added to the efficient frontier. Briefly, VaR at a given tolerance level α is the return (or the amount of money) that the client likes to have in all but the worst $\alpha\%$ of the cases. In the mean-variance diagram, the VaR constraint can be illustrated as a line with a slope of $\alpha\%$, which intersects the vertical axis at the level of return that the client likes to have in all but the worst $\alpha\%$ of the cases.[10] The VaR constraint divides the efficient frontier in two parts. All efficient portfolios on the right side of the constraint need to be excluded since in the worst $\alpha\%$ of the cases, their return is lower so that the client may lose more money than he can tolerate. The higher the probability α, the stronger the VaR constraint, the more efficient portfolios need to be excluded.

The optimal asset allocation is determined by the tangency of the efficient frontier and the investor's utility function reflecting his preferences. If this optimal portfolio is on the left of the VaR constraint, it is also in line with the client's risk ability. Technically, we say that the VaR is "not binding" (see left part of Figure 4.3). If, however, the investor's utility function tangents the efficient frontier on the right side of the VaR constraint (see right part of Figure 4.3), we

---

[10] Recall that mean-variance analysis can only guarantee rational decisions if returns are normally distributed. In that case, the VaR(α) is a linear function of the standard deviation.

say that the VaR constraint is "binding". The optimal asset allocation is then the efficient portfolio that satisfies the VaR constraint.

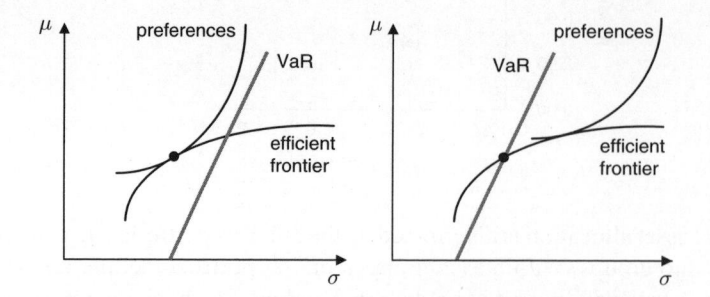

Figure 4.3 Risk ability in the mean-variance analysis

Within the mean-variance analysis, the transfer from the client's risk profile to his optimal asset allocation goes via the *two-fund-separation theorem*. It says that one part of the client's wealth should be invested in the tangency portfolio T (an optimally diversified mix of risk assets), and the rest should be invested in risk-free asset paying R_f according to the client's risk tolerance.[11] Thus, within the mean-variance analysis, the advisor evaluating a client's risk preferences needs to know only the client's risk tolerance. Based on this information he decides how to split the client's wealth between the tangency portfolio and the risk-free asset. Thereby the mix of risky assets in the tangency portfolio should not change with the risk tolerance of the client. Figure 4.4 illustrates the idea.

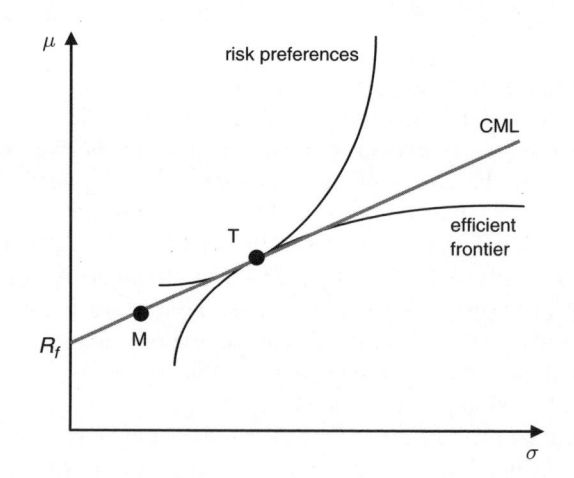

Figure 4.4 Mean-variance analysis with risk ability

---

[11] This is to say that the advisor needs to decide a point on the CML (e.g. point M) that corresponds to the client's risk tolerance.

4.6 INTEGRATING BEHAVIOURAL FINANCE IN THE RISK PROFILER

The main features of the client's risk profile are his risk ability, risk preferences, and risk awareness. In the following sections we show how one can use behavioural finance to assess them.

4.6.1 Risk ability

The risk ability represents a constraint for the optimization of the client's utility, which embodies his risk preference. In general, one would like to find an asset allocation that maximizes the client's utility while ensuring that he is able to finance his liabilities. In this respect, the advisor needs to find out two important things. First, is it possible to prioritize the client's liabilities in, say, "hard" (that wealth which is necessary to keep up the lifestyle) and "soft" (wealth to add plans and wishes that shall enhance the lifestyle). Second, the advisor needs to figure out whether some of the liabilities shall not be risked in any case, or whether a certain small probability of risking them is acceptable to the client. If the former case holds, one says the client wants *safety first*,[12] while in the latter case he may apply concepts like Value at Risk (VaR) or Conditional Value at Risk (CVaR).

Using VaR, one will accept positions as safe when in not more than α % of the cases one loses more money than one can afford. However, the VaR concept has some drawbacks. One will accept positions that with high probability are good, but that with a very small probability may lead to disastrous losses. Moreover, applying VaR for separate mental accounts is very problematic since adding up the VaR of different mental accounts may lead to erroneous conclusions with respect to the total risk exposure of the client.

An alternative measure that does not have these problems is the Conditional Value at Risk defined as $CVaR = E(x|x \leq VaR(\alpha))|$ (theorem by Artzner *et al.* (1999)). The CVaR is thus the conditional expectation of the random variable x below the VaR-level. The main advantages of this measure as compared to VaR are that it takes into account the size of losses and does not distort the risk exposure at portfolio level.

4.6.2 Risk preferences

The risk preferences of the client are described by his risk and loss aversion. Eliciting risk preferences shows considerable differences among individuals as Figure 4.5 shows.[13] The risk aversion of the individuals ranges between 0.39 and 1.15. The loss aversion reaches values up to 2.15.[14]

The calibrated risk aversion parameters for each of the participants in the Kahneman and Tversky's experiments are illustrated in Figure 4.6.[15]

---

[12] The safety first principle was been first suggested by Roy (1952). In general, it amounts to keeping the probability of a small loss. Hence as in VaR, some tolerance level α % could be introduced.
[13] The participants of this study conducted by BhFS were employees of the Zuercher Kantonalbank (Cantonal Bank of Zurich).
[14] The parameters are estimated using the piecewise power function, as suggested by Tversky and Kahneman (1992).
[15] The calibration is done by BhFS. The dot represents the calibrated parameters on the median decision maker. The values for the risk aversion parameter over losses α^- are presented here as positive numbers.

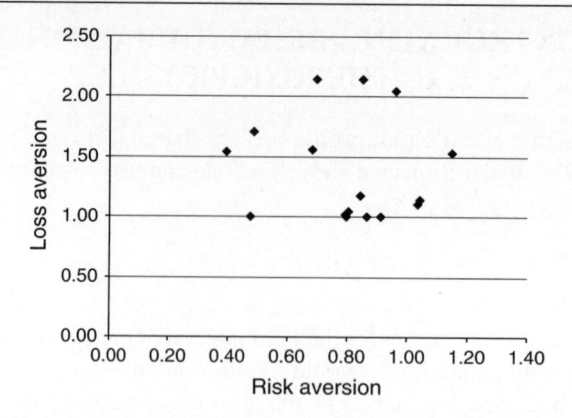

Figure 4.5 Heterogeneity in the individuals' risk and loss aversion assessed in a study at ZKB

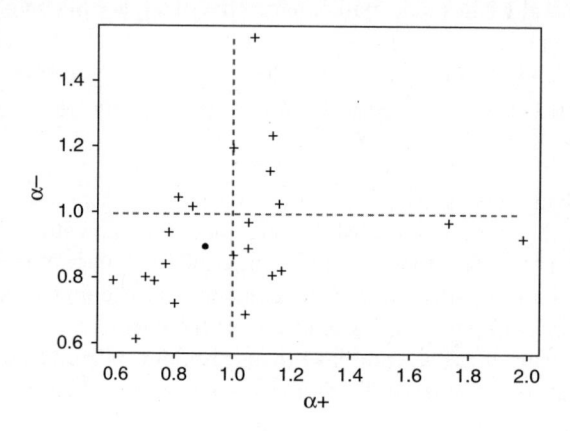

Figure 4.6 Heterogeneity in the individuals' risk aversion over gains α^+ and losses α^-

4.6.3 Risk awareness

Heterogeneity among individuals is also observed with respect to their risk awareness, i.e. their perception of probabilities for gains (γ^+) and losses (γ^-). This is illustrated in Figure 4.7.[16]

Overall, we conclude that individuals differ substantially with respect to their risk preferences and risk awareness. If one neglects these differences when assessing clients' risk profiles, one will probably recommend an asset allocation that will not fit the individual's needs.[17]

In Math Box 4.1, we provide an example of how to assess the preferences of behavioural investors in order to develop a risk profiler that fits with the client's understanding of risk.

---

[16] The parameters for each of the participants are calibrated by BhFS to Kahneman and Tversky's experiments. The dot represents calibrated parameters on the median decision maker. The dashed line is the 45 degree line.
[17] An asset allocation that is optimal for a risk averse investor is not necessarily optimal for another investor who is loss averse.

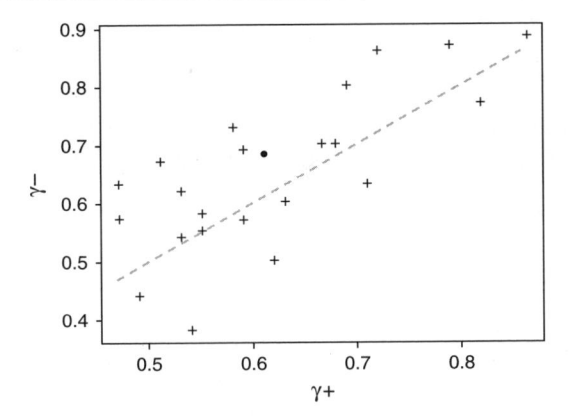

Figure 4.7 Heterogeneity in the individuals' perception of probabilities

---

Math Box 4.1: Basic calibration of prospect theory parameters

Before we go through a real-life risk profiler based on prospect theory, we will briefly show how to compute the prospect theory parameters from elementary lottery questions. We will use the piecewise quadratic value function since it also has the advantage of leading to simple calculations for the prospect theory parameters.

Recall the piecewise quadratic utility function:

$$v(\Delta x) = \begin{cases} \Delta x - \dfrac{\alpha^+}{2}\Delta x^2 & \text{for } \Delta x > 0 \\ \beta\left(\Delta x - \dfrac{\alpha^-}{2}\Delta x^2\right) & \text{for } \Delta x > 0 \end{cases}$$

The first lottery question determines the risk aversion parameter over gains α^+.

Question 1: What would you be willing to pay (as a percentage of your investment) to have a 50 % chance of gaining 10 % on your investment, while otherwise you break even?

Suppose the investor answers 4 %. Then the equation to determine α^+ based on Q1 is: $0.5\left(10 - \dfrac{\alpha^+}{2}100\right) = 4 - \dfrac{\alpha^+}{2}16$, which yields $\alpha^+ = 1/17$.

The second lottery question determines the risk aversion parameter over losses α^-.

Question 2: Suppose you follow a strategy that can either have a loss of 10 % or can break even with equal probability. Which sure loss would you consider to be equivalent to the strategy?

Suppose the investor again answers 4 %. Then the equation to determine α^- based on Question 2 is: $0.5\beta\left(-10 - \dfrac{\alpha^-}{2}100\right) = \beta\left(-4 - \dfrac{\alpha^-}{2}16\right)$, which yields $\alpha^- = -1/17$.

The third lottery question determines the investor's loss aversion β.

Math Box 4.1: (Continued)

Question 3: Suppose you follow a strategy that can gain 10 % with a 50 % chance. What is the maximal loss that you find acceptable in the other 50 % cases so that the strategy is acceptable?

Suppose the investor again answers 4 %. Then the equation to determine β based on Q3 is: $0.5\left(10 - \frac{\alpha^+}{2}100\right) + 0.5\beta\left(-4 - \frac{\alpha^-}{2}16\right) = 0$, which yields $\beta = 2$.

The final lottery question determines whether probabilities are perceived in a biased way as captured by the parameter γ:

Question 4: What percentage of your investment would you consider to be equivalent to a strategy that with 1 % chance achieves an 8 % gain and otherwise breaks even?

Suppose the investor answers 0.5 %. Then the equation to determine γ based on Q4 is:[18]
$$\frac{0.01^\gamma}{(0.01^\gamma + 0.99^\gamma)^{1/\gamma}}\left(8 - \frac{1}{34}64\right) = \left(0.6 + \frac{0.6}{34}\right), \text{ which yields } \gamma = 0.44.$$

4.6.4 Case study: Risk profiler by BhFS Behavioural Finance Solutions

The BhFS risk profiler recognizes various notions of risk.

- Is the client concerned with the standard deviation of asset returns, i.e. the uncertainty over what the future returns will be?
- What is the client's attitude toward losses?
- Is the client concerned with the ambiguity of assets returns, i.e. the difficulty in quantifying future returns?

Before starting an assessment of the client's risk preferences, the risk profiler asks questions about the client's type (retail, private or affluent) and his risk ability. The latter is particularly important, because it represents a constraint that should not be violated in any case.

Question 1: Investment amount and liabilities

a) How much do you intend to invest ....., 000 USD
b) Of this amount, how much do you require for future expense (e.g. children's education, retirement, business needs, lifestyle, and unexpected family events)? ....., 000 USD

The answer to part b) can be used to restrict the investment amount so that the client is sure to retain at least this amount.

---

[18] For simplicity, we have not used normalized prospect theory (NPT) but prospect theory (PT) here (see Chapter 2 for a description of both theories).

The second question is related to the client's *experience*.

Question 2: Investment experience

How many years have you been investing in the following asset classes?

- money markets
- global bonds
- global equities
- hedge funds
- global real estates
- commodities

The answer to this question is usually interpreted in the following way: a more experienced investor can hold more risky assets than an inexperienced investor since inexperienced investors tend to overestimate their risk tolerance. This point is used in the last question assessing the client's risk preferences.

One possible justification for this advice lies in the *ambiguity aversion* as shown by the Ellsberg paradox. Inexperienced investors see a lot of ambiguity in risky investments while experienced investors have more precise beliefs about the return distributions. To give an example, which is even simpler than the one Ellsberg used, suppose you have the choice between lotteries, one with a 50 % chance of winning while on the alternative lottery you win the same amount if one of two states with unknown probabilities occurs. Imagine for example the states are determined by drawing a ball from an urn with two types of balls in an unknown proportion. Most people are ambiguity averse and would thus prefer the lottery with known probabilities. Experience would then mean that someone had the chance to play the ambiguous lottery very often so that he can quite well estimate the relative proportion of the two types of balls.

The next question evaluates the *investment options* for the client. The question allows the client to define the investment universe he specifically wishes to exclude, or insists on including from his portfolio.

Question 3: Investment options

All of the selected asset classes will be considered for your portfolio. Please indicate if you have a strong feeling that you do not want to hold more than a certain maximum investment in a particular asset class (in %)

- hedge funds (e.g. CS/Tremont Hedge Funds Index)
- commodities (e.g. SPGSCI Total Return)
- money markets (e.g. BBA 3 Month Dollar Deposit)
- global bonds (e.g. JPM Global Bond Index)
- global equities (e.g. MSCI World Index)
- global real estates (e.g. EPRA/NAREIT Global Index)

122   Behavioural Finance for Private Banking

Thereafter, the *investment horizon* is evaluated.

Question 4: Time horizon

Over how many years do you wish to invest?

- 1 year
- 2 years
- 3 years
- 4 years
- 5 years
- 6 years
- 7 years
- 8 years
- 9 years
- 10 years
- more than 10 years

This question is important because the risk-return characteristics of risky assets (and thus the optimal portfolio) change with the investment horizon. This is closely linked to the effect known as *time diversification*, according to which the risk-return ratio improves with the length of time the investor plans to stay with it.

To illustrate the time diversification effect, we use monthly price data of the S&P 500 index for the time period from January 1871 until January 2007 and build 15 portfolios with a time horizon of 1, 2, ..., and 15 years.[19] This gives a total of 1453 returns for each portfolio. The mean and the variance of their log-returns are illustrated in Figure 4.8 together with the mean and variance of portfolio returns under a random walk.[20]

If the returns follow a random walk, then the mean and the variance of the portfolios increase proportionally with the time horizon. In this case, the optimal asset allocations of investors should not depend on the planning horizon. This is because, under a random walk, the investment problem of a long-term investor is simply a scaled-up short-term problem. We show this in more detail in Chapter 6. In reality, however, the variance of the S&P 500 does not increase as rapidly with the length of the investment horizon as the mean of the investment returns (see Figure 4.8). Hence, the optimal asset allocations of investors with different time horizons should not be the same.

It is also important to know the client's time horizon in order to prevent the client from falling into the trap of *myopic loss aversion*. A key point in prospect theory is that investors react to losses more strongly than to gains. Thus, the more often losses are experienced, the more risk averse the client is. The frequency of experiencing losses depends on the length of

---

[19] We get the price data from Robert Shiller's home page: www.econ.yale.edu/~shiller/.
[20] The portfolios with the shorter investment horizon are on the left side, the portfolios with the higher investment horizon are on the right side of the figure.

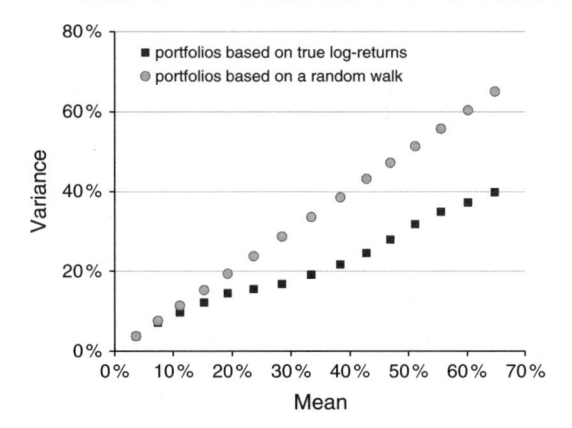

Figure 4.8 Time diversification: The longer the investment horizon, the better the return-risk ratio

the evaluation period. By focusing on short periods, myopic investors are exposed to a higher risk of experiencing a loss. The next example illustrates the point.[21]

Example 4.1:

Consider an asset that offers either a 20 % gain or a 10 % loss with equal probabilities. Thus, if one invests 1000 in this asset, the return will be either 1200 or 900 after 1 period. Thus, if an investor holds the asset for 1 period, the probability of a loss is 50 %.

In contrast, an investor with a time horizon of 2 years can get either 1440 or 1080 or 810. Thus, the probability of a loss in this case is 25 %, half as large as the probability for a loss that an investor with a time horizon of 1 year needs to face.

In the example above, the probability of a loss decreases with the length of the evaluation period. The effect can be also seen in real data. Consider, for example, the annual returns of Fama/French stock portfolios and the returns of Treasury Bills for the period between 1925 and 2005. We build 10 portfolios with an investment horizon of 1, 2, 3, ..., and 10 years respectively. Each of these portfolios contains either stocks or Treasury Bills. Then we compare the returns of the stocks and Treasury Bills portfolios with different time horizons. Figure 4.9 shows the probability that the return of each portfolio with Treasury Bills is greater than the return of the corresponding portfolio containing stocks.

We see that the probability of Treasury Bills being more attractive than stocks decreases with the time horizon. Hence, loss averse investors with a short investment horizon who decide between stocks and bonds will shun equities and forgive the equity premium. To examine this effect, we consider an investor with medium loss aversion and risk tolerance. Under the assumption that this investor desires to hold only bonds, equities and cash, we calculate his optimal asset allocation for different time horizons. The results summarized in Figure 4.10 show that the investor's exposure to stocks increases with the time horizon while his bond holdings decreases.

---

[21] See also Example 3.15.

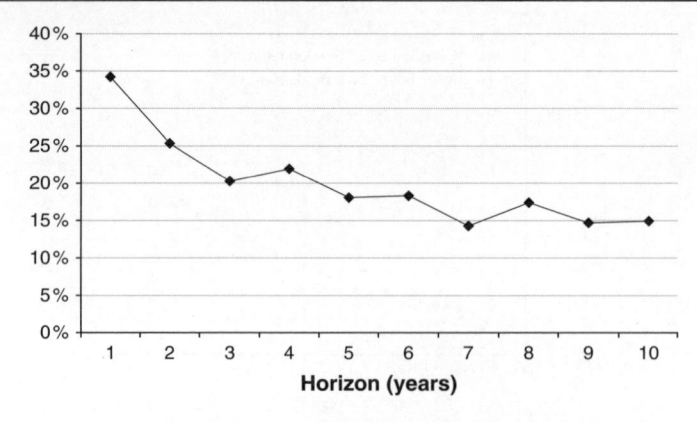

Figure 4.9 Probability for bonds beating stocks for portfolios with different time horizons

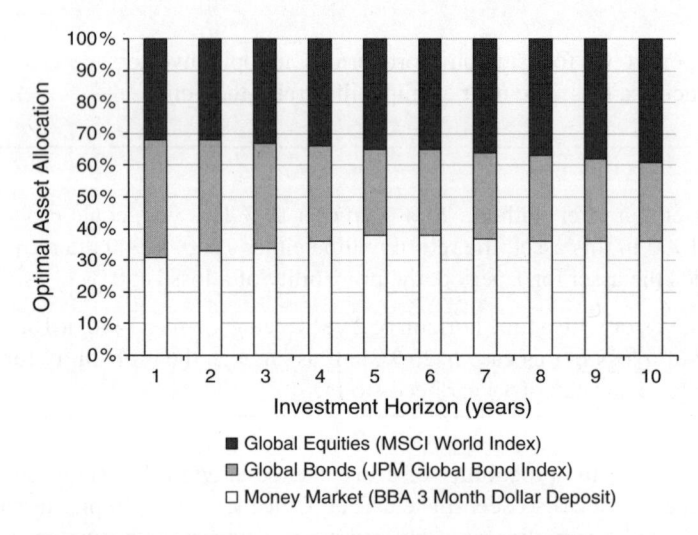

Figure 4.10 Optimal asset allocation over different time horizons

The next question evaluates the client's *expectations*. This question is necessary because the client will most likely judge the result of the investment by the expectations he had at the outset: They define his reference points. Moreover, the client's expectations represent useful anchors for his risk-taking behaviour.

Question 5: Expectations

Which return p.a. does the client expect under normal conditions? (aspiration level, AL%)

Below which return p.a. would the client view the investment as a loss? (reference point, RP%)

Before we evaluate the client's risk preferences, it is necessary to take into account how the client makes decisions. Some clients may prefer to make a choice by comparing different alternatives (qualitative clients). Others may prefer to be more precise in their answers (quantitative clients). Depending on the client's classification, the following questions assessing client's risk preferences are designed in a different manner.

Question 6: Decision making style

How do you make your investment decisions?

- By considering various options to make a choice.
- By defining my portfolio's performance numerically.

If the client is of the qualitative type, the next question assessing client's loss aversion is expressed as follows.

Question 7a: Attitude to losses of qualitative clients

What is your investment goal?

- capital preservation
- regular income
- regular income with some capital growth
- capital growth
- above average growth

The investment goals listed above provide different trade-offs between the downside risk and upside potential. Note that the answer to this question is used to determine the client's loss aversion. It does not define objectives for his optimal asset allocation.

If the client is of the quantitative type, his loss aversion is assessed with the following question.

Question 7b: Attitude to losses of quantitative clients

Suppose your portfolio is giving you a return of AL% over one year in the best-case scenario. In the worst case scenario, would you be willing to accept a AL% loss?

(*Ask the question above, repeating it, reducing the percentage each time, until the percentage loss is acceptable to the client. Input the accepted percentage below.*)
____ %

The client is offered a portfolio that achieves the average return he expects under normal conditions (see Question 5). If gains and losses are equally felt, the client would be indifferent between a portfolio offering AL % on average and a portfolio with a loss of AL %. The question is repeated by lowering the loss of AL % until the client becomes indifferent or chooses to buy this portfolio. The lower the accepted loss, the higher the client's loss aversion is.

The next question aims to evaluate the client's attitude to *uncertainty* or his *risk aversion*. It is designed to assess how much risk the client is willing to accept in order to have the potential for higher returns. The question asks how much the client is willing to pay (how much potential return the client is willing to give up) in order to avoid taking a risk (holding a risky portfolio).

For qualitative clients, the question is specified as follows.

Question 8a: Attitude to uncertainty of qualitative clients

My investment return

- can be 1 % annually if the return is guaranteed;
- can vary between $-a$ % and b %;
- can vary between $-c$ % and d % annually.

These clients have the choice between three different investments, each with two equally likely outcomes. Moreover, the payoffs (a %, b %, c %, and d %) are defined depending on the client's expectations revealed in Question 5 and his loss aversion evaluated with Question 7. Moreover, the investment with lower (higher) investment returns is specified also to have a lower (higher) risk. The answer to this question is mapped on to a predefined level of risk aversion.

If the client is quantitative, his risk aversion can be calculated more precisely. In particular, it uses the reference point and the aspiration level of the client revealed in Question 5 to increase the perceived relevance of the question and to motivate the client to give the best answer.

Question 8b: Attitude to uncertainty of quantitative clients

You have the choice between a risky portfolio and a safe deposit. The risky portfolio gives either a return of AL+(AL-RP) % or a return of RP %.

Would you choose the safe deposit if its yearly return is 0.0 %?

(*Ask the question above, repeating it, raising the percentage returns until the client is happy with the safe deposit. Input the accepted percentage below.*)

_____ %

The lower the client's answer, the stronger is the curvature of his value function, the stronger is his risk aversion.

The final question aims to check the client's risk preferences in the case of extreme losses. It is motivated by the notion that the recommended asset allocation should be strategic, i.e. it should remain fixed despite the ups and downs of the market. One could assume that all clients look for investment returns that are above their reference point at the end of the investment horizon. However, there might be clients who are concerned with temporary losses even though the portfolio they hold is matched with their risk profile. Therefore, a client's tolerance to temporary losses needs to be considered in determining the optimal portfolio.

Question 9: Market dynamics

Assume that after 10 years of good performance, the value of your diversified portfolio declined by x % over the past year.[22] How would you react?

- I would immediately change to more conservative options.
- I would wait at least 3 months before changing to more conservative options.
- I would wait at least 1 year before changing to more conservative options.
- I would not change my portfolio.

Depending on the client's answer to this question, the client may be "upgraded" to a safer portfolio.

Having assessed the client's risk ability, his investment universe, his experience, and investment horizon as well as his risk and his loss aversion, one can then compute the optimal asset allocation based on prospect theory and the bank's view of the asset classes.[23]

4.7 CASE STUDY: COMPARING RISK PROFILES

4.7.1 Case description

Christine Kuhn, mentioned in Case Study 4.1, needs advice on how to invest her inherited wealth in the best way. The following extended information is available.

Christine Kuhn is 40 years old, married with no children and has no plans to start a family. Her family income is CHF 203 000, out of which she can save CHF 25 000 p.a. She is an IT specialist. Her pension fund is decided and well secured. Her investment horizon is at least seven years. She would like to achieve a return of about 5 % p.a. as she always did before. However, she will be disappointed if she loses money. Apart from her inheritance of CHF 150 000, her total financial assets are CHF 100 000. She owns property worth around CHF 1 000 000. She has no debt or other liabilities. In seven years, she needs her financial capital to buy a cottage for CHF 200 000. Five years ago, she invested CHF 10 000 in a stock market product called Ladder Pop. At the time she expected to get 10 % p.a. out of this investment and she was aware that with the same probability she could have lost up to 5 % in total over five years. If she did invest the full amount of her inheritance in a product giving her a 50 % chance to gain 10 % p.a. and gaining her usual 5 % in the other 50 % cases, she would consider this to be equivalent to a safe investment giving her 7.5 % p.a. for sure. She is confident she can tolerate temporary losses of −10 % for one year. Christine Kuhn likes all asset classes; however she does not really understand how hedge funds work and limits her exposure to them by 10 %.

---

[22] The suggested value of the loss depends on the client's loss aversion and his aspiration level.
[23] For further details visit the webpage: www.bhfs.ch

4.7.2 The advice of former Bank Leu

Using the information above we complete the questionnaire to estimate Christine's risk profile.

Question 1
Think about the largest investment in your portfolio that you have made in recent years:

*only one answer per question is possible

a) What return were you aiming to achieve with this investment?

	Points*
Less than 4%	☐ 10
4–6%	☒ 20
6–8%	☐ 30
8–10%	☐ 40
More than 10%	☐ 50

b) At the time, what did you estimate the maximum return to be?

	Points*
Less than 4%	☐ 10
4–6%	☐ 20
6–8%	☐ 30
8–10%	☒ 40
More than 10%	☐ 50

c) In your opinion at that time, what was the greatest loss that the investment could incur?

	Points*
0–6%	☒ 10
6–15%	☐ 20
15–25%	☐ 30
25–40%	☐ 40
More than 40%	☐ 50

10	Smallest number of points of all answers given
	Transfer value to the box on the evaluation sheet

Question 2
You would like to invest CHF 1,000,000. With this investment you have a 50% chance of either gaining CHF 1,000,000 within a year or ending up with less than CHF 1,000,000. How much of the CHF 1,000,000 would you need to be left with, in a worst case scenario, for you to continue to invest?

*only one answer per question is possible

	Points*			Points*
1,000,000	☐ 0	at least	750,000	☐ 30
at least 940,000	☐ 10	at least	600,000	☐ 40
at least 850,000	☒ 20	less than	600,000	☐ 50

20	Points total for answer to question 2
	Transfer value to the box on the evaluation sheet

Question 3
Possibly you may wish to be able to dispose of your invested assets* at a specific date in order to buy something, or there is a possibility you may need this sum again.
*By invested assets we mean the sum of securities and cash that you currently have invested with financial institutions.

°several answers per question possible

a) When do you plan to use or estimate that you will use your assets?

Definitely in…	Points°
Less than 3 years	☐ 40
3 years	☐ 30
4 years	☐ 20
5 years	☐ 10
6 years	☒ 5
8 years and over	☐ 0

Probably in…	Points°
Less than 3 years	☐ 40
3 years	☐ 30
4 years	☐ 20
5 years	☐ 10
6 years	☐ 5
8 years and over	☒ 0

b) Amount of the sum invested I will need is

	Factor
a quarter	☐ ¼
a half	☐ ½
three quarters	☐ ¾
the entire sum	☒ 1

5	Highest number of points of all answers given

5	Please multiply the points from question 3a) by the factor from question 3b)
	Transfer value to the box on the evaluation sheet

Risk Profiling   129

Question 4
In the course of a life unforeseen events occur. In such cases, money may be needed.

°several answers per question possible

a) In which of the following events would you need access to your financial engagements?

	Points°		Points°
Purchasing a house for an attractive price	☒ 10	Founding my own company	☐ 10
		If I was unable to work	☐ 10
Increase in mortgage interest rates	☐ 10	Serious illness	☐ 10
Marriage or divorce	☐ 10	Temporary loss of employment for about ½ year	☐ 10
In the event of my death, the heirs would need access to the sum	☐ 10	None of the above cases will occur	☐ 10
Children's education	☐ 10	I do not need the sum invested for any of the above reasons	☐ 10
Early retirement	☐ 10		

10	Sum of answers to question 4a)

b) Amount of the sum invested I will need is

	Factor
a quarter	☐ ¼
a half	☐ ½
three quarters	☐ ¾
the entire sum	☒ 1

10

Please multiply the points from question 4a) by the factor from question 4b)

Transfer value to the box on the evaluation sheet

Question 5
Problems can occur in everyday life where you need to have access to your invested assets.

°several answers per question possible

a) In which of the following events would you need access to your financial engagements?

	Points°
Car accident where the insurance does not pay and I have to buy a new car	☐ 50
I make an expensive purchase for the home – furniture for example	☐ 50
Temporary loss of employment for about 1 month	☐ 50
None of the above cases will occur	☒ 0
I do not need the sum invested for any of the above reasons	☒ 0

0	Sum of answers to question 4a)

b) Amount of the sum invested I will need is

	Factor
a quarter	☐ ¼
a half	☐ ½
three quarters	☐ ¾
the entire sum	☐ 1

0

Please multiply the points from question 5a) by the factor from question 5b)

Transfer value to the box on the evaluation sheet

Question 6
In order to integrate the invested assets in an overall financial plan, we need the following personal information.

a) Your age in years

	Points
Under 30	☐ 0
30–60	☒ 10
Over 60	☐ 0

b) Are you

	Points
Self-employed	☐ 0
A retiree	☐ 10
A blue-collar worker	☐ 0
A salaried employee	☒ 0
A manager	☐ 10

c) Number of children (young children or children in full-time education)

	Points
0	☒ 0
1–3	☐ –10
More than 3	☐ –20

130 Behavioural Finance for Private Banking

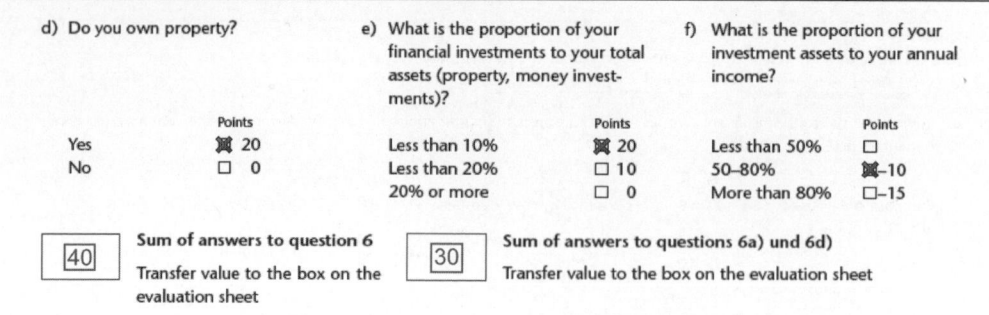

d) Do you own property?

	Points
Yes	☒ 20
No	☐ 0

e) What is the proportion of your financial investments to your total assets (property, money investments)?

	Points
Less than 10%	☒ 20
Less than 20%	☐ 10
20% or more	☐ 0

f) What is the proportion of your investment assets to your annual income?

	Points
Less than 50%	☐
50–80%	☒ –10
More than 80%	☐ –15

40 Sum of answers to question 6
Transfer value to the box on the evaluation sheet

30 Sum of answers to questions 6a) und 6d)
Transfer value to the box on the evaluation sheet

The answers are evaluated as follows.

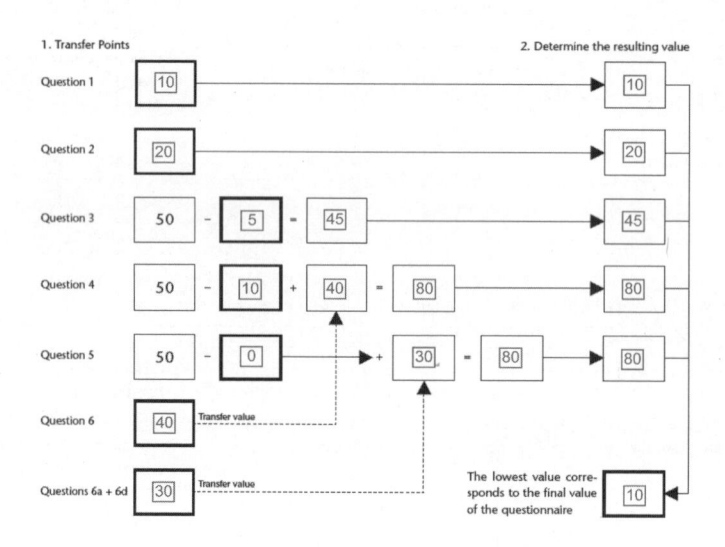

1. Transfer Points
2. Determine the resulting value

Question 1: 10 → 10
Question 2: 20 → 20
Question 3: 50 − 5 = 45 → 45
Question 4: 50 − 10 + 40 = 80 → 80
Question 5: 50 − 0 + 30 = 80 → 80
Question 6: 40 Transfer value
Questions 6a + 6d: 30 Transfer value

The lowest value corresponds to the final value of the questionnaire: 10

Hence, her optimal asset allocation is "25 % equity" (see Figure 4.11).

Points	Maximum 8	8 to 18	18 to 28	28 to 40	more than 40
	"100% Fixed Income"	"25% Equity"	"50% Equity"	"75% Equity"	"100% Equity"
Breakdown by asset class in %					
Cash CHF	5	5	5	5	5
Bonds CHF	60	48	29	12	
Bonds EUR	35	22	16	8	
Equities Switzerland		10	19	27	33
Equities Europe		7	15	23	28
Equities USA		6	11	17	22
Equities Japan		2	4	6	8
Equities Emerging Markets			1	2	4

Figure 4.11 Investment advice of the former Bank Leu

The result is driven by Christine's risk awareness (answer to Question 1). As she has invested in a stock market product called Ladder Pop, expecting to get 10 % p.a., she was aware that with the same probability she could have lost up to 5 % in over five years. This perception of low risk for losses leads to a more conservative strategy consisting of 25 % equities, 5 % cash, and 70 % bonds.

4.7.3 The advice of BhFS

Question 1: Investment amount and liabilities

a) How much do you intent to invest?
   150 000 USD
b) Of this amount how much do you require for future expense (e.g. children's education, retirement, business needs, lifestyle, unexpected family events)?
   0 USD

Question 2: Investment experience

How many years have you been investing in the following asset classes?

- money markets
- global bonds
- global equities   **5 years**
- hedge funds
- global real estates
- commodities

Question 3: Investment options

All of the selected asset classes will be considered for your portfolio. Please indicate if you have a strong feeling that you do not want to hold more than a certain maximum investment in a particular asset class (in %)

- hedge funds (e.g. CS/Tremont Hedge Funds Index) **10%**
- commodities (e.g. SPGSCI Total Return)
- money markets (e.g. BBA 3 Month Dollar Deposit)
- global bonds (e.g. JPM Global Bond Index)
- global equities (e.g. MSCI World Index)
- global real estates (e.g. EPRA/NAREIT Global Index)
- emerging markets (e.g. MSCI Emerging Markets)

Question 4: Time horizon

Over how many years do you wish to invest?

- ○ 1 year
- ○ 2 years
- ○ 3 years
- ○ 4 years
- ○ 5 years
- ○ 6 years
- ✓ 7 years
- ○ 8 years

> **(Continued)**
>
> - 9 years
> - 10 years
> - More than 10 years
>
> **Question 5: Expectations**
>
> Which return p.a. does the client expect under normal conditions? **AL = 5 %**
> Below which return p.a. would the client view the investment as a loss? **RP = 0 %**
>
> **Question 6: Decision making style**
>
> How do you make your investment decisions?
>
> - By considering various options to make a choice
> - ✓ By defining numerically my portfolio's performance
>
> **Question 7b: Attitude to losses of quantitative clients**
>
> Suppose your portfolio is giving you a return of 5 % over one year in the best-case scenario. In the worst-case scenario, would you be willing to accept a 5 % loss?
> **2.5 %**
>
> **Question 8b: Attitude to uncertainty of quantitative clients**
>
> You have the choice between a risky portfolio and a safe deposit. The risky portfolio gives either a return of 10 % or a return of 0 %.
> Would you choose the safe deposit if its yearly return is 0.0 %?
> **5 %**
>
> **Question 9: Market dynamics**
>
> Assume that after 10 years of good performance, the value of your diversified portfolio declined by 10 % over the past year. How would you react?
>
> - I would immediately change to more conservative options.
> - I would wait at least 3 months before changing to more conservative options.
> - ✓ I would wait at least 1 year before changing to more conservative options.
> - I would not change my portfolio.

The result of the profile's assessment is an optimal asset allocation over the asset classes commodities (SPGSCI Total Return), hedge funds (HFRI Fund of Hedge Funds Conservative), money market (BBA 3 Month Dollar Deposit), global bonds (JPM Global Bond Index), emerging markets (MSCI Emerging Markets), global equities (MSCI World Index), global real estate (EPRA/NAREIT Global Index), and private equity (LPX 50 TR Index). The optimal asset allocation is illustrated in Figure 4.12.

Based on the provided answers and using five predefined risk profiles, the client can be classified as conservative (see Figure 4.13).

Finally, we compare the asset allocation recommended by BhFS and the former Bank Leu (see Table 4.2).

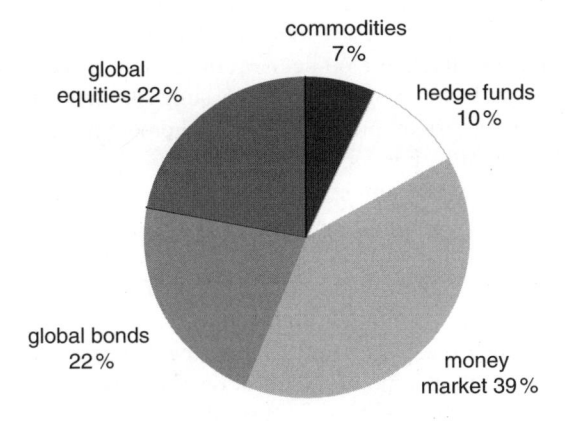

Figure 4.12 Optimal asset allocation of Christine Kuhn according to BhFS

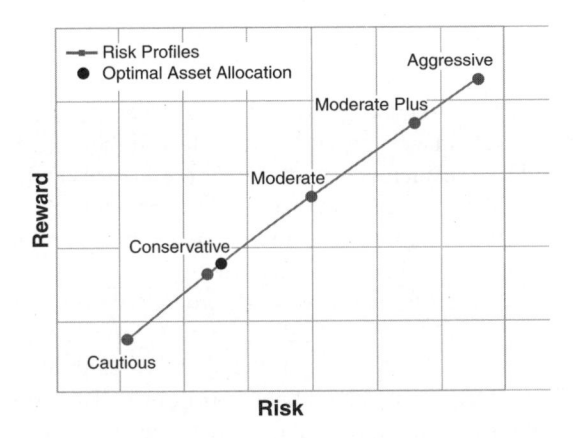

Figure 4.13 Client's classification based on predefined risk profiles

Table 4.2 Summary investment advice of BhFS and the former Bank Leu

	BhFS (conservative)	Former Bank Leu (conservative to moderate)
Commodities	7.00 %	0.00 %
Hedge funds	10.00 %	0.00 %
Money market	39.00 %	5.00 %
Global bonds	22.00 %	70.00 %
Emerging markets	0.00 %	0.00 %
Global equities	22.00 %	25.00 %
Global real estates	0.00 %	0.00 %
Private equity	0.00 %	0.00 %

The two pieces of investment advice are more similar than in the *Stocks* article. However, they still exhibit significant differences. While the former Bank Leu considers only three asset classes (bonds, equities, and money market), BhFS suggests investing also in hedge funds and commodities. Global real estate, private equity, and emerging markets are considered as sub-optimal for the client by all advisors.

The main differences in the recommendations appear in the weight of equities and bonds. While BhFS recommends underweighting equities and holding more hedge funds, the former Bank Leu focuses exclusively on traditional asset classes. Its asset allocation is composed of an allocation to fixed income-like investments, and an allocation to investments with equity-like risks. Hedge funds, commodities, and real estate are looked at as substitutes for either bonds or equities, depending on their risk parameters, and are therefore not recommended separately. For the former Bank Leu, the outcome of the questionnaire never resulted in a detailed asset allocation, but rather indicated the client's preferred allocation to equity and equity-like assets. The detailed determination of the final allocation always involved personal judgment by the relationship manager and depended on the bank's current market outlook.

4.8 CONCLUSION

Assessing clients' preferences and restrictions in a risk profiler is essential for providing customized advice. Behavioural finance provides valuable insights into which aspects of the clients' behaviour should be considered as part of their preferences and which aspects should be corrected during the wealth management process. It is the advisor's duty to make this distinction and consider the preferences of behavioural clients in an appropriate way in order to derive an asset allocation that fits with the clients' needs.

There are many ways to structure and use a risk profiler. Within the mean-variance analysis, the risk profiler should ask how strong the client's aversion against fluctuations in the returns is. This information can be used to split the client's wealth between a risk-free asset and a diversified mix of risky assets (the tangent portfolio). If there is no risk-free asset, the optimal asset allocation is determined by the client's aversion against returns above or below their average and some constraints such as the client's risk ability. The optimal asset allocation is then a portfolio on the efficient frontier, which may be one of a few master portfolios.

From behavioural finance' point of view, clients' risk preferences are not completely described by the concept of risk aversion. Additional features such as the client's loss and ambiguity aversion should also be considered in a risk profiler. Furthermore, one should be aware that there are also other factors (e.g. experience) that may influence the client's perception of his own preferences. Hence, if the risk preferences of the client are not double-checked, the recommended asset allocation may become sub-optimal with the ups and downs of the market. Implementing these ideas in the risk profiler allows one to derive a customized asset allocation that is consistent with the client's notion of risk and responds optimally to biases in the client's perception of risk.

5
Product Design

One important service banks offer to their clients is the development of investment products that best suit the clients' preferences. This service is profitable to the bank because it sells its expertise and superior access to financial markets to its clients. That is to say, clients buy structured products to get access to risk-return trade-offs that are not directly available on the market. As the hedging costs of private clients are usually higher than the hedging costs of a bank (e.g. because the bank can use economies of scale) and clients may lack the expertise to structure financial products, the bank is able to make a profit.

Indicators for the attractiveness of structured products are, for example, the assets under management compared to other asset classes and the number of listed products. In Switzerland, more than 340 billion Swiss francs are invested in structured products as of November 2007. This corresponds to 6.5 % of all assets under management invested in traditional asset classes (e.g. equities and funds). In 2007, there were more than 20 000 listed structured products on the Swiss stock exchange, 87 % more than in the previous year.

Crucial success factors for keeping the profits high are the costs of reconstruction and the benefits offered to potential buyers. The costs are typically calculated with the help of arbitrage-theoretical tools. The benefits are determined by the clients' possible utility gains from the financial product.

One straightforward way to capture a client's utility is to use expected utility theory and model the client's behaviour as perfectly rational. However, we have already seen that real-life human decision-making behaviour is not governed by the axioms of rationality (see Chapters 2 and 3). In particular, prospect theory provides a model to describe the behaviour of natural investors. Since *a priori*, it is not clear whether a typical client resembles more the expected utility or the behavioural type, developers of investment products need to know both views.

With respect to product development, at least the following three main differences between an expected utility maximizer and a prospect theory maximizer are important. While expected utility maximizers with a CRRA trade off losses against possible gains, behavioural investors are very sensitive to losses. Moreover, from their point of view, a loss is a shortfall behind a reference point that itself is a crucial aspect of their preferences. The second major difference is that rational investors focus on their returns independent of the market returns or the bank's profit, while a behavioural investor has a clear sense of fairness from which he derives a sense of how returns on a certain investment should be divided between him and the bank. Finally, a rational investor either likes to take or to avoid risk while the risk taking of a behavioural investor depends on whether payoffs below his reference point are possible and on how he weights probabilities.

These differences have important implications for product development. While a rational investor typically is interested in market exposure at minimal costs which, for example, could be achieved by buying exchange traded funds (ETFs), a behavioural investor is willing to pay for structured products that protect him from falling short behind his reference point, give a fair participation on the upside potential, and may, moreover, involve some gambling for a very attractive return even when the probability of success is extremely low. Concerning the willingness to pay, from a behavioural point of view, it is always better to pay indirectly in terms of opportunity costs than paying out of pocket. Figure 5.1 shows the payoff diagram with these three components that best suits a behavioural investor.

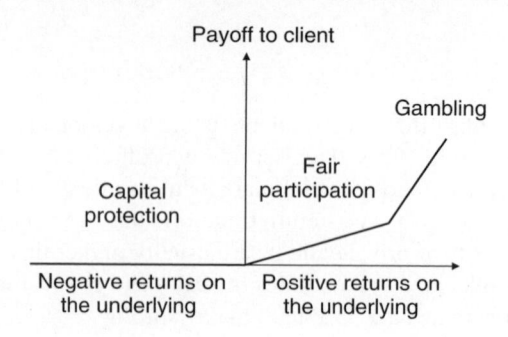

Figure 5.1 Optimal payoff from the perspective of behavioural investors

The first component is capital protection. Behavioural clients dislike returns that are below their reference point. Hence, structured products offering non-negative returns, when the value of the underlying is below its initial level, are perceived as more attractive than investments in the underlying. The higher the loss aversion of the clients, the stronger is their willingness to pay something for this capital protection. Because of the diminishing utility of higher wealth, the best way to ask the clients paying for capital protection is to suggest that they abandon some upside potential of the underlying while keeping their participation fair. This fairness in the upside participation is the second component of an attractive payoff from the perspective of behavioural clients. The last component is gambling. It gives the clients the chance to achieve very attractive returns while probability for these returns is very low. As behavioural investors tend to overestimate small probabilities, a structured product with a gambling component is likely to be perceived as more attractive as an investment in the underlying asset.

In the following two case studies, we compare the attractiveness of different structured products for expected utility maximizers and for behavioural investors. Afterwards, we analyze the problem of product design from a more general perspective while focusing on behavioural clients.

5.1 CASE STUDY: "LADDER POP"

The basic idea of investment houses offering structured products for their clients is to provide payoffs reflecting clients' needs in situations associated with different risks for the clients. Capital protected products, for example, are based on the notion that investors dislike losses. These products are designed in a way that allows participation only in the upward movements of the underlying asset.

To evaluate such products, we could use at least two approaches, one based on the theory of rational choice and another based on behavioural considerations. The differences in the results are discussed in the following case study, which highlights the importance of capital protection. Gambling due to probability weighting and the optimal participation rates will not be considered, since these aspects are not dealt with in the real life product we have chosen for this case study.

Consider the investment product called "Ladder Pop".[1] The product was constructed to follow the SMI over almost 4.9 years (issue date: 22 January 2002, expiration date: 12 December 2006). The floor was set at 80 %. That is, at maturity, investors got at least 80 % of their money back. Additionally, investors participated in the upward movements of the SMI.

To be more precise, we study the payoff of the Ladder Pop in detail. According to the product's fact sheet, the return of the Ladder Pop depends on two factors:

- the maximal underlying value achieved over the 4.9 years period and
- the underlying value at the end of the period.

Let (the first return factor) a be the return of the underlying achieved when the underlying breaks the next level (of 10 %). For example, if the SMI return is 10 %, then the investor gets 5 %, half of it. If the SMI breaks the next level and achieves 20 %, then the investor gets 10 %.

Thus, $a = N \cdot 5\%$, where N is the number of levels achieved by the underlying. The underlying reaches the next level every time when it realizes an additional 10 % return. Hence, the factor a can be interpreted as half of the maximum underlying return over the whole period truncated to the lower decimal level (if the SMI maximum return is 45 %, then $N = 4$ and $a = 20\%$).

The second return factor of the Ladder Pop is the percentage increase of the underlying over the whole period, which we denote as b. This is equivalent to the buy-and-hold return of an investor holding only the underlying.

The nominal value of the Ladder Pop is then obtained by the following version of the formula found in the product fact sheet.[2]

$$5000 \cdot (0.8 + a + \max(0, b - a))$$

where 5000 is the nominal of the Ladder Pop at the beginning and the investor starts at a floor of 80 %. This is logically equivalent to

$$5000 \cdot (0.8 + \max(a, b)).$$

Hence, starting at 80 %, the investor obtains the higher of the two returns at maturity. Figure 5.2 summarizes the payoff of the Ladder Pop at maturity.

The dashed line represents the payoff of the Ladder Pop, given that the buy-and-hold return b of the index is higher than half of the maximum index return over the whole period (truncated to the lower decimal level). In this scenario, the Ladder Pop pays 20 % less than the return achieved by the index. However, if the index is very volatile, i.e. it reaches high levels before maturity but it falls down at the time of maturity, then half of the maximum index return achieved over the whole period may be larger than the buy-and-hold return. In this case, the Ladder Pop payoff is determined by the number of levels achieved over the holding period. For example, if the maximum index return over the whole period is 65 % (index value of 160 %), then $N = 6$ and $a = 30\%$ so that the payoff of the Ladder Pop return is 10 %, i.e. $100 \cdot (0.8 + 0.3) - 100$.

The product takes the maximum between a and b, and adds it to the floor of 80 %. Hence paying a *disagio* of 20 %, the investor gets the return of the SMI to maturity or if it is higher, the investor gets half the maximal increase during the next 4.9 years.

From today's perspective, investors who decided to buy the Ladder Pop on 22 January 2002 and then held it until maturity did not make a good decision. During the first year until spring 2003, the SMI lost up to 40 %, whereas the loss of Ladder Pop investors was limited

---

[1] The product was offered by Bank Wegelin&Co. Privatbankiers.
[2] The formula presented in the product fact sheet is $5000 \left(N \cdot 5\% + \max \left(0\%; \frac{S_{final} - S_{initial}}{S_{initial}} - N \cdot 5\% \right) \right)$ where S_{final} is the closing price of SMI at maturity and $S_{initial}$ is the index value at the issuance day.

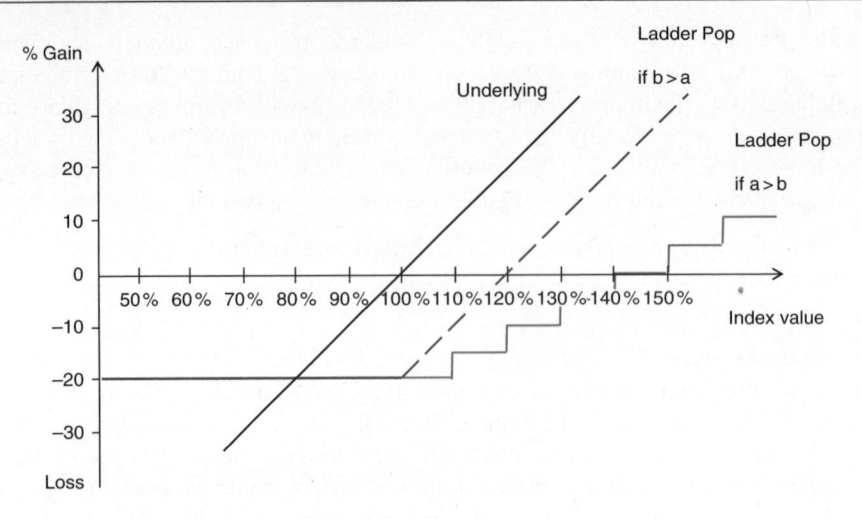

Figure 5.2 Payoff of the Ladder Pop at maturity

to 21 %. However, over the whole period of 4.9 years, the Ladder Pop investment was worse than a buy-and-hold strategy. The return of the latter was 38.2 %. In contrast, Ladder Pop investors paid 20 % disagio in the hope of getting half of the maximum return over these 4.9 years. Unfortunately, the SMI was not so volatile, so that the maximum index return up to maturity was lower than the buy-and-hold payoff. At maturity, Ladder Pop investors got the buy-and-hold return minus 20 % disagio, or 18.2 % (see Figure 5.3).

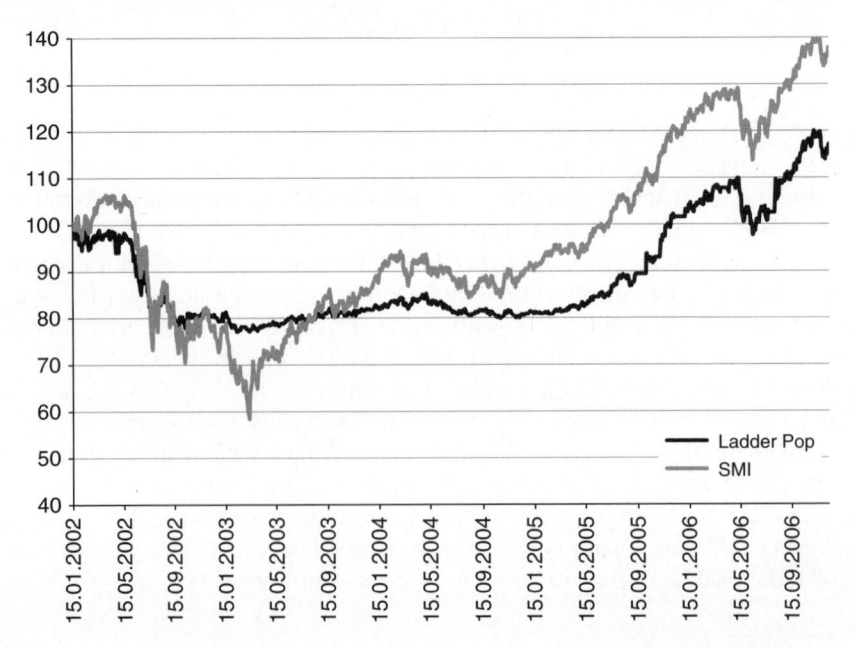

Figure 5.3 SMI and Ladder Pop prices (indexed) from 15.01.2002 to 12.12.2006 (*Source*: Bank Wegelin & Co.)

Even though the price of the product is set at 80% of the nominal, its price decreased below this level due to the time value of money. This is discussed in more details in Math Box 5.1.

Math Box 5.1: Dynamics of structured products:

When one buys a government bond, one is fairly sure that at maturity at least the money will be returned. And yet, before maturity, it may happen that the bond can only be sold at a loss. Why is this so? Consider the following example: one invests 10 000 in a bond for two years delivering an interest of 4 % p.a. Hence, without touching the bond, the account shows 10 400 after the first year and 10 810 after the second year. However, if one needs to sell the bond after the first year and if at that time interest rates have increased to, say 10 %, then there will be a loss of 167.27, which is a gain of 400, comprised of interest from the first year minus a capital loss of 567.27. Why? Because, seen from that point in time, one has two ways to continue: either you sell the bond and reinvest for 10 % or keep going with 4 %. Hence, (10 400 − 567.27) appreciating at 10% equals the alternative to hold the 10 400 in the form of the bond paying 4 % interest (see Figure 5.4). That is to say, the combination of marking to market and no-arbitrage leads to a negative time value before maturity.

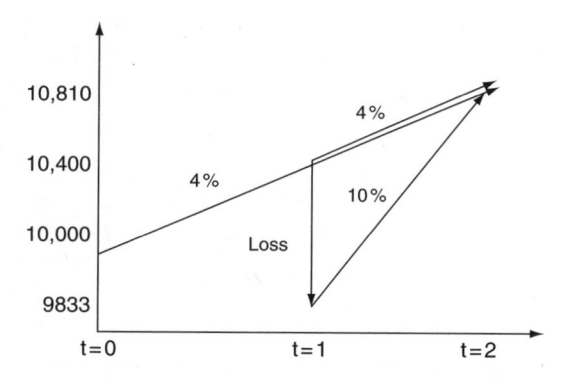

Figure 5.4 Two ways of achieving 8.1 % return after two years: Investing at 4 % each year or changing to 10 % after the first year

Structured products with capital protection like the Ladder Pop discussed above share this unfortunate feature with bonds. As we have seen, the value of the Ladder Pop at maturity cannot be below 80 %. The return it yields is given by $(0.8 + \max(a,b))$, where a is the ladder component and b is the buy-and-hold return. Since the term a is non-negative, the 80 % is secured. Yet, as Figure 5.1 has shown, the investors who wanted to sell the Ladder Pop could not have achieved at least the 80 % in the period of January to July 03.

Many individual investors do not really understand these dynamics of structured products; they feel cheated by the bank and then sell their structured products prematurely. If a bank is interested in keeping its clients for the long term, it should recognize that clients do not always understand negative time values. Brochures for structured products should thus include this important aspect.

Clearly, in advance, when the market is unpredictable so is the payoff of the Ladder Pop. However, evaluating different scenarios allows us to draw conclusions on at least two questions:

1. does the bank make a profit and
2. what type of investors would buy this product?

5.1.1 A simple setup

For simplicity,[3] consider two scenarios for the underling (SMI) and a bond as an alternative. These are summarized in Figure 5.5.

	t=0	t=1	t=2	t=3	t=4
SMI positive	100	110.0	150.0	175.0	170.0
SMI negative	100	105.0	120.0	90.0	85.0
Bond (risk-free)	100	102.4	104.9	107.4	110.0

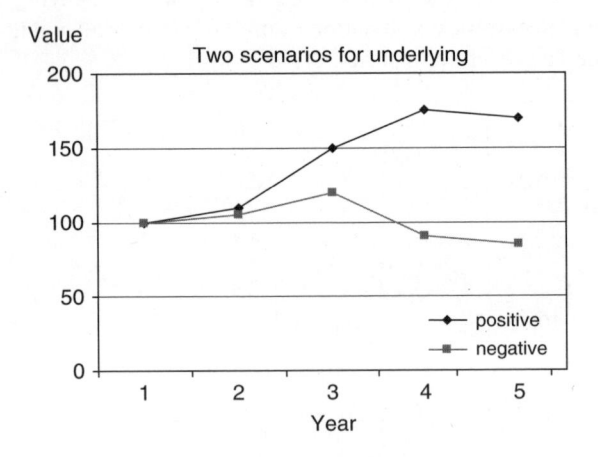

Figure 5.5 Scenarios setup

To determine whether the bank makes a profit by offering the Ladder Pop, we first determine the payoffs for the underlying, the Ladder Pop, and the bond (assuming 10 % interest) for the whole investment period of 4.9 years. According to our scenarios, the value of the underlying can either increase to 170 or fall to 85. Respectively, the return of the Ladder Pop can be either 70 % or −10 %, which gives the nominal 150 in the first scenario and 90 in the second scenario. More precisely, the payoffs of the underlying and the Ladder Pop with a nominal of 100 are:

SMI positive: max return ($t=3$): 75 %, $a=35\%$
return at the end: 70 %, $b=70\%$
Ladder Pop value: $100 \cdot (0.80 + 0.70) = \mathbf{150}$ or 50 %
SMI negative: max return ($t=2$): 20 %, $a=10\%$
return at the end: −15 %, $b=-15\%$
Ladder Pop value: $100 \cdot (0.80 + 0.10) = \mathbf{90}$ or −10 %

---

[3] See Yeniavci (2002) for an evaluation of the Ladder Pop based on the standard Black and Scholes model.

To answer the first question, whether the bank makes a profit, we assume that asset prices are determined so that arbitrage is excluded. Then, we get that the bank offering the Ladder Pop at 100 does not run a deficit as intuitively assumed. To see this, calculate a hedge portfolio as the combination of the underlying (S) and the bond (B) so that

$$170 \cdot S + 110 \cdot B = 150 \text{ and}$$
$$85 \cdot S + 110 \cdot B = 90.$$

Taking the difference of both equations gives $S = 0.706$. Inserting this result in the first equation, we get $B = 0.273$. The hedging costs of the bank are therefore equal to 97.86. Hence, the bank does run a deficit by selling the product for 100. The bank hedges the risk of the product and earns 2.14 ($100 - 97.86 = 2.14$) on each unit sold.

5.1.2 The product from an investor's perspective

Would an investor without hedging possibilities buy this product? To answer this question, we can apply the expected utility or the behavioural approach. In general, the optimal portfolio for a client is determined by two variables; the average client's income and his risk aversion.

Consider an investor with an initial wealth of 100. His utility is determined by the function $u(w) = \frac{w^\alpha}{\alpha}$, where w is his final wealth and α is a parameter indicating his risk aversion. Hence, this investor has a CRRA of $\alpha = -1$. He can choose between investing his wealth into the underlying, the Ladder Pop, or in a bond. Which product would he prefer?

To answer this question, we compare the expected utility of the client if he would invest his wealth into each of these products. The value of the products at maturity is depicted in Table 5.1.

Table 5.1 Final wealth with the underlying, the Ladder Pop, and a bond

Initial Wealth: 100	Value Underlying	Value Ladder Pop	Value Bond
Up State	170	150	110
Down State	85	90	110

Assuming that the probability for the up state is 0.35, the investor with a CRRA has an expected utility of $E_u = 0.35 \left(\frac{w_u^\alpha}{\alpha} \right) + 0.65 \left(\frac{w_d^\alpha}{\alpha} \right)$, where w_u is the investor's final wealth in the up state and w_d is the investor's final wealth in the down state. The certainty equivalent of the investor is then $CE = (\alpha E_u)^{1/\alpha}$.

Using the values from Table 5.1, we find that an investor with a CRRA would choose either the underlying or the bond (in dependence on his risk aversion), but not the Ladder Pop (see Table 5.2).

How would behavioural clients choose? To answer this question, we use the normalized prospect theory (NPT) to calculate the expected utility of a behavioural client E_{NPT} investing in one of the products. Recall, that NPT is defined as

$$NPT_v = \frac{w(p)}{w(p) + w(1-p)} v(\Delta x) + \frac{w(1-p)}{w(p) + w(1-p)} v(\Delta x),$$

Table 5.2 Expected utility and certainty equivalents of a CRRA investor

Expected utility/Certainty equivalent	Underlying	Ladder Pop	Bond
Most realistic case with $\alpha = -1$	−0.00971	−0.00956	−0.00909
	103.030	104.651	110.000
Bernoulli utility with $\alpha = 0$	4.68525	4.67860	4.70048
	108.338	107.619	110.000
Cramer utility with $\alpha = 0.5$	21.11229	20.90610	20.97618
	111.432	109.266	110.000

where $v(\Delta x)$ is specified as the quadratic value function as described in Chapter 2. The certainty equivalent of the behavioural investor is the solution of the equation $v(CE) = E_{NPT}$ or

$$CE = \frac{1 - \sqrt{1 - 2\alpha^+ E_{NPT}}}{\alpha^+} + 100.$$

The parameters of the median investor from the experiments of Kahneman and Tversky transferred to the quadratic value function yields[4]:

- risk aversion over gains $\alpha^+ = 0.21512$;
- risk aversion over losses $\alpha^- = -0.18469$;
- loss aversion $\beta = 2.25$;
- probability weighting over gains $\gamma^+ = 0.63154$; and
- probability weighting over losses $\gamma^- = 0.73620$.

Using these parameters and the returns of the products (see Table 5.3), we get the prospect utilities (respectively certainty equivalents) as summarized in Table 5.4.[5]

Table 5.3 Product returns

	Return underlying	Return Ladder Pop	Return bond
Up state	70 %	50 %	10 %
Down state	−15 %	−10 %	10 %

Table 5.4 Prospect utility and certainty equivalents of a behavioural investor

	Underlying	Ladder Pop	Bond
Prospect utility	0.0379	0.0404	0.0989
Certainty equivalent	100.0381	100.0405	100.1000

---

[4] The parameters β and γ can directly be taken from Kahneman and Tversky's piecewise power function. However, the parameter α needs some care; take an elementary lottery as described in the risk rulers of the previous chapter, answer it for the median PT-investor with piecewise power value function, and then interpret the answer using the piecewise quadratic value function.

[5] Assume that the investors' reference point is 0 %.

Thus, behavioural investors would choose the risk-free asset since it is associated with the highest utility. The same conclusion also holds for other value functions like the piecewise power value function of Kahneman and Tversky.

5.1.3 Portfolio considerations

At first glance, the results above seem to be a contradiction to our previous intuitive judgment that the structured product is attractive for loss-averse investors. The normalized prospect theory utility of investing in the riskless asset is higher than the utility from investing in the structured product and the investor is ready to pay. This apparent contradiction is due to the fact that we compared the utility of the product with the utility of investing in the bond but not with the utility of investing in the underlying. In fact, these two assets do not seem to belong to the same mental account. The reason is that people usually build portfolios dividing the assets into classes such as, for example, "riskless" and "upside potential". Following this idea, we could assume that structured products such as the Ladder Pop better suits investors' needs in the "upside potential" class where the underlying also belongs. Thus, we are allowed to separate the riskless bond from the other assets and compare the attractiveness of the Ladder Pop relative to the underlying. In this case, investors would prefer the structured product to the underlying (see Table 5.4).

Note also that unless there are high transaction costs, this preference cannot be explained; nobody would pay 100 to the bank if the replication costs are only 98 as in the case above, because the replication portfolio is a simple long-only portfolio.

5.1.4 Scientific assessment of the Ladder Pop

The bank makes a profit of 2.14 for each unit of the Ladder Pop it sells, since the hedging costs (97.86) are below the price of the Ladder Pop (100). But is the Ladder Pop really the optimal structured product the bank could have designed?

The Ladder Pop mainly builds on loss aversion. This is certainly one of the most important aspects of prospect theory. Moreover, the participation rate of 50 % implemented in the Ladder Pop will certainly be judged as fair by most clients. The Ladder Pop does not, however, consider probability weighting, and thus could be extended by incorporating an attractive lottery component. Finally, the worst aspect of the Ladder Pop is the large implicit up front cost by setting the floor 20 % below par. We would imagine that even in 2002, when the Ladder Pop was issued, only a few market participants had the view that the SMI would appreciate significantly more than 40 % over the next 4.9 years.

5.2 CASE STUDY: "DAX SPARBUCH"

Consider the investment product called "DAX Sparbuch".[6] Its underlying is the German equity index (DAX). The DAX Sparbuch targets private investors who usually save money in certificates of deposit but still want to take part in the stock market game without, however, taking risks. For any month, the DAX Sparbuch offers a bonus p.a. that is equal to half the DAX appreciation of that month but a maximum of 5 %. That is to say, if the DAX appreciates

---

[6] The product was offered by the Postbank (Germany). A "Sparbuch" is a savings account.

by $x\%$ in a given month, then approximately $x/2\%$ p.m. or $x/24\%$ p.a. is the bonus for that month. The price paid for this opportunity is that only half of the rate given on certificates of deposit is guaranteed as the base interest rate in the DAX Sparbuch.

For example, the DAX Sparbuch bonus from November 2006 to November 2007 was as shown in Table 5.5.

Table 5.5 DAX return per month and DAX bonus for that month (Nov. 2006–Dec. 2007) (*Source*: Postbank)

Month	DAX on the day before the last day of each month	DAX return (in %)	DAX bonus (in %) p.a. for this month
Nov 2006	6.363,80	1.69	0.84
Dec 2006	6.573,96	3.30	1.65
Jan 2007	6.788,23	3.26	1.63
Feb 2007	6.819,65	0.46	0.23
March 2007	6.897,08	1.14	0.57
Apr 2007	7.378,12	6.97	3.49
May 2007	7.764,97	5.24	2.62
June 2007	7.921,36	2.01	1.01
July 2007	7.456,31	−5.87	0.00
Aug 2007	7.519,94	0.85	0.43
Sept 2007	7.853,79	4.44	2.22
Oct 2007	7.977,94	1.58	0.79
Nov 2007	7.765,19	−2.67	0.00
Dec 2007	7.869,19	1.34	0.67

The problem with this representation is that the DAX bonus is represented per annum while the basis for its calculation is the *monthly* DAX returns. The fair way of representation should be therefore as shown in Table 5.6.

Table 5.6 DAX return and DAX bonus per month (Nov. 2006–Dec. 2007)

Month	DAX return (in %)	DAX bonus (in %)
Nov 2006	1.69	0.07
Dec 2006	3.30	0.14
Jan 2007	3.26	0.14
Feb 2007	0.46	0.02
March 2007	1.14	0.05
Apr 2007	6.97	0.29
May 2007	5.24	0.22
June 2007	2.01	0.08
July 2007	−5.87	0.00
Aug 2007	0.85	0.04
Sept 2007	4.44	0.19
Oct 2007	1.58	0.07
Nov 2007	−2.67	0.00
Dec 2007	1.34	0.06

Product Design   145

The attractiveness of the product decreases further if one compares the return on the DAX Sparbuch with a buy-and-hold strategy with the DAX on an annual basis, and also with the 12-months interest rate in Germany (see Table 5.7).

Table 5.7 DAX return and DAX Sparbuch return on annual basis (*Source*: Postbank and Datastream)

Year	DAX return	DAX Sparbuch return	12 months money market interest
2001	−17.96 %	3.08 %	4.72 %
2002	−44.03 %	3.19 %	3.34 %
2003	27.70 %	3.71 %	2.73 %
2004	5.91 %	2.50 %	2.30 %
2005	26.02 %	2.96 %	2.32 %
2006	21.04 %	2.58 %	2.84 %
2007	20.75 %	3.10 %	4.01 %

5.2.1 A simple setup

For simplicity, consider two equally probable scenarios: a bull and a bear market. The risk-free rate of return is a %. Assume also that in the bull market, the DAX increases by u % and in the bear market it decreases by $\frac{1}{1+u}$ %. Thus, the monthly return of the DAX Sparbuch in a bull market is $0.5\left(a+\frac{u}{12}\right)$ %, respectively $0.5a$ % in a bear market (see Figure 5.6).

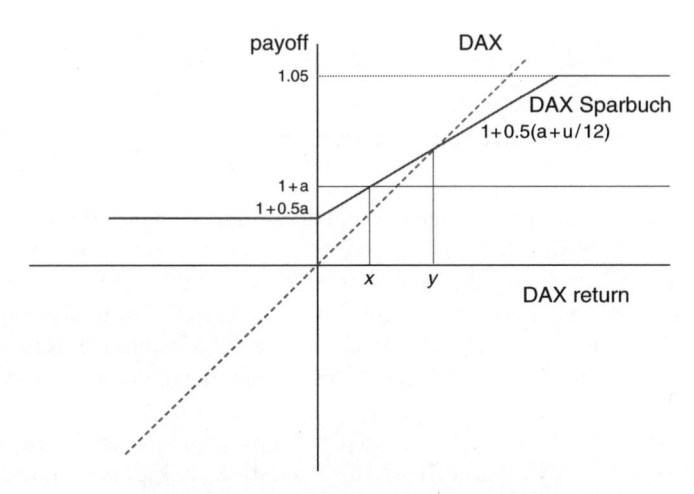

Figure 5.6 Payoff DAX Sparbuch per month

For further analysis we assume that the risk-free rate of return is 4 % p.a. or 0.333 % p.m. The first question we analyze is whether the DAX Sparbuch is profitable for the bank. In particular, we study for which degree of volatility of the DAX the product is offered at a price not below its fair value. To answer this question, we first construct a hedge portfolio consisting of a position with the risk-free asset (R) and a position with the DAX (D) that replicates the payoff of the DAX Sparbuch. Then we find the maximal monthly appreciation of the DAX for which the bank does not run a deficit by offering the product.

> **Math Box 5.2:** Appreciation of the underlying and the bank's profit
>
> Since we assume that there are two possible states, there are two conditions for the hedge portfolio that need to hold:
>
> (1) $R(1+a) + D(1+u) = 1 + 0.5\left(a + \dfrac{u}{12}\right)$ and
>
> (2) $R(1+a) + D\dfrac{1}{1+u} = 1 + 0.5a$.
>
> Thus, $D = \dfrac{1}{24}\dfrac{1+u}{2+u}$ and $R = \dfrac{1 + 0.5a - \dfrac{1}{24(2+u)}}{1+a}$. Hence, for $a = 0.33\%$ we get $R = 0.9983 - \dfrac{1}{24.08(2+u)}$ and the value of the hedge portfolio is $R + D = \dfrac{1}{24}\dfrac{1+u}{2+u} + 0.9983 - \dfrac{1}{24.08(2+u)}$, where u is the percentage of appreciation of the DAX per month.
>
> To find the value of u one needs to make sure that value of the hedge portfolio is not greater than 1 otherwise the bank makes a loss. This is $R + D \leq 1$, which holds if $u \leq 0.0796$.
>
> Hence, the monthly appreciation of the DAX should not exceed 7.96 %; otherwise the bank makes a loss in that month.

5.2.2 The product from an investor's perspective

Now we focus on the question of whether the DAX Sparbuch is attractive for an expected utility maximizer with CRRA and for behavioural investors. To answer this question, one must first look at the payoff of the structured product; its underlying and the risk-free asset (see Figure 5.6). The DAX Sparbuch is the best alternative only if the DAX returns remain within a certain range ($x\%$ and $y\%$ as shown in Figure 5.6). If the DAX returns are very low (smaller than $x\%$), the risk-free asset is more attractive than the DAX Sparbuch. Respectively, if the DAX returns are very high (above $y\%$), it is better to hold the underlying than the structured product.

On the other hand, the higher the expected monthly appreciation of the DAX (u), the more attractive is the DAX Sparbuch as the solid line in Figure 5.6 becomes steeper and the range ($x\%, y\%$) widens. This determines the attractiveness of the structured product relative to its underlying and the risk-free asset, which is analyzed in more detail below.

Consider first an investor maximizing the CRRA utility $u(w) = \dfrac{w^\alpha}{\alpha}$, where w is the investor's final wealth and α is his risk aversion. If the investor starts with EUR 40 000, $u = 7.96\%$ (the maximum appreciation of the DAX per month, for which the bank does not make a loss as calculated above) and $a = 0.333\%$ p.m., the final wealth of the investor holding one of the assets is as shown in Table 5.8.

Product Design

Table 5.8 Final wealth of a CRRA investor

	Probability	Risk-free asset	DAX	DAX Sparbuch
Up state	0.5	40 133	43 184	40 199
Down state	0.5	40 133	37 051	40 067

The expected utilities and certainty equivalents of clients with different CRRA associated with the investments are then as shown in Table 5.9.

Table 5.9 Expected utilities and certainty equivalents of CRRA investors

Expected utility/Certainty equivalent	Risk-free asset	DAX	DAX Sparbuch
Most realistic case with $\alpha = -1$	−0.0000249169	−0.0000250733	−0.0000249172
	40 133.33	39 883.01	40 132.88
Cramer utility with $\alpha = 0.5$	400.6661120	400.2932338	400.6642480
	40 133.33	40 058.67	40 132.96
Bernoulli utility with $\alpha = 0$	10.599962523	10.596634733	10.599952536
	40 133.33	40 000.00	40 132.93

Hence, the best product for a client with a CRRA is the risk-free asset.

At this point, one could ask what the minimum value of u is so that the DAX Sparbuch becomes attractive for a CRRA investor. In other words, we ask what the minimum appreciation in a month would be that would motivate CRRA investors to prefer the DAX Sparbuch to a risk-free investment. The answer to this question is the solution of the inequality

$$0.5 \frac{1}{\alpha} \left(1 + 0.5 \left(a + \frac{u}{12}\right) 40\,000\right)^{\alpha} + 0.5 \frac{1}{\alpha} ((1 + 0.5a)\, 40000)^{\alpha} > \frac{1}{\alpha} ((1 + a)\, 40\,000)^{\alpha}.$$

Table 5.10 Minimum appreciation of the underlying required by CRRA investors

	Minimum u
Most realistic case with $\alpha = -1$	8.0133 %
Cramer utility with $\alpha = 0.5$	8.0032 %
Bernoulli utility with $\alpha = 0$	8.0066 %

Thus, if the DAX is expected to appreciate by more than 8 % in a month, expected utility maximizers will prefer the DAX Sparbuch over the risk-free asset. However, if the bank shares the same expectations, it cannot offer the product without running a deficit.

Consider now the median behavioural investor of Kahneman and Tversky. As in the previous case study, we use the piecewise quadratic value function. In particular, the preferences of the median behavioural investor are described by the following parameters:

- risk aversion over gains $\alpha^+ = 2.1511$;
- risk aversion over losses $\alpha^- = -1.8469$;

- loss aversion $\beta = 2.25$;
- probability weighting over gains $\gamma^+ = 0.63154$; and
- probability weighting over losses $\gamma^- = 0.73620$.

Additionally, we assume that the investor can have two alternative reference points equal to 0 and the return of the risk-free asset. Assume also that $u = 7.96\%$.

If the reference point is zero, then the expected utility and certainty equivalents of the behavioural investor are calculated as in the previous case study (see Table 5.11).

Table 5.11 Prospect utility of behavioural investors with an absolute reference point

	Risk-free asset	DAX	DAX Sparbuch
Prospect utility	0.003321382	−0.0456432	−0.004330847
Certainty equivalent	40 000.0033	39 999.9564	40 000.0044

Thus, a behavioural investor would choose the DAX Sparbuch. This is true for all investors who are loss averse.

However, behavioural investors with the risk-free asset as a reference point decide differently. The best product for these investors is the risk-free asset (see Table 5.12).

Table 5.12 Prospect utility of behavioural investors with a relative reference point

	Risk-free asset	DAX	DAX Sparbuch
Prospect utility		0.0503352	0.00116134
Certainty equivalent	40 000.000	39 999.9521	39 999.9988

For these investors, the DAX Sparbuch is more attractive than the risk-free asset only if the underlying is sufficiently volatile. More precisely, the DAX Sparbuch is more attractive than the risk-free if the DAX is expected to appreciate in a month by more than 13.8%. However, if the bank shares the same expectations, it cannot offer the product without running a deficit. This is possible only if behavioural investors do not compare the returns of the structured product with the returns of the risk-free asset. In this case, the required minimum monthly appreciation of the DAX is 2.86% (increasing with the level of loss aversion) as shown in Table 5.13.

Table 5.13 Minimum appreciation of the underlying required by behavioural investors with an absolute reference point

	Minimum u
Behavioural investor with $\beta = 2.25$	2.8591%
Investor with $\beta = 1.5$	6.1504%

Thus, the bank is able to offer the structured product without running a deficit and behavioural investors with an absolute reference point will prefer to buy it instead of following a buy-and-hold strategy with the underlying or investing in the risk-free asset.

5.2.3 Portfolio considerations

If we consider the investor's attitude to separate investments in a "risk-free" account and an "upside potential" account, we may conclude that the behavioural investor prefers the DAX Sparbuch to its underlying in any case (see Tables 5.11 and 5.12). The reason is the investor's loss aversion. It drives the investor's preferences toward products with positive payoffs such as the DAX Sparbuch. In contrast, the typical expected utility maximizer with a CRRA prefers the DAX to both other assets (see Table 5.9) because he has a stronger focus on the returns of the investment than on the risk of falling below a certain benchmark.

5.3 OPTIMAL PRODUCT DESIGN

After having analyzed the advantages and disadvantages of different structured products in case studies, we study now the problem of designing products as the only way to invest in a more general setting. Overall, adding some structured products to clients' portfolios cannot be considered as a way to achieve an overall optimal portfolio since the correlation structure of the various products may be quite complex. It is preferable to design a client's whole portfolio rather than one structured product.

If the client has behavioural preferences, the starting point is the value function. If investors are loss averse and have diminishing utility from obtaining more money or making larger losses, then they will prefer to give up some portion of their gains in order to be protected from small to medium losses. In other words, behavioural investors are ready to accept a product with a limited participation if it eliminates as compensation the returns just below the reference point, while large negative returns need not to be excluded because the disutility of the investors does not increase significantly after losses have reached a certain level (see Figure 5.7). However,

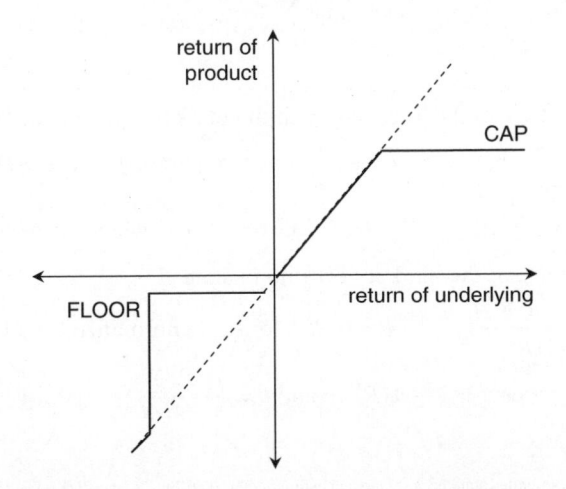

Figure 5.7 Payoff of a barrier-like structured product

the extremes receive more weight since investors with a biased perception of probabilities overestimate very unlikely events, so that only a numerical analysis can show which effect dominates.

Bonus certificates (a certain type of structured products) offer a similar payoff. They guarantee capital protection as long as the price of the underlying does not fall below a certain threshold, which is called a "barrier level". Once the price of the underlying falls below the threshold, the capital protection is gone and it does not recover later on when the price of the underlying increases above the barrier level.

In the following, we describe how to find a payoff function that is optimal for a behavioural client. The task is to maximize the utility of the client under the restriction that the price of the product is equal to the expenditures decided for the structured product. Hence, when one designs the payoff of the structured product in a state described by the payoff of the underlying, one needs to find a balance between the utility derived from that payoff and the price paid for that payoff. A more precise description of the design procedure is offered in Math Box 5.3.

Math Box 5.3: Designing optimal structured products

Let the return of the underlying be x. The return of the structured product as a function of the return of the underlying is then denoted by $y(x)$. In the case of $s = 1, \ldots, S$ states of the world, in each state the return of the structured product is y_s and the state probability is p_s; its decision weight $w(p_s)$.

The problem of designing optimal structured products is equivalent to finding an optimal function $y(x)$ that maximizes the utility of the client from holding the structured product under the restriction that the costs of the structured product equal the budget allocated to it. Formally, this is

$$\underset{y_s}{\text{Max}} \sum_{s=1}^{S} w(p_s) v(y_s)$$

$$\text{such that } \sum_{s=1}^{S} y_s \pi_s^* = B,$$

where the price of a payoff in a state s is denoted as π_s^*.[7] In the CAPM, for example, π_s^* is increasing with p_s and decreasing with the market portfolio x_s. More precisely, in that case we have $\dfrac{\pi_s^*}{p_s} = a - bx_s$, for some positive parameters $a, b > 0$ such that the no arbitrage conditions $\sum_{s=1}^{S} \pi_s^* x_s = R_f$, the CAPM formula (where R_f denotes the risk-free rate and R_s^M the return of the market portfolio in state s)

$$\sum_s p_s x_s - R_f = \frac{\text{cov}(x, R^M)}{\sigma^2(R^M)} \left(\sum_s p_s R_s^M - R_f \right) \text{ for some normalized stock prices } \sum_s \pi_s = 1$$

are satisfied. This gives $a = 1 + \mu(R^M)b$ and $b = \dfrac{\mu(R^M) - R_f}{\sigma^2(R^M)}$

---

[7] The probabilities π_s are the so-called state prices. One can estimate their distribution, the state price density, from option data. The probabilities p_s are the subjective beliefs of the returns for the underlying. One can estimate them from standard econometric models. See Detlefsen, Härdle and Moro (2007) for details.

Since the utility is increasing with y_s, we face the following trade-offs: suppose first that state probabilities are equally likely and that the utility is perfectly linear, i.e. $v(y_s) = y_s$. Then one would buy the total payoff of the structured product in that state with the lowest state price, i.e. in the state with the highest value of the underlying.

Supposing next a decreasing marginal utility of payoffs, one would also buy the structured products payoffs in other more expensive states since across all states, the ratio of the marginal utility from additional payoffs to the price of the payoffs needs to be equal. Moreover, supposing that the probabilities of the states might differ, one needs to shift relatively higher payoffs into those states with higher probability.

Finally, noting that the utility function might be s-shaped, as it is in prospect theory, one can no longer take the marginal utility as a criteria, since in the loss area the agent prefers to have his wealth concentrated in some states instead of being spread out among various loss states. Hence, we are left with numerical solutions as demonstrated by Hens and Rieger (2008).

Consider, for example, an investor with CRRA (e.g. an investor with the power utility function $v(x) = \frac{x^\alpha}{\alpha}$). The optimal structured product for this investor on a CAPM market is shown in Figure 5.8. The payoff of the structured product is strictly convex. For this investor, the optimal structured product exhibits a "smooth" capital protection and an increasing participation in gains.

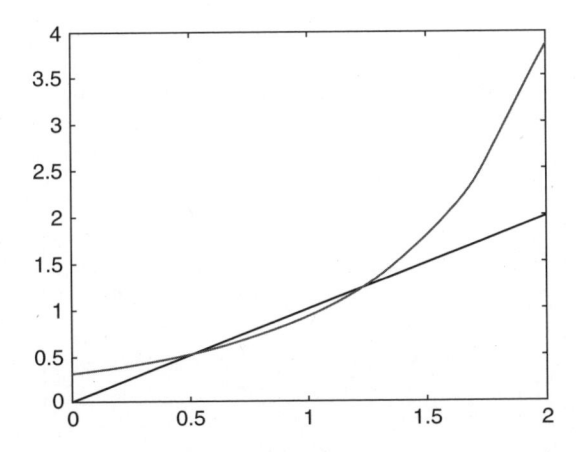

Figure 5.8 Optimal structured product of a CRRA investor with $\alpha = 0.8$ (*Source*: Hens and Rieger (2008))

Consider now an investor with a piecewise quadratic utility function. In the special case where this investor behaves as a mean-variance investor, i.e. (in the notation of our quadratic prospect theory model) e.g. with $\alpha^+ = \alpha^- = 0.1$, $\beta = 1$, and $\gamma = 1$, the optimal payoff of the structured product is linear with decreasing participation in the gains as well as the losses of the underlying (see Figure 5.9).

Math Box 5.3: (Continued)

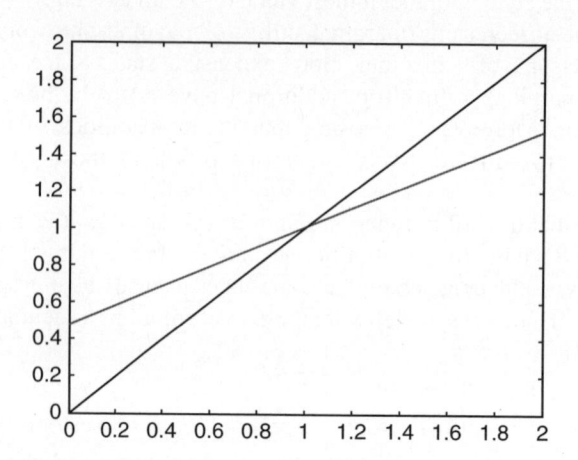

Figure 5.9 Optimal structured product for a mean-variance investor (*Source*: Hens and Rieger (2008))

In contrast, if this investor is behavioural and loss averse with $\beta = 2$, the structured product is optimal only if it protects the investor from losses of the underlying. The stronger the investor's loss aversion, the stronger the capital protection should be. As in the previous case, the optimal participation in gains of the underlying is decreasing (see Figure 5.10).

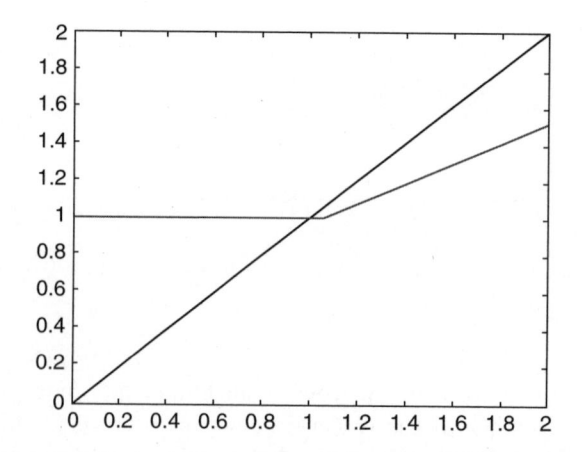

Figure 5.10 Optimal structured product for a behavioural investor with $\beta = 2$ (*Source*: Hens and Rieger (2008))

No capital protection is needed if the behavioural investor is risk averse but not loss averse, i.e. with $\alpha^+ = -\alpha^- = 0.1$, $\beta = 1$ and $\gamma = 1$. The optimal payoff of the structured product in this case is illustrated in Figure 5.11.

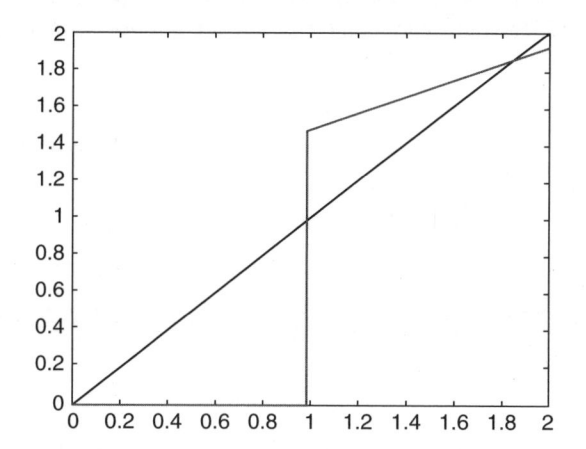

Figure 5.11 Optimal structured product for a behavioural investor with $\beta = 1$ (*Source*: Hens and Rieger (2008))

Consider now an investor with a probability weighting, e.g. with $\gamma = 0.5$. This investor overweights small probabilities and underweights high probabilities. From his perspective, the best-structured product is one with a strongly increasing payoff as the return of the underlying becomes greater or lower than the average (see Figure 5.12). As the probability of very likely payoffs is under-weighted, the investor is ready to accept a lower than average payoff of the underlying.

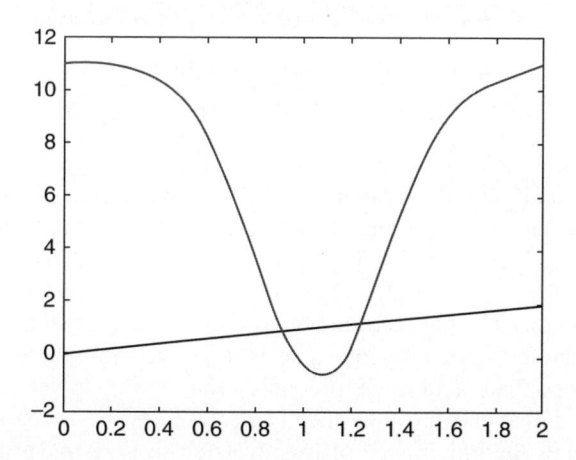

Figure 5.12 Optimal structured product of an investor with biased perception of probabilities (*Source*: Hens and Rieger (2008))

Some structured products are simple and beneficial to the typical client (which is most likely a behavioural one) and they are transparent and easy to understand. Most structured products are, however, complicated combinations of derivatives that the typical client only buys because he does not really understand the workings thereof. To improve the understanding of structured products, Marc Oliver Rieger and Thorsten Hens, in collaboration with the Swiss Design Institute for Finance and Banking, have designed a multi-touch-table that visualizes the construction of structured products.

After an introduction into the main aspects of structured products, there is a short questionnaire to check the understanding of the client. Then, at the heart of the device, one finds the payoff diagram which the client and the advisor can change interactively and discuss the pros and cons of capital protection or upside potential (see Figure 5.13).

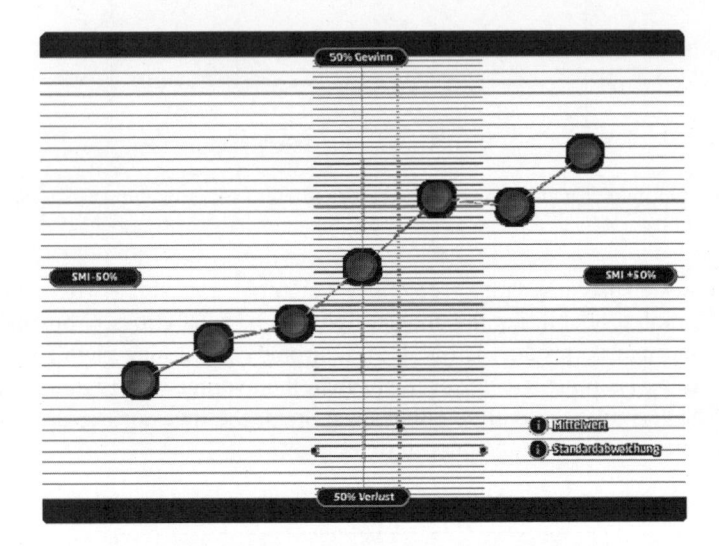

Figure 5.13 Interactive multi-touch table

The client will understand that there are trade-offs since whenever he raises the payoff for some returns of the underlying, the program readjusts the payoffs in all areas so that the same budget is spent for the structured product. Having an initial idea of the structured product the client likes most, one can then back-test its performance in relation to the underlying in various market scenarios.[8]

During a presentation at a public exhibition, visitors could try the device and design their personally structured product. More than 600 people took part. Afterwards we conducted a rough categorization of their products. The most popular types are shown in Table 5.14.[9] The fact that the most frequently designed types resembled capital protected products underlines the importance of loss aversion in investment decisions of private investors.

---

[8] An Internet based version of the multi-touch-table can be found at: http://www.sdfb.ch/projects/2008/sp_editor/.
[9] For an explanation of the product please visit: www.svsp-verband.ch.

Table 5.14 Structured products chosen by participants of a field study where structured products could be designed freely with a special editor

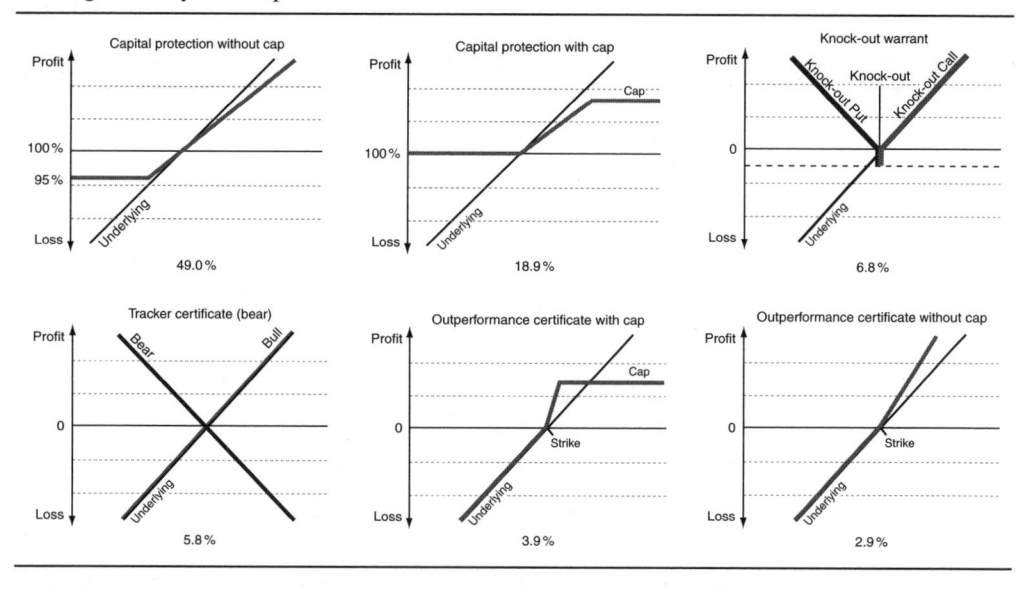

5.4 CONCLUSION

Product design is about structuring assets in a way that serves the needs of the client in the future or over the client's life cycle. The desired payoff can be achieved either with derivative instruments like structured products, or with traditional assets such as bonds and equities. The main advantage of structured products is that they can offer capital protection with a fair participation on the performance of the underlying. These criteria are particularly important for behavioural clients who are ready to give up some gain potential in order to prevent losses that they would need to realize with a direct investment in the underlying. At first glance, structured products with a capital protection appear attractive for clients with behavioural preferences. However, the average behavioural client would be better to buy and hold the underlying unless its returns are too volatile. In this case, the structured product is a better alternative.

If investors' preferences are known, the payoff of the structured product can be optimally designed. For investors with CRRA, the best product is one with a convex payoff structure. For the mean-variance investor, the optimal payoff increases linearly with the gains of the underlying. If, however, the investor is loss averse, the optimal structured product needs to offer some capital protection. The higher the investor's loss aversion, the higher is the capital protection needed.

6
Dynamic Asset Allocation

In the previous chapter, we learned how to find an asset allocation that is in line with the client's risk ability, risk preferences, investment horizon, and risk awareness. Now we determine how to change this asset allocation in the course of investment when financial markets go up and down. There are three prominent views on this question:

(1) Buy-and-hold, i.e. do nothing and let the portfolio run with the market.
(2) Rebalance, i.e. undo the market fluctuations and make sure that you always hold a portfolio in those proportions that you have decided to be optimal for you.
(3) Market timing, i.e. recalibrate your portfolio whenever new information arrives or when you get closer to or further away from your target.

The question of which of these three approaches is the best belongs to an old debate. The following ideas will help you to find your own standpoint on it.

In the simplest case, a multi-period decision can be seen as a sequence of independent two-period problems. We call the resulting mix of investment assets the "Tactical Asset Allocation" (TAA). The key question then is whether the client changes his TAA in the course of the ups and downs of the market. Of course if the wealth is eroding so far that the risk ability is eroded, the agent has to react and to reduce risk. In this chapter, we ask whether there are other reasons to react to the ups and downs of the market.

If the client anticipates that taking decisions at an early stage of the investment process affects the best decisions he will take later on, his optimal asset mix is called "Strategic Asset Allocation" (SAA). We will see in Section 6.2 how far the strategic asset allocation differs from the tactical asset allocation. The key question there is whether investing on a longer horizon leads to holding more risky assets, i.e. whether there is time diversification.

Throughout this chapter we will distinguish two types of investors: those who have no specific investment goals and care mainly for an appropriate growth of their wealth, and those who invest in order to achieve some targets. The former are best described as "expected utility maximizers" while the latter are "prospect utility maximizers".

In Section 6.1, we answer the question of what causes different clients to adjust their asset allocations to the market outcome. We shall see that, on a random walk, the expected utility investor with CRRA would follow a rebalancing strategy so that the share of risky assets remains the same over time. This is because, for an investor with a CRRA utility function, the asset allocation is independent of the investor's wealth and, on a random walk, returns are unpredictable, so that the investor cannot infer anything from the ups and downs of the market. This strategy is optimal for the expected utility maximizer but it is not necessarily the best for the behavioural prospect utility investor. Only if the behavioural investor updates his reference point every period will he effectively be solving a sequence of identical optimization problems and hence chooses a "fix-mix" strategy. If, however, he adjusts his reference point sluggishly[1] then he would adjust his asset allocation even if the current market realization does not provide any additional information for the future. The reason is that the behavioural client does not have a constant relative risk aversion, but he is loss averse and evaluates uncertain outcomes differently, depending on whether they result in gains or losses. For a fixed reference point, whether the investor will finally end up with a gain or a loss depends, however, on what has happened before. Moreover, if returns are predictable, then both clients would time the market depending on the probabilities of future realizations.

In Section 6.2, we answer the question whether one should hold more risky assets by planning strategically, i.e. whether one can profit from time diversification. We will see that, on a random walk, the long-term expected utility maximizer with CRRA does not profit from time diversification, i.e. he holds the same proportion of risky assets as in the short-term. In contrast, a behavioural investor, who determines his asset allocation in advance and keeps his reference point at its initial wealth, would invest almost all his wealth in risky assets if he plans for more than one period. On a mean reversion, both investors hold more risky assets if they plan strategically over the entire investment horizon rather than period by period. This is because, with mean reversion, the long-term risk increases less than proportionally to the long term return.

6.1 THE OPTIMAL TACTICAL ASSET ALLOCATION

Being aware of the psychological biases discussed in Chapter 3, advisors are able to correct them and develop an optimal asset allocation. To perform this task, advisors are required to know the client's preferences and, in particular, be able to isolate psychological effects distorting the client's perception. To understand the dynamics of asset allocation, we suggest the following simple model.

Assume that there are two assets and two states: a safe deposit paying 2 % interest rate in any state and a risky asset doubling the investment in the one state and losing 50 % in the other state. The probabilities of "good" (+) and "bad" (−) states going from one year to the next are summarized in a matrix, called the "Markov matrix" (see Figure 6.1 for examples). The matrix

t−1 \ t	+	−
+	b	1−b
−	c	1−c

t−1 \ t	+	−
+	1/3	2/3
−	2/3	1/3

Mean reversion

t−1 \ t	+	−
+	1/2	1/2
−	1/2	1/2

Random walk

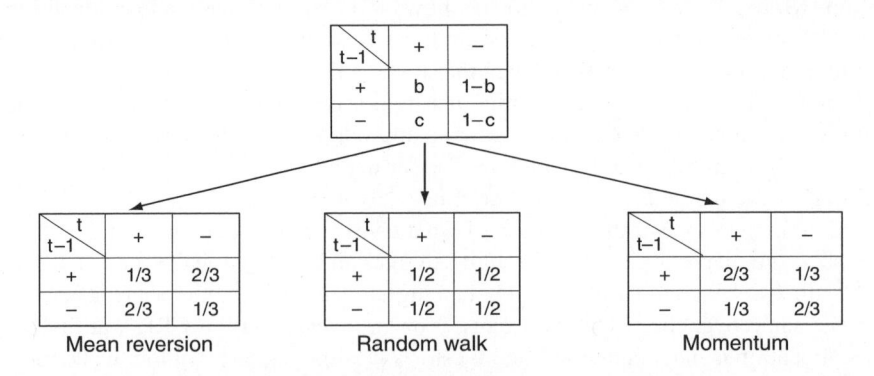

t−1 \ t	+	−
+	2/3	1/3
−	1/3	2/3

Momentum

Figure 6.1 Example of Markov matrices

---

[1] Based on the TV-show "Deal or No Deal", Post et al. (2008) have shown that this is the most realistic case.

has two rows (one for each condition: previously a "good" or previously a "bad" state) and two columns (one for each condition next year is a "good" or next year is a "bad" state), in which each row gives the respective transition probabilities. If $b<c$ ($b>c$) the matrix describes a mean-reverting (averting) process. For $b=c$ the process is a random walk.

Note that all three processes have the same limit distribution (1/2, 1/2). That is to say, following the trajectories of any of these processes leads one to observe "good" outcomes half of the time and "bad" outcomes half of the time.[2]

If the transition probabilities depend on the previous realization as, for example, in a mean-reversion (see Math Box 6.2) then we can distinguish between two cases. In the first (second) case, there is an upward (downward) movement in the first period, so that the probabilities after three years are:

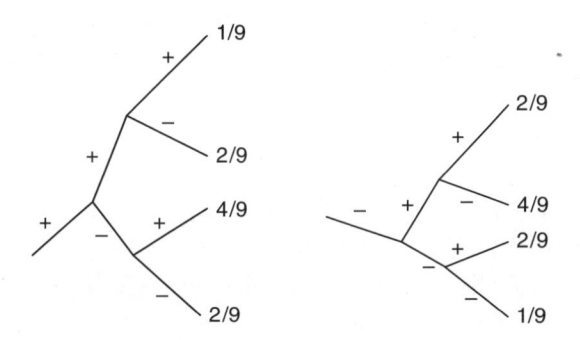

For example, if the process is mean-reverting, the probability of an upward movement in $t=1$, given that there was an upward movement in $t=0$, is 1/3 (see the Markov matrix). The probability of an upward movement in $t=2$ depends only on the state realized in $t=1$ since the process is Markov. Thus, the probability for two subsequent "good" realizations, given that there was a "good" realization, is equal to $1/3*1/3 = 1/9$. The probabilities of the other three states conditional on the realization in $t=0$ are calculated in a similar way.

In the following section, we construct the asset allocation of two model investors. One is called "CRRA investor", the other one is called "behavioural investor". Note that the difference between the investors is not the rationality of their decisions but their risk preferences. The CRRA investor is an expected utility investor with CRRA. His utility is given by

$$u(w) = \frac{1}{\alpha} w^\alpha$$

where w is the wealth and α is a parameter reflecting the investor's degree of risk aversion. His asset allocation is defined in $t=1$ for the whole investment period depending on the process driving asset returns.

---

[2] Let μ^t be the probability of being in a "good" state at period t. Then the product $(\mu^t, 1-\mu^t)$ times the Markov matrix $\begin{bmatrix} b & 1-b \\ c & 1-c \end{bmatrix}$ gives the next period probabilities for the two states, i.e. $(\mu^{t+1}, 1-\mu^{t+1})$. The limit distribution is then $[\mu^\infty, 1-\mu^\infty] \begin{bmatrix} b & 1-b \\ c & 1-c \end{bmatrix} = [\mu^\infty, 1-\mu^\infty]$. Note that for $b+c=1$ we get $(\mu^\infty, 1-\mu^\infty) = (\frac{1}{2}, \frac{1}{2})$.

The behavioural investor as defined by prospect theory has a utility given by

$$v(\Delta x) = \begin{cases} (\Delta x)^\alpha & \text{for } \Delta x \geq 0 \\ -\beta(-\Delta x)^\alpha & \text{for } \Delta x < 0 \end{cases}$$

where α is again a parameter indicating his risk aversion and β is a parameter reflecting his loss aversion.[3] Additionally, the behavioural investor uses the probability weighting function $w(p) = \frac{p^\gamma}{(p^\gamma + (1-p)^\gamma)^{\frac{1}{\gamma}}}$ to calculate his prospect utility.[4] Note that decisions of the behavioural investor are not influenced by any behavioural biases. Except for probability weighting, he decides as rationally as the CRRA investor.[5]

Although both clients may share the same view regarding the process driving asset returns, their optimal asset allocations differ for several reasons. First, in contrast to the CRRA investor, the behavioural one evaluates payoffs as gains or losses with respect to a reference point and he is loss averse. Additionally, the behavioural investor perceives probabilities in a biased way. In this chapter, we assume that the reference point is fixed at the starting wealth. This assumption is relaxed in the next chapter, where the behavioural investor updates his reference point in each period.

6.1.1 The optimal tactical asset allocation of an expected utility client with CRRA

As mentioned above, if asset returns follow a random walk, previous realizations are irrelevant for the probabilities of the next period realizations. Alternatively, one can say that on a random walk, asset returns are not predictable. Thus, an investor cannot learn anything from the ups and downs of the market, and market timing does not make sense. Moreover, if the investor has CRRA then his asset allocation is independent of his wealth. Thus, the CRRA investor would follow the strategy: when the asset price goes up, the investor sells part of his holdings of that asset, and when the price goes down, he purchases more of this asset in order to keep the share of wealth invested in this asset fixed over time.

In Example 6.1 below, for a realistically risk averse CRRA investor,[6] the optimal share of risky assets is 22.4%. This strategy is called "fix-mix" and the corresponding behaviour is called "rebalancing".

Math Box 6.1: Fix-mix strategy in TAA

The result that, in a world with constant investment opportunities $b = c$, a CRRA expected utility maximizer chooses an asset allocation that is independent of the time-uncertainty structure, can be proved in the following way. Suppose the investor is currently in state

---

[3] Here we use the piecewise power function because it compares better to the standard finance case of constant relative risk aversion which is usually used in dynamic asset allocation models.
[4] Note that in these optimization problems we do not need to normalize probabilities as suggested by NPT. This is because the solution of the problem is independent from multiplication of the objective function with some constant. As mentioned in Chapter 2, NPT is, however, important when comparing different sets of probabilities, e.g. different lotteries.
[5] See Chapter 2 for more detail on the rationality of decisions made by behavioural investors.
[6] It has been found that a CRRA of -1 is most realistic.

$s \in \{+,-\}$ and plans ahead for one more period (myopic behaviour). Then, the investor is solving the following optimization problem:

$$\max_{\lambda_t} \sum_{s=1}^{S} p_s \frac{1}{\alpha} \left(\sum_{k=0}^{K} R_s^k \lambda_{k,t} w_t \right)^{\alpha}$$

$$\text{s.t.} \sum_{k=0}^{K} \lambda_{k,t} = 1$$

where R_s^k is the return of asset k in the state s, $\lambda_{k,t}$ is the percentage of wealth invested in asset k at time t and w_t is the investor's wealth at time t. Since the transition probabilities $p_s = 1,\ldots,S$ are independent – both, over time and across previous realizations, the latter only influences the current wealth of the investor. But for a CRRA agent, the level of his wealth is irrelevant for his optimal asset allocation λ_t because w_t^{α} factors out in the optimization problem.

Example 6.1: A CRRA investor on random walk

To show how to compute the optimal asset allocation of an expected utility maximizer with CRRA, we make use of the results just stated and need only compute the asset allocation in one two-period decision problem. To do this explicitly, we now assume that his risk aversion is -1 and his wealth at the beginning of the investment period is 1 million.

To compute the optimal asset allocation, i.e. the mix of risky and risk-free assets that maximizes the expected utility of the investor, we proceed as follows. First, we determine the expected utility as a function of his asset allocation λ, i.e. the percentage of wealth he invests in the risky asset. Since $u = \frac{1}{\alpha} w^{\alpha}$ and $\alpha = -1$ we get:

$$E_u = p \frac{-1}{w^+} + (1-p) \frac{-1}{w^-} = p \frac{-1}{w((1+r^+)\lambda + (1+r^f)(1-\lambda))}$$

$$+ (1-p) \frac{-1}{w((1+r^-)\lambda + (1+r^f)(1-\lambda))}.$$

The percentage of wealth that should be optimally invested in risky assets, i.e. λ, is determined by calculating the first derivative of the expected utility with respect to λ and setting it equal to 0.

In our example with $p = 0.5$ as in the case of a random walk, $r^+ = 100\%$, $r^- = -50\%$, $w = 1$ and $r^f = 2\%$, we get

$$E_u = -\frac{1}{2w(2\lambda + 1.02(1-\lambda))} - \frac{1}{2w(0.5\lambda + 1.02(1-\lambda))}$$

$$\frac{\partial E_u}{\partial \lambda} = -\frac{1}{2w} \left[\frac{0.98}{(1.02 + 0.98\lambda)^2} - \frac{0.52}{(1.02 - 0.52\lambda)^2} \right] = 0$$

Example 6.1: (Continued)

$$\Leftrightarrow \frac{0.98}{(1.02 + 0.98\lambda)^2} = \frac{0.52}{(1.02 - 0.52\lambda)^2}$$

$$\Leftrightarrow 0.98 (1.02 - 0.52\lambda)^2 - 0.52 (1.02 + 0.98\lambda)^2 = 0$$

The quadratic equation has two solutions: -9.0940 and 0.22449. Since short sales are not allowed, the solution of the optimization problem is 0.22449, i.e. the investor should invest 22.4 % of his wealth in risky assets.[7]

The calculations can be also done by using the solver in MS Excel.[8] The results of the calculations are summarized in Figure 6.2.

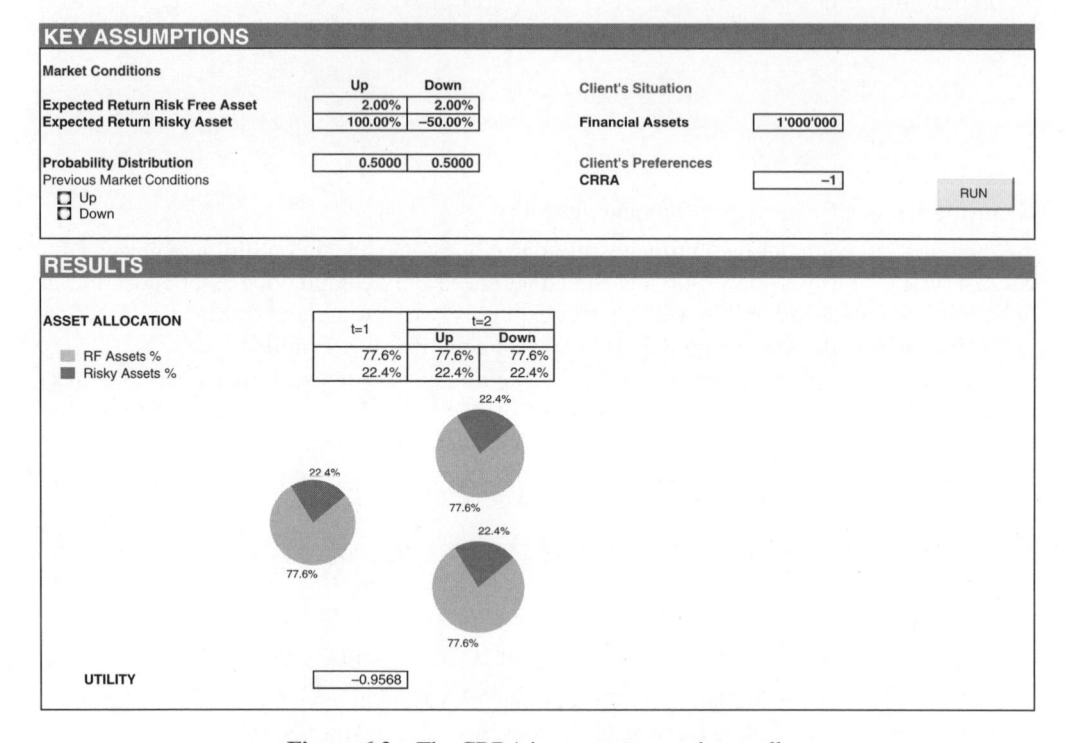

KEY ASSUMPTIONS

Market Conditions	Up	Down	Client's Situation	
Expected Return Risk Free Asset	2.00%	2.00%		
Expected Return Risky Asset	100.00%	−50.00%	Financial Assets	1'000'000
Probability Distribution	0.5000	0.5000	Client's Preferences	
Previous Market Conditions			CRRA	−1
☐ Up				
☐ Down				

RESULTS

ASSET ALLOCATION	t=1	t=2 Up	t=2 Down
■ RF Assets %	77.6%	77.6%	77.6%
■ Risky Assets %	22.4%	22.4%	22.4%

UTILITY	−0.9568

Figure 6.2 The CRRA investor on a random walk

Now, if asset returns follows a *mean reversion* instead of a random walk, an expected utility maximizer with CRRA should try to time the market and adjust his asset allocation in dependence on the most recent realized state. On a mean reversion, if the market has

---

[7] In general, we neglect extreme solutions with $\lambda = 0$ or $\lambda = 1$.
[8] Please visit our website www.bfpb.ch to download the tools performing these calculations.

gone up previously, the probability of a move downward in the following period is greater than 50 %, (see the Markov matrix for the transition probabilities). Given this information, the best strategy of an investor with CRRA maximizing his expected utility is to decrease (increase) the share of risky assets after positive (negative) returns as illustrated in the examples below.

Example 6.2: A CRRA investor on mean reversion

We use the same setting as in Example 6.1 however, here the probabilities depend on the current state.

After a "good" year, the expected probability of the investor from investing λ percentage of his wealth in risky assets and the rest, i.e. $1 - \lambda$, in the risk-free asset, is

$$E_u = -\frac{1}{3w}\left[\frac{1}{2\lambda + 1.02(1-\lambda)} + \frac{2}{0.5\lambda + 1.02(1-\lambda)}\right].$$

Then

$$\frac{\partial E_u}{\partial \lambda} = -\frac{1}{3w}\left[\frac{0.98}{(1.02+0.98\lambda)^2} - \frac{2*0.52}{(1.02-0.52\lambda)^2}\right] = 0$$

$$\Leftrightarrow \frac{0.98}{(1.02+0.98\lambda)^2} - \frac{1.04}{(1.02-0.52\lambda)^2} = 0$$

$$\Leftrightarrow 0.98\,(1.02-0.52\lambda)^2 - 1.04\,(1.02+0.98\lambda)^2 = 0$$

The solutions of the quadratic equation are negative. Since short sales are not allowed, the investor should invest all his wealth in the risk-free asset.

In the second period, after a "bad" year, the investor solves

$$E_u = -\frac{1}{9w}\left[\frac{2}{2\lambda + 1.02(1-\lambda)} + \frac{1}{0.5\lambda + 1.02(1-\lambda)}\right].$$

Then

$$\frac{\partial E_u}{\partial \lambda} = -\frac{1}{9w}\left[\frac{2*0.98}{(1.02+0.98\lambda)^2} - \frac{0.52}{(1.02-0.52\lambda)^2}\right] = 0$$

$$\Leftrightarrow \frac{1.96}{(1.02+0.98\lambda)^2} - \frac{0.52}{(1.02-0.52\lambda)^2} = 0$$

$$\Leftrightarrow 1.96\,(1.02-0.52\lambda)^2 - 0.52\,(1.02+0.98\lambda)^2 = 0$$

The solutions of the quadratic equations are: 101.52, 0.4827. Since the investor is not allowed to borrow money, the optimal percentage of wealth that should be invested in risky assets is 48.27 %.[9] This is illustrated in Figure 6.3.

Using the same procedure as before, we calculate the optimal asset allocation for the case that the year prior the investment starts was "bad". This means that the probability for the current year being "good" is 2/3 (see Figure 6.4).

---

[9] The same comment as in the previous footnote applies.

Example 6.2: (Continued)

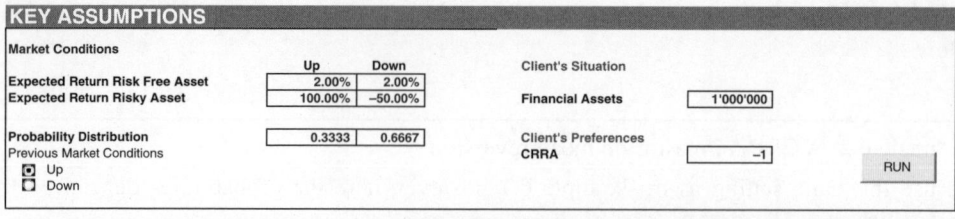

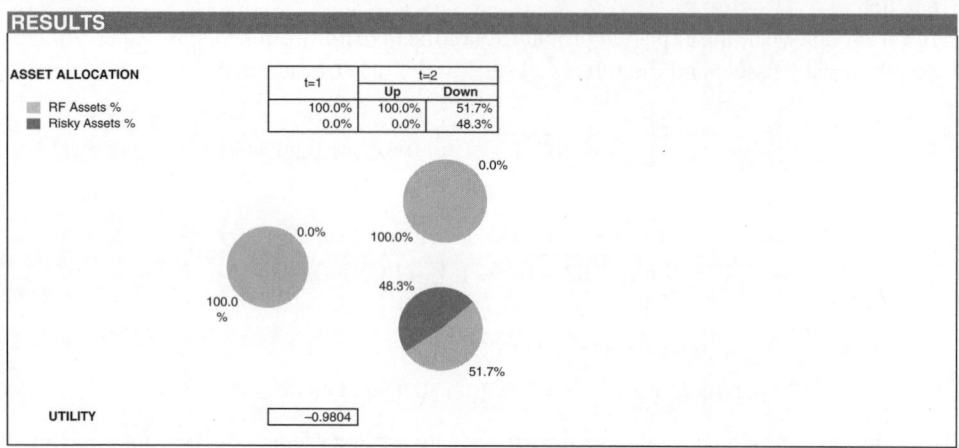

Figure 6.3 TAA of the CRRA investor on mean reversion after "good" times

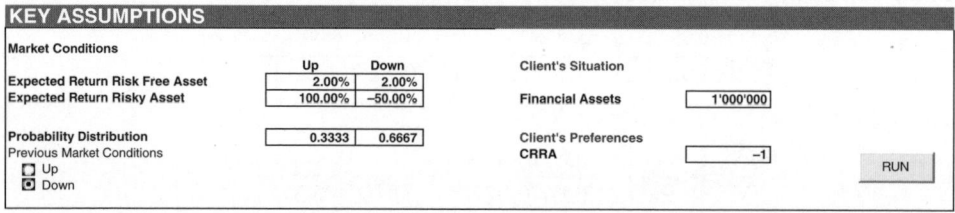

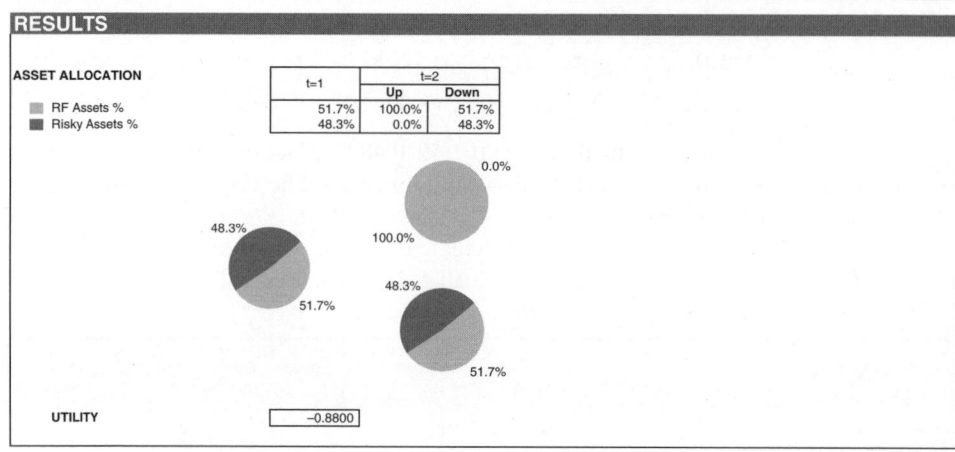

Figure 6.4 TAA of the CRRA investor on mean reversion after "bad" times

Note that, on average, the CRRA investor holds more risky assets on a mean reversion than on a random walk. Since, on average, the process is half of the time in a "good" state, the average holdings in risky assets on a mean reversion are $\frac{48.3}{2}\%$ which is greater than 22.4%, i.e. the average holdings in risky assets under random walk. The intuition for this result can be seen by referring to the extreme case of a mean reversion in which $b=0$ and $c=1$. Then after a "good" ("bad") realization, the investor would not at all (totally) go into the risky asset so that, on average, he holds 50 % of it. Since with a CRRA of -1, he holds less than 50 % in a random walk with $b=c=0.5$. If he were less risk averse, we might get that he holds more on average on a random walk than in the case of a mean reversion. Hence, the finding is different to the time diversification effect described in Section 6.2.1, which holds for any degree of risk aversion.

Rebalancing versus buy-and-hold

On a random walk or on a mean reversion, an investor with CRRA should follow a countercyclical investment strategy. How can the popular buy-and-hold advice be reconciled with this view? If asset returns follow a random walk, a buy-and-hold strategy can be justified when the investor's risk aversion decreases with wealth or when the investor's risk ability determines the portfolio on a continuous basis. Since the first case is not realistic, we consider the second case in more detail. When markets go up (down) the investor's risk ability improves (worsens) so the investor may not rebalance but decide to hold more (less) of the risky asset – maybe exactly as much as he gets from the market movement. As a result, the investor would simply hold on to his position. Finally, a buy-and-hold strategy can also be optimal for an investor with CRRA when the markets follow a momentum. In this case, the investor does not need to rebalance after gains (losses), as the market is likely to become more (less) favourable.

6.1.2 The optimal tactical asset allocation of a behavioural client

Although both investors share the same beliefs regarding the process driving asset returns, their optimal asset allocations are not likely to be the same since both clients have different preferences. The main differences arise from the fact that the behavioural investor is loss averse, evaluates outcomes differently for gains and losses, and uses a probability weighting function to evaluate the probabilities of events.

On a simple random walk, the distortions in perceived probabilities are so small that the optimal asset allocation of the behavioural investor is mainly determined by his loss and risk aversion as well as his reference point. We assumed that the reference point of the behavioural investor is his initial wealth. If he plans myopically, i.e. period by period, his optimal asset allocation changes in dependence on the realized gains and losses. Two effects determine his choice.

The first is the so-called *house money effect*. It originates from the observation that after a gain the investor has moved to the right of his reference point. Hence, investing in risky assets becomes less dangerous because it is then less likely to fall below the reference point. The opposite is true after a loss. Hence, the house money investor behaves pro-cyclically.

The second aspect affecting the optimal asset allocation of the behavioural investor on a random walk is the *disposition effect*. Briefly, it describes the tendency of investors to keep losses too long and realize gains too early. This is equivalent to saying that losses make investors less risk averse and gains motivate them to reduce risks. The argument for the disposition effect is based on the change in risk aversion after a gain and a loss. Since the value function is concave for gains, after a gain the investor is risk averse, so he may take profits. While the value function is convex in the loss region he may even risk more than before to have the chance to break even – which is called *break-evenitis*. Which of these effects dominates depends on the investor's loss and risk aversion and also on the expected asset returns.[10]

In our example, for $\alpha = 0.88$, $\beta = 2.25$, $\gamma = 0.65$, the behavioural investor increases his risk exposure after positive returns, i.e. the house money effect takes place.

Example 6.3: A behavioural investor on a random walk

The behavioural investor maximizes his prospect utility in much the same way as the expected utility maximizer. However, his utility function is defined over gains and losses where the reference point is his current wealth and he also weights probabilities.

The prospect utility function of the behavioural client is $PT_v = w(p)v(\Delta w) + w(1-p)v(\Delta w)$ where $w(0.5) = 0.439$ and

$$v(w_1 - w_0) = \begin{cases} \left(w_0\left((1+r)\lambda_0 + (1+r_f)(1-\lambda_0)\right) - w_0\right)^{0.88} \\ \quad \text{for } (1+r)\lambda_0 + (1+r_f)(1-\lambda_0) \geq 1 \\ \\ -2.25\left(-w_0((1+r)\lambda_0 + (1+r_f)(1-\lambda_0)) - W_0)\right)^{0.88} \\ \quad \text{for } (1+r)\lambda_0 + (1+r_f)(1-\lambda_0) < 1 \end{cases} \text{ and}$$

$r = r^+ = 100\%$ or $r = r^- = -50\%$ in our example.

Thus, in the "good" year, the investor makes a gain since $2\lambda + 1.02(1-\lambda) \geq 1$ for any λ; however, in the "bad" year, the investor can make a loss depending on his holdings in risky assets. To avoid making losses, the investor should hold less than 3.846% in risky assets because

$$0.5\lambda + 1.02(1-\lambda) > 1 \quad \text{for } \lambda < 0.03846.$$

The solution of the optimization problem for the first period is $\lambda_0 = 3.79\%$.

In the next period, the asset allocation is determined in a similar way.

In a "good" (+) year, the asset allocation is determined by maximizing the utility expected to be achieved with the asset allocation (λ^+ is percentage of the wealth is invested in risky assets). The utility in each of the final states is given by

---

[10] Hens and Vlcek (2005) have, however, recently shown that optimizing a prospect theory value function in the way explained in this chapter almost never produces the disposition effect. That is why in Chapter 3 we explained it with mental accounting. See also Barberis and Xiong (2008).

$$v(w_2 - w_0) = \begin{cases} \left(w_1\left((1+r)\lambda^+ + (1+r_f)(1-\lambda^+)\right) - w_0\right)^{0.88} \\ \quad \text{for } (1+r)\lambda^+ + (1+r_f)(1-\lambda^+) \geq 1 \\ -2.25\left(w_0 - w_1((1+r)\lambda^+ + (1+r_f)(1-\lambda^+))\right)^{0.88} \\ \quad \text{for}(1+r)\lambda^+ + (1+r_f)(1-\lambda^+) < 1 \end{cases}$$

with $r = r^+ = 100\%$ or $r = r^- = -50\%$.

Maximizing the expected utility (the sum of the utilities in the final states weighted with the biased probabilities), we get that the optimal percentage of wealth invested in risky assets after a "good" year is $\lambda^+ = 14.03\% > \lambda_0$. After a gain, the behavioural investor increases his exposure in risky assets since potential negative returns are perceived as diminishing gains instead of a loss. This is the house money effect.

In a "bad" year $(-)$, the optimal asset allocation is to keep the asset allocation almost unchanged, $\lambda^- = 3.85\%$. The results are summarized in Figure 6.5.

KEY ASSUMPTIONS

Market conditions	Up	Down	Client's Situation	
Expected Return Risk Free Asset	2.00%	2.00%	Financial Assets	1'000'000
Expected Return Risky Asset	100.00%	−50.00%		
Probability Distribution	0.5000	0.5000	Client's Preferences	
Previous Market Conditions			alpha	0.88
☐ Up			beta	2.25
☐ Down			gamma	0.65

RESULTS

ASSET ALLOCATION	t=1	t=2 Up	t=2 Down
RF Assets %	96.2%	86.0%	96.2%
Risky Assets %	3.8%	14.0%	3.8%

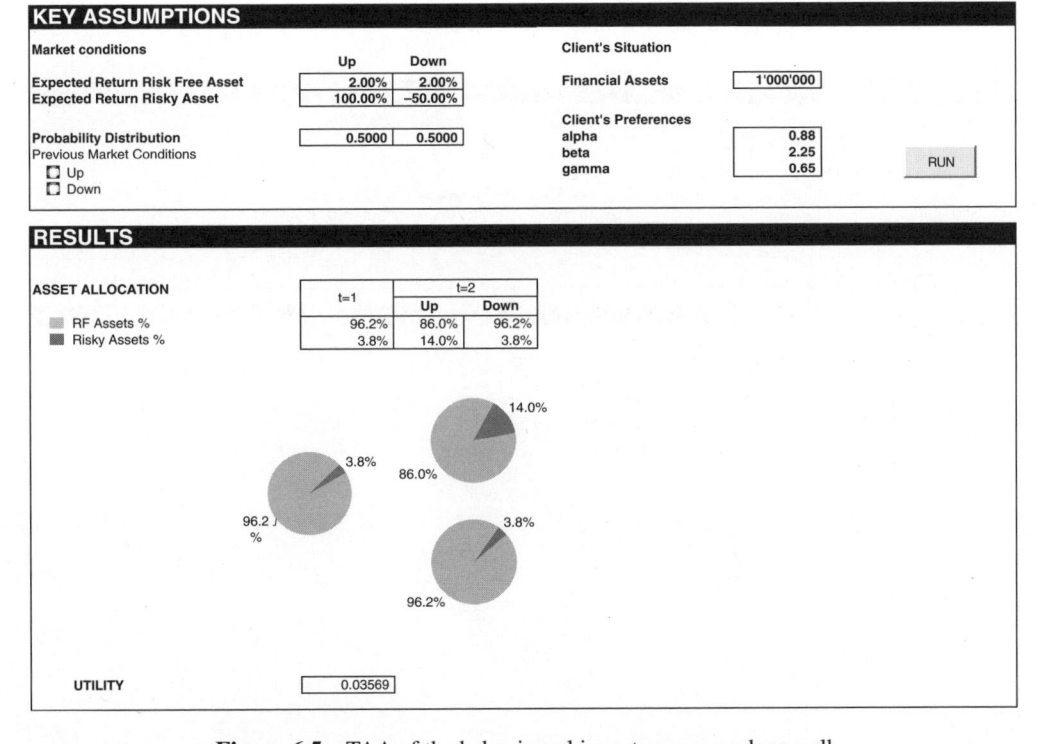

UTILITY: 0.03569

Figure 6.5 TAA of the behavioural investor on a random walk

On a mean reversion, the behavioural client also times the market as the CRRA investor does. After "good" times, he reduces his risk exposure to 2.1% until "bad" times come. Then he invests all his wealth in risky assets. This result is discussed in more detail in Example 6.4.

Example 6.4: A behavioural investor on mean reversion

To calculate the optimal asset allocation of the behavioural investor, we follow the procedure discussed above.

The prospect utility of the behavioural client at the beginning of the investment period is again $PT_v = w(p)v(\Delta w) + w(1-p)v(\Delta w)$ where $p = 1/3$ under mean reversion so that $w(p) = 0.344$ and $w(1-p) = 0.540$.[11]

The value function is the same as in the example before.

Consider first the case that the client starts the investments after "good" times. Since the probability for having a "bad" time in the current period is 2/3, which is perceived as 0.540, the investor reduces his risky holdings. The solution of the optimization problem for the first period is $\lambda_0 = 2.14\%$.

The next period's asset allocation depends on the asset allocation after a "good" year and after a "bad" year. If the next period is "good" (+), the investor increases slightly his risk exposure $\lambda^+ = 6.3\%$. In contrast, if the next period is "bad" (−), the investor invests all his wealth in risky assets $\lambda^- = 100\%$ in the expectation of positive returns.

These results are summarized in Figure 6.6.

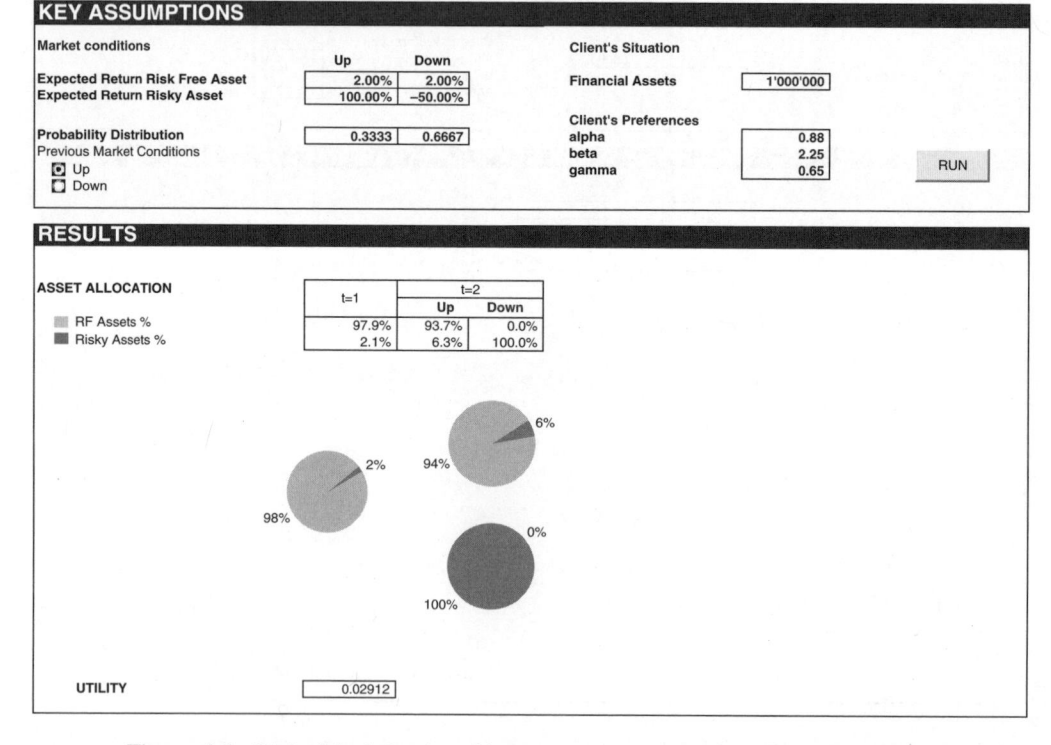

Figure 6.6 TAA of the behavioural investor on mean reversion after "good" times

---

[11] The same comment as in the previous footnote applies.

Consider now that the client starts the investment after "bad" times. In this case, the probability for ending up in a "good" state in the current period is 2/3, which is perceived as 0.540. Note that this is higher than the perceived probability under a random walk (0.434). As a result, the investor decides to invest all his wealth in risky assets, i.e. the optimal asset allocation is $\lambda_0 = 100\%$.

If the next period is "good", then the client timing the market decides to half his risk exposure to $\lambda^+ = 55.5\%$. If the next period is "bad", the client's optimal asset allocation is to keep his risk exposure maximal $\lambda_0 = \lambda^- = 100\%$. This is summarized in Figure 6.7.

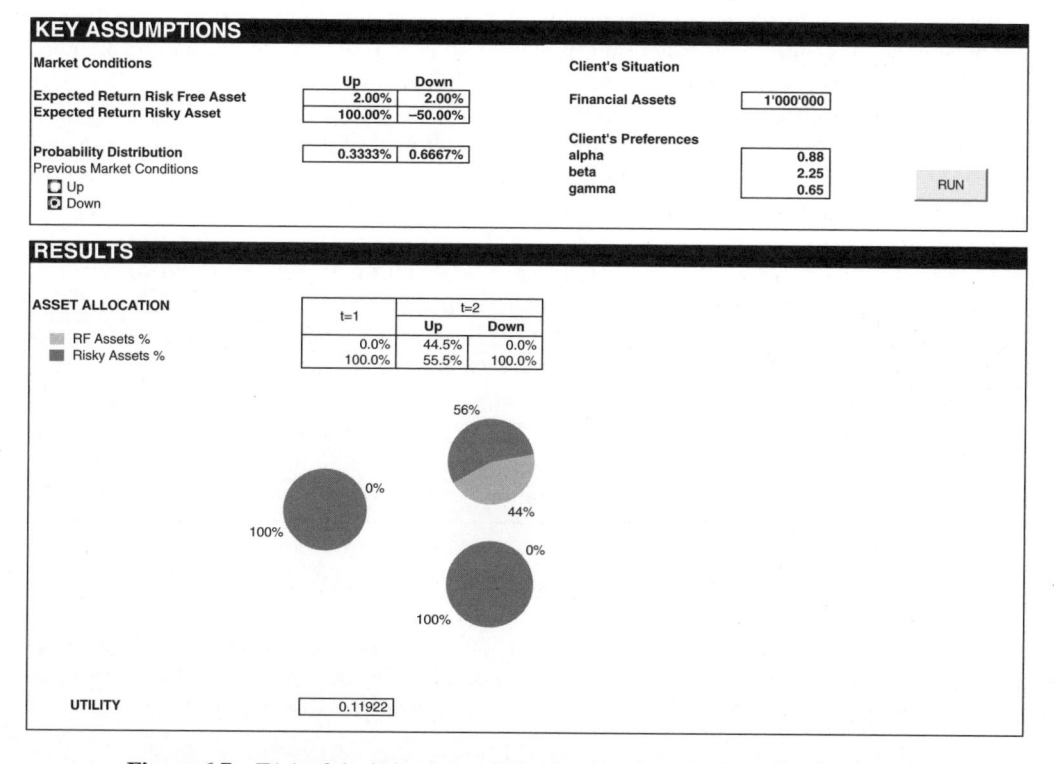

Figure 6.7 TAA of the behavioural investor on mean reversion after "bad" times

To get a better understanding of the rebalancing strategy of investors with different preferences, consider Example 6.5.

Example 6.5: Dynamic asset allocation for behavioural investors

A behavioural investor wants to buy a cottage in the Swiss Alps in five years from now. A small cottage costs 1 million Swiss francs, a big one 1.5 million Swiss francs. Currently, the investor has 0.9 million Swiss francs. He is also strongly loss averse, i.e. he will not take too many risks in order to earn a lot of money and buy the big cottage if, in the worst case scenario, he

Example 6.5: (Continued)

will not be able to buy even the small one. For this reason, the investor decides to follow a conservative strategy. After three years, his wealth increases to 1.2 million Swiss francs due to the good performance of the stock market. Should the investor rebalance his portfolio and reduce the increased share of equities?

The answer is no. As the house money effect predicts, the investor should not reduce the share of equities in his portfolio because the probability that at the end he will not be able to buy the small cottage is now very small (he has 0.2 million Swiss francs above his target).

Suppose now that, after three years, the investor who follows a conservative strategy does not have enough wealth to buy anything. What would he do? He would change the strategy and take more risks because this is the only way to achieve his target.

Consider now a different scenario. Suppose that the investor is less loss averse, but very risk seeking after he makes a loss. In this case, he decides to follow an aggressive strategy at the beginning and hold more equities. After three years, he accumulates 1.5 million Swiss francs. Should the investor rebalance his portfolio and reduce the increased share of equities?

The answer is yes. His wealth is above the target so that his risk seeking attitude in the case of losses does not have any impact on his asset allocation.

To compare, consider now the investment behaviour of the CRRA investor. His aim is to generate as much wealth as possible. He started also with 0.9 million Swiss francs and, after three years, realizes that his wealth has increased. As he does not follow any specific target, this wealth increase does not motivate him to change his investment strategy. He knows that he cannot learn anything from the past equity price movement so he rebalances in order to keep the share of equity as defined at the beginning.

Table 6.1 summarizes the results so far. If the returns of the risky assets are not predictable, then the CRRA investor would follow a fix-mix strategy. This strategy is not optimal for the behavioural investor under a random walk.[12] He holds more risky assets after realizing gains, i.e. he gambles with the "house money". Under mean reversion, both investors time the market; however, the behavioural investor seems to follow a more aggressive timing strategy.

Table 6.1 The tactical asset allocations of CRRA and behavioural investors under a random walk and a mean reversion

	Random Walk		Mean Reversion			
			After "good" times before starting investments		After "bad" times before starting investments	
CRRA investor	22.4%	22.4%	0%	0%	48.3%	0%
		22.4%		48.3%		48.3%
Behavioural investor	3.8%	14.0%	2.1%	6.3%	100%	55.5%
		3.8%		100%		100%

---

[12] The fix-mix strategy is however optimal for a behavioural client if he updates his reference point in each period.

6.2 THE OPTIMAL STRATEGIC ASSET ALLOCATION

Now we assume that the client does not optimize period-by-period, but anticipates his optimal future decisions in the plan he makes today. Such strategic planning helps the client, for example, to avoid forced liquidations, i.e. he does not need to sell when the market value of the assets is low. If he plans strategically, he anticipates that he will need to reduce the exposure on risky assets in the future and adjusts his asset allocation today.

We will see that for most investors,[13] the strategic asset allocation differs from the tactical asset allocation. The key question is whether investing on a longer horizon leads to holding more risky assets, i.e. whether there is *time diversification*. It is found that time diversification holds for all reasonably risk-averse rational investors if, and only if, the returns on the risky assets are mean-reverting (or mean averting). The intuition for this result is that on a mean reversion, variances increase less than proportionally to expected returns with the investment horizon, while the ratio of variances to expected returns remains constant on a random walk. A behavioural investor benefits from time diversification in any case. This is because, due to loss aversion and the s-shaped value function, he pays more attention to the probability of a loss than on the size of a loss. Hence, if one invests in risky assets with a positive drift, the probability that he will make a loss decreases over time. Note that on a mean reversion, the investors should time the market. The time diversification effect also holds, but less strongly if one restricts the investors to play a fix-mix strategy.

To illustrate how behavioural biases can affect the optimal asset allocation of clients planning over several periods, we use the same set up as in the previous section and compare the asset allocation decisions of the rational and the behavioural investor in different market situations.

The rational investor is an expected utility maximizer with CRRA. On a random walk, the optimal asset allocation of the rational investor is the fix-mix strategy. His asset allocation does not depend on his time horizon, but only on his risk aversion. We will see that the rational investor can benefit from time diversification only under mean reversion.

The behavioural investor is the average investor in the experiment of Kahneman and Tversky. He is loss averse and evaluates uncertain situations with respect to a reference point, which can be fixed at the initial wealth or adjusted to the wealth achieved in each period. In the following section, we assume that the reference point is fixed. The behavioural investor can plan myopically or anticipate his optimal decisions in the future.

6.2.1 The optimal strategic asset allocation of an expected utility maximizer with CRRA

If the risky assets have independent and identically-distributed (i.i.d.) returns, all means and variances are scaled up by the same factor. In other words, both short-term and long-term investors face the same mean variance choice scaled up or down by the same factor. For example (additive returns):

one period (short-term)   expected return $= \mu$, variance $= \sigma^2$
n periods (long-term)   expected return $= n \cdot \mu$, variance $= n \cdot \sigma^2$

The variance over two periods is, for example $\sigma^2(r_1 + r_2) = \sigma^2(r_1) + \sigma^2(r_2) + 2 \operatorname{cov}(r_1, r_2)$ where r_1, r_2 are the log-returns for the first, respectively the second period. If returns are i.i.d. then $\operatorname{cov}(r_1, r_2) = 0$ and $\sigma^2(r_1) = \sigma^2(r_2)$. On a mean reversion, $\operatorname{cov}(r_1, r_2) < 0$.

---

[13] An exception to this rule is the investor with logarithmic utility function, i.e. with $\alpha = 0$.

The effect is illustrated more precisely in Math Box 6.2.

Math Box 6.2: Mean reversion versus random walk over time

A stochastic process is mean-reverting if it tends to remain near a long-term average. One way to distinguish a mean reversion from a random walk is to compare the variance of the processes over different time horizons. Per definition, the variance of a random walk increases proportionally with time. To see this, we generate 100 random walks over 1000 periods (see Figure 6.8).

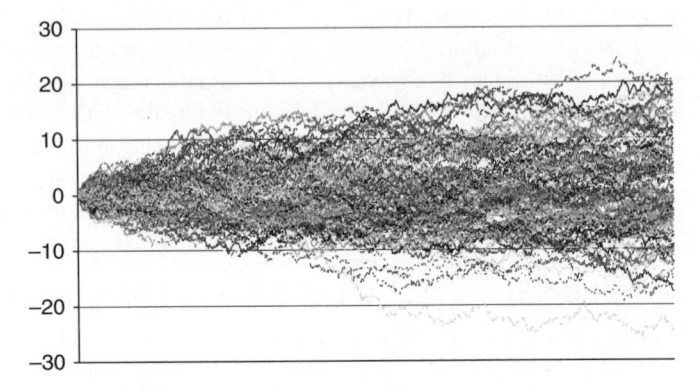

Figure 6.8 Sample paths of a random walk without drift

One can easily see that the variance of a random walk increases over time. Figure 6.9 shows this more precisely by comparing the variance of the generated random walks after 100, 200, 300, ..., and 1000 periods.

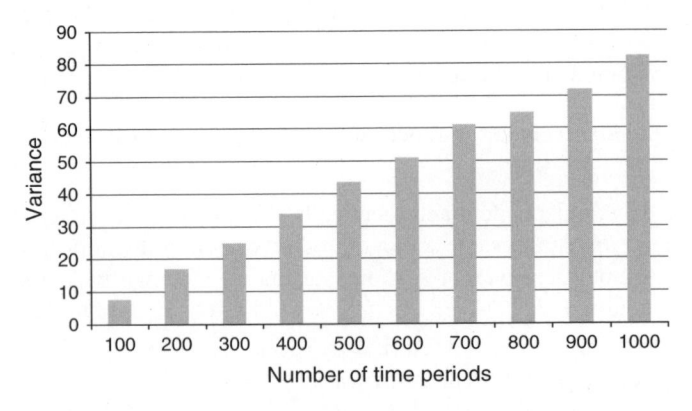

Figure 6.9 Variance of random walks over time

More interestingly, the mean-variance ratio of the random walks does not exhibit any patterns over time (see Figure 6.10). Thus, if an investor is concerned about the variance per unit of return, he should not expect it to decrease with his investment horizon.

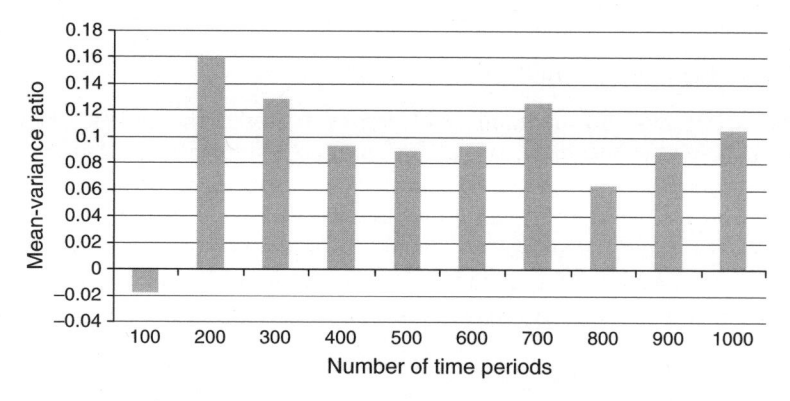

Figure 6.10 An example of mean-variance ratios of a random walk over different time horizons

In contrast, if the underlying process is mean-reverting, the mean of the returns increases proportionally with time, but their variance does not. In this case, the mean-variance ratio will increase over time.

This is illustrated in Figure 6.11 by using annual logarithmic S&P 500 returns over the period 1871 to 2007.[14]

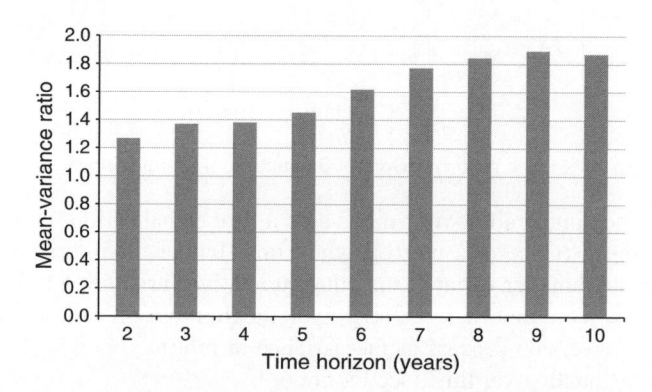

Figure 6.11 Mean-variance ratio of S&P 500 annual logarithmic returns (1871–2007)

The property of the variance to decrease/ increase over time if the process follows a mean reversion / mean aversion is further used in the so-called *variance ratio test*. The variance ratio test for k periods is given by

$$VR(k) = \frac{\sigma^2(r_{t,t+k})}{k\sigma^2(r_t)}$$

where $\sigma^2(r_t)$ is the variance of returns over one period starting at t and $\sigma^2(r_{t,t+k})$ is the variance of returns over k periods starting at t.[15] If the returns follow a random walk,

---

[14] We get the price data from Robert Shiller's home page: www.econ.yale.edu/~shiller/.
[15] The Variance Ratio should be adjusted for small-sample bias y dividing by the expected value of $VR(n)$, which is $E(VR(n)) = 1 - \left(\frac{2}{n}\right) \sum_{j=1}^{n} \frac{(n-j)}{(N-j)}$ where N is the number of observations.

Math Box 6.2: (Continued)

their variance grows with the number of periods k so that the variance of n-year is expected to be n times the one-year variance return and the Variance Ratio is expected to be 1. If the returns are generated by a mean-reverting (averting) process, the variance of returns with a longer horizon will grow slower (faster) than 1. Applying this statistic to real data, one can see that S&P 500 annual logarithmic returns from 1871 to 2007, for instance, are mean-averting in the short term (from 1–3 years) and mean-reverting in the long-term (from 5–10 years). This is illustrated in Figure 6.12.

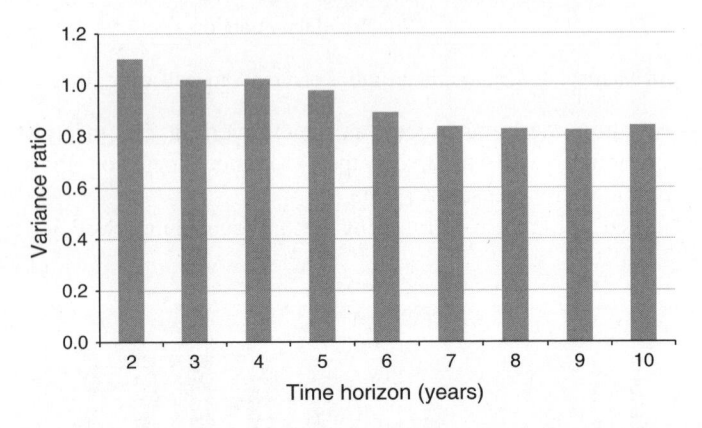

Figure 6.12 Variance ratios for S&P 500 annual logarithmic returns (1871–2007)

The decreasing variance ratio over time is also a further indication for the time diversification, i.e. the variance of a portfolio built on a longer time horizon, for example 10 years, exhibits a smaller variance than the cumulative variance of 10 portfolios built on a yearly basis. Note that there is time diversification only if returns follow a mean reversion / mean aversion process as the variance of returns following a random walk increases proportionally over time (see Figure 6.9).

Whether an investor can profit from the time diversification and increase his exposure to risky assets depends additionally on his risk preferences. Indeed, in Section 6.2.2, we will see that the behavioural investor can profit from time diversification even on a random walk.

Thus, if investors have CRRA utility functions, their asset allocation does not depend on their wealth, and since expectations and covariances are constant over time, both short-term and long-term investors should choose the same portfolio, i.e. the long-term investor acts myopically. In particular, if asset returns are unpredictable, the best strategy for an expected utility maximizer with CRRA planning over one or more periods is to buy and sell assets in order to hold the same portion of wealth invested in risky assets. This result is known as the *no time diversification theorem* which goes back to Samuelson (1969) and Merton (1969).

Dynamic Asset Allocation

Math Box 6.3: The no time diversification theorem

The No Time Diversification Theorem can be easily proved by considering a two-period economy with four possible states denoted by $\{R^+R^+\}$, $\{R^+R^-\}$, $\{R^-R^+\}$ and $\{R^-R^-\}$ where R^+ is a return after one "good" period and R^- is the return after one "bad" period. Let λ_0 represent the percentage of wealth invested in risky assets at the beginning of the investment, λ^+ the percentage of wealth invested in risky assets after a "good" period, and λ^- the percentage of wealth invested in risky assets after a "bad" period. Then, the final wealth of the investors in the four final states is: $(R^+\lambda^+)(R^+\lambda_0)w_0$, respectively $(R^-\lambda^+)(R^+\lambda_0)w_0$, $(R^+\lambda^-)(R^-\lambda_0)w_0$ and $(R^-\lambda^-)(R^-\lambda_0)w_0$. Note that R and λ are vectors so that $R\lambda = \sum_{k=0}^{K} R^k \lambda_k$. Thus, the investor with CRRA solves the following optimization problem.

$$\max_{\lambda_0, \lambda^+, \lambda^-} p^2 \frac{[(R^+\lambda^+)(R^+\lambda_0)w_0]^\alpha}{\alpha} + p(1-p)\frac{[(R^-\lambda^+)(R^+\lambda_0)w_0]^\alpha}{\alpha}$$
$$+ (1-p)p \frac{[(R^+\lambda^-)(R^-\lambda_0)w_0]^\alpha}{\alpha} + (1-p)^2 \frac{[(R^-\lambda^-)(R^-\lambda_0)w_0]^\alpha}{\alpha}$$

where p is the probability for a "good" period. We first observe that, $\lambda^+ = \lambda^-$ because $p\frac{(R^+\lambda_0 w_0)^\alpha}{\alpha}$ is a common factor in the first two terms and $(1-p)\frac{(R^-\lambda_0 w_0)^\alpha}{\alpha}$ is a common factor in the third and fourth term and what remains is just the same problem. Now that we have $\lambda^+ = \lambda^-$, we can show that $\lambda_0 = \lambda^+ = \lambda^-$. This is because, adding the first two terms of the problem, we get $\left(p\frac{(R^+\lambda^+)^\alpha}{\alpha} + (1-p)\frac{(R^-\lambda^-)^\alpha}{\alpha}\right)p\frac{(R^+\lambda_0 w_0)^\alpha}{\alpha}$ and adding the third and the fourth term of the optimization problem we get $\left(p\frac{(R^+\lambda^+)^\alpha}{\alpha} + (1-p)\frac{(R^-\lambda^-)^\alpha}{\alpha}\right)p\frac{(R^-\lambda_0 w_0)^\alpha}{\alpha}$. Hence, cancelling the common factor in the brackets, we have the same optimization problem again.

Example 6.6: A CRRA investor on a random walk (SAA)

Consider again two assets: a risk-free asset paying 2 % return in each state and a risky asset offering a return of 100 % or −50 %. The investor is an expected utility maximizer with CRRA of −1. His initial investment is 1 million. His planning horizon is 2 periods. The investor maximizes his utility from the final wealth. The portfolio weights are determined each period.

Let λ_0 represent the percentage of wealth invested in risky assets at the beginning and λ^+ (resp. λ^-) the percentage of wealth invested in risky assets in the next period given that the periods are "good" (+) and "bad" (−) respectively. The rest of the wealth is invested in the risk-free asset.

The expected utility of the investor at the beginning of the investment period is given by $E_u = p^2 \frac{-1}{w^{++}} + p(1-p)\frac{-1}{w^{+-}} + (1-p)p\frac{-1}{w^{-+}} + (1-p)^2 \frac{-1}{w^{--}}$ where w^{++} is the final wealth after two "good" (+) years, w^{--} is the final wealth after two "bad" (−) years, and w^{+-} resp. w^{-+} is the final wealth after changing "good" (+) and "bad" (−) years. In our example,

Example 6.6: (Continued)

$$w^{++} = w\left((1+0.02)(1-\lambda_0) + (1+1)\lambda_0\right)\left((1+0.02)(1-\lambda^+) + (1+1)\lambda^+\right)$$

$$w^{+-} = w\left((1+0.02)(1-\lambda_0) + (1+1)\lambda_0\right)\left((1+0.02)(1-\lambda^-) + (1-0.5)\lambda^-\right)$$

$$w^{-+} = w\left((1+0.02)(1-\lambda_0) + (1-0.5)\lambda_0\right)\left((1+0.02)(1-\lambda^-) + (1+1)\lambda^-\right)$$

$$w^{--} = w\left((1+0.02)(1-\lambda_0) + (1-0.5)\lambda_0\right)\left((1+0.02)(1-\lambda^-) + (1-0.5)\lambda^-\right)$$

the optimal asset allocation is determined using the MS Excel solver. The solution is $\lambda_0 = \lambda^+ = \lambda^- = 22.4\%$. The results are summarized in Figure 6.13.

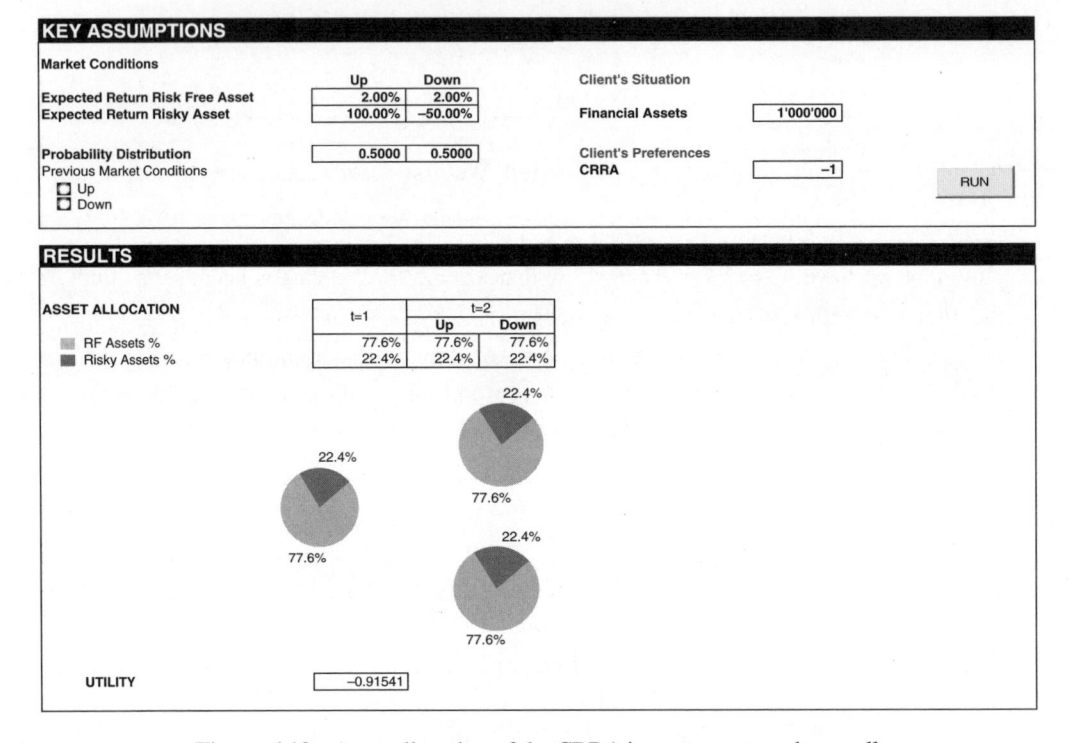

Figure 6.13 Asset allocation of the CRRA investor on a random walk

If asset returns are predictable, then the CRRA investor can profit from the ups and downs of the market and additionally benefit from time diversification. This can easily be seen by comparing the average holdings in risky assets of an investor planning period-by-period (myopically) and those of an investor planning over all periods. As in the case of myopic planning, on a random walk the CRRA investor holds on average 22.4 % invested in risky assets. However, on a mean reversion, the investor in each state holds more risky assets compared to the myopic case. This can be seen in Example 6.7.

Example 6.7: A CRRA investor on mean reversion (SAA)

Under mean reversion, the expected utility of the investor is given that the period before the investments was "good" (+) is

$$E_u = \frac{1}{3}\frac{1}{3}\frac{-1}{w^{++}} + \frac{1}{3}\frac{2}{3}\frac{-1}{w^{+-}} + \frac{2}{3}\frac{2}{3}\frac{-1}{w^{-+}} + \frac{2}{3}\frac{1}{3}\frac{-1}{w^{--}}.$$

If the period before the investment was "bad", the expected utility if the investor is

$$E_u = \frac{2}{3}\frac{1}{3}\frac{-1}{w^{++}} + \frac{2}{3}\frac{2}{3}\frac{-1}{w^{+-}} + \frac{1}{3}\frac{2}{3}\frac{-1}{w^{-+}} + \frac{1}{3}\frac{1}{3}\frac{-1}{w^{--}}.$$

Solving the maximization problem, we get that after "bad" times prior to the investment start, the optimal asset allocation in risky assets is $\lambda_0 = 52.3\%$. Then, if the market goes up, the investor sells all risky shares, i.e. $\lambda^+ = 0\%$ but if the market goes down again, the investor holds $\lambda^- = 48.3\%$ of his wealth invested in risky assets (see Figure 6.14).

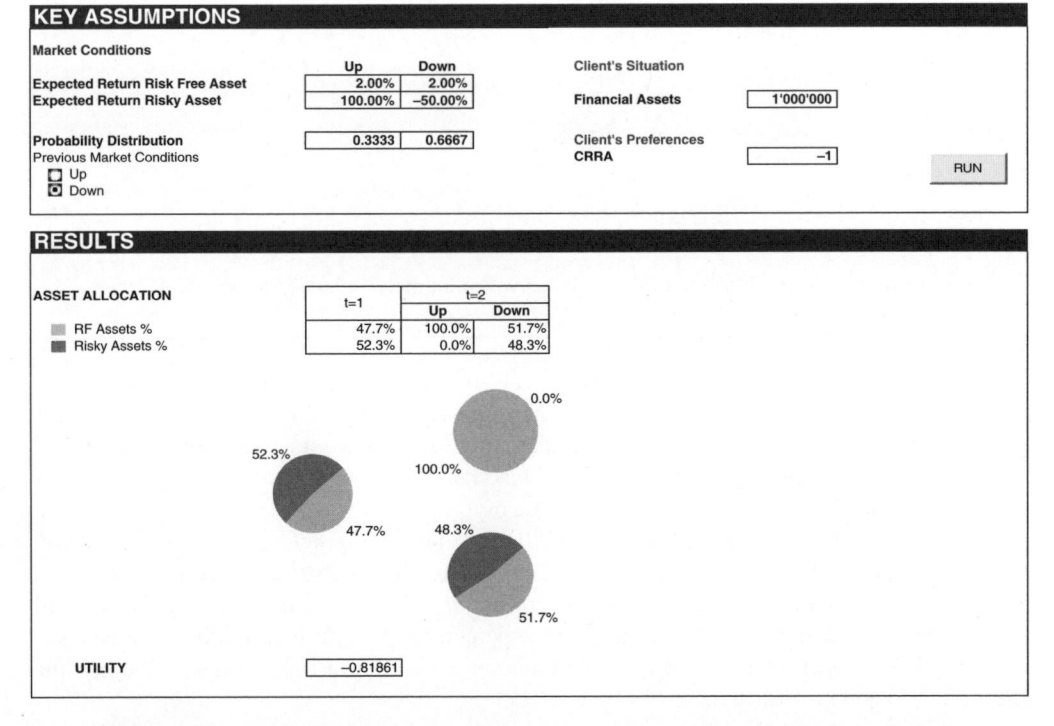

Figure 6.14 Asset allocation of the CRRA investor on mean reversion after "bad" times

After "good" times prior to the investment start, the optimal asset allocation is to hold few risky assets at the beginning, $\lambda_0 = 1.7\%$, but to increase them as soon as the market falls, $\lambda^- = 48.3\%$. If the market goes up, the investor should sell all risky assets, $\lambda^+ = 0\%$ (see Figure 6.15).

Example 6.7: (Continued)

KEY ASSUMPTIONS

Market Conditions

	Up	Down
Expected Return Risk Free Asset	2.00%	2.00%
Expected Return Risky Asset	100.00%	−50.00%

Probability Distribution	0.3333	0.6667

Previous Market Conditions
- ☒ Up
- ☐ Down

Client's Situation

Financial Assets: 1'000'000

Client's Preferences
CRRA: −1

RUN

RESULTS

ASSET ALLOCATION

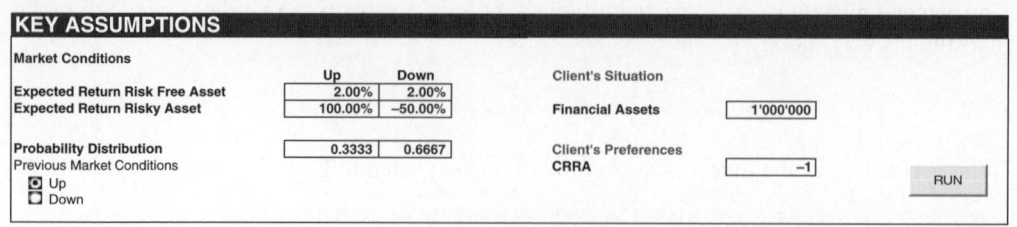

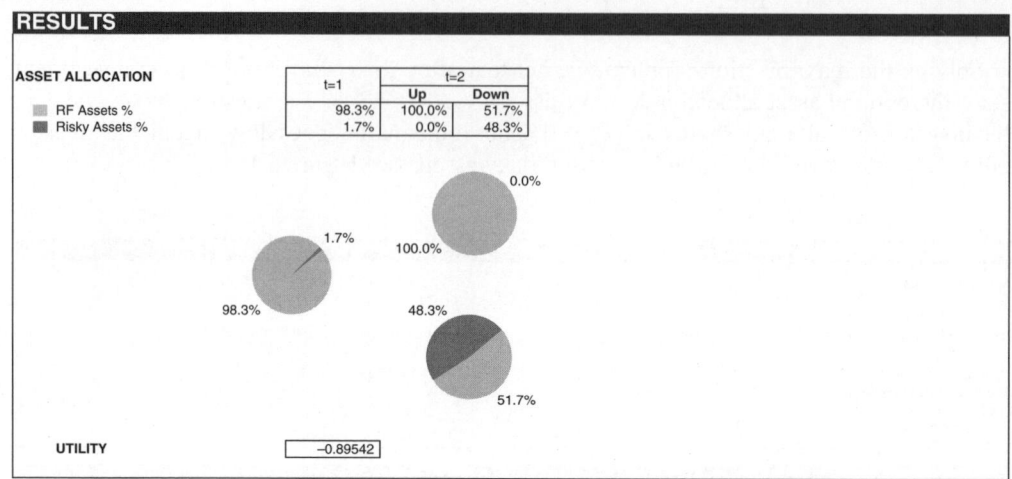

	t=1	t=2 Up	t=2 Down
RF Assets %	98.3%	100.0%	51.7%
Risky Assets %	1.7%	0.0%	48.3%

UTILITY: −0.89542

Figure 6.15 Asset allocation of the CRRA investor on mean reversion after "good" times

Thus, on a mean reversion, the investor can profit not only from timing the market but also from time diversification, i.e. after "good" times, he holds $\lambda_0 = 1.7\%$ in risky assets which is greater than 0%, which is the optimal asset allocation in risky assets in the myopic case, and after "bad" times, he holds $\lambda_0 = 52.3\%$ in risky assets, which is greater than 48.3%, which is the optimal asset allocation in risky assets in the myopic case.

If the investor is not endowed with the skills to time the market, i.e. to shift his market exposure in the "right" moment, it is perhaps better for him not to time the market and to hold a fix-mix portfolio. If a fix-mix is imposed (i.e. $\lambda_0 = \lambda^+ = \lambda^-$), then the investor can still profit from time diversification, i.e. the average percentage wealth invested in risky assets is 27.5%, which is still greater than the optimal asset allocation in risky assets in the myopic case (22.4%) and his utility increases.

Example 6.8: A CRRA forced holding a fix-mix

If a fix-mix is imposed, then $\lambda_0 = \lambda^+ = \lambda^-$. The expected utility, given that the period before the investments was "good" (+), is

$$E_u = \frac{1}{3}\frac{1}{3}\frac{-1}{w^{++}} + \frac{1}{3}\frac{2}{3}\frac{-1}{w^{+-}} + \frac{2}{3}\frac{2}{3}\frac{-1}{w^{-+}} + \frac{2}{3}\frac{1}{3}\frac{-1}{w^{--}}.$$

If the period before the investment was "bad" (−), the expected utility of the investor is

$$E_u = \frac{2}{3}\frac{1}{3}\frac{-1}{w^{++}} + \frac{2}{3}\frac{2}{3}\frac{-1}{w^{+-}} + \frac{1}{3}\frac{2}{3}\frac{-1}{w^{-+}} + \frac{1}{3}\frac{1}{3}\frac{-1}{w^{--}}.$$

Imposing a fix-mix λ changes the final wealth as follows:

$$w^{++} = w\left((1+0.02)(1-\lambda) + (1+1)\lambda\right)\left((1+0.02)(1-\lambda) + (1+1)\lambda\right)$$
$$w^{+-} = w\left((1+0.02)(1-\lambda) + (1+1)\lambda\right)\left((1+0.02)(1-\lambda) + (1-0.5)\lambda\right)$$
$$w^{-+} = w\left((1+0.02)(1-\lambda) + (1-0.5)\lambda\right)\left((1+0.02)(1-\lambda) + (1+1)\lambda\right)$$
$$w^{--} = w\left((1+0.02)(1-\lambda) + (1-0.5)\lambda\right)\left((1+0.02)(1-\lambda) + (1-0.5)\lambda\right)$$

The optimal weights of the risky asset are $\lambda = 17.4\%$, given that the previous market conditions were "good" (see Figure 6.16) and $\lambda = 37.6\%$, given that the previous market conditions were "bad" (see Figure 6.17). On average, the investor holds $(17.4\% + 37.6\%)/2 = 27.5\%$ but his utility is lower.

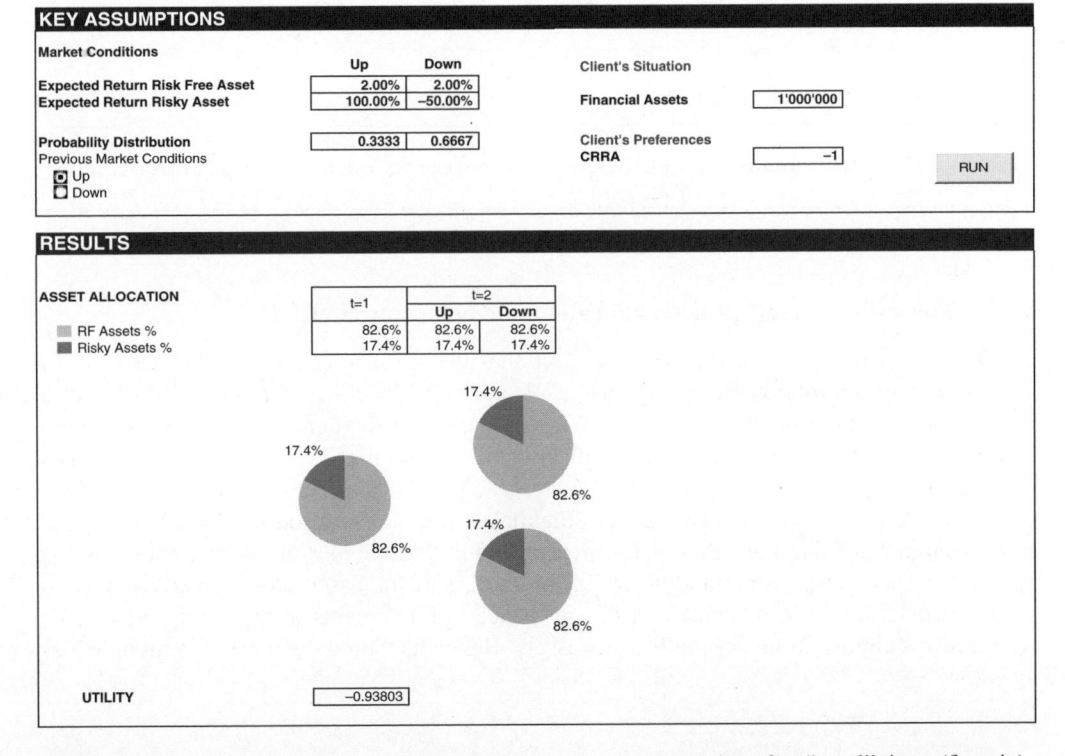

Figure 6.16 Asset allocation of the CRRA investor on mean reversion after "good" times (fix-mix)

Example 6.8: (Continued)

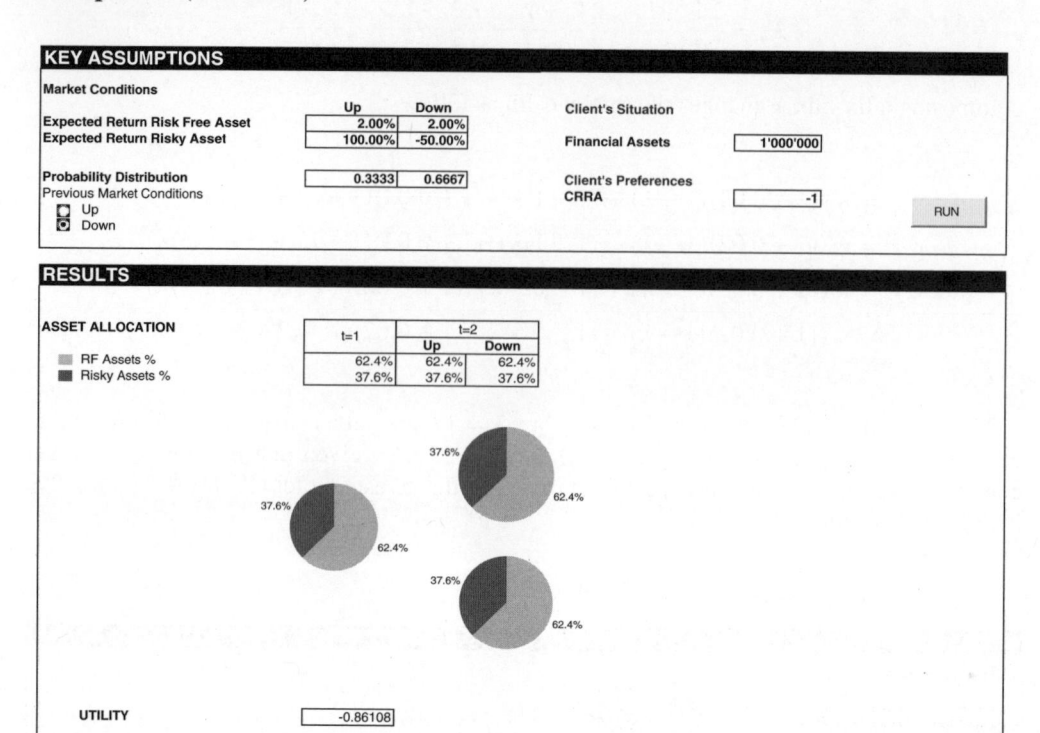

KEY ASSUMPTIONS					
Market Conditions		Up	Down	**Client's Situation**	
Expected Return Risk Free Asset		2.00%	2.00%		
Expected Return Risky Asset		100.00%	-50.00%	Financial Assets	1'000'000
Probability Distribution		0.3333	0.6667	Client's Preferences	
Previous Market Conditions				CRRA	-1
☐ Up ☒ Down					RUN

RESULTS

ASSET ALLOCATION	t=1	t=2 Up	t=2 Down
■ RF Assets %	62.4%	62.4%	62.4%
■ Risky Assets %	37.6%	37.6%	37.6%

UTILITY -0.86108

Figure 6.17 Asset allocation of the CRRA investor on mean reversion after "bad" times (fix-mix)

6.2.2 The optimal strategic asset allocation of a behavioural client

In contrast to the CRRA investor, we expect that the asset allocation of the behavioural investor is affected by myopic loss aversion. We consider the case where his reference point is fixed to the wealth of the first period. We will show that the behavioural investor cannot benefit from time diversification if his utility is affected by narrow framing or myopic loss aversion.

Myopic behaviour means that the investor makes decisions period by period. We recall from Section 6.1.2 that the behavioural investor would hold 22.4 % if his reference point is updated in each period on a random walk. In contrast, if the asset allocation in the second period is determined in advance and the reference point remains at the initial wealth, he would invest almost all his wealth in risky assets. Hence he would overcome his myopic loss aversion.[16]

---

[16] Recall Example 3.15 illustrating the effect.

The following example illustrates the results in more detail.

Example 6.9: A behavioural investor on a random walk (SAA)

The behavioural client determines his asset allocation in advance by maximizing his expected prospect theory utility defined as

$$PT_v = w(p)^2 v(W^{++} - W) + w(p)w(1-p)v(W^{+-} - W)$$
$$+ w(1-p)w(p)v(W^{-+} - W) + w(1-p)^2 v(W^{--} - W)$$

where $v(.)$ is the value function defined over the gain or loss in wealth, i.e. the difference between the final wealth accumulated over time and the initial wealth. For $p = 0.5$, $w(p) = 0.4388$ in our example.

The risky asset holdings that maximize the prospect utility of the behavioural client under random walk are $\lambda_0 = 99.4\%$, $\lambda^+ = 98.3\%$, and $\lambda^- = 100\%$. This result is summarized in Figure 6.18.

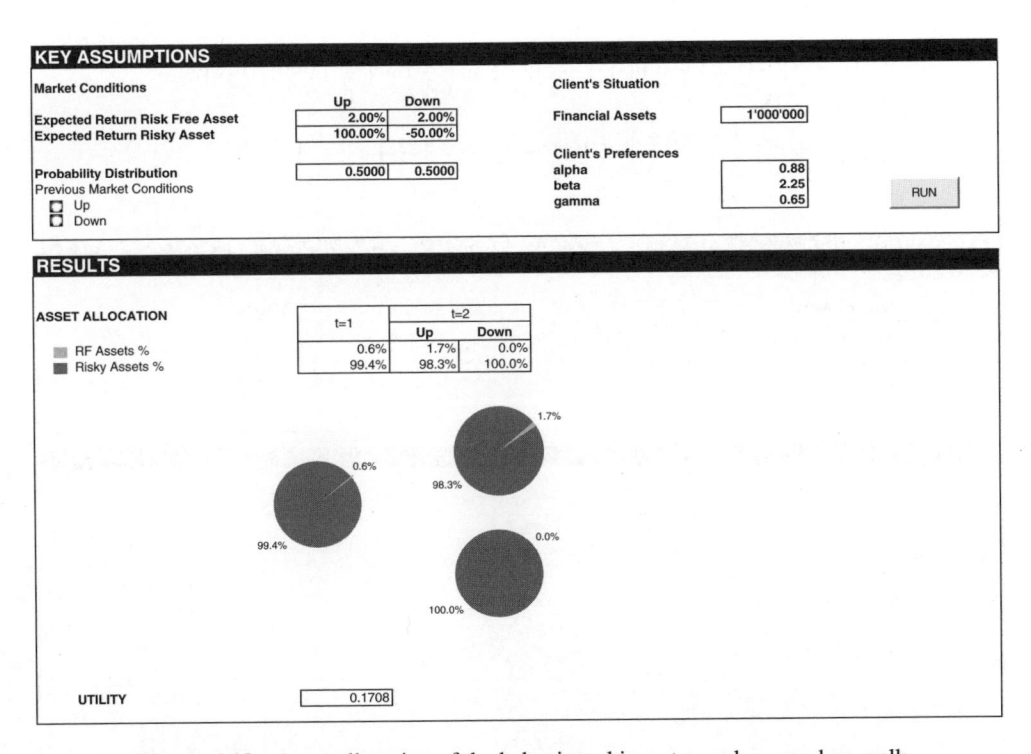

Figure 6.18 Asset allocation of the behavioural investor under a random walk

Thus, if the behavioural investor plans on a longer horizon, he would hold more risky assets. This effect is not driven by the process driving asset returns (it is a random walk); but rather by the myopic loss aversion of the client as illustrated in Example 3.15.

In the case of a mean reversion, there is also an additional effect that increases the average position in risky assets held by the behavioural investor.

Example 6.10: A behavioural investor on mean reversion (SAA)

Under mean reversion, the utility of the client also depends on whether the year before starting the investment was "good" or "bad".

If the year was "good" (+), the prospect utility of the client is

$$PT_v = w\left(\frac{1}{3}\right) w\left(\frac{1}{3}\right) v(W^{++} - W) + w\left(\frac{1}{3}\right) w\left(\frac{2}{3}\right) v(W^{+-} - W) +$$

$$+ w\left(\frac{2}{3}\right) w\left(\frac{2}{3}\right) v(W^{-+} - W) + w\left(\frac{2}{3}\right) w\left(\frac{1}{3}\right) v(W^{--} - W)$$

If the year was "bad" (−), the prospect utility of the client is

$$PT_v = w\left(\frac{2}{3}\right) w\left(\frac{1}{3}\right) v(W^{++} - W) + w\left(\frac{2}{3}\right) w\left(\frac{2}{3}\right) v(W^{+-} - W) +$$

$$+ w\left(\frac{1}{3}\right) w\left(\frac{2}{3}\right) v(W^{-+} - W) + w\left(\frac{1}{3}\right) w\left(\frac{1}{3}\right) v(W^{--} - W)$$

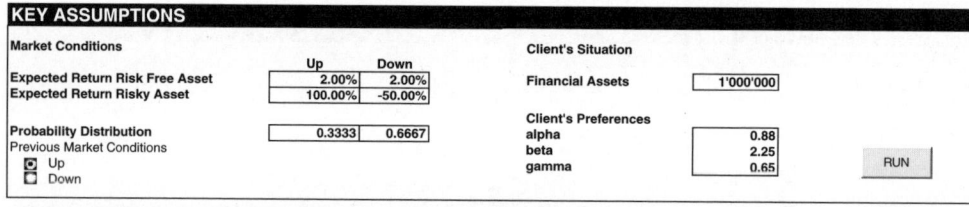

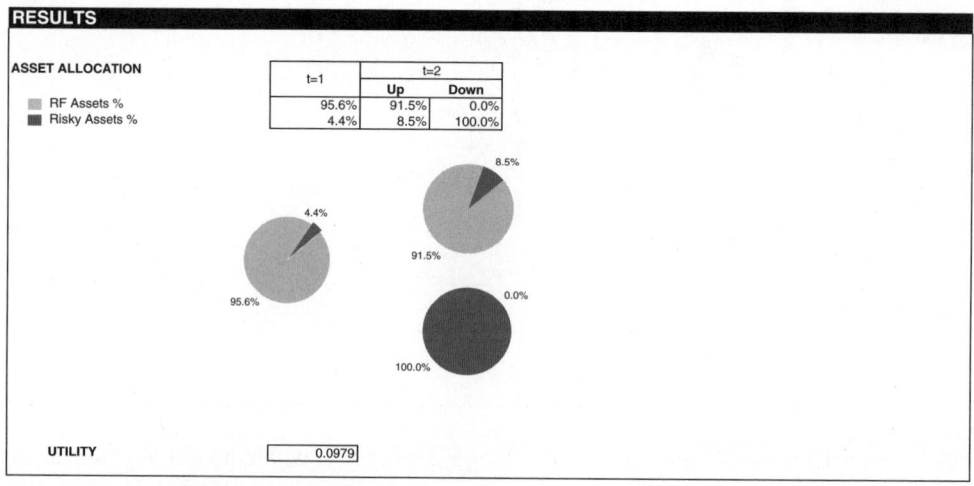

Figure 6.19 The behavioural investor on mean reversion after "good" times

where $\nu(.)$ is the investor's utility from changes in wealth defined over the difference between the final accumulated wealth and the initial wealth. Further, $w(1/3) = 0.344$ and $w(2/3) = 0.540$ in our example.

After "good" times, the asset allocation that maximizes the prospect utility of the client is $\lambda_0 = 4.4\%$, $\lambda^+ = 8.5\%$, and $\lambda^- = 100\%$. This is summarized in Figure 6.19.

After "bad" times, the asset allocation that maximizes the prospect utility of the client is: $\lambda_0 = 99.8\%$, $\lambda^+ = 5.5\%$, and $\lambda^- = 100\%$. This is summarized in Figure 6.20.

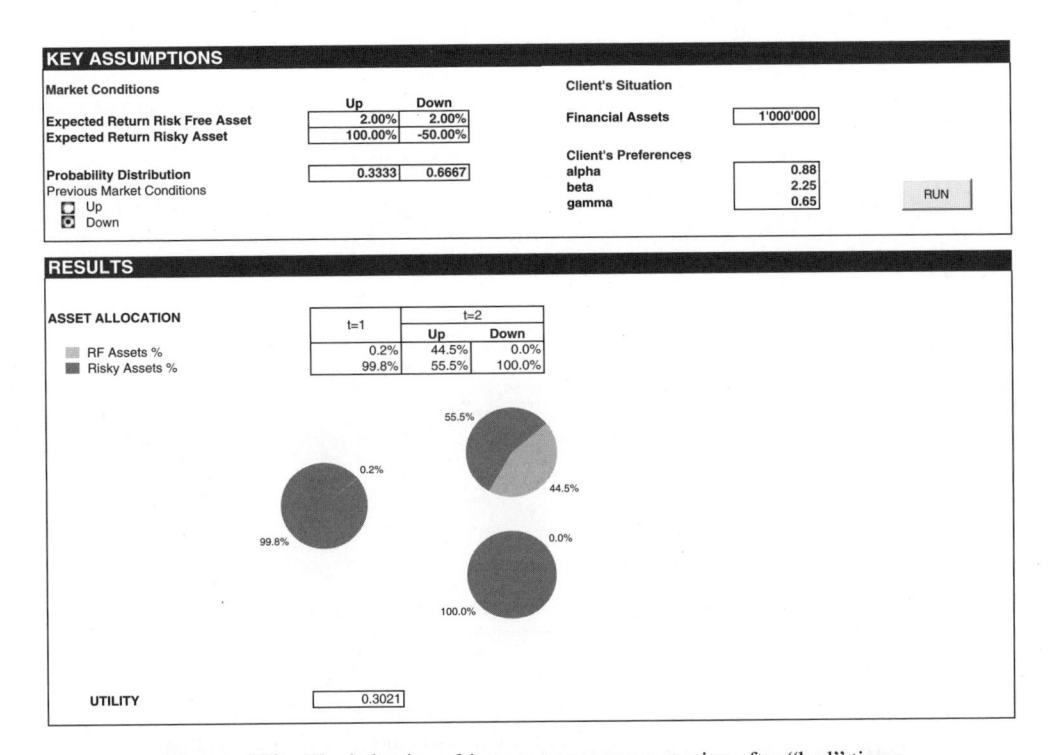

Figure 6.20 The behavioural investor on mean reversion after "bad" times

On average, the behavioural investor holds on mean reversion 52.1 % of his wealth invested in risky assets. If the behavioural investor times the market, he would hold, on average, fewer risky assets than in the case of a random walk.

Given that the behavioural investor is not a good timer, it might be better to hold a fix-mix even on mean reversion. If a fix-mix is imposed on the investor, he would hold, on average, 52 % ((3.8 % + 99.1 %)/2) of his wealth invested in risky assets.[17] Hence, forcing the client to hold a fix-mix instead of timing the market does not change his holdings in risky assets significantly. This is because the behavioural investor rationally anticipates his next period optimal allocation and adjusts his current positions accordingly.

---

[17] The calculations are not reported here, they are done in a similar way as the calculations in the previous examples.

However, compared to the myopic case with a reference point adjusting to the current wealth, keeping the reference point to the initial wealth and planning over more periods motivates the behavioural investor to hold more risky assets on a random walk (99.4 % vs. 3.8 %) and on a mean reversion (52.1 % on average vs. 51.1 % on average).

6.3 CONCLUSION

The main results of the strategic asset allocations of both investors under different market conditions are summarized in Table 6.2 and 6.3.

Table 6.2 Strategic asset allocations of CRRA and behavioural investors under a random walk and mean reversion

	CRRA Walk		Mean Reversion		Mean Reversion / Forced Fix-Mix	
			After "good" times before starting investments	After "bad" times before starting investments	After "good" times before starting investments	After "bad" times before starting investments
CRRA investor	22.4 %	22.4 % 22.4 %	1.7 % 0 % 48.3 %	52.3 % 0 % 48.3 %	17.4 %	37.6 %
Behavioural investor	99.4 %	98.3 % 100 %	4.4 % 8.5 % 100 %	99.8 % 55.5 % 100 %	3.8 %	99.1 %

Recall the optimal asset allocation of *myopic* investors.

Table 6.3 Optimal asset allocations of myopic investors under a random walk and mean reversion

	Random Walk		Mean Reversion			
			After "good" times before starting investments		After "bad" times before starting investments	
CRRA investor	22.4 %	22.4 % 22.4 %	0 %	0 % 48.3 %	48.3 %	0 % 48.3 %
Behavioural investor	3.8 %	14.0 % 3.8 %	2.1 %	6.3 % 100 %	100 %	55.5 % 100 %

Expected utility maximizers can profit from time diversification on mean reversion even if they are forced into a fix-mix strategy. But, independent of the time horizon, they hold the same fraction of risky assets on a random walk. In contrast to the latter result, the behavioural investor also holds more risky assets on a random walk when his investment horizon increases, since he then overcomes his myopic loss aversion. On a mean reversion, like the CRRA investor the behavioural investor also times the market and benefits from time diversification but he holds more risky assets than the expected utility maximizer, i.e. he profits more from timing and time diversification. If investors are forced to hold a fixed mix of assets on a mean reversion, they both hold, on average, almost the same risky assets as in the case of timing, but they can still profit from time diversification since they plan their asset allocation over all periods.

This chapter has shown that the optimal dynamic asset allocation depends on the type of risk preferences, the characteristics of market returns and, of course, the risk ability of the investor. One may argue that the main difference between an expected utility maximizer and a prospect theory investor is whether the investor has a specific target (the reference point in prospect theory) or whether he "just" wants to get richer in a steady way. In Chapter 8, we will see that both objectives could be true for one investor so that he will manage his wealth in separate accounts according to different risk preferences.

7
Life Cycle Planning

The very idea of life cycle investment is to plan your asset allocation over your complete life. Thus, by definition of the planning problem in this section, we will assume that investors plan strategically. A new aspect here is that withdrawals for consumption have to be included in the planning. Moreover, it is natural in life cycle planning to assume that the reference consumption level is updated over time. This leads to the effect of *habit formation*, i.e. one gets used to a previously high consumption level. Finally, we will have to say how future consumption is discounted to present consumption. The rational way is exponential discounting – like taking compounded interest – while behavioural agents might discount the future against the present even more, as in the concept of hyperbolic discounting first introduced in Chapter 3. In addition to the previous chapter, we will now have to consider an exogenous flow of wealth (human capital or labour income) that is hump-shaped (highest in the middle period).

The following questions will be addressed from a rational (intertemporal expected discounted utility maximizer) and a behavioural (prospect theory maximizer with hyperbolic discounting adjusting his reference point over the life cycle) investor.

- What is the best consumption/savings path along the life cycle?
- What is the best proportion of risky assets to financial capital over the life cycle?
- Does it make sense to lock the investor into a life cycle product?

The following case study shows what can go awry when investors plan their consumption and investments throughout their life cycle.

7.1 CASE STUDY: WIDOW KASSEL

Widow Kassel died in 2007 at the age of 92. She left 30 million Euro to the University of Frankfurt. In 1975, she had inherited 2 million Euro in the form of about 30–40 German stocks. She never touched these stocks and lived solely from the dividends in a small rented apartment in Frankfurt Lerchesberg. The performance of her portfolio coincided approximately with the performance of the M-DAX.

Let's first analyze whether Widow Kassel could have achieved a higher final wealth by investing in bonds instead of investing in stocks. The answer to this question depends on the investment horizon (see Figure 7.1).

Could Mrs Kassel have achieved higher consumption by going into bonds? The answer to this question depends again on the investment horizon. From 1974 to 2007, dividend yields of stocks were smaller than the interest on bonds, but stocks appreciate faster. Since

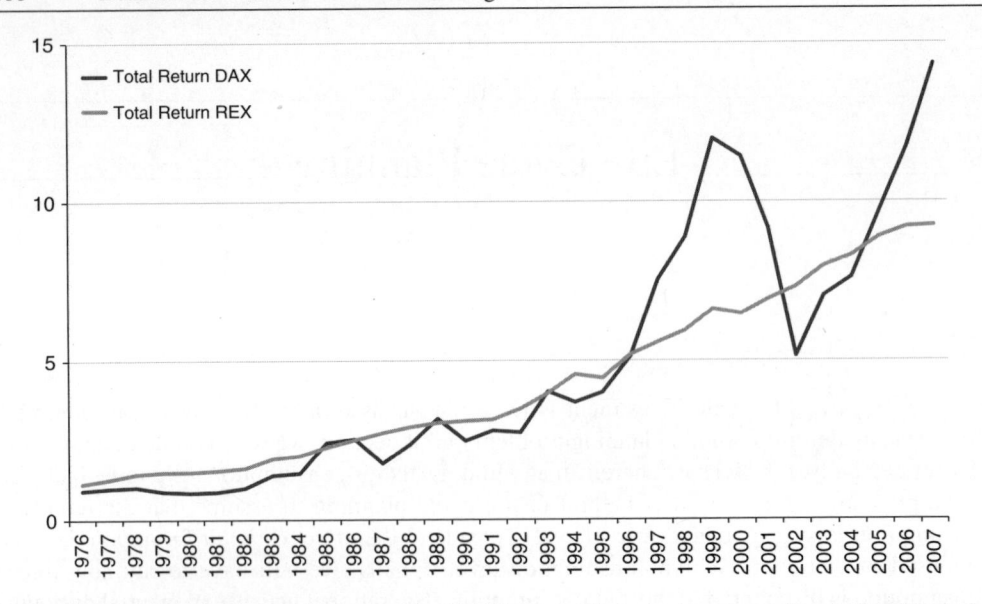

Figure 7.1 Performance of German stocks (DAX) versus German government bonds (REX index)

Mrs Kassel decided not to dip into the capital and to live from the dividends, we see that her consumption could have been higher if she had lived on the interest from bonds rather than on the dividends from the stocks (see Figure 7.2). Thus, given the mental accounting rule to live only on the cash flows from the investments (dividends respectively interest payments), bonds would have been a better choice with respect to consumption and stocks would have

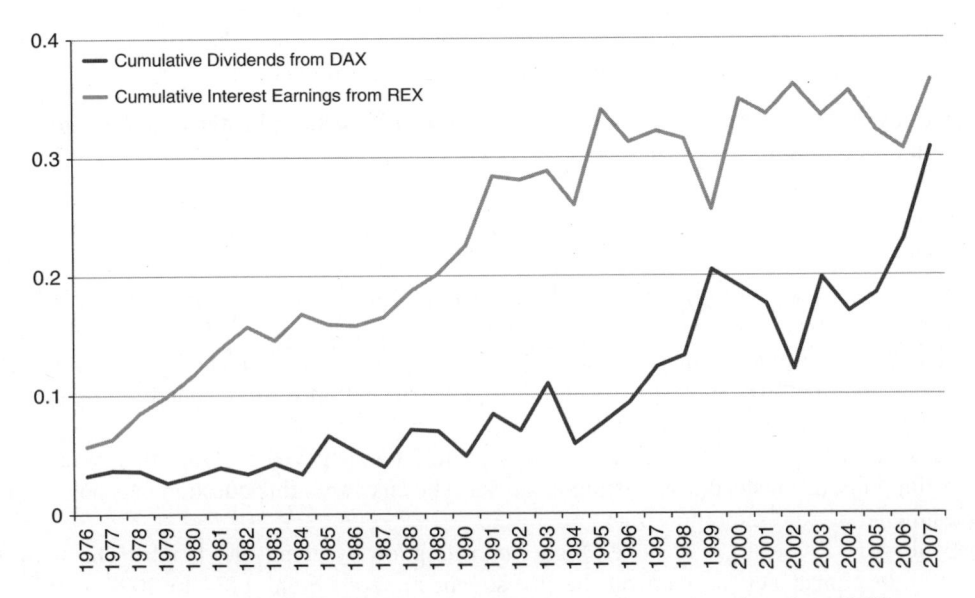

Figure 7.2 Cumulative dividends from DAX versus interest earnings from REX

been a better choice with respect to final wealth. Hence the lesson of this case study is that the University of Frankfurt benefited from the mental accounting of Widow Kassel while a financial advisor trained in behavioural finance could have helped Widow Kassel to improve upon her simple mental accounting rule.

In the following, we consider life cycle planning problems, like that of Mrs Kassel, in a more general setting.

7.2 MAIN DECISIONS OVER TIME

Over time, each investor has to make two types of decisions. First, he needs to decide how much of his income to consume and how much to save. This question is discussed in Sections 7.3, 7.4, and 7.5. Second, he needs to decide how to finance the consumption plan; to borrow and to invest, he can choose among credits, mortgages, certificate of deposit, bonds, stocks, real estate, and durable goods. The optimal asset allocation of investors with different preferences is discussed in Sections 7.6, 7.7, and 7.8.

Overall, we can say that the higher the savings today, the lower the current consumption, and the higher the income (and consumption) in the future. In the end, everything is consumed and/or inherited. We will assume that the investor derives utility from final wealth and do not distinguish here whether this utility results from consuming or inheriting the wealth.

7.3 CONSUMPTION SMOOTHING

One of the main empirical observations on individuals' consumption behaviour is the so-called *permanent income hypothesis*. It asserts that consumption (and saving) responds to *permanent* changes of income and hardly at all to transitory ones. Further, households do care about having a *smooth* consumption over their whole life so that transitory income changes have little impact on their consumption (and savings) path.

Why do households care about a smooth consumption? The reason is that—as already suggested by Bernoulli—individuals have a decreasing marginal utility of consumption, i.e. the additional utility gained from one unit of consumption decreases with the consumption level. To get an understanding of the link between consumption smoothing and the utility of consumption, consider Example 7.1.

Example 7.1.

Consider two alternative consumption plans:

(1) equal amount of consumption in each of two periods;
(2) consuming all in one period and nothing in the other.

Which consumption plan is more attractive for individuals with a decreasing marginal utility of consumption (concave utility function)?

Agents with a concave utility function would be better off by transferring some consumption from the period of plenty to the period of starvation. This is because the loss in the utility in the period of plenty is more than compensated for by the gain in utility in the period of starvation. This is illustrated graphically in Figure 7.3. The dotted arrows indicate the consumption transfer.

Example 7.1: (Continued)

Let C_2 be the consumption in the period of plenty and C_1 be the consumption in the period of poverty, i.e. $C_2 > C_1$. We can easily see that the reduction of utility $u(C_2) - u(C_{smooth})$ in the period of plenty is smaller than the increase of utility $u(C_{smooth}) - u(C_1)$ in the period of poverty.

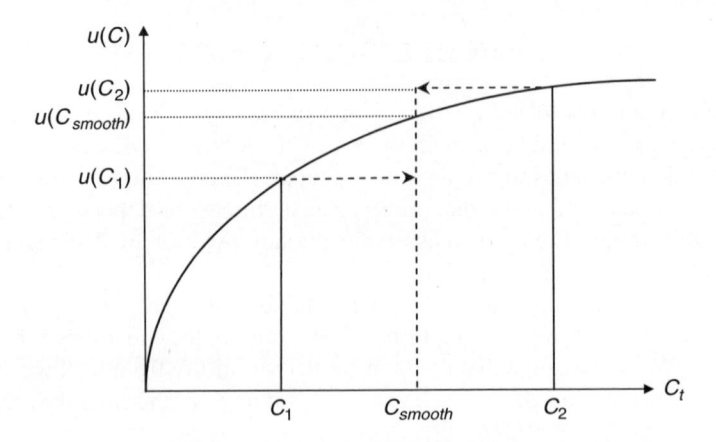

Figure 7.3 Consumption smoothing

The implications of consumption smoothing on the individual saving behaviour are illustrated in Example 7.2.

Example 7.2: Consumption smoothing

Consider two brothers identical in every aspect; one earns most of his money early in his life (e.g. a tennis professional), the other earns most of his money late in his life (e.g. a manager). If they consume without planning, i.e. if they consume whenever income is available, the one (tennis professional) would consume more in the early years, the other one (manager) would consume more in the later years. However, if they plan their consumption over their life cycles, their consumption would be smoother. The tennis professional should save when he earns more to increase consumption later in his life. The manager should borrow from his future high income to finance consumption today.

7.4 THE LIFE CYCLE HYPOTHESIS

The assumption that people have unequal income over time and that they try to smooth this out is the basis of the life cycle hypothesis developed in the 1950s and 1960s. It deals with the question of why people save. One answer to this question is that people live longer than they can generate income. If people want to keep spending, they need to save and accumulate assets during the period they work so that they can sell the assets when they retire. The next example illustrates the point.

Example 7.3: Consumption and saving over the life cycle

Suppose a 20-year-old person plans to retire at 60 and expects to die when he is 70 years old. His yearly income is $30 000. Thus, over the period of 40 years when he works, he will be able to generate $1 200 000.[1] If the person wants to be able to spend the same amount over his whole life (also after retirement) and does not want to leave wealth after his death, he needs to restrict his spending to $24 000 each year. To be able to spend this amount also after he retires, he will need to save $6000 per year (or 20 % of his yearly income) during his 40 years of working.

Suppose that the person wins $200 000 from playing lotto when he is 20 years old. Then his total income at retirement will be $1 400 000 and over the 50 years of living he will be able to spend $28 000 per year, i.e. $4000 more compared to the case without the win.

Thus, consumption can be financed through income (or through the sale of assets), and the income increase should increase consumption.

If the economic agents even out consumption over the whole life span as suggested by the life cycle hypothesis, one should not observe any changes in people's spending after retirement.

The observed behaviour of retirees seems not to jibe with these theoretical implications. Elderly people seem to severely reduce consumption after retirement. They do not appear either to stop accumulating wealth at all or to spend savings at a rate fast enough to keep up with consumption. Moreover, whereas according to standard theory, investors decide once and for all on holdings of bonds and stocks and then stick to this ratio, common investment advice[2] suggests that the investment behaviour depends on the investment horizon. Young people with a long investment horizon should invest more in risky assets while older people with a shorter investment horizon should switch to non-risky assets.

To understand why people do not behave according to standard economic models, one needs to add behavioural elements such as self-control, mental accounting and framing to the analysis. Hyperbolic discounting that has been discussed in previous chapters can cause investors to spend more today at the expense of saving tomorrow. As a result, they become ill prepared for retirement and, by myopic loss aversion, the degree of risk in their portfolios is inappropriate and the portfolios cannot make up for the lost time. A further problem of people applying simple rules like "consume from dividends but do not dip into capital" to overcome self-control problems is that their asset allocations are not balanced, i.e. there are too many income-producing assets. Moreover, investors with a self-control bias lose sight of financial principles such as compounding of interests so that, in general, they are unable to deal with the financial aspects of retirement questions.

In the following section, we show how these behavioural aspects of life cycle planning affect investors' decisions by using the behavioural life cycle hypothesis of Shefrin and Thaler (1988).

---

[1] Assume for the moment that the income is held in cash and does not earn any interest.
[2] A prominent rule is the "age rule" according to which the share of equity in one's portfolio should be equal to 100 minus the age of the investor.

7.5 THE BEHAVIOURAL LIFE CYCLE HYPOTHESIS

In the behavioural life cycle hypothesis of Shefrin and Thaler (1988), households have difficulties in postponing consumption until retirement because of a lack of self-control. Furthermore, they treat components of their wealth as non-fungible or non-interchangeable. In particular, households are observed to divide wealth into three mental accounts: current spendable income, current assets, and future income. These accounts are important because households encounter a variety of temptations to spend from them.[3] At a given time, the marginal propensity to consume is typically highest out of income (I), lowest out of future income (F), and somewhere in between for current assets (A). This is illustrated graphically in Figure 7.4.

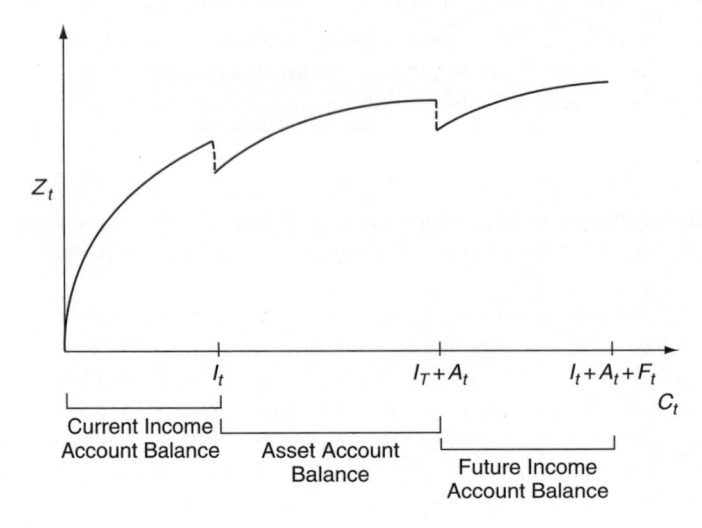

Figure 7.4 Utility derived from consumption drawn from different mental accounts. (*Source*: Shefrin and Thaler (1988))

At the beginning, consumption is financed from the current income account (I). As consumption increases, the psychological costs of resisting temptation (willpower effort) decreases so that the total utility Z (equal to the pleasure from consumption + pain from willpower effort) increases, but at a diminishing rate. When the entire balance of the current income account is consumed, the next marginal unit of consumption is financed out of the asset account (A). However, when accessing this account, the consumer needs to pay an entrance fee, which reduces his total utility Z at the beginning. Similar remarks apply when the next account F is accessed.

An application of the different marginal propensity to consume out of the mental accounts is that the saving rate of the households can be affected by the way wealth is "framed". In particular, an income paid in the form of a lump sum bonus is treated differently than a regular payment even if the bonus is expected.

---

[3] This is in contrast to the permanent-income hypothesis that says that wealth and income should be treated in the same way as long as they are permanent.

7.5.1 Hyperbolic discounting

People's intertemporal decisions of consumption and saving (investing) are additionally influenced by the discount factors used to determine the current value of future consumption. Laboratory and field studies find that discount rates used by decision-makers are much greater in the short run than in the long run, which contradicts the predictions of a utility function with stationary, fixed discount rates. This is why some people prefer "one apple today" to "two apples tomorrow", but at the same time they prefer "two apples in one year and one day" to "one apple in one year". To express these time-inconsistent preferences in a formal way, economists assume that individuals make decisions based on the following utility function that we also referred to in Chapters 2 and 3:

$$U(c) = u(c_0) + \beta \left[\delta u(c_1) + \delta^2 u(c_2) + \ldots + \delta^T u(c_T) \right].$$

In the utility function suggested above, $0 \leq \beta \leq 1$ is the hyperbolic and $0 \leq \delta \leq 1$ is the exponential discount factor. To see the effect of the hyperbolic discounting factor, compare the utilities of consumption between two subsequent periods over time. For example, the utility of current consumption $u(c_0)$ is $\beta\delta$ times greater than the utility of consumption one period ahead $u(c_1)$, but the utility of consumption in period 2 $u(c_2)$ is only δ times greater than the utility of consumption one period ahead $u(c_3)$. As a result, the consumption c_1 is discounted more strongly than the consumption c_3 compared to a period before. Consequently, in period 0 the agent would prefer to consume immediately but, after arriving in period 2, the agent would prefer to postpone consumption until the next period. Such preferences are called *time-inconsistent*.

7.5.2 Habit formation

Intertemporal decisions are additionally influenced by habit formation. Habitual behaviour can be defined as behaviour displaying a positive relation between past and current consumption. In particular, a higher level of consumption in the previous period results in a higher level of consumption in the current period, holding wealth constant. For example, a given standard of living usually provides less utility to persons who became accustomed to a higher standard in the past.

To model the effect of habit formation, we could choose a function like this one:

$$U(c) = u(c_0) + \beta \left[\delta \left(u(c_1)(1-h) \right) + hv(c_1 - c_0) + \delta^2 \left((1-h)u(c_2) + hv(c_2 - c_1) \right) + \ldots \right]$$

where $0 \leq \beta \leq 1$ is the hyperbolic discount factor, $0 \leq \delta \leq 1$ is the time-consistent discount rate, h is a coefficient determining whether the utility is driven by habit formation, and $v(.)$ is the prospect theory value function.[4]

From the habit formation perspective, the reference point is the previous period consumption. Depending on the coefficient h, the client's utility depends on the current consumption on the one hand and, on the other, on the consumption growth. For $h = 0$, only the consumption level matters, for $h = 1$, only the consumption growth is important.

Figure 7.5 illustrates how habit formation separates risk preferences and risk ability (dependent on overall wealth). The wealth level determines the risk ability but the prospect theory preferences determine the risk preferences.

---

[4] Blending in prospect theory into intertemporal excepted utility was first suggested by Barberis Huang and Santos, 2001.

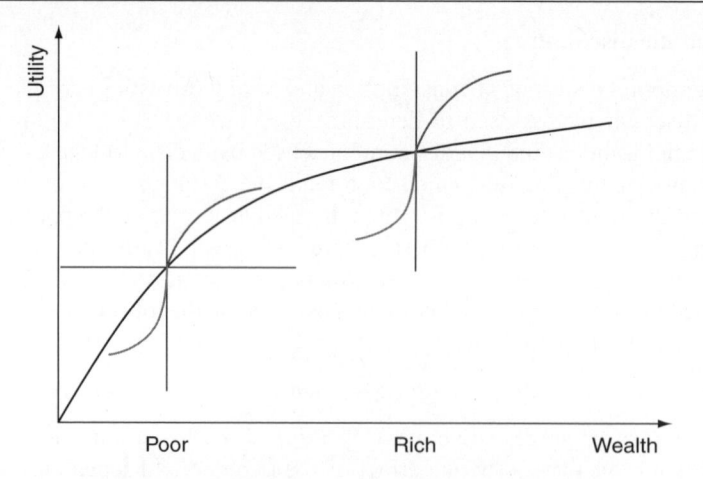

Figure 7.5 Separating risk preference from risk ability

7.5.3 Implications for product design

To motivate people to save (and invest) more, one should probably focus on product design. Benartzi and Thaler (2004), for example, suggest a program called *Save More Tomorrow (SMarT)*. The basic idea of the program is to give workers the option of committing themselves to increasing their savings rate each time they get a raise. The plan has the following ingredients. First, employees are asked to increase their contribution rates a considerable time before their scheduled pay increase. Because of hyperbolic discounting, the lag between the time when they sign up and the start-up date should be as long as feasible. Second, if employees join, their contribution to the plan is increased, beginning with the first payment after a raise. This feature mitigates the perceived loss aversion of a cut in the payment employees are able to take home. Third, the contribution rate continues to increase on each scheduled raise until the contribution rate reaches a pre-defined maximum. In this way, inertia and status quo bias help to keep the employees in the plan. Fourth, the employee has the option to opt out of the plan at any time. This feature makes employees feel more comfortable about joining the program. According to the authors, the initial experience with the SMarT plan has been remarkably successful. Most of the people decided to use it and to stick with it. As a result, their saving rates tripled (see Benartzi and Thaler, 2004).

7.6 THE LIFE CYCLE ASSET ALLOCATION PROBLEM

In the following section, we study the optimal consumption and investment strategy of two investors, one with a CRRA and one behavioural investor, under the assumption that asset returns follow a random walk. As a first result, we show that rational investors with CRRA utility hold more of any type of investment assets (e.g. bonds, equities, etc.) in their financial capital when young. This result is supported by the fact that individuals have two sources of capital: *human capital* and *financial capital* so that

Total Capital (TC) = Human Capital (HC) + Financial Capital (FC)[5]

---

[5] In the following, "Capital" of any sort and in any period t is understood as the present value of that capital for the rest of the life cycle.

Whereas financial capital is steadily increasing, human capital decreases at some point in time. If, as in the case of CRRA, the percentage of total capital invested in a particular asset is a constant, say α, then the percentage of financial capital invested in this asset is equal to $\frac{\alpha(HC+FC)}{FC}$. Hence, individuals with a greater proportion of human capital (HC) relative to financial capital (FC) invest a higher portion of their financial capital in a particular asset. Note that this does not imply that the ratio of bonds to stocks, for example, is changed over time because the formula applies equally to any asset. This sounds reasonable but there are some caveats.

- Wouldn't the investor like to adjust his percentage of risky assets to his consumption needs? For example, he might consume more when young and hence has less capital left to invest in risky assets.
- What is the consumption effect on the proportion of risky capital to financial capital?

To get some insights into these important questions, we again consider a three period investment problem with two assets, one risk-free with 2 % interest and one risky that can either double or halve the money. In this example, we restrict attention to a random walk since the main point can be made there.

The exogenous wealth (HC) is chosen to be (1 million, 2 million, 0). Hence the investors have little wealth to begin with, highest wealth in between and zero wealth when old. Initially the investors also have some financial wealth that in our computations was chosen to be 1 million.

The rational investor is reasonably risk-averse and the behavioural investor is slightly risk-averse but additionally loss averse. Both investors discount exponentially with 0.9 and the behavioural investor discounts hyperbolically in addition to that with 0.9 in our examples.[6] His reference point is the previous period's wealth, i.e. the investor updates his reference point in each period. Otherwise, the behavioural investor is as described in the previous chapter.

7.7 THE LIFE CYCLE ASSET ALLOCATION OF AN EXPECTED UTILITY MAXIMIZER

The expected utility maximizer has, as given above, a hump-shaped human capital flow and little financial capital to begin with. He chooses his consumption rate and his portfolio composition over time so as to maximize his discounted expected utility.

Consider first the simplest case, where assets do not pay any returns and the client is indifferent between consuming today or tomorrow ($\delta = 1$). He has no requirements with respect to the level of consumption over time. The investor starts with 1 million and he does not have any additional income (no human capital). In this case, the client would split his wealth equally over time in order to smooth out his consumption. Splitting wealth equally over time means that the client desires to consume 1/3 of his wealth today and the rest tomorrow, so that in each state he realizes he can consume the same portion of wealth, i.e. 1/3. This is *perfect consumption smoothing* (see Figure 7.6).

---

[6] The impact of hyperbolic discounting is discussed in Section 7.8.

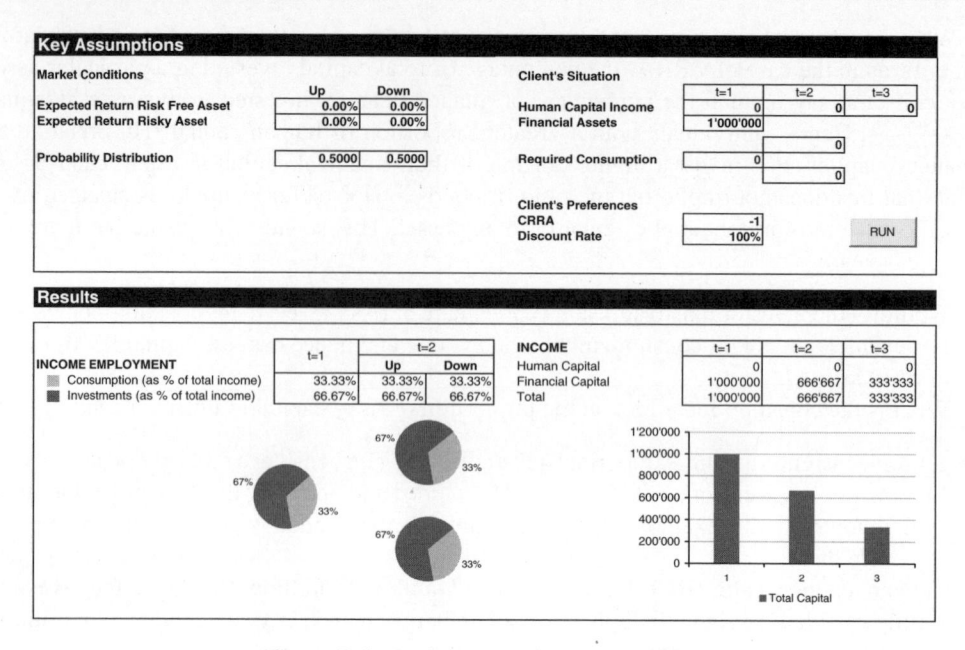

Figure 7.6 Perfect consumption smoothing

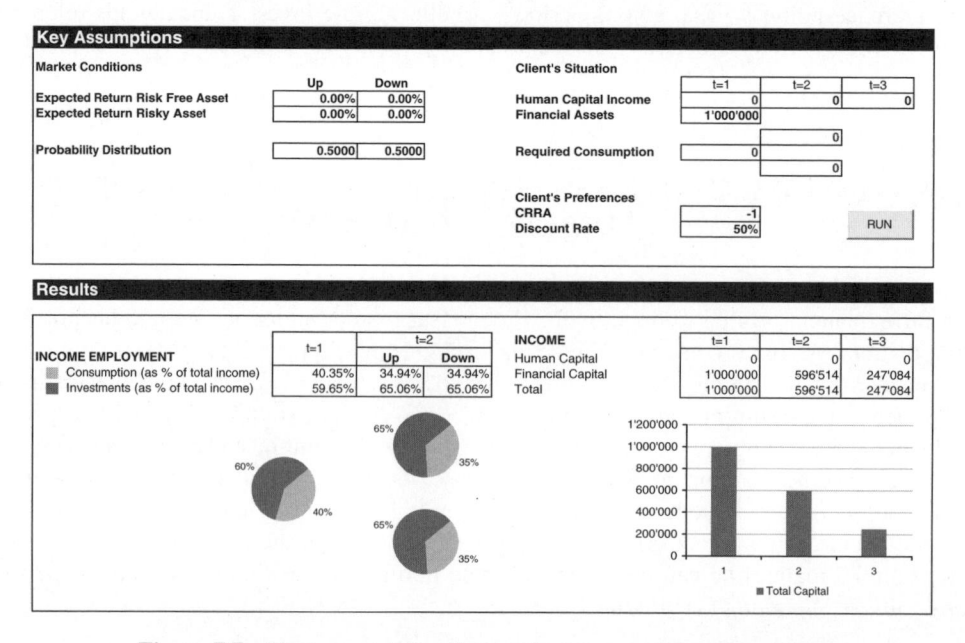

Figure 7.7 The impact of the discount factor on current consumption

Now consider the case where the discount factor decreases to 50 %, meaning that future consumption is of less value to the investor than consumption today.

In this case, the investor decides to increase current consumption from 33 % to 40 % (see Figure 7.7). The lower the discount rate is, the lower the utility from future consumption, the higher the current consumption. For example, if the discount factor is 20 %, the current consumption increases to 47 %.

Up to this point, we have assumed that risky assets do not pay any returns so that the client holds only riskless assets and decides upon his consumption according to his time preferences. Now we assume that the client has the opportunity to invest in risky assets. With this investment, he can either double his wealth (achieve 100 % return) or lose half of it (lose 50 %). Then the optimal allocation of wealth over risky and riskless assets depends on the client's preferences with respect to his consumption path. The client has two options:

(1) he can decide his asset allocation and his consumption simultaneously, or
(2) he can define a consumption path he would like to achieve, and then determine the optimal asset allocation that maximizes his utility given the required consumption.

7.7.1 Life cycle consumption and asset allocation without consumption requirements

Consider the first case where the client does not have any restrictions regarding his consumption path and the client is indifferent between consuming today and tomorrow, i.e. the discount rate is equal to 100 %.

In this case, as seen in the previous chapter, the client should hold a fix-mix portfolio of 22.4 % risky assets that allows him also to slightly increase his current consumption to 34 % (see Figure 7.8). Higher consumption in the current period means less investment in the future. As the asset allocation is fixed over time the portion of financial capital invested in the risky asset decreases.

The optimal fraction of risky assets to the financial capital changes depending on the human capital. Assume, for example, the case where the client's human capital in the current period is 1 million and in the second period is 1.5 million. In this case, the optimal asset allocation in risky assets increases from 22.4 % (the case without human capital) to 62.8 % in the current period (see Figure 7.9). This is because the total capital increases with the human capital. To keep the proportion of risky assets to the total capital constant, the client has to *increase* his exposure in risky assets. This is why the proportion of risky assets to the financial capital increases from 14.8 % (the case without human capital) to 51.4 % in the current period and from 11.1 % to 23.6 % and 40.5 % in the next period. Over time, the proportion of risky assets to financial capital decreases as in the previous case without human capital.

7.7.2 Life cycle consumption and asset allocation with consumption requirements

Consider now the second case, where the client has specific requirements on his current and future consumption, for example, to consume 500 000 in each state, or 50 % of his wealth instead of 34.1 % and 41 % instead of 33 %, which was the optimal consumption path in the case where the client didn't have any consumption restrictions. In this case, the client should

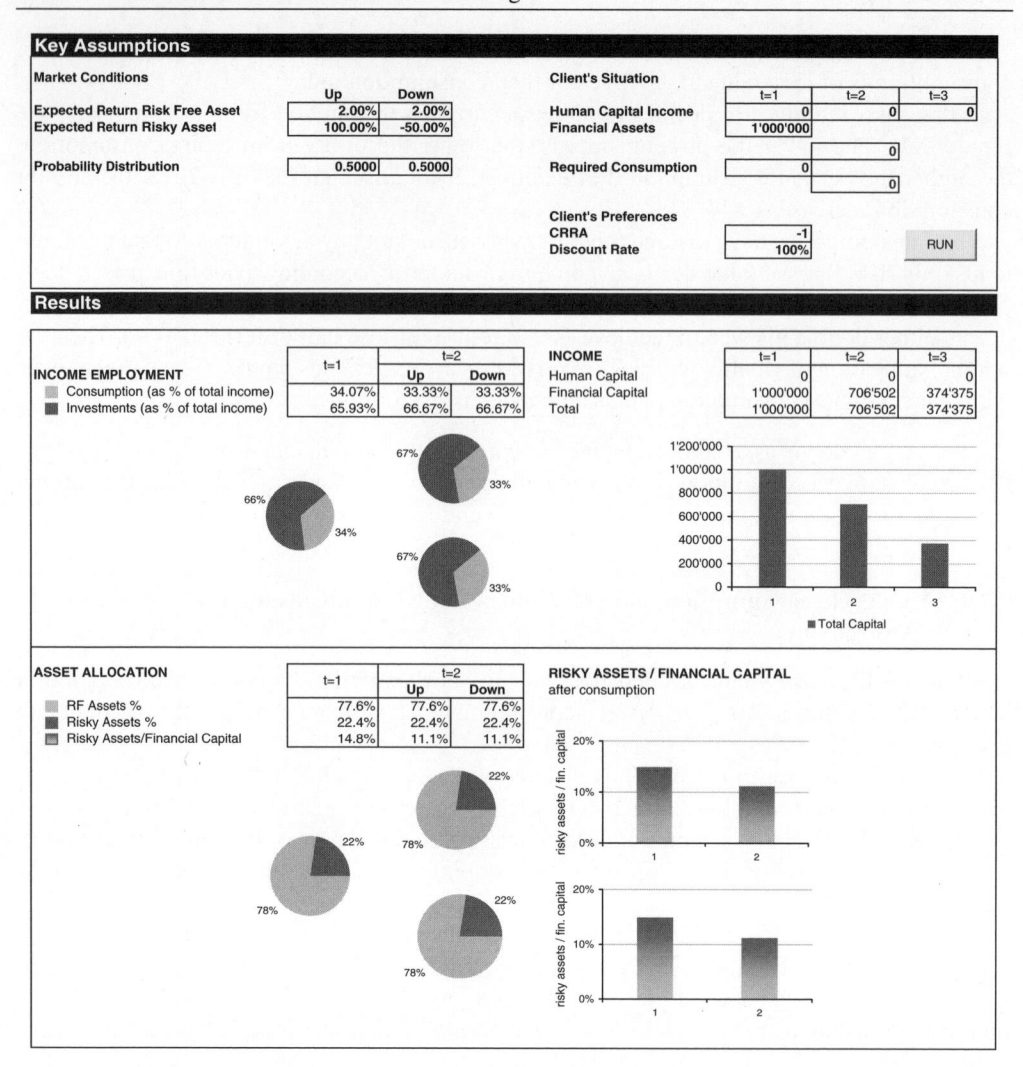

Figure 7.8 The impact of asymmetric returns on consumption and asset allocation of a CRRA investor

increase his current investments in risky assets from 22.4 % to 90.8 % (see Figure 7.10); as in the previous case, the proportion of risky assets to financial capital decreases over time.

7.8 THE LIFE CYCLE ASSET ALLOCATION OF A BEHAVIOURAL INVESTOR

The behavioural investor differs from the expected utility maximizer in several aspects. First, he is loss averse and evaluates payoffs relative to a reference point. Second, he may discount

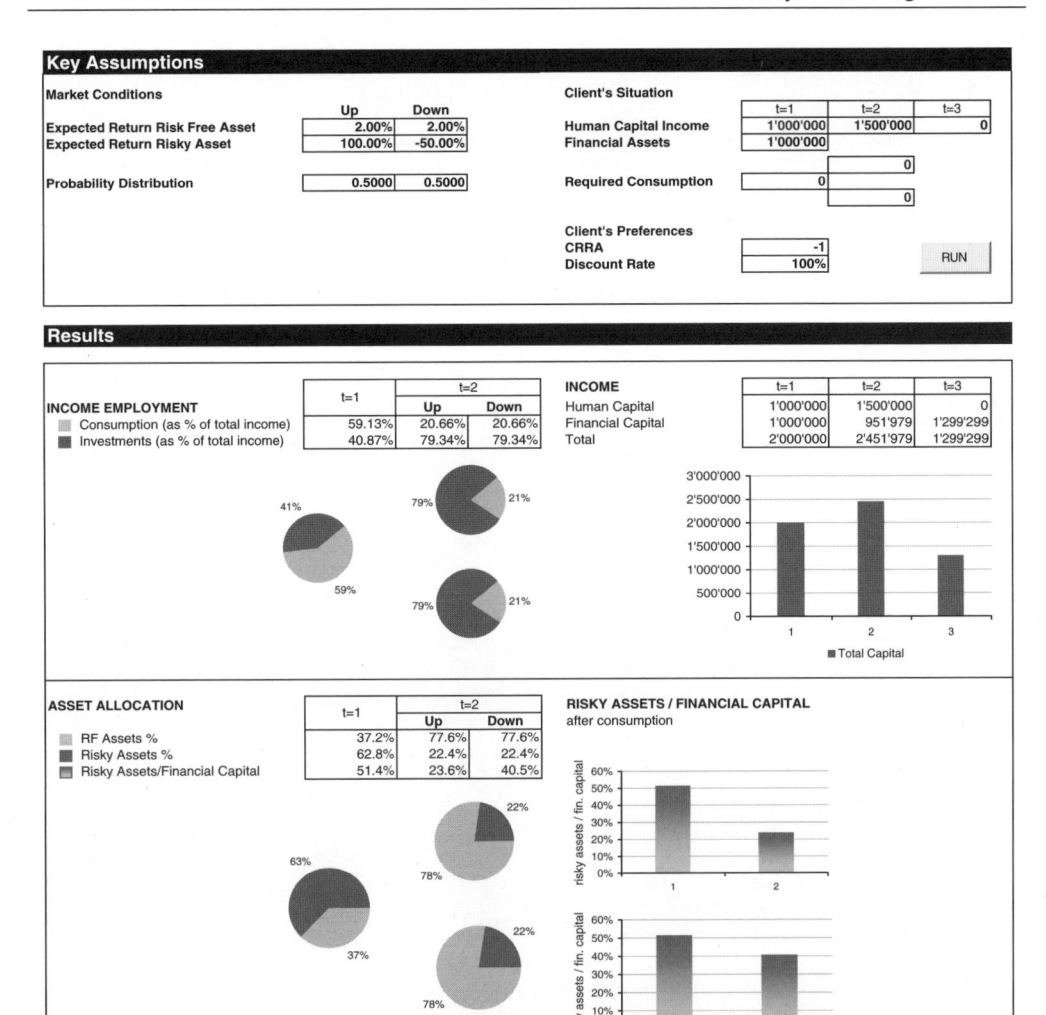

Figure 7.9 Impact of human capital on consumption and asset allocation of a CRRA investor

consumption streams hyperbolically. Finally, the behavioural investor may evaluate consumption streams by habit formation, applying the prospect theory value function to changes in consumption.

Consider first the simplest situation of assets with symmetric returns, no uncertainty, no interest, no discounting, and no human capital. If, in the beginning, habit consumption is equal to zero then the optimal consumption of the behavioural client coincides with the optimal consumption of the expected utility maximizer. Both clients smooth consumption perfectly, i.e. they consume 1/3 of their wealth in each state (see Figure 7.11).

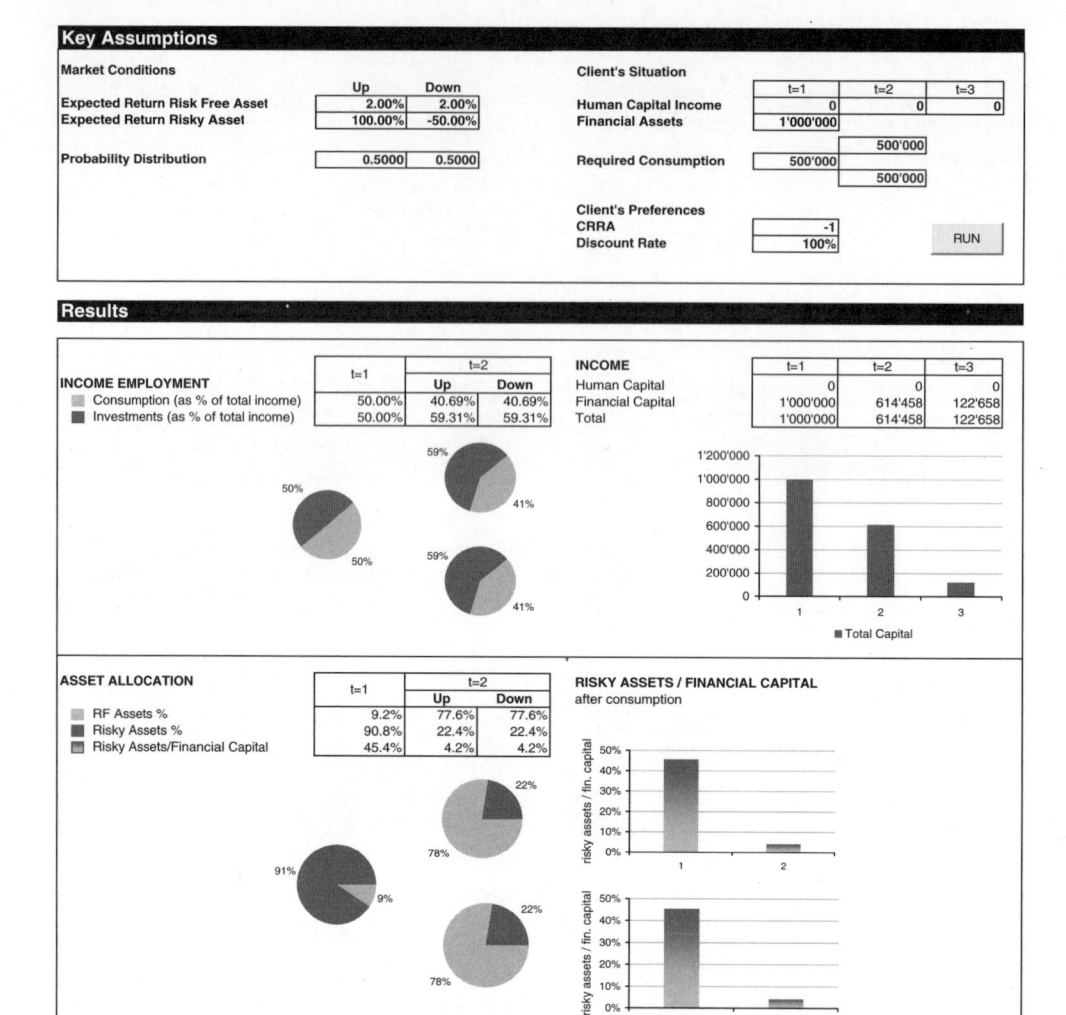

Figure 7.10 Impact of required consumption on the optimal asset allocation of a CRRA investor

However, if the coefficient indicating the effect of habit formation is, for example, 0.2, meaning that 80% of the utility is determined by the level of consumption and 20% is determined by the change in consumption, then the investor would decrease his consumption today (from 33% to 14%) in order to be able to experience increasing consumption in the future (see Figure 7.12).

The higher the coefficient h, the stronger is the reduction in current consumption levels. If, for example, $h = 0.3$, then the optimal consumption decreases to 6.4% of the total income; however, for any $h > 0$, the consumption increases over time.

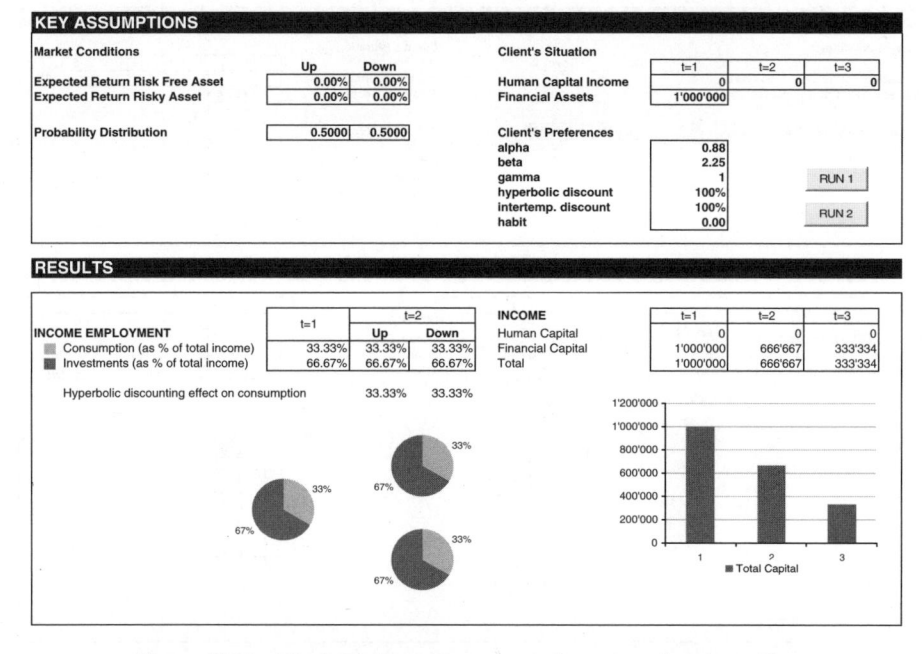

Figure 7.11 The behavioural investor and consumption smoothing

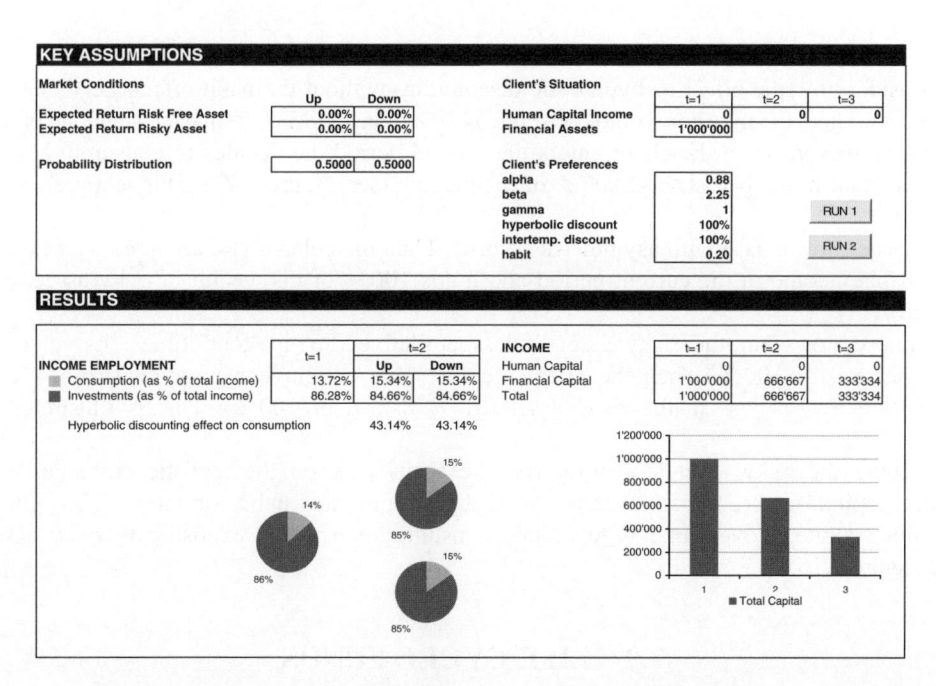

Figure 7.12 The habit formation effect on the optimal consumption over time

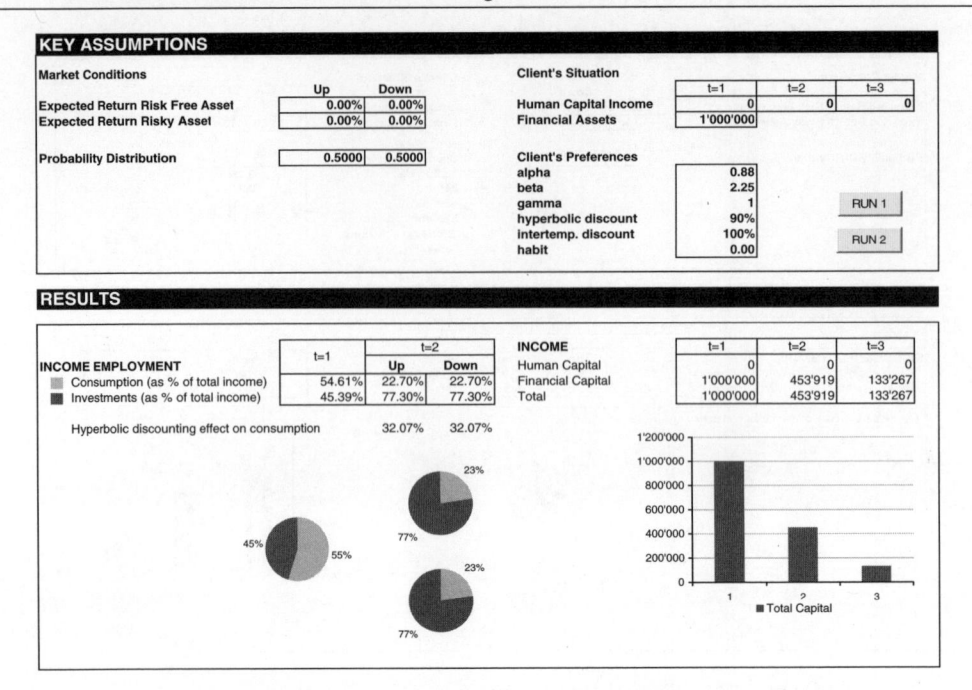

Figure 7.13 The effect of hyperbolic discounting on consumption

Consider now the effect of hyperbolic discounting without the habit effect, i.e. $\beta = 90\%$ and $h = 0$. Then, the investor would consume 54.6 % today and 22.7% in each state one period ahead. However, when the client enters the second period, he decides to consume, both in the good and in the bad state, 32.07 % of his income (see Figure 7.13). This is a preference reversal.

Consider now a case with asymmetric returns. Then the behavioural client consumes only 4 % of his income in the current period and holds 100 % of his wealth in risky assets (see Figure 7.14).

Suppose now that the risky asset is less attractive, i.e. in good times, its return is 60 % instead of 100 %. Then the client increases his current consumption (from 4 % to 26 %) and invests less in the risky asset (81 % instead of 100 %). This is illustrated in Figure 7.15.

Keeping the risky asset less attractive, we focus now on the realistic case, i.e. with human capital, hyperbolic and intertemporal discounting, and habit formation. The optimal investor's strategy over time is to reduce consumption and the exposure to risky assets (see Figure 7.16).

7.9 LIFE CYCLE FUNDS

While structured products target the current needs of the clients, life cycle products aim to meet the changing needs of clients over time. Life cycle funds are built on the premise that individual investors are historically bad at creating a diversified portfolio and react sluggishly

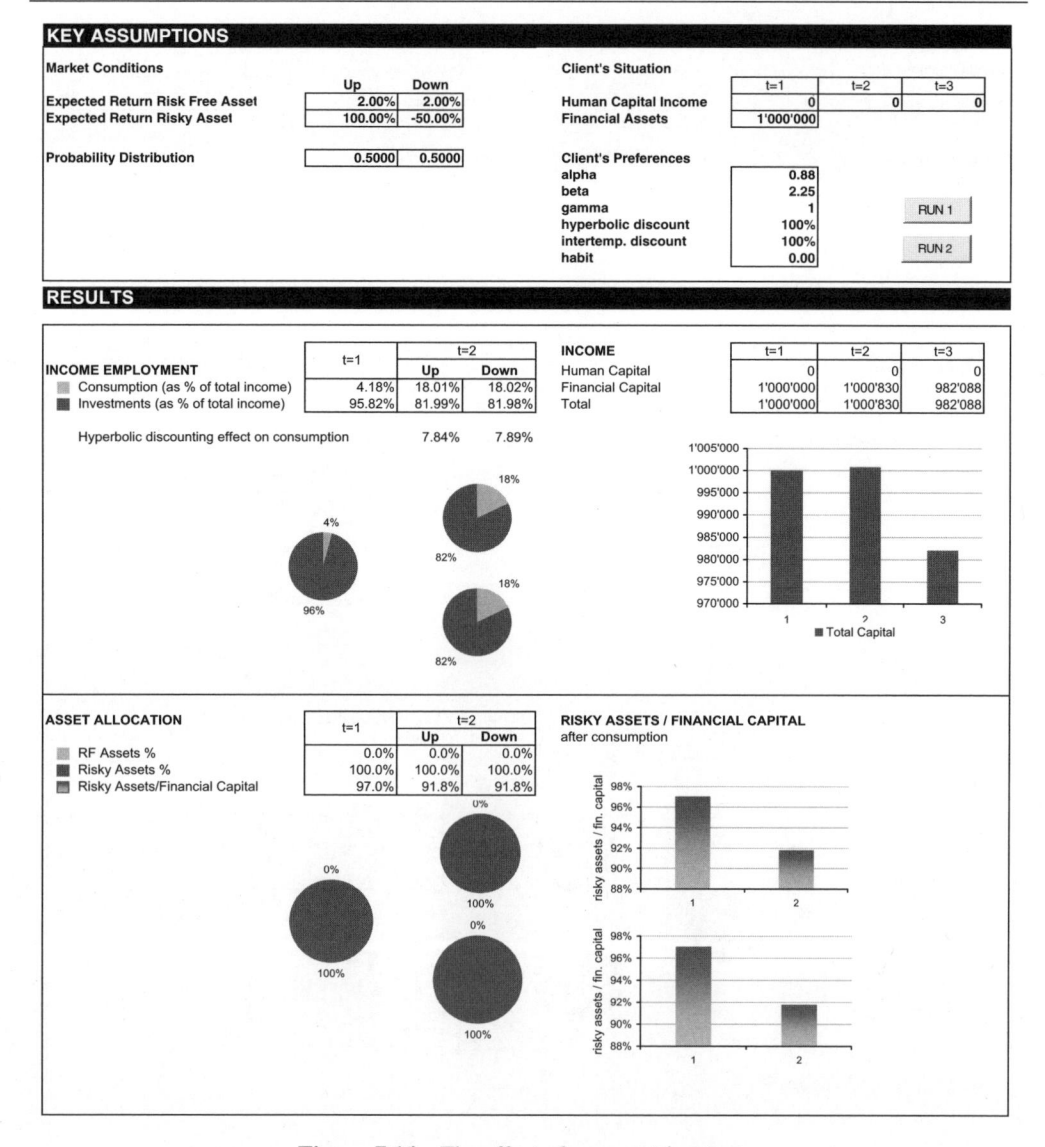

Figure 7.14 The effect of asymmetric returns

to rebalance their portfolios in response to the ratio of human capital to financial assets. Life cycle products do it all. Investors get a portfolio they never have to think about until retirement.

The products begin with an aggressive mix of risky assets such as stocks and bonds, and rebalance to maintain the portfolio diversification and limit the risk with the time left to the retirement date. For example, the Fidelity Freedom 2030 fund features 80 % stocks (65 % domestic and 15 % international equity), 11 % investment-grade bonds, and 9 % high-yield bonds, while the Fidelity Freedom 2010 fund features around 50 % stocks (40 % domestic and

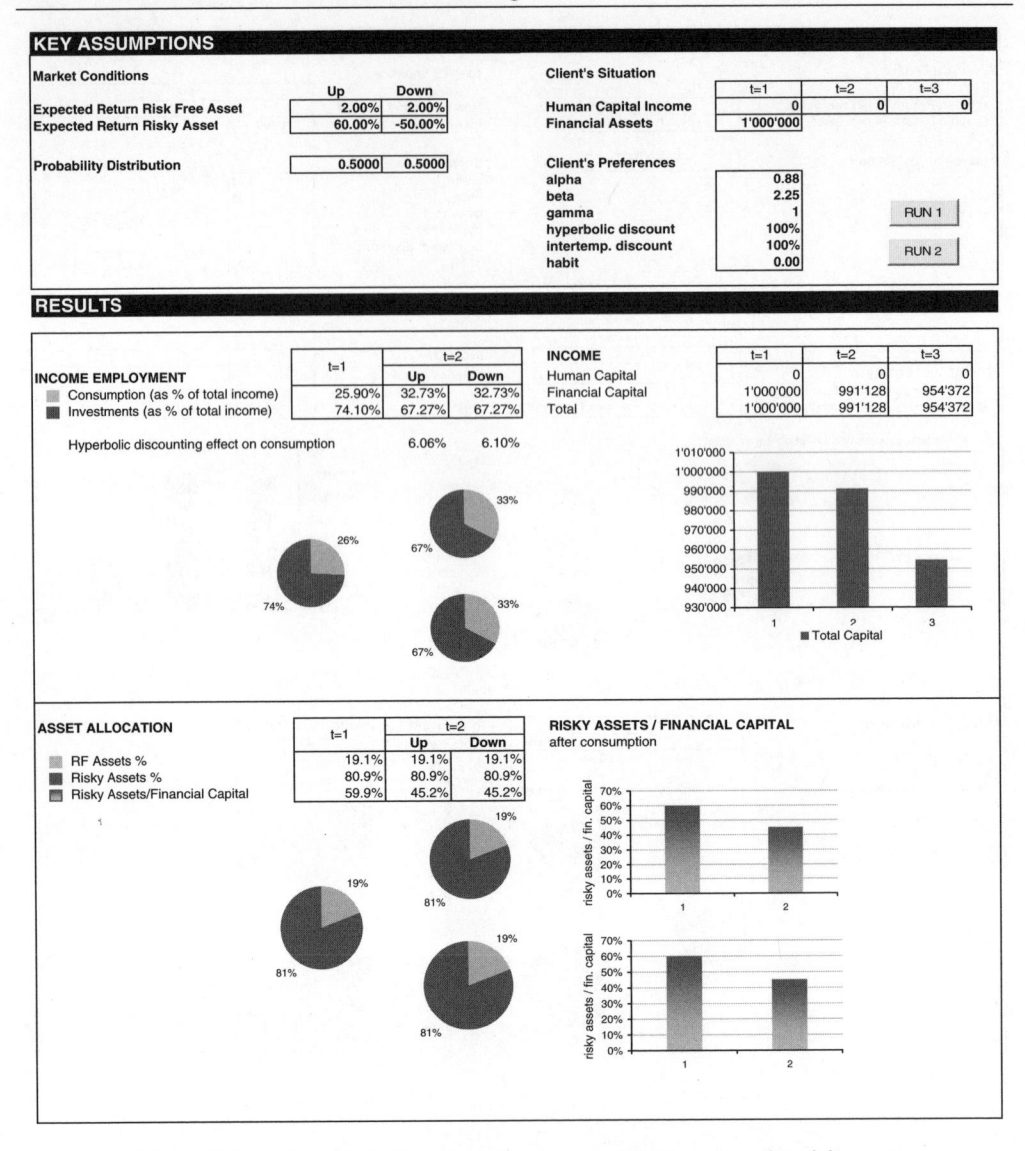

Figure 7.15 The effect of asymmetric returns with a less attractive risky asset

10 % international equity), 35 % investment-grade bonds, 5 % high-yield bonds, and 10 % cash (as of December 2007).[7]

These products reduce the exposure to risky assets with the length of the investment horizon. This is optimal for all investors unless they are CRRA investors and believe that markets are unpredictable. For these investors life cycle funds are not attractive unless the investors plan

---

[7] Other providers of life cycle products are: American Century (American Century My Retire Funds), Barclays (Barclays Global Investment Funds), Dreyfus (Dreyfus Life Time Funds), Charles Schwab (Schwab Retirement Income Fund), T. Rowe Price (T. Rowe Price Retire Funds), and Vanguard (Vanguard Target Retirement).

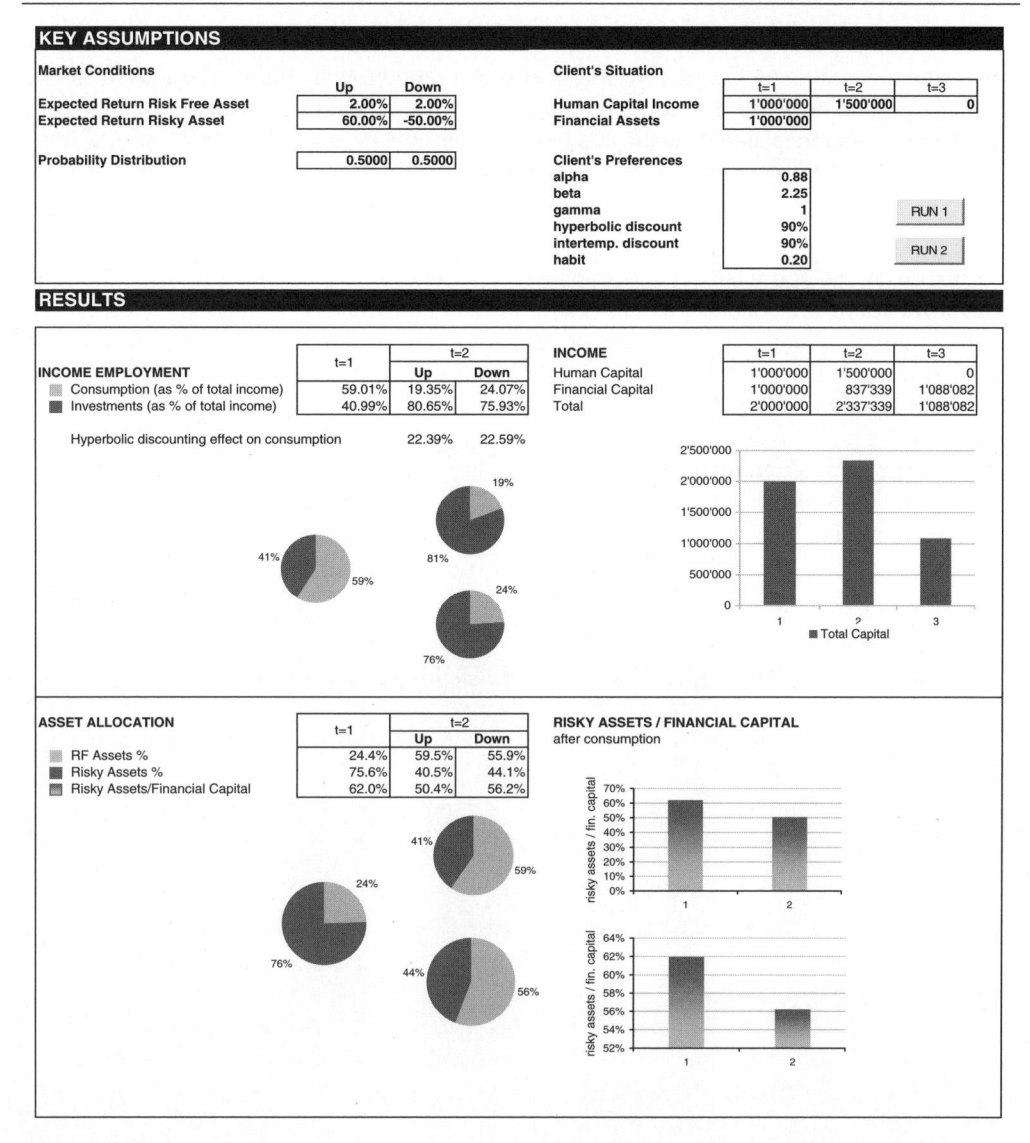

Figure 7.16 The cumulative effect of human capital, hyperbolic and intertemporal discounting, and habit formation

to withdraw funds for consumption or consider additional income as human capital in their planning.

The main problem of these products is that they are designed as stand-alone offerings. If investors do not allocate all of their wealth there, they need to decide on the rest of their money. In fact, only 34 % of the owners of Vanguard life cycle funds used them as the intended one-stop shopping investment choice.[8] Some people buy other funds in addition to the life-cycle

---

[8] See How America Saves 2007 report on Vanguard 2006 defined contribution plan data.

fund, while others own multiple life cycle funds or trade frequently in or out of the fund. In either situation, one may hurt the overall investment without realizing it. The reason is that, for many people, their retirement plan through their work is the largest, but it might be only one of many different accounts dedicated to retirement.

7.10 CONCLUSION

The analysis of the optimal asset allocation over the life cycle of different investors allows us to make the following conclusions: the importance of the current consumption increases with the discounting rate applied to estimate the value of future consumption, current consumption increases also with the asymmetry seen in the returns of risky and risk-free assets, which is also a reason to hold risky assets. Both the current consumption and the investments in risky assets increase if the investor with CRRA has human capital. In contrast, behavioural investors with time-inconsistent preferences due to hyperbolic discounting prefer to reduce the planned savings and increase consumption in the future. Habitual investors prefer consumption that increases over time.

These insights lead to the following steps in life cycle planning advisory:

1. Convince your client to overcome hyperbolic discounting and to start planning his investments now.
2. Make a financial plan for the client that includes his income and liabilities over the life cycle.
3. Point out potential gaps and discuss his consumption needs. By doing so, be aware of habit formation.
4. Use a decision support tool, e.g. extensions of the one used here to illustrate the various aspects and to generate investment strategies over the life cycle.

8
Structured Wealth Management Process

Managing wealth is a difficult task since assets on a financial market never offer bargains; only trade-offs. To find the best solution, one has to combine the trade-offs that the market offers with the preference of the investor, given the constraints of his personal financial situation. Study of behavioural finance is worthwhile in this respect, since it makes one aware of the typical mistakes in investing. It is difficult to say which mistakes are the most severe, because a major disaster typically results from the combination of many aspects which, in isolation, may not even be mistakes in other circumstances. For example, reference point behaviour and mental accounting may be useful in some circumstances, but when applied simultaneously, they may lead to a loss of money as Example 2.3 shows. Box 8.1 lists the behavioural traps that a structured wealth management process enables you to avoid, from fundamental factors to the more sophisticated ones.

Box 8.1: The five main mistakes in wealth management

1. A lack of planning
   The most fundamental mistake in wealth management is not planning your wealth-related decisions. Of course, planning takes time and asking for advice may be expensive. As a consequence, many clients try to hitch a free ride by imitating what others are doing, or they prefer to postpone the planning to another time. As the concept of hyperbolic discounting has shown, in the short run this looks attractive, but ultimately, without proper planning, you will end up in an unfortunate situation.
2. Incorrect framing of the situation
   Knowing how to frame a decision is a powerful skill once you master it. To a great extent, marketing specialists make money from providing a framing that influences the customers' decisions in whichever way the firm wants. Frames in wealth management should be based on the stocks and flows of money, the risk scenarios, and the alternatives one has. The frame should be forward-looking, i.e. previous decisions (such as at which price you bought an asset) should not be used as a reference point for future decisions. Moreover, frames should not be too narrow. The wealth should not be split up into many mental accounts and changes of wealth over time should be integrated so that myopic loss aversion can be avoided.
3. Inefficient risk management, e.g. false diversification
   Diversification is the most powerful tool to master the ups and downs of the financial markets. A well diversified portfolio will always lose on some assets but also always win on others. It is possible to diversify in such a way that on average your wealth grows. Single bets, like buying stocks of one company only, may be exciting but they

> **Box 8.1:** (Continued)
>
> are definitely not worth risking a large amount of your wealth on. Mental accounting may hinder good diversification and quantitative tools should be used to avoid naïve diversification.
>
> 4. Not following a strategy
>   You should be aware that in the course of investing, events will happen that could not have been anticipated before. But be aware that these things will always happen, so there is no need to over-react to them. To avoid being swept away by the hectic nature of the markets, you should follow a strategy of future investments in what has already been proven to achieve the characteristics that suit your preferences and constraints. Also, you should not believe that you can find a perfect response to the ups and downs of the markets. A good strategy is typically less volatile than the markets. Whenever something happens, double-check whether your fundamental investment premises and your constraints are still satisfied in a long-run perspective.
> 5. Wrong performance attribution
>   When the best investors have luck and know that they have had luck, they set moderate goals for the future. Success carries the risk of making you too proud and overconfident so you do not perceive risks effectively. Finding a correct performance attribution is important for improving your strategy. Emotions like greed, fear, pride, and regret may hinder a balanced evaluation of the situation.

These five points seem pretty obvious on a general level. But when it comes to more specific situations, this is less so. The structured advisory process that we outline in this text will help you avoid most of the behavioural traps.

The main ingredients of such a process can be summarised as follows.

- needs analysis
- personal asset and liability management
- risk profiling
- choosing and implementing an optimal asset allocation
- documentation and reporting

Independent financial advisors have to carry out all five steps on their own. They may try to get some support by using a questionnaire as a checklist for assessing the clients' risk preferences and risk awareness, they may purchase an asset liability tool, and they should apply a portfolio optimization tool. They also have to form a good understanding of the future risk-returns the various asset classes offer. All these tasks are quite ambitious if they are to be carried out by a single advisor. In a large organization, some specialization reflecting the comparative advantages of various specialists can be exploited. Here we will argue that for a large organization, a high degree of standardization is required in the wealth management process in order to guarantee good quality advice to all clients and to benefit from this specialization.

The purpose of private banking is to bridge the gap between the clients and the market. The client advisor therefore needs to have a double talent. He needs to understand the clients and also the market. Since time is a scarce resource to any client advisor, allocating time to the clients and to the market is a delicate balance. In the traditional approach, the client advisor is seen as a market specialist who mostly concentrates on understanding the market. This approach is based on the wrong idea that there is something like "the best" investment strategy that is the same for all clients. Indeed, most newspapers give the impression that the art of investing is to find this universal best investment strategy. Experts can easily be classified as being pro stocks, pro bonds, or pro hedge funds. The same is definitely true for client advisors. Some are intrigued by stocks, others by bonds, and still others by hedge funds, for example. Hence, it should not come as a surprise that client advisors make biased recommendations according to their personal style of investing. The truth, however, is that the market offers trade-offs: the more return one can achieve on a market, the higher the risk one has to take. Hence, there is nothing like "the best" investment strategy that can be found independent of knowing the risk tolerance and the risk preference of the client. The right approach to private banking is therefore to reveal these trade-offs to the client and then to assess the client in order to find the best balance for him. Since there are very strong economies of scale in understanding the market, the time of the client advisor should mainly be reserved for understanding the client. Many specialists can easily work together to understand the market but only a few people (the client advisor and some specialists on taxes, inheritance, etc.) can work together to understand the client. This fact calls for a clear division of labour in which client advisors devote most of their time to understanding the client. Understanding the client goes beyond having a good personal relationship with the client, which is, however, a necessary pre-requisite for doing private banking. It also involves assessing the client's risk ability and his risk preference in a systematic way. These important characteristics of the client determine his asset allocation.

8.1 THE BENEFITS OF A STRUCTURED WEALTH MANAGEMENT PROCESS

A structured process clearly reduces the freedom of the client advisors. Moreover, it makes the client advisors more controllable, and it requires from them the filling in of forms and data sheets and also the ability and willingness to handle new IT. This involves high costs. So are they worth paying? The answer is definitely "yes". Without a structured process, the high degree of heterogeneous advice (as found in the Christine Kuhn case study) will erode the client's trust in private banking. Clients will then focus only on the costs they have to pay and they might ultimately all end up with low cost "solutions" such as the Internet. A structured process, on the other hand, guarantees service quality through standardization, and it exploits economies of scope by focusing on comparative advantages. Finally, only with a structured process is an organization able to learn and improve collectively. This last aspect will become the competitive edge in an ever more rapidly changing world.

To illustrate the idea of comparative advantages, reconsider the trade-off faced by the client advisor. He could either spend most of the time in understanding the market or in understanding the client. A client advisor has to allocate time and effort so that the total value he is able to create from these two activities is maximized. Now, even if the investment committee (IC) is worse in both activities of understanding the client (which is certainly true) and understanding the market (which may not be true), then it would still make sense for the client advisor to specialize in what he can do *relatively* better: i.e. understanding the client. This is illustrated in Figure 8.1.

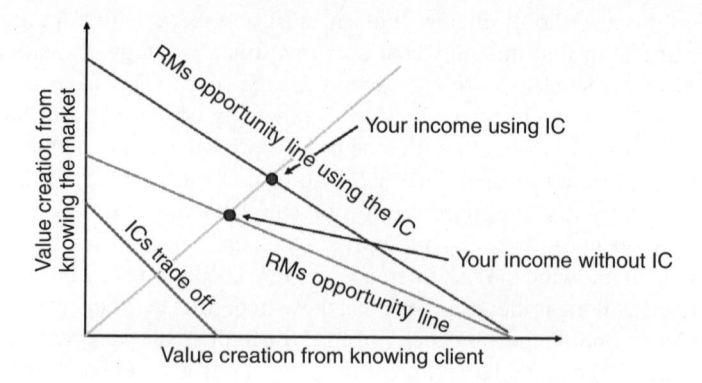

Figure 8.1 Exploiting the comparative advantage of the relationship manager (RM) vis-à-vis the investment committee (IC)

The same argument can, of course, also be made by showing that the IT department should specialize in providing a good IT platform and by showing that the analysts should specialize in giving effective appreciation of stocks and bonds. But since we got used to these specializations, we might have forgotten that they originate from the same principle in which client advisors should specialize in understanding clients.

8.2 PROBLEMS IMPLEMENTING A STRUCTURED WEALTH MANAGEMENT PROCESS

Client advisors and their clients have to optimally adjust to a given process. The transition requires some effort on both sides. Most likely one would expect to experience the usual J-curve effect; first things will become worse and eventually things will greatly improve.

One should be aware that some participants will seek "the easy way out". That is, they will fill in the required forms without interviewing the client, and they will try to complete them in such a way that the asset allocation they have recommended before turns out to be optimal.

8.3 IMPACT OF THE NEW PROCESS ON CONFLICTS OF INTERESTS

How does a structured process change the possible conflicts between the parties involved? With regard to the client advisors and the bank, it restricts the freedom of the client advisors; it redefines their core competences and it requires them to fill in forms and handle a new IT system. On the other hand, the client advisors will get a good IT system which also helps in the client reporting. Last but not least, a structured process binds the clients more to the bank and less to the client advisors. Concerning the clients and the bank, the former can be sure of getting less random advice. However, the IT system may also introduce more trading. Finally, concerning client advisors and specialists, one has to find a way of making sure that using the service of specialists to the client advisors is not for free, since this may result in an inefficient over-use of these free goods.

8.4 LEARNING BY "CYCLING" THROUGH THE PROCESS

Only a structured process allows an organization to learn collectively. Using the data provided to the IT system by the client advisor, the bank can do systematic studies in order to spot possible problems. Concerning the individual client, one has to check his risk ability and his risk preference regularly, since the gains and losses obtained through the investment process do change the client's free assets, and they will make him more experienced!

8.5 CASE STUDY: CREDIT SUISSE

Each bank has its own way of structuring the wealth management process; some go through four steps (e.g. Merrill Lynch[1]) while others use a five-step analysis (e.g. Credit Suisse). As the number of different stages is not decisive for the quality of the provided advice, we illustrate how to structure the wealth management process by using the approach of Credit Suisse, one of the largest banks in Switzerland. Additionally, we provide some ideas for improvement from the behavioural finance perspective.

The five steps in the wealth management process of Credit Suisse are illustrated in Figure 8.2 and discussed below.

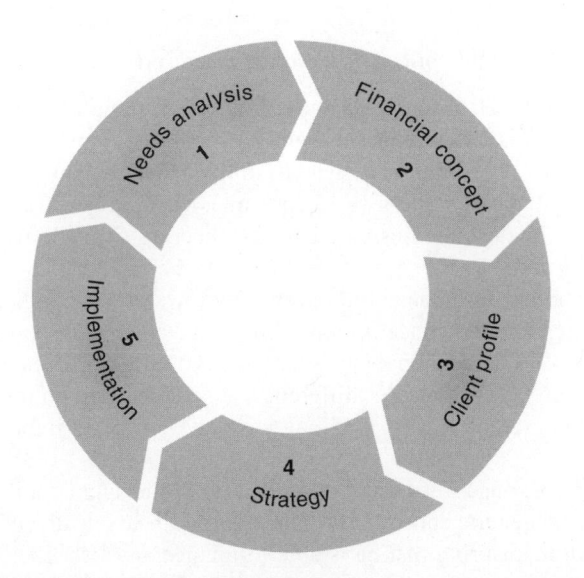

Figure 8.2 The wealth management process of Credit Suisse

---

[1] In the first step, the client advisor establishes the client's objectives. The second step sets an investment strategy. The third step implements a solution and in the last step the progress is reviewed.

8.5.1 Needs analysis

Good advice starts with an assessment of a client's needs. These are closely related to the client's life cycle and in particular to some turning points such as unemployment, a move to another country, marriage, children, inheritance, etc. These turning points are important because they can trigger the client's decision to ask for investment advice. Therefore, it is strongly recommended that client advisors should understand which needs arise at which stage of the client's life cycle in order to be able to keep the current clientele and acquire new customers.

At this stage, there are some important questions to be answered:

- Does the client want a quick fix or all-encompassing advice?
- Does the client want to delegate the wealth management completely, partially, or not at all? If the client wishes to delegate the management partially, he will expect to receive advice; if the client prefers not to delegate the investment decisions, then his needs are usually covered by an appropriate tool assisting him in making investment decisions (e.g. e-banking).
- How deep should the wealth management process go? Broadly structured processes offer clients the choice between some roughly defined categories. The process can be also structured on the basis of stereotypes which offer the client the possibility of choosing from some fixed menus. If the process is constructive, then each client receives a tailored asset allocation.

The major aim of the needs analysis is to assess whether the client can benefit from professional advice and, if so, which level and type of planning would be appropriate.

8.5.2 Developing a financial concept: Personal asset and liability management

In accordance with the level of planning chosen, the next stage of the wealth management process requires a careful assessment of the client's personal assets and liabilities. Professionals describe this approach as "Personal Assets and Liability Management" (PALM). It is based on the notion that from a financial point of view a person is very similar to a firm, i.e. the personal financial situation can be described using a balance sheet, as firms do when they report their financial position. In particular, one balance sheet can be used to assess the current assets and liabilities, and another to manage the in- and outflows of wealth that are determined by income, taxes, housing, and the consumption needs of the client. The following balance sheet is a fictional example of a personal balance sheet for a Credit Suisse client (see Figure 8.3).

This information can be evaluated in different ways, depending on the needs analysis and in particular, on the degree of planning. In any case, the PALM is important in determining the agent's risk ability.

The risk ability sets a constraint for the optimization of the agent's utility, which embodies his risk preference. In general, one should aim to find an asset allocation that maximizes the agent's utility while ensuring that he is able to finance any liabilities. In this respect, the advisor needs to find out two important things. First, how to determine a client's preferences, i.e. his risk profile which is discussed in Section 8.5.3. Second, is it possible to prioritize the client's liabilities in say, hard liabilities (e.g. necessary wealth to keep up the lifestyle) and soft liabilities (e.g. wealth to accomplish plans and wishes that would enhance the lifestyle)? Box 8.2 illustrates how Credit Suisse uses the asset split in PALM.

Structured Wealth Management Process 213

CREDIT SUISSE Private Banking **Advisory Report**
09.07.2008
Assets and Liabilities

Client number:
Reporting currency: CHF

Assets		Due Date	CHF	Liabilities	Due Date	CHF
Bankable assets with us			500'000	Mortgages with us		2'000'000
		500'000		· Credit Suisse	2'000'000	
Bankable assets with other				Loans/credits with us		-
banks			4'622'300	Guarantees with us		-
· DBS	1'136'100			Liabilities with other banks		-
· Rabobank	3'236'200	01.12.2009		Other liabilities		-
· HSBC	250'000					
Real estates			900'000			
· Owner occupied apartment, Zürich	900'000					
3rd Pillar			54'000			
· Credit Suisse	54'000					
2nd Pillar			250'000			
· Pension Fund	250'000	01.01.2023				
Life insurance policy			-			
Other assets			-			
Total			6'326'300	Total		2'000'000

Figure 8.3 Example of a personal balance sheet

Box 8.2: Asset split of Credit Suisse

In the asset split process the total bankable assets are split into dedicated assets and free assets. The hard liabilities are matched with the safe dedicated assets and the free assets can then be invested in more risky assets. That is to say, Credit Suisse introduces two mental accounts to one of which the safety first principle is applied; to the other, Credit Suisse uses the concept of Value at Risk. The idea is illustrated in Figure 8.4.

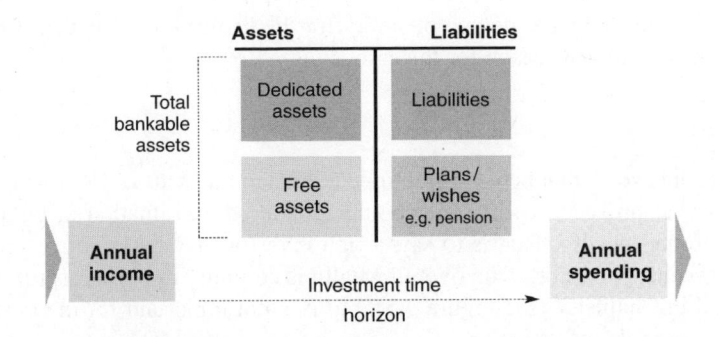

Figure 8.4 Assets split (*Source*: Credit Suisse)

The asset split gives the clients a higher utility since they know that their hard liabilities are no longer in danger. Moreover, it can be seen as a risk management technique, as the following argument shows.

Box 8.2: (Continued)

By integrating free and dedicated assets into one class of assets, one can try to make use of the fact that typically different assets are not perfectly correlated. Hence, by using the classical mean-variance diversification, a higher expected return can be achieved, even under a Value at Risk (VaR) constraint.

In a mean-variance diagram, the intended solution can be displayed as on the left of Figure 8.5.

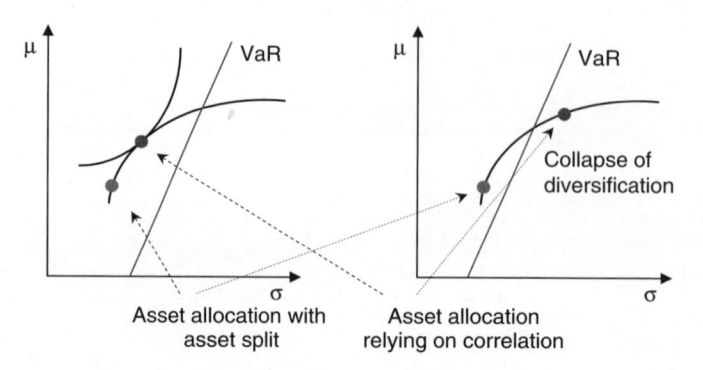

Figure 8.5 The asset split protects the client from a collapse of diversification

If assets are actually more strongly correlated than expected, then the solution that looks safe from a mean-variance perspective turns out to be treacherous because diversification is no longer possible. In effect, the result is as depicted in the right part of Figure 8.5. Some of the dedicated assets will be lost. Hence, whether one can benefit from the diversification effect depends on how good the estimates of the co-variances are. It is wise to use a higher degree of safety for the dedicated assets than for the free assets, which is a rational reason for the asset split.

One very important aspect that behavioural finance adds to the issue of PALM and risk ability is that, according to prospect theory, one should separate the evaluation of gains and losses from the background wealth. That is to say, a rich investor may be as angry about a loss of 10 % as a less wealthy investors. The overall wealth is certainly important for the risk ability, as we explained in Chapter 7 (see Figure 7.5), but it is not important for the risk preference, which is addressed in the next section.

8.5.3 The client profile

Wealth managers aiming to provide tailored asset allocations are required to assess the risk ability, the risk preference, and the risk awareness of each of their clients. The *risk ability* is determined by the personal asset and liability situation as discussed above. It depends on the client's financial strength, financial flexibility, and the extent to which he is able to bear short-term fluctuations of his investments. Using insights from prospect theory, wealth managers are able to estimate the *risk preferences* of the client. The risk preferences address the willingness of the client to take risks and possible losses. The extent to which clients are *aware* of the risks they take with their investment decisions depends on the client's inclination to certain biases. A detailed discussion on risk profiling is offered in Chapter 4.

8.5.4 Investment strategy

The optimal investment strategy is determined on the one hand by the risks and opportunities offered on the market, and on the other by the preferences and restrictions of the client. Questionnaires are helpful to elicit the latter. Previous return realizations of the assets included in the asset allocation provide information on the risks and the opportunities on the market.[2] By combining both pieces of information, one gets the optimal asset allocation of the client (see Figure 8.6).

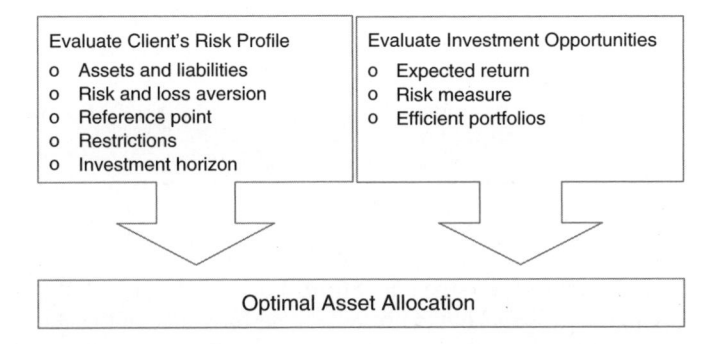

```
┌─────────────────────────────────┐  ┌─────────────────────────────────┐
│ Evaluate Client's Risk Profile  │  │ Evaluate Investment Opportunities│
│   o  Assets and liabilities     │  │   o  Expected return            │
│   o  Risk and loss aversion     │  │   o  Risk measure               │
│   o  Reference point            │  │   o  Efficient portfolios       │
│   o  Restrictions               │  │                                 │
│   o  Investment horizon         │  │                                 │
└─────────────────────────────────┘  └─────────────────────────────────┘
                    ↘                          ↙
                    ┌──────────────────────────────┐
                    │  Optimal Asset Allocation    │
                    └──────────────────────────────┘
```

Figure 8.6 Finding an optimal investment strategy for the client

8.5.5 Implementing and managing the optimal portfolio

Once the investment strategy has been determined, the client advisor implements the investment decisions. The investments are reviewed on a regular basis to make sure that they match the client's risk profile, particularly over major turning points of the client's life.

A typical advisory process will determine the client's optimal asset allocation, which is then implemented by the relationship manager choosing appropriate assets and investment products. For some clients, the process of assets and products selection is particularly valuable. Other clients prefer a passive approach and choose cost-efficient index solutions like Exchange Traded Funds (ETFs). In any case it is important to monitor whether the risk-reward characteristics of the client's portfolio match those of his best asset allocation.

8.5.6 Documentation and reporting

For each step of the process, specific information needs to be stored. This is important for at least three reasons. First, storing information used to take a particular investment decision is

---

[2] One can also use more sophisticated methods to forecast the moments of the return distribution of the assets than simply looking in the past.

necessary for performing double checks, but is also significant in the case of opinion revisions. Second, storing the information which was relevant at the time the decisions have been taken helps to avoid cognitive dissonances, i.e. the irrational regret once decisions have been taken. Moreover, it prevents the hindsight bias from occurring. Third, in certain cases, stored information might be useful as a protection against legal claims.

Before we go into these aspects in more detail, we shall first have a closer look at the example given below, which aims to show the effects of "aggregation" and "segregation" of payoffs.

Example 8.1:

Consider an investor who decides to hold cash and invest in bonds, stocks, and hedge funds. For simplicity, we will assume that all assets are equally weighted.

Asset	Weight	Return	Performance
cash	25 %	2.00 %	0.50 %
bonds	25 %	3.00 %	0.75 %
stocks	25 %	6.00 %	1.50 %
hedge funds	25 %	−4.00 %	−1.00 %

Since we now have an understanding of prospect theory, we can evaluate the different ways of presenting the investment result to the client from a behavioural point of view.

The main issue with reporting is how to present the performance of the client's investments so that he fully understands and feels good about it. From the perspective of traditional finance, this question does not make sense since the way information is presented does not affect its evaluation. However, from the perspective of a behavioural investor, reporting matters.

Example 8.1: (Continued)

To see why reporting matters, assume that the client is a behavioural client[3] with risk aversion over gains $\alpha^+ = 2.1511$, risk aversion over losses, $\alpha^- = -1.8469$ and loss aversion of 2.25.

If the client faces the performance of the whole portfolio his utility is 0.017171, which results in a certainty equivalent of 1.75 %. By comparing the utility levels resulting from alternative reporting strategies, one can see that this reporting scenario is the best from the client's perspective. Hence, if some of the investments realize small losses it is always better to report them together with the gains achieved by other investments.

We will now apply the same intuition to a slightly different scenario with a greater loss on the hedge fund investment (−8 % instead of −4 %).

---

[3] As before, we assume the piecewise quadratic value function.

Assets	Weights	Return	Performance
cash	25 %	2 %	0.50 %
bonds	25 %	3 %	0.75 %
stocks	25 %	6 %	1.50 %
hedge funds	25 %	−8 %	−2.00 %

In this case, it is better to report the performance of the hedge fund investment separately from all other assets. The prospect utility of the client is then 0.00897, which is greater than the utility of reporting all assets together (0.00744). The respective certainty equivalents are 0.7500 % and 0.9058 %. The reason is the decreasing marginal disutility from reporting losses, i.e. it is better to report losses separately instead of presenting them together with the gains realized by other assets.

8.6 MENTAL ACCOUNTING IN THE WEALTH MANAGEMENT PROCESS

Thaler (1999) defines mental accounting as "the set of cognitive operations used by individuals and households to organize, evaluate, and keep track of financial activities". In the context of wealth management so far, we have not used mental accounts since we assumed that the clients consider all assets as interchangeable and that they have one overall goal according to which they arrange all financial affairs. In the mean-variance approach, this goal is steered by a number describing the desire for having high returns on average relative to the aversion against deviations from the average investment return. In prospect theory, this overall goal depends on the reference point, the loss aversion, and the risk aversion.

It is very questionable whether clients can give one such an overall goal. Most likely their financial affairs include several goals such as capital protection, long term growth, or being able to afford certain specific wishes like early retirement, education of children, etc. Moreover, clients may separate assets into different asset classes (risk free, save, moderately risky, capital appreciation) so that they do not see them as perfectly interchangeable. In this section, we introduce mental accounts in the wealth management process, both for the separation of assets and also for allowing several investment goals.

In the easiest case one can associate one subset of assets for each investment goal (risk free for capital protection, ..., stocks for long term growth) and hence, the two ways of forming mental accounts coincide. One such example for the easy case is given by the portfolio pyramid (see Figure 3.10). Each layer of the portfolio pyramid, where each layer is associated with a particular goal or particular attitude toward risk. Investors' portfolios are then built as a pyramid of assets, layer by layer. In general, the clear association of assets to investment goals may, however, not be possible and all assets may be needed for each goal so that the two implementations of mental accounts do not coincide.

In the next section, we first look at mental accounts in the form of asset classes. There in particular, we ask the question of what would be the best way of grouping assets into mental accounts in order to achieve the highest utility. The surprising finding is that the highest utility is not achieved without mental accounts, i.e. by putting all assets into one group but the highest utility typically results if the risk free asset is separated from the risky assets. We know this because of two observations; by the law of decreasing marginal utility from gains, it is always better to have two separate gains than one total gain, and due to loss aversion, it is better to offset losses by gains, i.e. to diversify risky assets in one portfolio. This observation can also be seen as a solution to the asset allocation puzzle: Since the risk free asset has no diversification effect, it is better to separate it from the risky assets in order to benefit at the highest degree from the sure gain derived from it.

In Section 8.6.3, we then show how to do goal-based wealth management in a consistent way so that no irrationalities arise from several goals that might conflict with each other. Here the key insight is to use a two-stage approach, i.e. to optimize each goal separately and then to combine the goals on a higher level. The wealth management process will reflect this principle by using "portfolio risk profilers" for each goal and then using a "client risk profiler" for the combination of the goals.

8.6.1 Mental accounting among assets and the asset allocation puzzle

Here we analyze whether an investor benefits from separating assets into different accounts. Of course he would only lose by doing this if his utility did not reflect this account structure because using mental accounts would be a restriction to achieve his overall utility. Instead we consider here the case that the client forms different mental accounts and also evaluates them account by account. We will see that if a behavioural client uses mental accounts while determining his asset allocation, then it is typically optimal for him to use two mental accounts: one including all risky assets, i.e. equities, bonds, etc., and another one including the risk-free assets. The optimal allocation of risky assets is then determined within the first account. Consequently, the client's risk aversion would be reflected in his risky assets mix, i.e. investors with higher risk aversion would allocate more funds to assets with a lower risk and less funds to assets with a higher risk.

Following this observation, the asset allocation puzzle can also be explained with *optimal mental accounting*. The idea of optimal mental accounting is closely related to the *hedonic editing (framing) principle* (Thaler, 1985) describing how people code events.

Using the idea of hedonic editing, we can show that choosing the mental accounts in a way that maximizes the prospect utility of the investor implies separating the risk-free asset from the risky assets. This is illustrated in the following example:

Example 8.2:

Suppose that there are three assets; two risky assets and one risk-free asset. The risk-free asset pays 2 % p.a. in each state. Again, the payoff structure of the assets is as shown in Table 8.1.

Table 8.1 Asset payoffs

	Cash	Asset A	Asset B
Scenario 1	2 %	8 %	−2 %
Scenario 2	2 %	−1 %	6 %

What are the best mental accounts from the perspective of an average behavioural investor with a reference point equal to 0 % and $\alpha^+ = 2.1511$, $\alpha^- = -1.8469$, and $\beta = 2.25$? For simplicity, assume that the investor does not decide about an optimal asset allocation but splits his wealth among the three assets equally. Assume further that the weight of each mental account in the utility function is equal to one.

Table 8.2 Prospect utilities and certainty equivalents with different mental accounting rules

Combination	Prospect utility	Certainty equivalent
v(cash) + v(asset A) + v(asset B)	0.01816	1.853%
v(cash) + v(asset A + asset B)	0.02459	2.527%
v(cash + asset A) + v(asset B)	0.02006	2.051%
v(cash + asset B) + v(asset A)	0.02216	2.272%
v(cash + asset A + asset B)	0.02432	2.500%

Comparing the investor's prospect utilities with different mental accounting rules, we conclude that the best way to view the assets is to split the risky assets from the cash.

An intuitive explanation for this result can be given by considering the curvature of investor's utility function over gains. Splitting assets in two mental accounts (risky assets in one account and cash in another one) means, that investor's utility in each scenario is determined by the returns of two portfolios, i.e. one with risky assets and one with cash. Consider first Scenario 1. The portfolio return in the account with risky assets is 2 %, the return of the cash account is 0.67 %. The return of all assets on one portfolio is equal to 2.67 %. Since the investor's utility over gains is concave, we get $v(2\%) + v(0.67\%) > v(2.67\%)$. Similar considerations apply for Scenario 2 as well. The account with risky assets yields 1.67 % and the cash account yields 0.67 %. The account with all assets yields 2.33 %. Hence, by the concavity of the investor's utility function, we get $v(1.67\%) + v(0.67\%) > v(2.33\%)$. Hence, in each scenario, investors applying the mental accounting rule "risky assets in one account and cash in another one" achieve a higher expected utility than investors evaluating all assets in one account.

Math box 8.1 shows how to write the optimization problem with mental accounts in the general case.

Math Box 8.1: Optimization with mental accounts among assets

To formalize the decision problem with mental accounting among assets, let the set of all assets $\{1, ..., K\}$ be partitioned into $j = 1, ..., J$ mental accounts, which are subsets, K^j, of $\{1, ..., K\}$. Suppose the agent assigns a weight $w(K^j)$ to each such mental account. Then his portfolio optimization problem is:

$$\underset{\lambda_k}{Max} \sum_{j=1}^{J} w(K^j) \sum_{s=1}^{S} p_s u \left(\sum_{\substack{k=1 \\ k \in K^j}}^{K} R_s^k \lambda_k w \right) s.t. \sum_{k=1}^{K} \lambda_k = 1.$$

As shown in Chapter 2, the mean-variance case can be included in this optimization problem by choosing a quadratic utility, u. Moreover, one may want to generalize the optimization problem by allowing for different utility functions for the different asset accounts. Investors may be fine when they lose on stocks but they may be really disappointed when they lose on AAA-bonds, as the sub-prime crisis showed.

Is mental accounting among assets irrational, i.e. does it contradict the axioms of von Neumann and Morgenstern? The answer is "no" if the separation of assets is part of the investor's preferences. This is most easily seen in the state-preference approach. In that

> **Math Box 8.1:** (Continued)
>
> approach, as shown by Savage (1954) and Hens (1992), for example, a utility function is of the expected utility type if it can be written as the expected value of utility derived in the various states.[4] But this is definitely the case even with mental accounting.
>
> $$E_u = \sum_{j=1}^{J} w(K^j) \underbrace{\sum_{s=1}^{S} p_s u \left(\sum_{\substack{k=1 \\ k \in K^j}}^{K} R_s^k \lambda_k w \right)}_{U^j} = \sum_{s=1}^{S} p_s \underbrace{\sum_{j=1}^{J} w(K^j) u \left(\sum_{\substack{k=1 \\ k \in K^j}}^{K} R_s^k \lambda_k w \right)}_{U_s}$$
>
> Hence, as in the lottery approach, deviations from expected utility only arise from probability weighting, which is a key feature of prospect theory. The prospect theory utility function with mental accounting can accordingly be written as:
>
> $$PT_v = \sum_{j=1}^{J} w(K^j) \underbrace{\sum_{s=1}^{S} w(p_s) v \left(\sum_{\substack{k=1 \\ k \in K^j}}^{K} R_s^k \lambda^k w - RP^j \right)}_{V^j}.$$

8.6.2 The goal-based wealth management approach

In this section, we analyze the case that clients have several investment goals and that each of them can, in principle, be pursued with all assets. This gives a foundation for suggestions of practitioners like Brunel (2003, 2006), for example, who recommend a multi-strategy framework in which each strategy matches to a different investment goal. These goals are defined as: "liquidity", "income", "capital preservation", and "growth". The individual needs are then a combination of the four fundamental goals. Nevins (2004) takes these recommendations further into risk profiling. He suggests separating a client's risk tolerance for several goals rather than estimating an overall risk tolerance for each client. Investment strategies leading to specific investment goals should increase a client's confidence in the strategies. As strategies are aligned with the client's own objectives, clients would not feel as though they are being "boxed into" a long-term asset allocation, which they have difficulties associating with. Moreover, following this goal-based investment approach, clients would be also better prepared for bear markets and more likely to keep their perspective and remain disciplined. Finally, when strategies are evaluated based on the progress towards a specific goal, the performance measurement becomes more meaningful.

A potential drawback of the approach suggested by Nevins (2004) and Brunel (2003, 2006) is that mapping separate risk profiles into one investment strategy that serves different goals may lead to an overall risk exposure which exceeds the risk tolerance or even the risk ability of the client. To take account of this issue, we argue that clients should form goal specific portfolios that need, however, to be coordinated from a general perspective. The goal specific portfolios can be formed as outlined before. For each goal, a portfolio risk profiler determines the risk

---

[4] Compare The Representation Theorem of Expected Utility given in Chapter 2.

preferences of the client and a decision support tool suggests the optimal asset allocation. The various portfolio risk profilers then need to be coordinated by the client's risk ability and his weighting of the various goals. The latter is a very difficult but important step in order to get an overall consistency by a client risk profiler.

If a coordination of separate decisions is missing, the resulting decision may become irrational. This has been illustrated in Example 2.3, in which the typical decision-maker wastes money because he typically selects among two pairs of lotteries without seeing the overall connection. A second example showing the need for coordination among separate mental accounts refers to problems of the Value-at-Risk as a risk measure in different mental accounts. Applying the VaR for separate mental accounts is very tricky since adding up the Value-at-Risk of different mental accounts may lead to erroneous conclusions with respect to the total risk exposure of the client. In particular, it is possible that the investment risks in each account are within the limit but the cumulated risk over all accounts is not (see Artzner et al., 1999).

8.6.3 Solving the goal-based investment problem

In this section, we show that goal-based decisions are completely rational if they are pursued correctly. Indeed, we will give a solution technique for goal-based decisions that resemble the two levels: portfolio risk profiler and client risk profiler.

In the beginning, we define the goal-based investment problem and show that it is rational since it is consistent with expected utility maximization.

Math Box 8.2: Goal-based decisions: rational or not?

Consider the state-preference approach,[5] i.e. consider $s = 1, ..., S$ scenarios or states of the world occurring with probability p_s and $k = 1, ..., K$ assets with returns R_s^k. Suppose the client has $g = 1, ..., G$ goals, each of which he evaluates according to an expected utility function $\sum_{s=1}^{S} p_s U^g(w_s^g)$, where w_s^g is the wealth the client has obtained out of his asset allocation λ^g for goal g, i.e. $w_s^g = \sum_{k=1}^{K} R_s^k \lambda_k^g$, $s = 1, ..., S$, where we assume that the initial wealth is normalized to 1. The client's overall budget constraint is $\sum_{g=1}^{G} \sum_{k=1}^{K} \lambda_k^g = 1$, i.e. his total wealth of 1 has to be allocated to the G goal-specific portfolios.

The following optimization problem summarizes the goal-based portfolio approach:

$$\max_{\lambda_k^g} \sum_{g=1}^{G} \delta^g \sum_{s=1}^{S} p_s U^g(w_s^g)$$

s.t.

$$w_s^g = \sum_{k=1}^{K} R_s^k \lambda_k^g, s = 1, ..., S, g = 1, ..., G$$

$$\sum_{g=1}^{G} \sum_{k=1}^{K} \lambda_k^g = 1.$$

The numbers δ^g are the relative weights the client attaches to each goal. Moreover, it makes sense to add a risk ability constraint, e.g. as a "safety first" constraint

---

[5] In the special case of quadratic utilities, this approach encompasses the mean-variance approach as shown in Chapter 2.

> **Math Box 8.2:** (Continued)
>
> $\sum_{g=1}^{G} w_s^g \geq \underline{w}, s = 1, ..., S$, where $\underline{w}$ is the wealth that need to be secured. Note that the objective function is completely rational, as it is an expected utility. This can be seen by rearranging terms:
>
> $$\sum_{g=1}^{G} \delta^g \sum_{s=1}^{S} p_s U^g(w_s^g) = \sum_{s=1}^{S} p_s \sum_{g=1}^{G} \delta^g U^g(w_s^g)$$

Before we show how to solve the goal-based portfolio problem in two stages, we need to mention two variations of it: a generalization including state dependence and a specification – the mean-variance case.

State dependence can arise from two sources. It may be that the client has some exogenous wealth, $\widetilde{w}_s^g$ which is state-dependent. This stochastic wealth may lead to an insurance need, which can then be formulated as one of the client's goals. Moreover, it may be that the client's utility depends on the states of the world even though his wealth does not. For example, the client may care about issues like global warming, poverty, etc. and may then have a goal to generate wealth, e.g. for a charity, taking care of these issues.

> **Math Box 8.3:** State dependence
>
> Lets $\widetilde{w}_s^g$ be the exogenous wealth which is state-dependent and let the utility function be also state-dependent, i.e. $u_s^g(w_s)$. Then the following optimization problem summarizes this general goal-based portfolio approach.
>
> $$\max_{\lambda_k^g} \sum_{g=1}^{G} \delta^g \sum_{s=1}^{S} p_s U_s^g(w_s^g)$$
>
> s.t.
>
> $$w_s^g = \widetilde{w}_s^g + \sum_{k=1}^{K} R_s^k \lambda_k^g, s = 1, ..., S, g = 1, ..., G$$
>
> $$\sum_{g=1}^{G} \sum_{k=1}^{K} \lambda_k^g = 1.$$

The goal based portfolio problem for the case of mean-variance can be derived from the expected utility case as illustrated in the following math box:

> **Math Box 8.4:** The mean-variance goal-based portfolio problem
>
> The mean-variance case follows for goal specific utility functions of the form $u^g(w_s^g) = w_s^g - \frac{\alpha^g}{2}(w_s^g)^2$. In this case, the expected utility is

$$\sum_{s=1}^{S} p_s U^g(w_s^g) = \mu(w_s^g) - \frac{\alpha^g}{2}\mu\left[\left(w_s^g\right)^2\right], \text{ which by definition of the variance gives}$$

$$\sum_{s=1}^{S} p_s U^g(w_s^g) = \mu(w_s^g) - \frac{\alpha^g}{2}\left[\sigma^2(w_s^g) + \mu^2(w_s^g)\right] = V^g\left(\mu(w_s^g), \sigma^2(w_s^g)\right).$$

However, for practical reasons one may also want to work with more general mean-variance goal-based decision problems of the form:

$$\max_{\lambda_k^g} \sum_{g=1}^{G} \delta^g V^g(\mu(w^g), \sigma(w^g))$$

s.t.

$$w_s^g = \widetilde{w}_s^g + \sum_{k=1}^{K} R_s^k \lambda_k^g, s = 1, ..., S, g = 1, ..., G$$

$$\sum_{g=1}^{G} \sum_{k=1}^{K} \lambda_k^g = 1.$$

Thus, a goal-based investor with quadratic utility maximizes the mean-variance trade-off for each goal and allocates wealth to each goal according to the relative importance of the goals, δ^g, and the satisfaction with each goal per unit of wealth.

It is important to note the difference from a mean-variance optimizer without multiple goals; such an investor would try to keep the variance of his total wealth small while a goal-based mean-variance investor tries to reduce the weighted sum of the variance of each goal. Thus, he does not benefit from covariance-diversification across goals.

In the following section we show that the complexity of the huge optimization problem given in Math Box 8.2 can be reduced by solving it in two stages. First, one needs to find an asset allocation that maximizes the investor's expected utility of achieving each specific goal. The optimal asset allocation for each goal determines the budget for this goal. In the second stage, one needs to make sure that the budgets are divided in an optimal way among the different goals. The aim is achieved if the investor's overall expected utility from the budgets, weighted with the relative importance of each goal, is maximal. Additionally, the overall wealth generated by the goal-based asset allocations should cover the minimum required by the investor. These two steps are specified in Math Box 8.5:

Math Box 8.5: Two-stage approach for solving the goal-based investment problem

To this end, let b^g be the budget allocated to goal g and consider the goal-g-portfolio problem.

$$\max_{\lambda_k^g} \sum_{s=1}^{S} p_s U^g(w_s^g)$$

s.t.

> **Math Box 8.5:** (Continued)
>
> $$w_s^g = \sum_{k=1}^{K} R_s^k \lambda_k^g, s = 1, ..., S, g = 1, ..., G$$
>
> $$\sum_{k=1}^{K} \lambda_k^g = b^g$$
>
> Let $\lambda_k^g(b^g)$ be the solution of the problem and let accordingly $U^g(b^g) = \sum_{s=1}^{S} p_s u^g \left(\sum_{k=1}^{K} R_s^k \lambda_k^g(b^g) \right)$ be the expected utility derived from budget b^g allocated to goal g. Then in a second stage, we can ensure overall optimality by optimally allocating the overall budget on the goals $g = 1, ..., G$.
>
> $$\max_{b^g} \sum_{g=1}^{G} \delta^g U^g(b^g)$$
>
> s.t.
>
> $$\sum_{g=1}^{G} \sum_{k=1}^{K} R_s^k \lambda_k^g(b^g) \geq \underline{w}, s = 1, ..., S, g = 1, ..., G$$
>
> $$\sum_{g=1}^{G} b^g = 1$$
>
> A similar two-stage approach can be done in the mean-variance case.

Hence, the huge optimization problem can be resolved by solving several smaller and easier-to-understand optimization problems. This mathematical insight is of very high practical importance since clients can more easily understand the recommendations of the bank by focusing on their goals.

We close this section by giving an analytical example of this general result. The next section will then summarize the goal-based wealth management approach in a diagram.

Example 8.3:

Suppose there are three equally likely states and also three assets, so that the return matrix is

Table 8.3   Asset returns

	Risk-free asset	Market	Option
State 1	$1+r$	u	0
State 2	$1+r$	m	0
State 3	$1+r$	d	e

where $e > u > 1 + r > m > d > 0$. The first asset is risk-free, the second will be called the "market", and the third will be called an "option". As a general notation, we use R_s^M and O_s for the returns of the second and the third asset.

Suppose the client has three goals: "safety" ($g = 1$), "participation" ($g = 2$) and "gambling" ($g = 3$). To model these goals we use the following utility functions: $u^1(w_s^1) = \frac{(w_s^1)^\alpha}{\alpha}$, $u^2(w_s^2) = -(w_s^2 - R_s^M)^2$ and $u^3(w_s^3) = w_s^3$. We will consider the case of extreme risk aversion $\alpha \to -\infty$ so that the utility function of an investor with goal "safety" is then $u^1(w_s^1) = \min\{w_1^1, w_2^2, w_3^3\}$.

Now we solve the problem for the three goal portfolios:

$$\max_{\lambda_k^1} \min\{w_1^1, w_2^1, w_3^1\}$$

s.t.

$$w_s^1 = \sum_{k=1}^{3} R_s^k \lambda_k^1, s = 1, 2, 3$$

$$\sum_{k=1}^{3} \lambda_k^1 = b^1$$

Referring back to the asset returns in Table 8.3, we see that investing in assets other than the risk-free asset does not make sense for the "safety" goal. Hence, the optimal asset allocation for this goal is $\lambda^1 = (b^1, 0, 0)$.[6]

For goal "participation" we have

$$\max_{\lambda^2} -(w_s^2 - R_s^M)^2$$

s.t.

$$w_s^2 = \sum_{k=1}^{3} R_s^k \lambda_k^2, s = 1, 2, 3$$

$$\sum_{k=1}^{3} \lambda_k^1 = b^2.$$

Again, we have an obvious solution $\lambda^2 = (0, b^2, 0)$.

Finally, we solve

$$\max_{\lambda^3} w_s$$

s.t.

$$w_s^3 = \sum_{k=1}^{3} R_s^k \lambda_k^3, s = 1, 2, 3$$

$$\sum_{k=1}^{3} \lambda_k^1 = b^3.$$

Supposing $e > u + m + d$, the solution is $\lambda^2 = (0, 0, b^3)$.

Hence, the overall budget allocation problem is

$$\max_{b^1, b^2, b^3 > 0} \delta^1 b^1 - \delta^2 \left[(u + m + d)(b^2 - 1)\right]^2 + \delta^3 e b^3$$

s.t.

$$(1 + r)b^1 + R_s^M b^2 + O_s b^3 \geq \underline{w}, s = 1, 2, 3$$

$$b^1 + b^2 + b^3 = 1.$$

Suppose we solve the risk ability constraint by the risk-free allocation, i.e. suppose $(1 + r)b^1 \geq \underline{w}$. Then, the optimal allocation b^2, b^3 can be obtained from

$$\max_{b^2} -\delta^2 \left[(u + m + d)(b^2 - 1)\right]^2 + \delta^3 e(1 - b^1 - b^2)$$

that yields $b^2 = 1 - \frac{\delta^3 e}{2\delta^2 (u+m+d)^2}$ so that $b^3 = \frac{\delta^3 e}{2\delta^2 (u+m+d)^2} - \frac{\underline{w}}{1+r}$ if $(1 + r)b^1 = \underline{w}$.

---

[6] Note if $e > u > m > 1 + r > d > 0$ then a combination of the market portfolio and the option might be the solution to goal 1. Hence, this would be a case in which some assets are useful for more than one goal.

In the following diagram, we summarize the goal-based wealth management process.

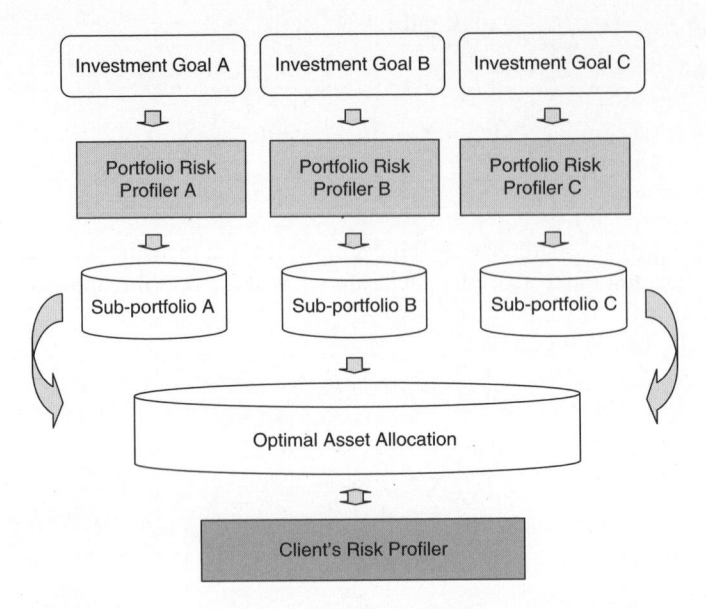

Figure 8.7 Integrated goal-based wealth management approach

In the first step, advisors evaluate whether the client has specific goals he aims to reach with his investment (see Figure 8.7). This is important as the investment goals represent reference points upon which loss-averse clients judge investment performance. As it is possible that the investor exhibits different aversions toward uncertainty and different loss aversion depending on the goal in question, it is advantageous to separate the goals into different mental accounts and specify a risk profile for each of them. On this basis, advisors can define optimal sub-portfolios serving the pre-defined investment goals. The optimal asset allocation of the client is derived by combining the sub-portfolios into a whole. The weights can be determined depending on the relative importance of the goals for the client. Finally, to make sure that the overall risk exposure of the client is in line with the client's risk profile, the asset allocation is fine-tuned according to the overall risk preferences and risk ability of the client.

Overall, the portfolio risk profiler makes use of the positive aspects of mental accounting while the client risk profiler avoids the negative aspects.

8.7 CONCLUSIONS

Following a structured wealth management process has clear advantages. First, it supports advisors in their attempt to help clients overcome several behavioural biases. The most prominent examples of such biases are the lack of financial planning, incorrect framing, inefficient risk management, not following a clear strategy, and incorrect performance attribution. Further, a bank following a structured wealth management process is in a position to guarantee service quality through standardization, thereby benefiting from economies of scope. Ultimately, advisors following a structured wealth management process have the opportunity to learn and improve collectively.

Each bank has its own way of designing the wealth management process but its basic structure is very similar to a typical decision-making process. In the beginning, the client's needs are determined. This is the basis for the further analysis of the client's personal financial situation (assets and liability management). This step is essential for the proper risk management of the client's investments as it defines objective criteria for the optimal asset allocation. The subjective criteria according to the client's risk preferences are reflected in his risk profile. Ultimately, the optimal asset allocation is implemented.

Although the structure of the typical wealth management process makes sense intuitively, one needs to be aware of some behavioural effects that may significantly influence its quality; the most important one is mental accounting. It is a powerful rule of decision-making, in particular for complex problems, but it should be applied very carefully as it may lead to sub-optimal decisions. In general, using mental accounting is rational if it is applied properly. Additionally, mental accounting can be used to structure the decision problem according to the client's investment goals. An optimal portfolio is formed for each of the goals, taking into account the client's risk profile and his personal financial situation. Ultimately, the optimal asset allocation should be fine-tuned according to the client's risk profiler to make sure that his risk exposure is in line with his risk ability and risk preferences.

9
Conclusion and Outlook

9.1 RECAPITULATION OF THE MAIN ACHIEVEMENTS

In this book, we argued that behavioural finance not only gives a theoretical foundation for private banking, but also contains a highly practical relevance.

To persuade the reader of the validity of this claim, we first laid the foundation by reviewing the three main paradigms of decision theory: mean-variance analysis, expected utility theory, and prospect theory. Then we systematically surveyed the most important behavioural biases, including cultural differences. Finally, we extended the static decision theory and portfolio optimization view to dynamic asset allocation and also to life cycle planning. The main practical applications were outlined in our chapters on risk profiling, product design, and structured wealth management processes.

Risk profiling is at the heart of any structured wealth management process. It helps the financial advisor reach the same high service quality for all his clients. The advice he gives on the basis of risk profilers becomes more stable and more justifiable to outside parties (the regulator or a judge) – both across various clients and across time. Moreover, the information the bank obtains from the risk profilers is a useful tool for product design and for marketing.

Nowadays many banks have become "product pushers". Margins on structured products are high and the product shelves of the banks are so full that, for each client, one easily finds some product that he can feel confident buying. Some regulators have started to restrict this market severely. Our chapter on structured products shows how to design products that are beneficial to the bank and the client. We hope that these insights help the bank maintain a long-term relationship with its clients.

Structuring the wealth management process is one of the central tasks of bank management for private banks. As we have demonstrated, structuring along the decision process is nowadays a beneficial practice in private banking where each step can benefit from applying the knowledge of behavioural finance.

9.2 OUTLOOK OF FURTHER DEVELOPMENTS

Recently, the research field of behavioural finance has joined forces with neurology to merge into what is now called "neuro-finance". Neuro-finance researches the neurological foundations of decision theory. In particular it tries to detect which behavioural biases can be addressed by advice and which are hard-wired in our brain so that one should rather accept them as a restriction in the asset allocation process.

The bank management aspects touched upon in this book will further evolve by extending the main features of wealth management by lowering the wealth threshold to include more clients. The main focus of our book was on the average private banking client with a wealth of $2 to $5 million. One result of the standardization of wealth management that is possible by applying our Chapters 4, 5, and 8 is that advisory costs can be reduced so that banks will more effectively target the affluent clients with a wealth around or even below $1 million. On the other hand, as our section on goal-based wealth management suggests, we expect that on the other end of the wealth distribution, more sophisticated wealth management tools will be applied. Goals in this sector will be not only financial goals, but will also be a service for future generations, the environment, and the survival of mankind on this planet; goals that are far-reaching and can be pursued in the form of trusts and foundations.

References

Aaker, J. L. and P. Williams (1998). Empathy versus Pride: The Influence of Emotional Appeals across Cultures. *Journal of Consumer Research* **25**: 241–261.

Ackert, L. F., B. K. Church, J. Tompkins and P. Zhang (2004). What's in a Name? An Experimental Examination of Investment Behavior. FRB of Atlanta Working Paper No. 2003-12.

Artzner, P., F. Delbaen, J. M. Eber and D. Heath (1999). Coherent Measures of Risk. *Mathematical Finance* **9**: 203–228.

Banz, R. W. (1981). The Relationship Between Return and Market Value of Common Stocks. *Journal of Financial Economics* **9**: 3–18.

Barber, B. and T. Odean (2000). Trading is Hazardous to Your Wealth: The Common Stock Investment Performance of Individual Investors. *Journal of Finance* **55**: 773–806.

Barber, B. and T. Odean (2001): Boys will be Boys: Gender, Overconfidence, and Common Stock Investment. *Quarterly Journal of Economics* **116**: 261–292.

Barber, B. and T. Odean (2005). All that Glitters: The Effect of Attention and News on the Buying Behavior of Individual and Institutional Investors. Mimeo, Haas School of Business, Berkeley University.

Barberis, N., M. Huang, and T. Santos (2001). Prospect Theory and Asset prices. *Quarterly Journal of Economics* **116**: 1–53.

Barberis, N. and H. Ming (2004). Stocks as Lotteries: The Implications of Probability Weighting for Security Prices. AFA 2005 Philadelphia Meetings Paper.

Barberis, N. and W. Xiong (2008). Realization Utility. Working Paper.

Benartzi, S. and R. H. Thaler (1995). Myopic Loss Aversion and the Equity Premium Puzzle. *Quarterly Journal of Economics* **110**: 73–92.

Benartzi, S. and R. H. Thaler (2001). Naïve Diversification Strategies in Defined Contribution Saving Plans. *American Economic Review* **91**: 79–98.

Benartzi, S. and R. H. Thaler (2004). Save More Tomorrow: Using Behavioral Economics to Increase Employee Saving. *Journal of Political Economy* **112**: S164–S187.

Bernard, V. L. and J. K. Thomas (1990). Evidence that Stock Prices do not Fully Reflect the Implications of Current Earnings for Future Earnings. *Journal of Accounting and Economics* **13**: 305–340.

Berry, J. W., P. R. Dasen and T. S. Sarawathi (1997). *Handbook of Cross-Cultural Psychology*, 2nd edition. Allyn & Bacon.

Bontempo, R. N., W. P. Bottom and E. U. Weber (1997). Cross-Cultural Differences in Risk Perception: A Model Based Approach. *Risk Analysis* **17**: 479–488.

Brunel, J. L. P. (2003). Revising the Asset Allocation Challenge Through a Behavioral Finance Lens. *Journal of Wealth Management*, (Fall): 10–20.

Brunel, J. L. P. (2006). *Integrated Wealth Management: The New Direction for Portfolio Managers*, 2nd edition. Euromoney Institutional Investor Plc.

Brunnermeier, M. K. and S. Nagel (2004). Hedge Funds and the Technology Bubble. *Journal of Finance* **59**: 2013–2040.

Caliskan, N., E. De Giorgi, T. Hens and T. Post (2008). A Prospect Theory Explanation of Three Asset Pricing Puzzles. Mimeo, University of Zurich.

Capgemini and Merrill Lynch (2007). World Wealth Report.

Capgemini and Merrill Lynch (2008). World Wealth Report.

References

Campbell, J. Y. and L. M. Viceira (2002). *Strategic Asset Allocation*. Oxford University Press.

Canner, N., N. G. Mankiw and D. N. Weil (1997). An Asset Allocation Puzzle. *American Economic Review* **87**: 181–191.

Carhart, M. (1997). On Persistence of Mutual Fund Performance. *Journal of Finance* **52**: 57–82.

Chan, K., V. Covrig and L. Ng (2005). What Determines the Domestic Bias and Foreign Bias? Evidence from Mutual Fund Equity Allocations Worldwide. *Journal of Finance* **60**: 1495–1534.

Choi, I. and R. E. Nisbett (2000). Cultural Psychology of Surprise: Holistic Theories and Recognition of Contradiction. *Journal of Personality and Social Psychology* **79**: 890–905.

Chui, A. C. W., S. Titman and K. C. J. Wei (2005). Momentum Around the World. Mimeo, University of Texas.

Cocca, T. D. and H. Geiger (2007). The International Private Banking Study 2007. Available at www.isb.uzh.ch.

Daniel, K., D. Hirshleifer and A. Subrahmanyam (1998). Investor Psychology and Security Market under- and Overreactions. *Journal of Finance* **53**: 1839–1885.

De Bondt, W. F. M. and R. H. Thaler (1985). Does the Stock Market Overreact? *Journal of Finance* **40**: 793–808.

De Georgi, E., T. Hens and H. Levy (2004). Prospect Theory and the CAPM: A Contradiction or Coexistence? NCCR Working Paper No. 85, University of Zurich.

De Georgi, E., T. Hens and J. Meier (2006): A Behavioral Foundation of Reward-Risk Portfolio Selection and the Asset Allocation Puzzle, NCCR Working Paper No. 286, University of Zurich.

Detlefsen, K., W. Härdle and R. A. Moro (2007). Empirical Pricing Kernels and Investor Preferences. Discussion Papers SFB 649 DP2007-017, Humboldt University, Berlin.

Dimson, E., P. Marsh and M. Staunton (2003). Global Evidence on the Equity Risk Premium. *Journal of Applied Corporate Finance* **15 (4)**: 8–19.

Dimson, E., P. Marsh, and M. Staunton (2006). The Worldwide Equity Premium: A Smaller Puzzle. Working Paper, London Business School.

Douglas, M. and A. B. Wildavsky (1982). *Risk and Culture: An Essay on the Selection of Technical and Environmental Dangers*. Berkeley: University of California Press.

Eichberger, J. and I. R. Harper (1997). *Financial Economics*. Oxford University Press.

Eisenführ, F. and M. Weber (2003). *Rationales Entscheiden*. Berlin: Springer.

Fama, E. F. and K. R. French (1992). The Cross-Section of Expected Stock Returns. *Journal of Finance* **47**: 427–465.

Fama, E. F. and K. R. French (1998). Value versus Growth: The International Evidence. *Journal of Finance* **53**: 1975–1999.

Fan, J. X. and J. J. Xiao (2005). Cross-cultural Differences in Risk Tolerance: A Comparison Between Chinese and Americans. available at SSRN: http://ssrn.com/bstrct=939438.

Fischhoff, B. (1980). For Those Condemned to Study the Past: Reflections on Historical Judgments in: R. A. Shweder and D. Fiske: *New Directions for Methodology of Behavioral Sciences: Fallible Judgment in Behavioral Research*. San Francisco: Jossey-Bass.

French, K. R. and J. M. Poterba (1991). Investor Diversification and International Equity Markets. The American Economic Review 81(2). Papers and Proceedings of the Hundred and Third Annual Meeting of the American Economic Association: 222–226.

Griffin, J. M., X. Ji and J. S. Martin (2003). Momentum Investing and Business Cycle Risk: Evidence from Pole to Pole. *Journal of Finance* **58**: 2515–2547.

Grinblatt, M. and M. Keloharju (2001). How Distance, Language, and Culture Influence Stockholdings and Trade. *Journal of Finance* **56**: 1053–1073.

Gupta, V., P. J. Hanges and P. Dorfman (2002). Cultural Clusters: Methodology and Findings. *Journal of World Business* **37**: 11–15.

Haigh, M. S. and J. A. List (2005). Do Professional Traders Exhibit Myopic Loss Aversion? An Experimental Analysis. *Journal of Finance* **60**: 523–534.

Hens, T. (1992). A Note on Savage's Theorem with a Finite Number of States. *Journal of Risk and Uncertainty* **4**: 63–71.

Hens, T. and M. O. Rieger (2008). The Dark Side of the Moon: Structured Products from the Customers' Perspective. NCCR Working Paper No. 459, University of Zurich.

Hens, T. and M. Vlcek (2005). Does Prospect Theory Explain the Disposition Effect? NCCR Working Paper No. 247, University of Zurich.

Hens, T. and M. Wang (2007). Does Finance have a Cultural Dimension? in: B. Strebel-Aerni: *International Finance*. Zurich: Schulthess.

Hodges, S. H., R. G. Tompkins and W. T. Ziemba (2008). The Favorite-Longshot Bias in S&P 500 and FTSE 100 Index Futures Options: The Return to Bets and the Cost of Insurance. In *Handbook of Sports and Lottery Markets*. Elsevier.

Hofstede, G. (2001): *Culture's Consequences: Comparing Values, Behaviors, Institutions and Organizations across Nations*, 2nd edition. Sage Publications.

Huber, J. (2006). J-shaped Returns to Timing Advantage in Access to Information – Experimental Evidence and a Tentative Explanation. Working Paper, Yale University and University of Innsbruck.

How America Saves (2007). A Report on Vanguard 2006. Defined Contribution Plan Data.

Jagannathan, R. and Z. Wang (1996). The Conditional CAPM and the Cross-Sections of Expected Returns. *Journal of Finance* **51**: 3–53.

Jegadeesh, N. and S. Titman (1993). Returns to Buying Winners and Selling Losers: Implications for Stock Market Efficiency. *Journal of Finance* **48**: 65–91.

Jegadeesh, N. and S. Titman (2001). Profitability of Momentum Strategies: An Evaluation of Alternative Explanations. *Journal of Finance* **54**: 699–720.

Jungermann, H., H.-R. Pfister and K. Fischer (1998). *Die Psychologie der Entscheidung*. Heidelberg: Spektrum.

Kahneman, D., J. Knetsch and R. H. Thaler (1990). Experimental Test of the Endowment Effect and the Coase Theorem. *Journal of Political Economy* **98**: 1325–1348.

Kahneman, D. and A. Tversky (1979). Prospect Theory: An Analysis of Decision under Risk. *Econometrica* **47**: 263–291.

Kahneman, D. and A. Tversky (1992). Advances in Prospect Theory: Cumulative Representation of Uncertainty. *Journal of Risk and Uncertainty* **5**: 297–323.

Karmakar, U. S. (1978). Subjectively Weighted Utility: A Descriptive Extension of the Expected Utility Model. *Organizational Behavior and Human Performance* **21**: 61–72.

Keynes, J. M. (1936). *The General Theory of Employment, Interest and Money*. New York: Harcourt.

Kindleberger, C. (1978). *Manias, Panics, and Crashes: A History of Financial Crises*. New York: Basic Books.

Knight, F. H. (1921). *Risk, Uncertainty, and Profit*. Boston and New York: Houghton Mifflin.

Laibson, D. (1997). Golden Eggs and Hyperbolic Discounting. *Quarterly Journal of Economics* **112**: 443–477.

Lakonishok, J., A. Shleifer and R. F. Vishny (1994). Contrarian Investment, Extrapolation, and Risk. *Journal of Finance* **49**: 1541–1578.

Levinson, J. D. and K. Peng (2006). Valuing Cultural Differences in Behavioral Economics. SSRN Working Paper, available at http://papers.ssrn.com/sol3/papers.cfm?abstract_id=899688.

Markowitz, H. (1952). Portfolio Selection. *Journal of Finance* **7**: 77–91.

Merton, R. C. (1969). Lifetime Portfolio Selection under Uncertainty: The Continuous-Time Case. *Review of Economics and Statistics* **51** (August).

Montier, J. (2007). *Behavioural Investing: A Practitioner's Guide to Applying Behavioural Finance*. John Wiley and Sons Ltd.

Montier, J. (2002). *Behavioural Finance: A User's Guide*. John Wiley and Sons Ltd.

Nevins, D (2004). Goal-Based Investing: Integrating Traditional and Behavioural Finance. *The Journal of Wealth Management* **6 (4)**: 8–23.

Nisbett, R. E., K. Peng, I. Choi and A. Norenzayan (2001). Culture and Systems of Thought: Holistic vs. Analytic Cognition. *Psychological Review* **108**: 291–310.

Odean, T. (1998). Are Investors Reluctant to Realize Their Losses? *Journal of Finance* **53**: 1775–1798.

Papa, B. (2004). Stock Market Volatility: A Puzzle? An Investigation into the Causes and Consequences of Asymmetric Volatility. Master Thesis For the Master of Advanced Studies in Finance, University of Zurich and Swiss Federal Institute of Technology Zurich.

Pasteur, L. (2004). Was There a NASDAQ Bubble in the Late 1990s? Chicago Business School Working Paper.

Post, Th., M. J. van den Assem, G. Baltussen, and R. H. Thaler (2008). Deal or No Deal? Decision Making under Risk in a Large-Payoff Game Show. *American Economic Review* **98 (1)**: 38–71.

Prelec, D. (1998). The Probability Weighting Function. *Econometrica* **60**: 497–528.

PriceWaterhouseCoopers (2007). Global Private Banking/Wealth Management Survey.

Rieger, M. O. and M. Wang (2006). Cumulative Prospect Theory and the St. Petersburg Paradox. *Economic Theory* **28**: 665–679.

Rouwenhorst, K. G. (1998). International Momentum Strategies. *Journal of Finance* **53**: 267–284.

Roy, A. D. (1952). Safety First and the Holding of Assets. *Econometrica* **20**: 431–449.

Russo, J. E. and P. J. H. Schoemaker (1992). Managing Overconfidence. *Sloan Management Review* **33**: 7–17.

Samuelson, P. (1969). Lifetime Portfolio Selection by Dynamic Stochastic Programming. *Review of Economics and Statistics* **51 (3)**: 239–46.

Savage, L. J. (1954). *The Foundations of Statistics*. New York: Wiley and Sons Inc.

Shefrin, H. M. (2000). *Beyond Greed and Fear: Understanding Behavioral Finance and the Psychology of Investing*. Harvard Business School Press.

Shefrin, H. M. (2005). *A Behavioral Approach to Asset Pricing*. Academic Press.

Shefrin, H. M. and M. Statman (2000). Behavioral Portfolio Theory. *Journal of Financial and Quantitative Analysis* **35 (2)**: 127–151.

Shefrin, H. M. and R. Thaler (1988). The Behavioral Life-Cycle Hypothesis. *Economic Inquiry* **26 (4)**: 609–643.

Shleifer, A. (2000). *Inefficient Markets: An Introduction to Behavioral Finance*. Oxford University Press.

Siebenmorgen, N. and M. Weber (2003). A Behavioral Model for Asset Allocation. *Financial Markets and Portfolio Management* **17 (1)**: 15–42.

Sirri, E. R. and P. Tufano (1998). Costly Search and Mutual Fund Flows. *Journal of Finance* **53**: 1589–1622.

Stephan, E. and G. Kiell (1997). Urteilsprozesse bei Professionellen Akteuren im Finanzmarkt (Abschlussbericht einer experimentellen Studie mit Trade- und Sales-Personal einer Deutschen Geschäftsbank). University of Cologne.

Strohm, V. (2003). Die Suche nach der richtigen Bank. *Stocks* issue 41–42: 32–37.

Thaler, R. H. (1985). Mental Accounting and Consumer Choice. *Marketing Science* **4 (3)**: 199–214.

Thaler, R. H. (1999). Mental Accounting Matters. *Journal of Behavioral Decision Making* **12**: 183–206.

Thaler, R. H. and E. J. Johnson (1990). Gambling with the House Money and Trying to Break Even: The Effect of Prior Outcomes on Risky Choice. *Management Science* **36**: 643–660.

Thaler, R. H. and W. T. Ziemba (1988). Anomalies: Pari-mutuel Betting Markets: Racetracks and Lotteries. *Journal of Economic Perspectives* **2**: 161–174.

Tobin, J. (1958). Liquidity Preference as Behavior Towards Risk. *Review of Economic Studies* **25 (1)**: 65–86.

Tversky, A. (1969). Intransitivity of Preferences. *Psychological Review* **76**: 31–48.

Tversky, A. and D. Kahneman (1981). The Framing of Decisions and the Rationality of Choice. *Science* **211**: 455–458.

Tversky, A. and D. Kahneman (1992). Advances in Prospect Theory: Cumulative Representation of Uncertainty. *Journal of Risk and Uncertainty* **5**: 297–323.

Von Neumann, J. and O. Morgenstern (1944). *Theory of Games and Economic Behavior*. Princeton University Press.
Wang, M. and P. Fishbeck (2004). Similar in How to Frame but Different in What to Choose. *Marketing Bulletin* **15** Article 2: 1–12.
Weber, E. U. and C. K. Hsee (1998). Cross-Cultural Differences in Risk Perception, but Cross-Cultural Similarities in Attitudes towards Perceived Risk. *Management Science* **44**: 1205–1217.
Wright, G. N. and L. D. Phillips (1980). Cultural Variation in Probabilistic Thinking: Alternative Ways of Dealing with Uncertainty. *International Journal of Psychology* **15**: 239–257.
Yates, J. F., J.-W. Lee and H. Shinotsuka (1996). Beliefs about Overconfidence, Including Cross-national Variations. *Organizational Behavior and Human Decision Processes* **65 (2)**: 138–147.
Yeniavci, H. (2002). Die Bewertung und Analyse des Ladder-Pop. Master Thesis, University of Zurich.

Index

Advisors   6, 7–8, 63–4, 74–7, 87–8, 105–34, 207–27, 229–30
  anchoring bias   74–7, 105–6
  biases   74–7, 105–6, 209
  MiFID requirements   106
  regret aversion   87–8
  see also Private banking; Risk profiles; Wealth management
Aggregation of payoffs   216–17
Allais, Maurice   12, 13–14, 63–4
Allen, Woody   26
Ambiguity aversion, concepts   85, 98, 102, 104, 120–1, 134
Anchoring bias, concepts   74–7, 105–6, 124–5
Anticipation of clients' needs, service quality improvements   6, 7–9, 105–34, 209–27
Arab Bank   110
Arbitrage   139, 141
Arrow-Pratt measure of absolute risk aversion (ARA)   31–2
Asia Pacific
  behavioural biases   95–104
  high net worth individuals   4–5
Aspiration level reference points   36–7, 88, 98, 110, 112, 124–7, 135–6, 148–55, 160, 165–70, 171–85, 198–206, 207–27
Asset allocation   19–20, 50–8, 60–3, 85, 106–34, 135–55, 157–85, 189, 194–206, 208–27, 229–30
  life cycle planning   194–206
  optimal asset allocation   50–8, 60–2, 106–7, 114–17, 122–34, 141–3, 149–55, 157–85, 189, 194–206, 208–27
  puzzle   19–20, 85, 218–20
  structured products   60–3, 135–55
  see also Dynamic asset allocation
Asset increases, private banking   5–6, 208–27
Asset and liability management   208, 212–27
Asymmetric risk aversion   7, 8–9, 65–6, 69–70, 202–6
Availability bias, concepts   68, 70, 105–6
Average gains, concepts   55–8, 125–7, 207–8
Average losses, concepts   55–8
Axiom 0   26–35, 60
Axioms, rational behaviour   23–35, 60–6, 67, 135–55, 219–20

Balance sheets, asset and liability management   212–14
Bank Leu   109–14, 128–34
Bankruptcies   71
Banks, *see* Private banking
Barings   38
Bayes rule   34–5, 67, 75–6
Bear markets   145–9
Behavioural finance   1–9, 50–8, 60–2, 105–34, 135–55, 157–85, 194–206, 207–27, 229–30
  BhFS   108–9, 120–7, 131–4
  dynamic asset allocation   157–85, 202–4, 229–30
  life cycle planning   187–95, 198–206
  neuro-finance   229–30
  optimal asset allocation   50–8, 60–2, 106–7, 114–17, 122–34, 141–3, 149–55, 157–85, 194–206, 208–27
  optimal strategic asset allocation   171, 180–5
  optimal tactical asset allocation   159–60, 165–70
  outlook   229–30
  risk profiles   117–34, 208–27, 229–30
  service quality improvements   6–9, 209–27
  structured products   135–55
  wealth management   1–9, 105–34, 207–27
  see also Prospect theory
Beliefs   67–82
Benchmarks   36–7, 75–7
Bernoulli, Daniel   11, 12–13, 40–1, 67, 142, 147, 189–90
  see also Expected utility theory
BhFS (Behavioural Finance Solutions)   108–9, 120–7, 131–4
Biases   7, 35, 44–5, 67–104, 117–34, 153–5, 158–9, 165–85, 188–9, 191–206, 207–27, 229–30
  ambiguity aversion   85, 98–104, 120–7, 134
  anchoring bias   74–7, 105–6, 124–5
  availability bias   68–70, 105–6
  concepts   67–104, 117–34, 158–9, 229–30
  conservatism bias   74, 75–7, 100–1, 105–6, 169–70
  cultural differences   95–104, 229–30
  decision biases   67–8, 82–8
  decision evaluation biases   67–8, 87–8

Biases (*Continued*)
  disposition effect   84, 86, 166
  emotions   104, 106, 208
  endowment bias   85–6
  favourite long-shot bias   81–2
  framing bias   77–8, 82–4, 90, 104, 105–6, 180–5, 191–206, 207–27
  gambler's fallacy   73, 105–6, 136
  hindsight bias   87, 104, 106
  home bias   85, 101, 106
  house money effect   84, 165–7, 170
  illusion of control   81–2
  information processing biases   67–8, 70–82
  information selection biases   68–70
  intertemporal decisions   88–91, 101–2, 202–6
  mental accounting   8–9, 82–5, 106, 117, 166, 188–90, 191–206, 207–9, 217–27
  neuro-finance   229–30
  overconfidence bias   78–82, 91, 100–4, 106, 208–27
  PEAD   76–7
  psychological call options   87–8
  regret aversion   87–8, 208
  representativeness bias   71–4, 105–6
  risk profiles   105–6, 117–34, 208–27, 229–30
  self-attribution bias   104, 106, 208–27
  speculative bubbles   91–4
  splitting bias   78
  sunk costs   85, 86
  wealth management   207–27
Bills, *see* Government bonds
Black and Scholes option pricing model   140
Bonds   14–22, 31, 45–8, 55–8, 60–2, 77–8, 83–4, 87–8, 107, 121–7, 131–4, 139–55, 187–206, 209, 216–27
Bonus certificates   150–5
Book-to-market ratios   69–70
Booms   31
Break-evenitis   166
Brunel, J.L.P.   220–1
Bubbles   91–4
Buffet, Warren   69
Bull markets   145–9
Buy-and-hold strategies   137–55, 157–85

Call options   81–2, 87–8
Capital Asset Pricing Model (CAPM), concepts   16–17, 150–1
Capital Market Line (CML)
  concepts   18–22, 52–3, 116
  see also Sharpe ratio
Capital protection   136–55, 217–27
Capital sources   194–206

CAPM, *see* Capital Asset Pricing Model (CAPM), concepts
Cash, risk attitudes   19–21, 66, 83, 107, 121–7, 131–4, 217–27
CDs, *see* Certificates of deposit (CDs)
Certainty equivalent, concepts   29–32, 43–4, 142, 147–9
Certificates of deposit (CDs)   45–8, 143–4, 189
Clients
  experiences and differentiation strategies   5–7, 121–7, 131–4
  life cycle planning   9, 187–206, 212
  needs   6–9, 105–34, 136–55, 208–27
  risk profiles   7–9, 105–34, 208–27, 229–30
  wealth management   1–9, 105–34, 207–27, 229–30
CML, *see* Capital Market Line (CML)
Collectivist cultures, behavioural biases   95–104
Commitment evidence, intertemporal decisions   89–90
Commodities   121–2, 131–2
Comparative advantages, wealth management processes   208–10
Completeness axiom, preference relations   23–35
Concave utility functions   30–2, 40–1, 49–50, 166–70, 189–90, 219–20
Conditional probability, concepts   34–5, 71
Conditional Value at Risk (CVaR)   117
Confidential private banking   1–2
Conflicts of interest, wealth management   210–11
Conservatism bias, concepts   74, 75–7, 100–1, 105–6, 169–70
Consumption factors, life cycle planning   187–206
Consumption smoothing, concepts   189–90, 195–206
Continuous preferences axiom, preference relations   24–35
Contrarian investment strategies   72–3
Convex utility functions   30–2, 39–40, 49–50, 151–2, 166–7, 192–4, 219–20
Cost/income ratios, Swiss private banks   2–3
Covariance   223–4
CPT, *see* Cumulative prospect theory (CPT)
Credit cards   40–1
Credit Suisse   4, 109–10, 211–17
Cultural differences, behavioural biases   95–104, 229–30
Cumulative prospect theory (CPT)   43–4
Currencies   107
Current assets, understanding the clients   6–7
'Cushion hypothesis'   97–8
CVaR, *see* Conditional Value at Risk (CVaR)

Index

DAX Sparbuch case study 143–9
Decision analysis, definition 11
Decision biases, concepts 67–8, 82–8
Decision evaluation biases, concepts 67–8, 87–8
Decision-making processes 7, 35, 44–5, 67–104, 125–7, 153–5, 158–9, 165–85, 188–9, 191–206, 207–27, 229–30
    biases 7, 35, 44–5, 67–104, 153–5, 158–9, 165–85, 191–206, 227, 229–30
    cultural issues 95–104, 229–30
    typical schematic 67–8, 221
Decision-making styles 125–7, 132–3, 207–8
Decision support systems, concepts 11, 105–6
Decision theory
    basic insights 11–12, 66, 229–30
    concepts 6–9, 11–66, 229–30
    definition 12–13
    historical background 11–14
    normative/descriptive contrasts 11–12, 22–35, 64–6
    see also Expected utility theory; Mean-variance analysis; Prospect theory
Decreasing marginal utility from wealth law 12–14, 30–1, 189–94, 217–27
Derivatives 81–2, 154–5
    see also Futures; Options
Descriptive decision theory 11–12, 35, 64–6
    see also Prospect theory
Differentiation strategies, private banking 5–7
Discount rates 32–5, 88–91, 95, 98–104, 187–8, 193–206, 207–27
Disposition effect, concepts 84, 86, 166–70
Diversification 8–9, 40–1, 80–1, 106, 122–3, 127, 134, 171–85, 202–6, 207–8, 214–27
Dividends 92, 187–9, 191–206
Documentation/reporting processes, wealth management 208–9, 211, 215–17
Downside risk measures, concepts 8–9, 125–7
Dynamic asset allocation 88–9, 127, 157–85, 202–4, 229–30
    approaches 157–8
    concepts 157–85
    optimal strategic asset allocation 157–8, 171–85
    optimal tactical asset allocation 157–85

Economies of scale/scope, wealth management 208–10
Efficient frontiers
    calculations 20–1
    concepts 16–22, 52–3, 65–6, 115–17, 134
Efficient Market Hypothesis 69–70
Efficient portfolios, concepts 16–22, 52–3, 66, 115–17, 134
Ellsberg, Daniel 12, 13–14, 63–4, 121

Emerging markets 72–3, 121–2, 131–4
Emotions 104, 106, 208
Endowment bias, concepts 85–6
Equities 16–22, 31, 45–8, 77–8, 85, 92–4, 107, 121–7, 131–4, 169–70, 187–206, 209, 216–27
    dividends 92, 187–9, 191–206
    risk attitudes 16–22, 45–8, 83–4, 121–7, 131–4, 169–70, 187–206, 216–27
Equity premiums 14–15, 16–22, 102–4, 123–4
Errors of commission, regret aversion 88
Errors of omission, regret aversion 88
Europe
    behavioural biases 95–104
    high net worth individuals 4–5
European Markets in Financial Instruments Directive (MiFID) 106
Evaluation phase, prospect theory 35–58
Expected returns 15–22, 52–8, 112–14, 124–34, 160–85, 195–206, 215–27
Expected utility theory
    axioms 23–35, 63–6, 67, 219–20
    concepts 11–12, 13–14, 22–35, 37, 40–1, 47–8, 63–6, 95, 135–55, 157–65, 171–80, 184–5, 187, 189–206, 219–20, 222–7, 229–30
    critique 63–6, 95, 185
    dynamic asset allocation 157–85
    insurance 49–50, 64
    intertemporal decisions 32–5, 88–91, 193–206
    life cycle planning 187, 189–206
    lottery approach 22–4, 63–4
    mean-variance analysis 63, 64–6
    optimal strategic asset allocation 171–80
    optimal tactical asset allocation 160–5
    prospect theory 14, 37, 40–1, 47–8, 64–6, 135–55, 166, 185, 198–9
    structured products 135–55
    updated expectations 33–5
    wealth management 222–7
Expected value, concepts 11–12, 13–14, 41
Exponential discounting, concepts 32–5, 95, 187–206

Fama, E.F. 69, 123
Favourite long-shot bias, concepts 81–2
Feedback, decision-making processes 67–8, 87–8
Fidelity 19, 203–5
Financial capital, human capital 194–206
Financial concept, wealth management 212–14
Financial markets, lotteries 12–13
Financial products 60–3, 104, 135–55
Finter Bank 110
Fix-mix strategy 160–5, 171, 178–80, 184–5

Foreign investments, home bias   85, 101, 106
Framing bias, concepts   77–8, 82–4, 90–1, 104, 105–6, 180–5, 191–206, 207–27
Framing phase, prospect theory   35, 37, 46–7, 65–6, 77–8, 207–27
French, K.R.   69, 123
FTSE100   81
Fuller and Thaler Asset Management   76–7
Fundamental values, speculative bubbles   91–5
Funds, life cycle planning   202–6
Future performance, past performance   72–3, 207
Futures   81–2

Gains, prospect theory   7, 12, 13–14, 35–58, 64–6, 69–70, 88, 95–104, 119–27, 135–55, 157–85, 198–206, 207–27, 229–30
Gambler's fallacy   73, 105–6, 136
Gates, Bill   69
Globalization effects   104
Global Private Banking/Wealth Management survey 2007   3–6
Goal-based wealth management approach   220–7, 230
Government bonds   14–16, 55–8, 60–2, 123–7, 139–40, 203–6, 216–27
Greed   91, 208
Grimm brothers   23–4
Growth prospects, private banking   4–5, 220–7

Habits   90–1, 187, 193–206
Hedging   8, 36–7, 44–8, 60–3, 121–2, 132–4, 141–3, 145–9, 209, 216–17
Hedonic editing (framing) principle   218–19
Heuristics, concepts   67–8, 71–8
High net worth individuals, statistics   4–5
Hindsight bias, concepts   87, 104, 106
Histograms, returns   12–14, 44–5
Hofstede, G.   95–8
Home bias, concepts   85, 101, 106
House money effect, concepts   84, 165–70
Housing bubble   94
Human capital   194–206
Hyperbolic discounting   33, 89–91, 187–9, 193–206, 207–27

i.i.d. (independent and identically-distributed) outcomes   73, 171–2
Illusion of control   81–2
Independence axiom, preference relations   24–35, 62–6, 136
Indifference curves   51–2
Individualistic cultures, behavioural biases   95–104
Inflation rates   98–100

Information
   anticipation of clients' needs   8–9
   biases   67–104
   overreactions to new information   70, 72, 75–6, 80–2, 208
   underreactions to new information   75–7
Information processing biases, concepts   67–8, 70–82
Information selection biases, concepts   68–70
Initial Public Offerings (IPOs)   48–9
Innovations, speculative bubbles   91–5
Institutional asset management performance comparisons, private banking   4–5
Insurance, expected utility theory   49–50, 64
Interest rates   45–8
Internet stocks   81, 94
Intertemporal decisions
   biases   88–91, 98–101, 202–6
   concepts   32–5, 88–91, 187–206
Introduction   1–9
Investment committee (IC)   209–10
Investment options   121–7
IPOs, see Initial Public Offerings (IPOs)
Irrational behaviour, concepts   7–9, 11–12, 26–35, 37, 48–9, 67–8, 84, 95–104, 105–34, 165–70, 219–20, 229–30
IT   209–10

Jensen's inequality   30–1, 41, 49–50

Kahneman, Daniel   12, 22, 36, 40–3, 50–8, 77, 117–18, 142–3, 147–9, 171
   see also Prospect theory
Kassel, Widow   187–9
Kerviel, Jerome   38
Knock-out warrants   155
Kuhn, Christine   107, 127–34, 209
Kurtosis   69–70

Ladder Pop   130–1, 136–43
Latin America, high net worth individuals   4–5
Learning by 'cycling', wealth management   211
Leeson, Nick   38
LGT   55–8, 73–4
Liabilities, asset and liability management   208, 212–27
Liberal capital markets   1–2
Life cycle hypothesis   190–4
Life cycle planning
   asset allocation   194–206
   concepts   9, 187–206, 212, 229–30
   consumption smoothing   189–90, 195–206
   expected utility theory   187, 189–206
   funds   202–6
   human capital   194–206
   main decisions over time   189

mental accounting 191–206
product design 194, 202–6
prospect theory 187–95, 198–206
self-control problems 191–206
Widow Kassel case study 187–9
Liquidity goals 220–7
Loss aversion 7, 35, 39–58, 65–6, 67, 69–70, 91, 95–104, 106–34, 135–55, 160–85, 191–206, 207–27
Losses, prospect theory 7, 12, 13–14, 35–58, 64–6, 69–70, 88, 95–104, 119–27, 135–55, 157–85, 198–206, 207–27, 229–30
Lotteries, concepts 12–13, 22–8, 43–4, 49–50, 60–6, 119–20, 221
LSV-fund 69
Lucky Hans story 23–4

Marginal utility from wealth law 12–14, 30–1, 189–94, 218–27
Market timing dynamic asset allocation 157–85
Markov matrices 158–63
Markowitz, H. 14–16, 54
MBS 94
Mean reversion
concepts 158–85
random walks 171–4, 184
Mean-variance analysis
concepts 12, 14–22, 35, 50–3, 54–8, 59–63, 64–6, 114–17, 151–5, 214, 222–7, 229–30
critique 59–63, 64–6
expected utility theory 63, 64–6
mathematics 20–1
prospect theory 64–6
risk profiles 114–17
structured products 151–5
wealth management 214, 222–7
Mean-variance paradox 60, 65
Median behavioural investors, preferences 54, 147–9
Mental accounting
concepts 8–9, 82–5, 106, 117, 165–70, 188–90, 191–206, 207–9, 217–27
wealth management 207–9, 217–27
see also Disposition effect, concepts; House money effect, concepts
Merrill Lynch 19, 211
Merton, R.C. 14, 174
MiFID, see European Markets in Financial Instruments Directive (MiFID)
Miscalibration effect, concepts 79–82
Momentum investment strategies 72–3, 100–4, 158–60
Monitoring of clients' needs, service quality improvements 6, 7, 9, 209–27
Monty Hall Problem 33–4
Morgan, Jim 39

Morgenstern, Oskar 12, 13, 14, 25, 219–20
MSCI 60–2, 74, 102, 124, 132–4
MS Excel 162, 176
Multi-touch table, structured products 154–5
Mutual funds 72–4, 77–8, 101–4
Myopic loss aversion 90–1, 122–3, 165–70, 176–8, 180–5, 191–206, 207–27

NASDAQ 73
Needs of clients 6–9, 105–34, 136–55, 208–27
Negative time values, structured products 139
Neuro-finance 229–30
Nevins, D. 220–1
New York Times 19–20
Normal distribution assumptions 8–9, 14, 50–8, 59–63, 65–6, 69–70
Normalized prospect theory (NPT) 44–5, 48, 141–3
Normative decision theory 11–12, 22–35, 64–6
see also Expected utility theory
North America
behavioural biases 95–104
high net worth individuals 4–5
'No time diversification' theorem 174–5
NPT, see Normalized prospect theory (NPT)
Nuclear power 43

Objective probabilities, concepts 63–4
Optimal decisions 11–12, 17–22, 35, 48–9, 50–8, 60–2, 106–7, 114–17, 122–34, 141–3, 149–55, 157–85, 189, 194–206, 208–27
see also Normative decision theory
Options 81–2, 87–8
Outperformance certificates 155
Overconfidence bias, concepts 78–82, 91, 100–4, 106, 208–27
Overreactions to new information 70, 72, 75–6, 80–2, 208
Over-weighted probabilities 35–6, 41–58, 63–6, 81–2, 97–104, 142–3, 148–55, 165–85, 220

PALM, see Personal Assets and Liability Management (PALM)
Pascal, Blaise 11
Past performance, future performance 72–3, 207
PEAD, see Post-earnings-announcement-drift (PEAD)
Pension funds 77–8
Perceived probabilities, prospect theory 35–6, 41–58, 63–6, 97–104
Performance issues
future performance/past performance 72–3, 207
private banking 2–3, 4–5, 207–27

Personal Assets and Liability Management (PALM) 212–14
Piecewise exponential value functions 51–2
Piecewise power function 40–1, 50–1, 143
Piecewise quadratic value functions 52–4, 61–2, 65–6, 119–20, 141–3, 151–2, 219–20
Planning processes, wealth management 7–9, 105–34, 207–27
Portfolio choice 8–9, 14–22, 40–1, 48–9, 52–3, 54–8, 66, 80–1, 83–4, 106, 121–7, 134, 143, 149, 171–85, 202–6, 207–27
    concepts 14–22, 52–3, 66, 83–4, 143, 149, 217–27
    diversification 8–9, 40–1, 80–1, 106, 122–3, 127, 134, 171–85, 202–6, 207–8, 214–27
    efficient portfolios 16–22, 52–3, 66, 115–17, 134
    goal-based wealth management approach 220–7, 230
    pyramids 83–4, 217–18
    see also Asset allocation; Mean-variance analysis
Positive decision theory, see Descriptive decision theory
Post-earnings-announcement-drift (PEAD) 76–7
Preferences 9, 23–35, 54, 60–6, 67, 88–91, 106–16, 117–34, 157–85, 193–206, 209–27
    axioms 23–35, 60–6, 67, 219–20
    median behavioural investors 54, 147–9
Prescriptive decision theory, see Normative decision theory
PricewaterhouseCoopers (PwC) 3–6
Private banking 1–9, 18, 107, 208–27, 229–30
    asset increases 5–6, 208–27
    biases 209
    challenges 3–6, 208–27
    client experiences and differentiation strategies 5–7
    concepts 1–9, 208–27, 229–30
    definition 2–3
    functions 1–3, 208–27
    growth prospects 4–5, 220–7
    institutional asset management performance comparisons 4–5
    performance issues 2–3, 4–5, 207–27
    risk profiles 105–34, 208–27, 229–30
    service quality improvements 5–9, 209–27
    statistics 2–6
    surveys 3–6
    wealth management 1–9, 105–34, 207–27, 229–30
    see also Advisors; Wealth management
Probabilities 11–36, 41–58, 63–6, 71–2, 75–8, 81–2, 97–104, 142–3, 148–55, 165–85
Probability matching, concepts 78

Probability weighting function, concepts 42–58, 63–6, 97–104, 142–3, 148–55, 165–85, 220
Product design
    concepts 135–55, 194–206, 229–30
    DAX Sparbuch case study 143–9
    Ladder Pop case study 136–43
    life cycle planning 194, 202–6
    optimal design 149–55
Prospect theory
    concepts 7, 12, 13–14, 35–58, 64–6, 69–70, 88, 95–104, 119–27, 135–55, 157–60, 165–70, 171, 180–5, 198–206, 207–27, 229–30
    critique 64–6, 185, 229–30
    cultural differences 95–104, 229–30
    dynamic asset allocation 157–85, 202–4
    evaluation phase 35–58
    expected utility theory 14, 37, 40–1, 47–8, 64–6, 135–55, 165, 185, 198–9
    framing phase 35, 37, 46–7, 65–6, 77–8, 207–27
    life cycle planning 187–95, 198–206
    loss aversion 7, 35, 39–58, 65–6, 67, 69–70, 91, 95–104, 106–34, 135–55, 160–85, 191–206, 207–27
    mean-variance analysis 64–6
    optimal asset allocation 50–8, 60–2, 106–7, 114–17, 122–34, 141–3, 149–55, 157–85, 194–206, 208–27
    optimal strategic asset allocation 171, 180–5
    optimal tactical asset allocation 159–60, 165–70
    over-weighted probabilities 35–6, 41–58, 63–6, 81–2, 97–104, 142–3, 148–55, 165–85, 220
    phases 35
    probability weightings 35–6, 41–58, 63–6, 97–104, 142–3, 148–55, 165–85, 220
    reference points 36–7, 55–8, 65–6, 88, 98–104, 112, 124–7, 135–6, 148–55, 160, 165–70, 171–85, 198–206, 207–27
    reward-risk perspective 54–8, 66, 215–27
    risk profiles 119–27, 208–27, 229–30
    structured products 135–55
    utility functions 50–8, 159–60, 166–7, 218–27
    value functions 35–41, 50–8, 61–6, 96–104, 119–20, 141–3, 149–55, 165–70, 181–5, 199–206, 218–27
    wealth management 1–9, 105–34, 207–27, 229–30
Psychological call options, concepts 87–8
Put options 81–2

Qualitative decision-making styles   125–7, 132–3
Quantitative decision-making styles   125–7, 132–3, 208–27
Questionnaires, risk profiles   106–34, 208–9, 215, 229–30

Random walks
  concepts   73–4, 122–3, 157–85, 195–206
  meanreversion   171–4, 184
Rational behaviour
  axioms   23–35, 60–6, 67, 135–55, 219–20
  concepts   7–9, 11–12, 13–14, 21–35, 60–6, 78, 85, 95–104, 105–34, 135–55, 159–206, 221–7, 229–30
  see also Expected utility theory; Mean-variance analysis
Real estate   83–4, 121–2, 132–4, 189
Rebalancing dynamic asset allocation   157–85, 203
Recessions   31, 45–8
Reference points, prospect theory   36–7, 55–8, 65–6, 88, 98–104, 112, 124–7, 135–6, 148–55, 160, 165–70, 171–85, 198–206, 207–27
Regret aversion, concepts   87–8, 208
Regulations   229
Relative risk aversion   31–2
  see also Risk aversion
Representation theorem, concepts   24–5
Representativeness bias, concepts   71–4, 105–6
Return-on-equity (ROE), Swiss private banks   2–3
Returns   2–3, 7, 8–9, 12–22, 35–58, 100–4, 112–14, 121–34, 136–55, 160–85, 195–206, 215–27
  cultural differences   100–4, 229–30
  efficient portfolios   16–22, 48–9, 52–3, 66, 115–17, 134
  equity premiums   14–15, 101–4, 123–4
  expected returns   15–22, 52–8, 112–14, 124–34, 160–85, 195–206, 215–27
  histograms   12–14, 44–5
  mean-variance analysis   12, 14–22, 35, 50–3, 54–8, 59–66, 222–7, 229–30
  prospect theory   7, 12, 13–14, 35–66, 69–70
  risk   16–22, 54–8, 121–34, 208–27
Reward-risk perspective, prospect theory   54–8, 66, 215–27
Risk   7, 8–9, 14, 16–22, 29–32, 35, 43–4, 54–8, 63–4, 95–104, 121–34, 208–27, 229–30
  concepts   7, 8–9, 14, 16–22, 29–32, 35, 43–4, 54–8, 63–4, 95–104
  cultural issues   95–104, 229–30
  efficient portfolios   16–22, 48–9, 52–3, 66, 115–17, 134
  measures   7–9, 11–12, 31–2, 35, 63–4, 115–17, 119–27, 213–14, 221
  objective probabilities   63–4
  returns   16–22, 54–8, 121–34, 208–27
Risk ability, concepts   106–14, 117–34, 157–85, 209–27
Risk attitudes   7, 8–9, 14, 16–22, 25, 29–32, 35, 38–58, 83–4, 95–104, 105–34, 157–85, 187–206, 217–27
Risk aversion
  Arrow-Pratt measure of absolute risk aversion   31–2
  concepts   7, 8–9, 14, 16–22, 29–32, 38–58, 62–3, 65–6, 69–70, 95–104, 106–34, 141–3, 147–55, 158–85, 195–206, 216–27
  measures   31–2, 119–20, 141–3, 218–27
  relative risk aversion   31–2
Risk awareness, concepts   106–14, 118–34
Risk-free assets   8, 14–15, 18–22, 55–8, 116, 134–43, 145–9, 161–85, 217–27
Risk-loving decision makers   30–2, 98–9
Risk neutral decision makers   30–2
Risk premium, concepts   29–32, 102–4, 123–4
Risk profiles   7–9, 105–34, 208–27, 229–30
  Bank Leu   109–14, 128–34
  behavioural finance   117–34, 208–27
  benefits   106–7
  BhFS   108–9, 120–7, 131–4
  biases   105–6, 117–34
  comparisons case study   127–34
  concepts   105–34, 208–27
  definition   106
  design considerations   108–9
  implementation case study   109–14
  mean-variance analysis   114–17, 214
  prospect theory   119–27, 208–27
  questionnaires   106–34, 208–9, 215, 229–30
  wealth management   208–27
Risk-return opportunities, portfolio choice   16–22, 54–8, 121–34, 208–27
ROE, *see* Return-on-equity (ROE), Swiss private banks
Rules of thumb, *see* Heuristics, concepts

S&P 500   19–20, 81–2, 122, 173–4
SAA, *see* Strategic asset allocation (SAA), concepts
Safety first principle   117, 221–2
St Petersburg Paradox   12–13
Samples, representativeness bias   71–4, 105–6
Sarasin, Alfred E.   2
Save More Tomorrow program (SMarT)   194
Savings, life cycle planning   189–206
Segmentation criteria, needs of clients   6–7
Segregation of payoffs   216–17
Self-attribution bias   104, 106, 208–27

Self-control problems 89–91, 191–206
Self-esteem 100–1
Service quality improvements, private banking 5–9, 209–27
Sexual equality issues 95
Sharpe ratio
　concepts 18–22, 69–70
　see also Capital Market Line (CML)
Shefrin, H.M. 191, 192
Short fall probabilities 8
Short trades 19
Skewness 69–70
Smith, Vernon 7
Special investment vehicles (SIVs) 94
Speculative bubbles, biases 91–4
SPI, see Swiss Performance Index (SPI)
Splitting bias, concepts 78
Standard deviations 14–15, 20–1, 114–20
　see also Variance ratio test
Standardization needs, wealth management 208–27, 229–30
State preference approach, concepts 22–3, 25–6, 219–20
Stereotypes, representativeness bias 71–4, 105–6
Stocks 107, 134
Strategic asset allocation (SAA), concepts 157–8, 171–85
Structured products 60–3, 135–55, 202–6, 229–30
　asset allocation 60–3, 135–55
　behavioural finance 135–55
　DAX Sparbuch case study 143–9
　dynamics 138–40
　expected utility theory 135–55
　investor's perspectives 141–3, 146–9
　Ladder Pop case study 136–43
　mean-variance analysis 151–5
　multi-touch table 154–5
　negative time values 139
　optimal product design 149–55
　portfolio considerations 143, 149
　see also Product design
Structured wealth management, see Wealth management
Subjective probabilities, concepts 63–4
Sub-prime crisis 219–20
Sunk costs, concepts 85, 86
Surveys, private banking 3–6
Swiss Government Bonds (SGB) 55–8, 60–2
Swiss Performance Index (SPI) 55–8, 60–2
Swiss private banking 1–3, 18, 107

TAA, see Tactical asset allocation (TAA), concepts

Tactical asset allocation (TAA), concepts 157–85
Takeovers 71
Tangent portfolio
　calculations 21
　concepts 18–22, 115–16
　see also Capital Market Line (CML)
Thaler, R. 191–2, 217
Time consistency concepts 9, 32–5, 88–91, 193–206
Time-inconsistent preferences 9, 32–5, 88–91, 193–206
TMT bubble 94–5
Tobin, James 18, 20
Total payoffs, decisions 37
Tracker certificates 155
Transitivity axiom, preference relations 23–35
Tversky, Amos 12, 22, 36, 40–3, 50–8, 77, 117–18, 142–3, 147–9, 171
　see also Prospect theory
Two fund separation theorem 14, 18–22, 53–4, 116

Uncertainty 7, 22–3, 63–4, 95–8, 126–7, 132–4, 219–20
Uncertainty Avoidance Index 95–8
Underlying assets 135–55
Underreactions to new information 75–7
Understanding the clients, service quality improvements 6–9, 18, 209–27
Updated expectations 33–5, 76, 124–7
Utility functions, concepts 12–14, 30–2, 39–40, 49–58, 159–60, 166–7, 189–94, 218–27

Value functions 35–41, 50–8, 61–6, 96–104, 119–20, 141–3, 149–55, 165–70, 181–5, 199–206, 218–27
Value investors 69–70
Value at Risk (VaR) 8, 115–17, 213–14, 221
Vanguard life cycle funds 205–6
Variance ratio test 173–4
Variance uses 8–9, 12, 15–22, 171–4, 214, 222–7
　see also Mean-variance analysis
VaR, see Value at Risk (VaR)
Von Neumann, John 12, 13, 14, 25, 219–20

Warrants 155
Wealth management 1–9, 105–34, 207–27, 229–30
　asset and liability management 208, 212–27
　behavioural finance 1–9, 105–34, 207–27
　comparative advantages 208–10
　conflicts of interest 210–11
　Credit Suisse case study 211–17

documentation/reporting processes   208–9, 211, 215–17
economies of scale/scope   208–10
financial concept   212–14
goal-based approach   220–7, 230
implementation issues   210, 215–17
learning by 'cycling'   211
mean-variance analysis   214, 222–7
mental accounting   207–9, 217–27
mistakes   207–8
needs of clients   208–27

planning processes   7–9, 105–34, 207–27
risk profiles   208–27, 229–30
standardization needs   208–27, 229–30
steps   211–17
structured wealth management benefits   209–27, 229–30
see also Private banking
Widow Kassel case study   187–9
William T. Ziemba   81–2
World Wealth Report 2007/2008   3–6